THE PROPHETS AND THE PROMISE

BY

WILLIS JUDSON BEECHER

BAKER BOOK HOUSE
Grand Rapids, Michigan

Reprinted by Baker Book House from the
original edition made in 1905 by
Thomas Y. Crowell, New York.

Library of Congress Catalog Card Number: 63-19837

ISBN: 0-8010-0650-3

Paperback edition:

First printing, August 1975
Second printing, August 1977

Printed in the United States of America

NEW

INTRODUCTION

by

Walter C. Kaiser, Jr.

Our generation of Biblical readers and scholars have denied the center of the Scripture's message. The content of both Testaments is said to be varied and too diverse for any single approach, plan, theme, or center to serve the reader as a guide.

That is why this generation needs to be challenged once again to consider the central thesis of Willis J. Beecher. For him, there is a clear channel distinctly marked out and jointly shared by the writers of Scripture themselves. The Old Testament is more than just a happy hunting ground of scattered predictions whose mere word about the future remains isolated from the historic fulfillment until it suddenly arrives in Jesus the Messiah. Rather, there is an unfolding doctrine of the promise that embraces the predictive word; but it also links the intervening means by which God continued to give additional embellishments to that doctrine as well as concrete evidence in history that served as his "earnest" money until the final fulfillment arrived in Christ.

This view is not to be associated with any "double meaning" theory of prophecy, for it is closest to the old Antiochian School's position of *"Theoria."* For them, and for Beecher, the prophet had one meaning in mind, but it embraced at once the prophet's contemporary situation, the immediate future, and God's culminating act as divinely revealed in that feature of the on-going doctrine of the promise.

This thesis is tremendously important for the disciplines of Old Testament Biblical theology (Is there a center to Old Testament theology?), hermeneutics (Does the prophet speak better than he knows?), and the Old Testament's relationship to the New Testament (Does apostolic exegesis agree with prophetic truth-intention?).

In spite of the simplicity and elegance of style, certain passages (especially in Part II) are demanding since the Hebrew mode of thinking involves a corporate solidarity with an intruding individualization or a climaxing representative individual—all as part of a single concept—which is foreign to our mode of thought. But the effort invested is abundantly worth it.

Willis Judson Beecher was born to parents of New England decent on April 29, 1838, in Hampden, Ohio. They had settled there as home missionaries. In 1858, he graduated from Hamilton College (B.A.), Clinton, New York, and taught at Whitestown Seminary (New York) until 1861, when he entered Auburn Theological Seminary (New York). He was ordained to the Presbyterian ministry in 1864 and took a pastorate in Ovid, New York, for one year. He and his bride, Sara Maria (June 14, 1865), went to Galesburg, Illinois, to accept the chair of moral science and *belles-lettres* at Knox College, and stayed for four years. From 1869-71, he was pastor of the First Church of Christ (Congregational) in Galesburg, after which he held the post as professor of Hebrew language and literature at Auburn Theological Seminary from 1871-1908.

In 1902, he delivered the Stone Lectures at Princeton Theological Seminary, which were published in 1905 as *The Prophets and the Promise.* His next major achievement came in 1904, when he became president of the Society of Biblical Literature and Exegesis.

Most of Beecher's literary work can be found in extensive contributions to journals, encyclopedias, and newspapers. For example, he has numerous articles on the Old Testament in the *International Standard Bible Encyclopedia*; *Encyclopaedia Britannica* (1883-89); twelve articles on the postexilic history in the *Old and New Testament Student* (1889-90); "Critical Notes" on the lessons for many years in the *Sunday School Times*; and a series on matters of the Presbyterian ministry in *Johnson's Universal Cyclopedia* (1892-95).

His monographs include: *Farmer Tompkins and His Bibles* (1874); *Index of Presbyterian Ministers: 1706-1881* (1883); *Drill Lessons in Hebrew* (1883, 1886); *Old Testament Notes* (1897); *The Teaching of Jesus Concerning the Future Life* (1906); *The Dated Events of the Old Testament* (1907); and *Reasonable Biblical Criticism* (1911). He died at his home in Auburn, May 10, 1912.

Willis J. Beecher was known in his day as a "progressive conservative," and nowhere is the meaning of *progressive* more apparent than his two or three references to higher critical positions in *The Prophets and the Promise.* Nowhere in the Stone Lectures did he adopt the Wellhausian view, but unfortunately he did reflect the trend of the theology in his day. Since I presume he knows better now that he is in glory, the reader would be well advised to disregard these few asides made as concessions for the sake of a point of reference to what was deemed academically respectable in that day—and, sadly, such concessions still continue to this day.

March 1975

Walter C. Kaiser, Jr.
Professor of Semitics and Old Testament
Trinity Evangelical Divinity School
Deerfield, Illinois

PREFACE

In part the Stone lectures as delivered were a selection from the materials of this volume, and in part the volume is an expansion of the lectures. It is a product of studies accumulating during many years, rather than a predirected discussion of a subject, but I hope that it will not be found deficient in logical coherence.

The presentation it makes is essentially a restatement of the Christian tradition that was supreme fifty years ago, but a restatement with differences so numerous and important that it will probably be regarded, by men who do not think things through, as an attack on that tradition. If what I have said makes that impression on any one, and if he regards the matter as of sufficient importance, I ask him to consider it more carefully. I have tried to make my search a search for the truth, without undue solicitude as to whether its results are orthodox; but it seems to me that my conclusions are simply the old orthodoxy, to some extent transposed into the forms of modern thought, and with some new elements introduced by widening the field of the induction.

It follows, of course, that my position is antagonistic to that of the men who attack the older tradition. But I have tried not to be polemic. I have tried to give due consideration to the views of the men with whom I differ. Where practicable, I have preferred the broader statements, in which we are in agreement, to the narrower ones that would emphasize our differences.

CONTENTS

CHAPTER I

PRELIMINARY

PART I

THE PROPHETS

CHAPTER II

TERMS USED IN DESCRIBING THE PROPHETS

CHAPTER III

THE EXTERNAL HISTORY OF THE PROPHETS

vii

CHAPTER IV

THE PROPHET. A CITIZEN WITH A MESSAGE

CHAPTER V

*THE FUNCTIONS OF A PROPHET—NATURALISTIC
AND SUPERNATURALISTIC*

CHAPTER VI

THE PROPHET'S MESSAGE

CHAPTER VII

THE PROPHET AS A GIVER OF TORAH *AND WRITER OF SCRIPTURE*

PART II

THE PROMISE

CHAPTER VIII

THE PROMISE-DOCTRINE AS TAUGHT IN THE NEW TESTAMENT

CHAPTER IX

THE PROMISE AS GIVEN TO THE PATRIARCHS

CHAPTER XII

MESSIANIC TERMS. THE SERVANT

CHAPTER XIII

MESSIANIC TERMS. THE KINGDOM AND ITS ANOINTED KING

CHAPTER XIV

MESSIANIC TERMS. YAHAWEH'S HHASIDH. OTHER TERMS

CHAPTER XV

COLLATERAL LINES OF PROMISE-DOCTRINE

CHAPTER XVI

MESSIANIC EXPECTATION AND FULFILMENT

CHAPTER XVII

THE APOLOGETIC VALUE OF PROPHECY

THE PROPHETS AND THE PROMISE

CHAPTER I

PRELIMINARY

THE prophets of Israel: what manner of men they were, their functions, naturalistic or supernaturalistic, how their messages were given to them and how uttered by them, their part in the writing of the scriptures, the doctrine they taught concerning Israel's peculiar relations to Deity and to mankind, the messianic kingdom they heralded and its king, and the value of their mission for the current illustration and defence of the Christian religion, — this theme and these topics under it are certainly not new. They are familiar, trite, commonplace. Yet it seems to me that in this field a painstaking student may still hope to gather something. The older treatments seem to me inadequate, by reason of a certain lack of insight into the literary character of the sources and into the nature of historical movements, and by reason of too great reliance on traditional interpretations. The newer treatments seem to me yet more inadequate, by reason of the too easy rejection of portions of the testimony, and the too ready substitution of conjecture for evidence. Both leave something to be desired in this field of study, and something that is not beyond the reach of diligence and industry.

Without taking time to discuss thoroughly the principles that should govern such an investigation as this, I shall try to present, in this preliminary chapter, a few considerations touching the sources to be used and the interpretation of them, followed by a brief outline of the treatment that will be attempted.

I. The Old Testament is our one direct source of information concerning the prophets and their teachings.

Sources — Indirect sources are, first, the New Testament and other later writings, including the evidence of the monuments; second, analogies drawn from other religions, or from later times, or from our theories or opinions.

Of these sources the Old Testament, supplemented at some points by the New, is principal, and all others are subsidiary. Simple as this fact is, it is imperative that we pay it due attention. Our generation is much in the habit of substituting superficial reading for careful study. If a person has read a hundred volumes, in six or seven languages, concerning the prophets, he is in danger of fancying that he has done more work on the subject than if he had carefully examined all that the Old and New Testaments say about them. To avoid being misled, he should have it in mind that the hundred volumes contain very little real information save that which has been drawn from these principal sources. Nineteen-twentieths of all that we really know on this subject comes from the bible. Only the other twentieth comes from extrabiblical tradition, or from monuments, or from the analogy of other religions, or by inference from the theories we hold, or from our general knowledge of things and men.

The scriptures as a source

My purpose is, mainly, to reëxamine the evidence

found in the Old and New Testaments. To some this programme will seem exceedingly simple and rudimentary. They would think it a greater thing to read many books, and discuss the bearing of their contents on the subject in hand. But no amount of reading can supersede the necessity of examining for ourselves the direct evidence in the case. Just this has been more neglected than anything else in dealing with the subject of the prophets of Israel. Men of learning as well as others have neglected it. We must do this first of all, and do it with care, or all other study of the subject will be of little value to us.

Men have assumed that they were already familiar with what the Old Testament says concerning the prophets, when they were not really so ; and have hastened on prematurely to the examination of the collateral branches of the evidence. Many of the current statements as to what the Old Testament says are based on analogies, or on later traditions, to a much greater extent than on the actual testimony of the Old Testament. Such statements are instances of mistaken method. The direct evidence in the case is not only the most important, but it is essential to the correct understanding of the indirect evidence. The indirect evidence can genuinely assist in interpreting the direct only on condition of its being itself interpreted by the direct. In Old Testament studies, the thing now more needed than anything else is a more correct knowledge of what the Old Testament says. Always the beginner should begin by attaining to this correct knowledge ; and at present, in Old Testament work, this is the need of advanced scholars as well as of beginners.

At once we see the importance of the question of the degree of credence to be accorded to the testimony of In what   our principal sources. If we hold to a divine degree is the testimony inspiration that guarantees the remarkable credible?   truthfulness of all parts of the bible, it does not therefore follow that we must take this doctrine as a presupposition in our historical study of the prophets. And if one holds that the bible is full of mistaken statements, that does not justify him in an undiscriminating rejection of the statements concerning the prophets. Both as a matter of correct method, and for the sake of convincing those with whom we differ, we should waive, at the outset, all questions of inspiration, and treat our sources merely as literature that has come down to us from a remote past. In respect to trustworthiness we will make no stronger claim than this : that statements of fact found in the Old and New Testaments are to be provisionally regarded as true except as reasons appear to the contrary.

This is not an extravagant claim to make for the truthfulness of the scriptures. Our courts would accord as much credence as this, not to a reputable witness only, but even to a witness who is a jailbird or a harlot or a noted liar. If statements of fact are self-contradictory, or contrary to known truth, we will not accept them. Even if they are seemingly credible we will at the outset accept them only provisionally, till we can test them by their results when we bring them into combination with other truths. We will fully admit the principle that human historians often make mistakes. But this we must insist upon : that statements of fact are to be provisionally accepted unless there are substantial reasons for not accepting them.

It follows that in using the testimony of the Old and New Testaments on this and other questions, we ought to begin with a direct examination, and not with a cross-examination. We ought to take the trouble to understand what their statements mean, in the form in which they have come down to us, as preliminary to testing the truth of them, and either accepting or rejecting them. *Direct examination versus cross-examination*

As our investigation depends largely on the question of the historical correctness of the affirmations of the bible, so it depends indirectly on questions concerning the structure, the date, and the authorship of the books. For these have *Dependence on critical questions* their bearing on the question of historicity, and also on the question of the interpretation of the statements we find. Yet we need not wait till all these other questions are settled before we begin our studies concerning the prophets. Indeed, many of the questions concerning the prophets are more simple and primary than the others, and therefore ought to be studied first, that the results reached may assist us in our inquiries into matters that are less obvious.

Our first inquiry is: What are the representations of the Old Testament in regard to the prophets? In other words: What manner of men were the prophets, supposing the statements of the Old Testament concerning them to be historical, *The provisional point of view* so far as they purport to be so, and supposing them also to be correct? From the point of view of all parties this is a fair question. It is supposable that, in seeking the answer, we may find the statements of the Old Testament unsatisfactory, but at the outset the question is a fair one. On the supposition that the Old Testament gives a truthful account of the prophets of Israel, what is that account? We do not affirm that it gives a truthful account; we do not deny it; we simply suppose it.

It is wisest to start from this point of departure, not trying to settle beforehand all questions in regard to the character or the trustworthiness of our data, but using them at first as provisional, and as leading only to provisional results. We shall surely test the data as we advance. If they are not trustworthy, we shall find it out. If they are trustworthy, we shall see them to be so, and shall thus transform our provisional results into final results.

These last considerations are important. How shall we determine whether statements of fact found in any Use as a test source are to be depended upon? There is of evidence no better test than that of actual use. By carefully examining what the Old Testament says on such a subject as the prophets, we may form a judgment concerning the Old Testament as a source of evidence. Certain schools of criticism deny that these books are historically valid, asserting that they are full of anachronisms and inconsistencies and absurdities. In case this is so, we shall be pretty sure to find traces of the unhistorical character of the books, if we carefully examine some section of them, running through different chronological periods. Such a section for testing them is afforded in what they say concerning the prophets. This is found scattered through all the books, including a vast number of details and allusions, belonging to periods of time separated by centuries. It is conceivable beforehand that we may find these details so confused and inconsistent as to be incredible in many points, and that we may be compelled to estimate the books accordingly. On the other hand, if we find their account of the prophets to be throughout consistent and probable, that will be an argument of no little weight in favor of the historical trustworthiness of the books themselves.

Thus our attitude toward these writings and their testimony is at the outset neutral. It will not remain so. As the investigation proceeds we shall inevitably either gain or lose confidence in the witnesses.

II. In the interpretation of our sources, and especially of the Old Testament, there is one point in particular in which we need to be sedulously on our guard. That is the point where we are in danger of substituting an eisegetical treatment for an exegetical.

None of us come to this study as to a new and unfamiliar subject. We already have pretty distinct ideas concerning the prophets and their activities, Eisegesis is and in particular concerning messianic predic- to be avoided tion, and the meaning and use of the term Messiah. It is supposable that our preconceived ideas may be crude and misleading. We can decide this only by holding them in suspense until we can test them by the facts we find by study. We cannot be too jealously careful against the process of merely first putting our ideas into the Old Testament passages, and then dipping them out again. There is especial danger of eisegesis from two sources, Christian theology and theories of Comparative Religion.

We must avoid alike the carrying back of Christian ideas into the Old Testament and the neglecting of those ideas that belong to the Old Testament in common with Christianity.

When we are studying the Old Testament we ought not to import into it ideas drawn from the New Testament, or from some scheme of Christian messianic theology. This rule is nowadays often laid down; if we

violate it, we shall not do so for lack of being warned; but
it is a correct rule.   And we shall not properly observe
Eisegesis of it unless we take pains.   We are familiar, for
Christian example, with a certain interpretation of what
doctrine the New Testament says concerning Jesus
as the Messiah, and we go to the Old Testament looking for the same teaching expressed in similar terms.
In this way we are likely to find what we are looking
for, whether it is there or not.   We sometimes find
things where they are not.   We put the idea into the
passage, instead of looking to see what is already in the
passage; and then, by way of interpretation, we take out
just what we have put in, possibly a little miscolored by
the process.

This way of studying the Old Testament is all the
more dangerous because it is not altogether valueless.
The method of interpreting the Old Testament by the
light of the New is within its proper limits correct.
Even when the method is incorrectly used, such study
is study.   Though faulty, it may, especially in the case
of persons who have spiritual insight, result in the
reaching of truth.   Critically bad as this way of learning is, we cannot afford to forego it save as we can
replace it by something better.

Nevertheless it is logically bad.   It is contrary to
accepted laws of investigation.   There are grave objections to it.   First, it is needless.   All the truth it yields
is equally attainable by methods that will stand the test
of correct criticism.   Second, it is perilous.   The truth
we thus reach, though genuinely true, has yet been
inferred from premises that can be shown to be false.
There is danger that when we come to see that the
premises are false, our confidence in the truth will be
shaken.   Third, it is wasteful.   By this particular way

of learning the Old Testament through the New we obtain from it nothing but a pale reflection of the New. This is a great loss. In a wide range of truths the Old Testament is more rudimentary, and therefore simpler and fuller than the New. It is capable of illuminating the New, and not merely of being illuminated by it. When so much light is ready to glow, we cannot afford to take a point of view which brings the object perpetually into the shadow.

Equally true, however, and at present far more to the purpose, is the converse rule that, in studying the Old Testament, we should not drop out the ideas which we actually find there, merely because the same ideas are also found in the New Testament. We are just now in far greater danger of making this mistake than the other. There are men who are so afraid of reading into the Old Testament some more recent truth that does not belong there that they actually expel from it, in their interpretations, some of its simplest and most evident teachings. They say, for example, that the fatherhood of God is a New Testament teaching; and they affirm that the Old Testament passages which speak of God as father must be understood as meaning something less than they say. We are not infrequently told that the heart of the religious teaching of Jesus is his doctrine concerning love — to love God with the whole heart, to love our neighbors as ourselves, to love our enemies; and in this the religion of Jesus is contrasted with that of the Old Testament; and passages in the Old Testament which verbally teach just these doctrines are subjected to a squeezing process to expel from them this alleged impossible doctrine of love. Those who practise this style of interpretation ignore the fact that the doctrines of supreme love to God, equal love to men, and love to enemies are chiefly taught in the New Testament by direct citation from the Old, with distinct affirmation that these are the doctrines which are to be regarded as central in the Old Testament. The same style of interpretation is practised in many other instances, and in particular in the interpretation of the Old Testament statements concerning the prophets.

Against this I protest as being critically worse than even the current habit of reading New Testament meanings into the Psalms and the Prophets. We are to go to the Old Testament to find what is there, and not to find what we suppose ought to be there. Anything we find there is not removed from there by the fact, if such be the fact, that it is also found in the New Testament, or in the Vedas or the Sagas or the Chinese or the Greek literature. Not to speak at all of possibilities arising from the inspiration of the writers of the Old and New Testaments, nothing is more in accord with probability than that great truths should be repeated by the great minds of different ages.

Quite as baneful in its effect as any other form of eisegesis is the practice of unduly interpreting the biblical statements by the theories that one may hold as to the evolution of religions. To the evidence from the analogy of other religions we should allow just its proper value, and no more. There are scholars who reason on the assumption that certain propositions, inferred from the comparison of the various human religions, are to be regarded as ascertained scientific facts; so that biblical statements, if they conflict with these alleged facts, are thereby proved to be untrue. This is unscientific. The religion described in the bible is the one early religion

Eisegesis of theories of religion

in regard to which we have, on the whole, fuller and more trustworthy information than in regard to any other. Any generalizations on the rise and development of religions, made without using the data given in the bible, are, by that very circumstance, so far forth defective and unscientific. Again, no other known religion is so decidedly marked by its own peculiarities as the religion described in the bible. If generalizations were made by the comparison of all other known religions, still no one would be justified in arguing that these give us facts concerning the religion of Israel, in opposition to the specific evidence we have concerning that religion.

Here is the danger in one direction. On the other hand, the analogies of other religions may indirectly throw great light on the history of the religion of the bible. It is foolish to neglect this or any other source of possible evidence. In fine, these analogies are, in biblical questions, of the nature of remote evidence, and should be treated as remote evidence is properly treated in any investigation. They should neither be discredited, nor pushed into the chief place to the discrediting of the direct evidence.

This is the general rule. How much credit should be given to any particular scheme of Comparative Religion is another question. For instance, how shall we account a theory which assumes that the religion of Israel was primitive in the times of the judges, and advanced thereafter by certain specified steps from lower to higher? Do we know that the religion of the time of the judges was primitive? If the chronological opinions now current are correct, the times of the judges are modern compared with the earliest times in which splendid religious cults are known to have existed in Babylonia or Egypt. Who knows that the order of evolution in a religion is uniformly in an ascending series, according to some particular theory of ascent and descent?[1] It is obvious that conclusions derived from such processes need to be very cautiously used when they are set forth in contradiction to specific evidence.

In opposition to such methods as have just been discussed, the true method is to come to an Old Testament A true   passage with the question: What did this method   mean to an intelligent, devout, uninspired Israelite of the time to which it belongs? The Old Testament passage, whatever its date may be, is itself a monument of the Israelite mind of that time.   As a disclosure of Israelite religious thought in the time when it was written or in earlier times, it is more authoritative than any inferences we may draw from what we happen to know of the religious thought of the Iroquois or the Hottentots or the Chinese or the Thibetans. In order to understand the passage, we must bear in mind that it was uttered for thoughtful people, and was suited to their capacities. The great majority was then as now unintelligent and superficial in matters of religious thinking, and we are not to gauge the utterance by the likelihood that such would take an interest in it. If

[1] "Scholars of this class are in the habit of arranging all known races and cults in linear series, placing those which they consider the lowest at the bottom, and those which they consider the highest at the top, the others graduating between these two extremes. From this artificial series, proceeding on the assumption that the lowest must of necessity be the most ancient, they write the history of civilization and thought. This method is a radically pernicious one. The series of facts might be as easily read in the descending scale; . . . ' The history of religions should be based, not upon gratuitous assumptions . . . but upon such real historical facts as are obtainable." — Merwin-Marie Snell in *Biblical World*, September, 1896, p. 209.

there were miraculously inspired men in those days, they may supposably have understood the thought given in the passage in the light of all the future history of mankind; but it was not for such men that the utterance was chiefly given. The givers of the message claim to be inspired, but it was to uninspired though thoughtful men that the message was immediately directed. So far forth as we can assume their attitude, we are in shape to understand the utterances that were primarily designed for them.

III. The order of treatment adopted in this volume is based in part on a conception of the relative present-day importance of the several topics treated. Order of The greatest interest we feel in the prophets treatment arises from the doctrine they taught concerning the Messiah. On the basis of this fact, the subject separates into two principal parts, dealing respectively with the prophets as the men who promulgated the messianic promise and with the promise which they promulgated. In treating the first of these two parts we must necessarily begin by some discussion of the terms used. Then we pass naturally to a biographical and historical account of the succession of persons known as the prophets. Nowhere in history can we find a line of men more picturesque and interesting in themselves, or whose achievements have been more significant. They figure more prominently than any other men in the history of Israel. A series of the biographies of the prophets would be a complete history of Israel. This particularly attractive part of our subject, however, we must dismiss with a single chapter, instead of allowing it to expand into a volume. With the questions of the personal presentment and the functions of the prophet we must deal somewhat more fully. Further, the authorship of the

Old Testament is attributed to the prophets, alike in the Old Testament itself, in the New Testament, and in Jewish and Christian tradition. There is no studying the Old Testament or Old Testament criticism, apart from the prophets. We must discuss this claim, though briefly. These topics will occupy the first part of the volume, leading up to the consideration, in the second part, of the messianic promise. The second part naturally closes with the question of the bearing of the whole upon Christian Apologetics.

It may not be superfluous to mention a few matters of detail. Most of the scriptural passages used have Certain mat- been freshly translated. The translating has ters of detail been done with the fact in mind that readers are likely to have the current English versions within reach. The translations I have given are ordinarily more literal than those in the versions. In some cases I have deliberately made them so at the cost of literary smoothness. Occasionally, however, the variation from the common translation is made for the purpose of bringing out the point under discussion.

The use of Hebrew type has been avoided. In transliterating Hebrew words the attempt has been to make them look as little un-English as possible, and to avoid employing unusual type. Proper names and other words familiar to the eye of English readers have been retained in their traditional form. In words less familiar a more accurate transliteration has been used, though even in these the vocal *sh'was* are sometimes represented by a short vowel instead of an apostrophe. The continental vowel system has been used in transliterating, on account of the clumsiness of our English way of writing the vowels. Waw is represented by *w*, and Yodh by *y*. The quiescing Waw is omitted, save in special instances. The quiescing Yodh is omitted after Hhiriq, but retained after Tsere and Seghol, to distinguish these words from those that are spelled with Aleph. I have not thought it necessary to distinguish between Sin and Samekh, or between Taw and Teth. Readers who know even a little Hebrew can make these distinctions for themselves, and for others the matter is unimportant. Aleph and Ayin are commonly omitted in transliteration, though for distinction Aleph is sometimes represented by the spiritus lenis, and Ayin by the spiritus asper. Tsadhe is represented by *ts*, and Hheth by *hh*.

For the name of the national God of Israel I have used the form Yahaweh. No one should judge this name until he has first acquired the habit of pronouncing it correctly, according to the analogies commonly accepted in pronouncing Hebrew. Accent the last syllable, make the middle *h* distinctly a consonant, and pronounce the middle *a* so short as to make it a mere breathing. I do not care to discuss the question whether "Yahweh" is theoretically a more correct transliteration. Whoever tries to pronounce the word with this spelling will inevitably either accent the first syllable, or fail to sound the middle *h*, or introduce a slight vowel sound after it. The third is the correct alternative. If the word were rare, the best transliteration might be Yah'weh, but for a frequent word, Yahaweh pleases the eye better. For the rest, the purposes of this volume require that this word shall be distinguished as a proper name, and it seems to me that the correct form of the word is better for this purpose than the artificial combination " Jehovah."

As for other designations of the supreme Being. The name Yah should not be confounded with Yahaweh, as is done in the English versions.   Even if one holds that Yah is an abbreviated form of Yahaweh, he must also acknowledge that the two are used distinctively.   The Hebrew word El is most exactly our English word God, while Elohim is a more abstract term, like our English word Deity.   Sometimes in this volume Elohim is translated Deity, for distinction; but more commonly it is translated God, following the established practice.

PART I

THE PROPHETS OF ISRAEL

CHAPTER II

TERMS USED IN DESCRIBING THE PROPHETS

OUR English word " prophet " is, of course, the Greek word προφήτης, from πρό, and φημί. The word needs no discussion here, as it is fully considered in dictionaries and other accessible works.[1] It denotes, not one who speaks beforehand, though the prophet was believed to be a foreteller of events ; nor one who speaks in behalf of another, though the prophet ordinarily speaks in behalf of Deity ; but a person who speaks forth, speaks publicly, speaks out the word that he has to speak. When he predicts, he speaks forth the future verity that would otherwise remain in concealment. When he speaks for another, he speaks forth the message which the other has committed to him, and which would otherwise have remained unknown. The thing uttered is often a divinely given prediction, but the word " prophesy " does not signify to predict.

"Prophet" in Greek and English

In the Hebrew, the prophet and his functions are described in various terms. The standard term, the one that is most distinctive, is the noun *nabhi* and its cognates of the stem *nabha*. The words of this stem are used in every part of the Old Testament. In our English versions they are uniformly translated " prophet," " prophesy," " prophecy," and so

Nabhi and its cognates

[1] See the Greek lexicons of Cremer, Thayer, Liddell and Scott, etc. Or see the Century Dictionary, or Skeat's Etymological Dictionary, or similar books of reference.

forth.   Except in five verses, no other word is so translated.[1] The instances number some hundreds in all, and
they can readily be found for study by the aid of a concordance, either English or Hebrew.   We shall have
occasion to examine many of them, one by one, in our
present study of the prophets.   The lexicons attribute to
the stem an original physical meaning, " to boil up," and
from this derive the idea of fervid utterance as characterizing the prophets ; but this is an etymologist's conjecture, and is disputed by other etymologists.   It is too
uncertain to build upon.   What we know as to the
meaning of the word is inferred solely from the use of
it.   Fortunately, the usage is abundant and unequivo-
cal.   The whole of our study of prophecy will be really
a study of the meaning of the word.   We need not anticipate further than to say that the meaning of the Hebrew
term is well expressed in its Greek-English equivalent.

In our English versions two different Hebrew words
are translated " seer," and each of them has a group of
cognates widely used for expressing matters concerning
the prophets.

Of the two, the one most properly so used is *hhozeh*.
It is the active participle of a verb that is common to the
Hhozeh and   Hebrew and the Aramaic.   In the Aramaic
its cognates   it is the ordinary word for physical seeing,
but in Hebrew it is little used except to express thoughtful insight, or in connection with prophetic matters.
David's friend Gad is described as a seer (2 Sam. xxiv.
11 ; 1 Chron. xxi. 9, xxix. 29 ; 2 Chron. xxix. 25). Asaph
and Heman and Jeduthun are severally called seers
(2 Chron. xxix. 30, xxxv. 15 ; 1 Chron. xxv. 5).   The
term is applied to Jedo and Iddo and Jehu and Amos

---

[1] The five verses are Prov. xxx. 1, xxxi. 1; Isa. xxx. 10; Mic. ii. 6, 11.
The five verses contain in all ten instances.

(2 Chron. ix. 29, xii. 15, xix. 2; Am. vii. 12), and is also used in cases where no individual is mentioned (2 Ki. xvii. 13; Isa. xxix. 10, xxx. 10; Mic. iii. 7; 2 Chron. xxxiii. 18, 19).

The verb of this stem is commonly translated "see." It is often used in cases where an object is thought of as presented to the eye, but it does not necessarily imply that. It may denote any form of mental perception, whether through the senses or not. The following are examples. "The vision of Isaiah the son of Amoz, which he saw" (Isa. i. 1, cf. ii. 1, xiii. 1; Am. i. 1; Mic. i. 1; Hab. i. 1). "The diviners have seen falsely" (Zech. x. 2, cf. Lam. ii. 14; Ezek. xiii. 6, 7, 8; and the Aramaic of Dan. vii. 1, 2, 7, 13, etc.). In one passage the English versions render this noun and verb by "prophet" and "prophesy," in order to distinguish them from the other words for "seer" and "see" (Isa. xxx. 10).

Several different nouns of this stem are also in use, and each of them is sometimes rendered "vision" in the English versions.[1]

[1] The following are the nouns that occur most frequently:—

Hhazon, used thirty-five times. It commonly denotes a revelation given to a prophet, whether through an appearance presented to the eye or by some other method (1 Sam. iii. 1; 1 Chron. xvii. 15; Isa. xxix. 7; Jer. xiv. 14, xxiii. 16, etc.). Often the word is used as part of the literary title of a prophecy (Isa. i. 1; Nah. i. 1; 2 Chron. xxxii. 32).

Hhazoth (2 Chron. ix. 29). Part of a title of a writing.

Hhizzayon (2 Sam. vii. 17; Job iv. 13, vii. 14; Zech. xiii. 4, etc.). Like *Hhazon*, except that it is not used in literary titles.

Mahhazeh appears four times: "The word of Yahaweh was unto Abraham in the vision" (Gen. xv. 1 JE). Balaam habitually "saw the vision of Shaddai, falling, and being uncovered of eyes" (Num. xxiv. 4, 16 JE). "Have ye not seen a vain vision" (Ezek. xiii. 7).

Hhazuth, translated "vision" (Isa. xxi. 2, xxix. 11), "agreement" (Isa. xxviii. 18), "notable horn" (Dan. viii. 5, 8).

Add to these the Aramaic noun *Hhezev*, occurring only in Daniel,

The other noun translated "seer" is *roeh*. It is the active participle of the verb which is in most common
Roeh and its use for physical seeing. The persons who
cognates in the use of this word are called seers are Samuel, Zadok, and Hanani (1 Sam. ix. 9 et al.; 2 Sam. xv. 27; 2 Chron. xvi. 7, 10). The word is also used in this sense without particularly mentioning the person (Isa. xxx. 10). As a participle the word is used dozens of times. The stem is used hundreds of times.

The English versions make no difference in translation between this word with its cognates and *hhozeh* with its cognates. For the sake of distinction, even at the cost of somewhat ungainly English, I shall translate the words of this stem by the English words "behold," "beholder," "a beholding," "appear," "appearance," "semblance," reserving the words "see," "seer," "vision," for rendering the Hebrew words of the stem *hhazah*.

The verb in the simple active voice is used of a person beholding something, and thus receiving a revelation from Deity. Ezekiel says: "The heavens opened themselves, and I beheld divine beholdings" (i. 1). Zechariah says: "I lifted my eyes and beheld, and lo, four horns" (i. 18). Jeremiah is asked: "What art thou beholding?" He replies: "I am beholding a pot that boils, its face being from the direction of the north" (i. 13).[1] In the reflexive or passive stem the verb is used of Deity appearing to men for purposes of revelation. "Yahaweh appeared unto Abram;" "and Deity appeared unto Jacob again;" "Yahaweh appeared to Solomon the second time;" "the Angel of Yahaweh

eleven times in the sense of prophetic vision, and once (vii. 20) in the sense of outward appearance.

[1] See also Isa. xxx. 10; Dan. viii. 2, x. 8, etc., and the construct infinitive in 2 Chron. xxvi. 5.

appeared" unto Moses at the burning bush (Gen. xii.
7, xvii. 1, xviii. 1, xxxv. 1, 9; 1 Ki. ix. 2; Ex. iii. 2).
In the causative-active stem the verb is used of Deity,
causing one to behold something that constitutes a divine
revelation.   Amos says: "Thus the Lord Yahaweh
caused me to behold, and lo, he formed locusts."   Again
he says: "Thus the Lord Yahaweh caused me to behold, and lo, he called to contend by fire."   And again :
"Thus he caused me to behold, and lo, the Lord stood
beside a plumb wall, with a plumbline in his hand"
(vii. 1, 4, 7).   Jeremiah says: "Yahaweh caused me to
behold, and lo, two baskets of figs" (xxiv. 1).   Finally,
there are two nouns from this causative stem, a masculine, *mareh*, and a feminine, *marah* (măr-eh and măr-ah),
which denote either the divine process of causing one to
behold, or the human act of beholding so caused, or the
object which one is thus made to behold.[1]

[1] These nouns start in usage as the hiphil participle, "causing to behold," either in the sense of giving one power to behold or in that of an
object presenting itself to be beheld, and thus causing one to behold it.

Once the feminine noun denotes mirrors (Ex. xxxviii. 8).   A mirror
causes one to behold, in the sense of enabling one to see what would otherwise be invisible.   Elsewhere the noun is used only of revelations from
Deity.   It can always be translated, though in some instances awkwardly,
by the English noun "beholding," denoting either the divine enabling or
the human act or the object beheld.   The object is thought of as either
really or ideally presented to the eye.   The following are the instances : —

"And Deity said to Israel in beholdings by night" (Gen. xlvi. 2 E).

"In the beholding I will make myself known unto him; in the dream I
will speak with him" (Num. xii. 6 E).

"Samuel being afraid to declare the beholding unto Eli" (1 Sam. iii.
15).

"The heavens were opened, and I beheld beholdings from Deity"
(Ezek. i. 1).

"A spirit . . . brought me in to Jerusalem, with beholdings from Deity" (Ezek. viii. 3).

"With beholdings from Deity he brought me in unto the land of
Israel" (Ezek. xl. 2).

The nature of the functions denoted in these two groups of words is reserved for a future chapter. For the present we note that the words of the two stems are not properly interchangeable. At first sight, especially in the book of Daniel, the words of one stem seem to be confused with those of the other, but closer examination shows that this is not the case.

The uses of raah and hhazah

" Beholdings like the appearance which I had beheld " (Ezek. xliii. 3). See below under *mareh*.

Mareh, the masculine noun, is more widely used than its feminine. It appears participially, for example, " all that I am causing thee to behold " (Ex. xxv. 9; Ezek. xl. 4). Most commonly, however, it is a substantive, denoting the external aspect of persons or things, their looks, semblance, appearance. Like *marah* it implies either a real or an ideal presentation to the eye, or to the other senses. It is oftener translated by " appearance " than by any other word. In cases of revelation from Deity it has four different meanings. First, it has its usual signification, denoting the looks of anything. Second, it denotes an apparition, a visible semblance, of some particular person or thing. Third, it denotes more generally a manifestation or disclosure coming from Deity to a man. Fourth, it is sometimes used in the sense of *marah*.

The first and third of these meanings are illustrated in the following instance : —

" And the appearance of the appearance which I beheld was as the appearance which I had beheld at my coming in to destroy the city; and [there were] beholdings like the appearance which I had beheld at the river of Chebar; and I fell upon my face " (Ezek. xliii. 3). The meaning of this becomes clear if we translate : " And the aspect of the manifestations which I beheld was like that of the manifestations which I had beheld at my coming in to destroy the city; and [there were] beholdings like the manifestations which I had beheld," etc.

The following are additional instances of the third meaning. In each case notice that the word " appearance " denotes a manifestation, a disclosure, from Deity.

" That I may behold this great appearance " (Ex. iii. 3 E). Burning bush.

" And the appearance of the glory of Yahaweh as devouring fire at the head of the mountain " (Ex. xxiv. 17 P).

" There used to be over the *mishkan* as it were an appearance of fire, . . . and an appearance of fire by night " (Num. ix. 15–16 P).

For example, the verb *hhazah* never has *mareh* or *marah* as its object. When this verb is used of the seeing of a vision, the word for vision is always of its own stem.

"Mouth unto mouth I speak with him, and an appearance, and not in riddles" (Num. xii. 8 E). In contrast with *marah* of ver. 6.

"The glory of the God of Israel, according to the appearance which I beheld" (Ezek. viii. 4).

"And a spirit lifted me up and brought me in at Chaldea unto the exiles, in the appearance, by the Spirit of Deity; and the appearance which I beheld went up from upon me" (Ezek. xi. 24).

The second of the four meanings is frequent, and may be illustrated by the following instances. In some cases there may be room for doubt as between the second, third, and fourth meanings. Using the English word "appearance" for each, there is room for difference of judgment as to the meaning of the word.

"According to the appearance which Yahaweh made Moses behold" (Num. viii. 4 P). Is the "pattern" here a semblance, or a divine manifestation?

"And his face according to the semblance of lightning" (Dan. x. 6).

"And lo, there stood before me as it were the semblance of a person" (Dan. viii. 15). See also Ezek. i. 26, 27, viii. 2, 4.

In the book of Daniel the distinction between *mareh* and *marah* is not so consistently maintained as elsewhere. In the following instances I translate the masculine noun by "appearance," and the feminine by "beholding"; but the two alike denote a manifestation or disclosure by Deity.

"Gabriel, make this man to understand the appearance" (viii. 16).

"He understood the word, and had understanding as to the appearance" (x. 1).

"And the appearance concerning the evenings and the mornings, as hath been said, is truth ; and as for thee, close thou up the vision, because it is for many days" (viii. 26). The reference here is to what has been said concerning the "vision" and the 2300 "evening-mornings" (vv. 13-14).

"And I was astonished concerning the appearance" (27).

"And to understand the matter, and to give understanding in regard to the appearance" (ix. 23).

"And I Daniel myself alone beheld the beholding, while the men who were with me beheld not the beholding" (x. 7).

"And I beheld this great beholding" (x. 8).

"My lord, at the beholding my pangs are turned upon me, and I retain no strength" (x. 16).

The verb *raah*, however, a few times takes as its object
a word of the stem *hhazah*. "Your young men shall
behold visions" (Joel ii. 28 [iii. 1]). "As I Daniel was
beholding the vision" (Dan. viii. 15). In this context
in Daniel the reflexive voice of *raah* is also used with
derivatives of *hhazah*. "A vision appeared unto me
. . . after the one that had appeared unto me at the beginning" (viii. 1). But these expressions are explained
by the parallel expression, "I beheld in vision" (viii. 2,
2, ix. 21), and also by the use of the nouns in these chapters of Daniel. *Hhazon* here denotes the whole transaction (viii. 1, 2, 2, 13, 15, 17, ix. 21, x. 14, xi. 14). It is
something that can be put into written form, and sealed
or closed up (ix. 24, viii. 26). *Mareh* and *marah*, on the
other hand, designate certain parts of the transaction,
parts that may be thought of as presented to the eye
(viii. 15, 16, 26, 27, x. 1, 6, 18, 7, 7, 8, 16). The use of
the verbs is quite congruous with this. It is everywhere
true that the words of the *raah* stem imply the possibility of presentation to the eye or to the senses, while
those of the *hhazah* stem are capable of being used independently of that implication, in the sense of insight or
reflection or other mental processes, as distinguished
from physical seeing.[1] It further illustrates the difference to observe that the derivatives of *hhazah* are frequently employed, as we have seen, in the literary titles
of the prophetic writings, but the words from *raah*
never.

The phrase "man of God," *ish elohim, ish haelohim*,
occurs often in the Old Testament as the equivalent of
nabhi, and is probably never employed except in this

[1] The cases in which a preposition is used with a noun of either stem,
forming the phrase "in vision," afford no additional instance that is significant.

use. Moses is many times called a man of God (*e.g.*
Deut. xxxiii. 1 ; Josh. xiv. 6 ; 1 Chron. xxiii. 14).[1] So are
Samuel and Shemaiah and David and Elijah and Elisha
and many others (1 Sam. ix. 6, 7, etc. ; 1 Ki. Man of God
xii. 22, etc. ; 2 Chron. viii. 14, etc. ; 2 Ki. i. 9,
10, etc. ; 2 Ki. iv. 7, etc., and concordance). The Angel
that appeared to Manoah and his wife is by them
described as a man of God (Jud. xiii. 6, 8, JE). The
person who spoke against Jeroboam's altar (called Jadon
by Josephus, probably " Jedo the seer " of 2 Chron. ix.
29) is several times called "man of God," and once
"prophet " (1 Ki. xiii. 1, 4, 5, 6, 6, 7, etc., and 18, 23),
while the term " prophet " is uniformly used of the
resident prophet who brought him back (11, 18, 20,
etc.).

Corresponding in form to the phrase "man of God "
is the phrase "word of Yahaweh," *d'bhar yahaweh*,
the usual designation for a message given Word of
by Deity to or through a man endowed with Yahaweh
the prophetic gift. " The word of Yahaweh came unto
Abraham in a vision " (Gen. xv. 1, 4 E). Moses is represented as saying : " I stood between Yahaweh and
you at that time, to tell to you the word of Yahaweh "
(Deut. v. 5). Isaiah says : " Out of Zion law shall go
forth, and the word of Yahaweh from Jerusalem " (ii. 3).
The phrase appears in the titles of prophetic books :
" The word of Yahaweh that came to Micah " (Mic.
i. 1). It is habitually used for opening the prophetic
narratives : " The word of Yahaweh came unto Jonah " ;
" the word of Yahaweh came unto Jonah the second
time " (Jon. i. 1, iii. 1). The phrase is probably never
employed in any other meaning, and at least this is its

---

[1] The new tradition assigns Deut. xxxiii to a date earlier than J or E,
and Josh. xiv. 6 sq. to JE.

ordinary use.[1]   The parallel term "word of God,"
d'bhar elohim, or *d'bhar haelohim*, sometimes occurs,
though but seldom.

Cognate with this are the phrases of asseveration,
amar yahaweh and *n'um yahaweh*, each occurring hun-

Saith
Yahaweh

dreds of times, and in our versions both translated " saith Jehovah." Both are commonly,
perhaps exclusively, applied to prophetic utterances (*e.g.*
Jer. ii. 2, 5, iv. 3 and i. 8, 15, 19), though it is in many
cases doubtful whether *amar yahaweh* is used as an asseveration or as giving a mere statement of fact.   In
asseverations of this kind the word *elohim*, "God,"
" Deity," is not often used, except in combination with
other words.   The different expression *yomar yahaweh*,
"Yahaweh is saying," sometimes appears (*e.g.* Isa. i.
11, 18, xxxiii. 10, xl. 1), though it is not distinctively
translated in the English versions.   In numberless instances we find the merely descriptive statement that
Yahaweh, or Deity, spake, or said.

As the prophetic gift is constantly represented as
bestowed by the Spirit of Yahaweh (1 Ki. xviii. 12 ;

Man of the
Spirit

Isa. lxiii. 10, 11 ; Joel ii. 28–29; 2 Chron.
xv. 1 ; Num. xi. 25–29, etc.), the prophet is
very naturally designated by the descriptive phrase
"the man of the Spirit " (Hos. ix. 7).

The word *massa*, "burden," is used to denote a
prophecy of a certain kind, from the days of Elisha,

Massa

and later.   A *massa* is poetic in form, and
in most cases minatory in character, and
always relatively brief.   Jehu is represented as saying
to Bidkar his captain that Yahaweh had " lifted up this
burden " upon Ahab : —

[1] For additional instances see Isa. i. 10; 1 Ki. xvii. 2, 8, 16, 24; 1 Sam.
iii. 1, 21, xv. 23, 26; Ex. ix. 20, 21, and concordance.

" Surely the blood of Naboth and the blood of his sons
    I beheld yesterday, so saith Yahaweh !
And I will make requital to thee
    in this plat, so saith Yahaweh ! "

Jehu mentions this as a reason for casting the corpse
of Ahab's son, whom he has just slain, into the plat of
Naboth (2 Ki. ix. 25–26). In Isaiah, the " Burden of
Babylon," " Burden of Moab," " Burden of Damascus "
(xiii. 1, xv. 1, xvii. 1), are poems of threatening upon
those countries. The instances of "burdens" are numerous (*e.g.* Ezek. xii. 10; Nah. i. 1; Zech. ix. 1, xii. 1;
Mal. i. 1; Isa. xiv. 28; 2 Chron. xxiv. 27 and concordance). In Prov. xxx. 1, xxxi. 1, where the poems are
not minatory, the King James's version translates *massa*
in the title by " prophecy." The revised version everywhere proposes "oracle" as the alternative translation
of the word. *Massa* seems to be used in 1 Chron. xv.
22, 27, to denote the singing when David brought the
ark to Jerusalem, and this may possibly indicate the
nature of its use in matters prophetic.

Certain forms of the causative-active stem of *nataph*
are sometimes applied to prophetic utterance. The
verb means to drip, to fall in drops, as in *Hittiph,*
the case of drippings of honey, or a gentle *mattiph*
shower. When used of human speech (Prov. v. 3;
Cant. iv. 11; Job xxix. 22) the idea seems to be that of
sweet or smooth or persuasive talk. When the words
of this stem are applied to prophets (Am. vii. 16; Mic.
ii. 6, 11; Ezek. xx. 46 and xxi. 2 [xxi. 2, 7], they can
be forcibly translated by the English words " preach,"
" preacher." In Micah ii these words seem to be used
by enemies, and ironically.

" Preach ye not ! They will be preaching ! They shall not preach
to these ! One never ceaseth uttering reproaches ! "

And a few verses farther on appears this statement: —

"If a man going in wind and falsehood has lyingly said, I will preach for thee of wine and of strong drink, then he will become the preacher of this people " (Mic. ii. 6, 11).[1]

A prophet is also sometimes called an angel of Yahaweh (*e.g.* Hag. i. 13), or a shepherd or a servant Metaphor- or a watchman, or by other like names; but ical terms these terms are properly figures of speech rather than appellations. Other like forms of expression might be added.

Three general observations are to be made in regard to the use of these several terms in the Old Testament — observations that are equally true whether we apply them to the history or to the records that contain the history, and in the main equally true whether we follow the old tradition concerning the dates of the records, or follow some form of the newer tradition.

In the first place, there is no definite succession of dates at which the various terms describing the prophets The several come successively into use. In a general terms not sense it is true that all the principal terms confined to particular are employed in all parts of the record. dates One critic may infer from this that the prophetic phenomena were practically all in existence before the earliest records were written; and another may account for it by some theory of interpolation into the records by later writers; but in any case the fact exists. It is true that particular words have a limited range of use. For example, *roeh* in the sense of seer

[1] The English words " prophet," " prophesy," " prophecy," are used in the King James or the revised versions to translate *hittiph* in this passage, to translate *massa* in Prov. xxx. 1, xxxi. 1, and to translate the *hhazah* words in Isa. xxx. 10. Elsewhere they are restricted in these versions to words of the stem *nabha*.

appears only in the literature treating of the times from
Samuel to Isaiah ; while *hhozeh* first appears in the
history of David, and may possibly be said to supersede
roeh for the later times.   In the time of Samuel *roeh*
was the appellative in common use in place of *nabhi*
(1 Sam. ix. 9, 10, 11, *cf.* x. 5, 10, 11, 12, 13).   *Massa*
appears only from the time of Elisha and onward.   But
it is doubtful how far an absence of these terms from
any part of the Old Testament is really significant.
Their not being used in the writings which we have
for any period does not necessarily prove that they were
at that time unknown.   And one may see, by running
over the references given in this chapter, that the
phrase " man of God " is applied to Moses, and to other
men from his time on; and that the phrase " word of Yahaweh," with words of the stems *nabha*, *raah*, and *hhazah*,
are used in describing divine revelations to men from
the times of Abraham.   And these several terms are in
frequent use, not only in those parts of the Old Testament which the critics of the Modern View regard as of
relatively late origin, but in those which they assign to
the times of Amos and Hosea and earlier.   For example,
the references include passages from those parts of the
book of Judges that are regarded by the men of the new
tradition as early, and also passages from those parts of
the hexateuch which they assign to J or E or JE or
independent early sources.   Follow what critical theory
you please, there is a somewhat extensive vocabulary of
prophetic terms from a time as early as the earliest sur-
viving records of the earliest times in Israelitish history.
   Further, it is in general true that the terms we have
been considering are interchangeable, so far as their
application to any given person is concerned.   Each
term has of course its own differential meaning.   The

terms differ in meaning when they denote the functions of the prophet. The seers seem to be distinguished from the beholders. As we have seen above, the men who are spoken of by name as seers are different men from those who are spoken of as beholders. Samuel the beholder is specifically distinguished from Gad the seer, and beholders in general are distinguished from seers in general (1 Chron. xxix. 29; Isa. xxx. 10). But Samuel was both a *roeh* and a *nabhi*. Gad was both a *hhozeh* and a *nabhi* (1 Sam. xxii. 5; 2 Sam. xxiv. 11, etc.). So was Amos (Am. vii. 12–16). So probably was Jehu, the son of Hanani (1 Ki. xvi. 7, 12, etc., *cf.* 2 Chron. xix. 2), the alternative being that Hanani was both *roeh* and *hhozeh* (2 Chron. xvi. 7, 10, *cf.* xix. 2). With perhaps some limitation in the case of *roeh* and *hhozeh*, a person who was regarded as having certain supernatural gifts was called indifferently man of God, prophet, seer, beholder. One term may have been at certain times current, rather than another, the term *roeh*, for example, just before the prophetic revival under Samuel, but all four of the terms were current from very early times. The permanent differences between the terms were differences in the form of the thought, and not in the person designated.

Finally, it should be noted that these several terms are used in the Old Testament with different degrees of comprehension. First, they are applied to persons who are better known as prophets than in any other capacity, for example, Samuel or Elisha or Jeremiah or Isaiah. Such prophets were also eminent as judges, priests, statesmen, and the like ; but the mention of any one of these names suggests to us the services of the man as a prophet, rather than in any other capacity. Second, the terms are applied to

persons who are better known in some other capacity
than as prophets, but who exercised prophetic gifts.
Some of these, as Moses the lawgiver or David the
king, stand very high in the prophetic ranks. By
parity the character of prophet belongs to other men of
like position, for example, such men as Joshua and Solomon and Ezra and Nehemiah.   It will sometimes be
convenient, for distinction's sake, to call such men prophetic men, rather than prophets.   That is partly a
question of convenience in the use of language.   But
when we are discussing the prophets as a subject, we
must take into the account all persons who have the
prophetic character.   Third, the terms are applied to
persons who were prophets only in a secondary sense,
to the pupils or disciples or assistants of the men who
were strictly prophets.   As we advance in our study we
shall find much said concerning certain prophetic "companies," and certain so-called "sons of the prophets,"
men who were banded together into organizations under
such great prophets as Samuel or Elijah, men who were
recognized as disciples of such a prophet as Isaiah.   A
person of this type may naturally be spoken of as a
prophet or a man of God, especially when he is sent by
his superior on some prophetic errand.   The secondary
prophets were at times much more numerous than the
primary prophets, and it sometimes becomes important
to distinguish between the two.

In addition to these uses, many assert that the words
that denote the prophet and his functions are also used
to denote mere frenzied utterance, and that primarily
the prophetic gift is conceived of as a kind of insanity.
We shall find that there is no ground for this, and that
herein there is a difference between the prophets of
Israel and the prophets of the nations.

CHAPTER III

THE EXTERNAL HISTORY OF THE PROPHETS

THIS subject, though we must dismiss it with a single chapter, is a fascinating one. Some of the older treat-

The attractiveness of the subject ments of it are dull through the lack of imagination, or through the wrong use of imagination. They regard the prophets as unearthly revealers of the divine will, with no human blood in them. Some of the more recent treatments are yet more faulty, rejecting half the biblical data, filling in the gaps thus made from conjecture or by inference from theory, and thus giving portraits utterly different from those in the bible, and immeasurably inferior. In contrast with both these modes of treatment would be that of one who should simply take the trouble to find out just what the biblical statements mean, using his imagination only to render the facts distinct and vivid. What we need is a treatment at once correct and imaginative. Why does not some one write a history of Israel in the form of a series of biographies of the prophets, working it up, not from Bible Dictionaries, not from volumes, not from Josephus, not from commentaries, not from theories of the evolution of religion, but purely from the data given in the bible? There are no heroes in history more picturesque or interesting or full of vitality than these same prophets, provided we picture them rightly.

Many of the books of reference affirm that the succession of the prophets began with Samuel. In proof they cite passages from the Acts and from 1 Samuel. But the context in Samuel, as we shall see below, The division implies that prophecy was previously in exist- into periods ence, and that in the Acts affirms that prophecy had been in existence from the days of Moses, and, indeed, from the beginning of the world.[1] Other parts of the record give details in abundance. Certainly the biblical view is that what occurred in Samuel's time was not an origination but a revival. There was then a new beginning in the progress of an ancient institution.

The biblical presentation of the history of the prophets is in very clearly marked chronological periods. The first great period, that before Samuel, includes as subordinate periods the pre-Abrahamic times, the patriarchal times, the times of the exodus, and the times of the Judges before Samuel. The prophets of the second great period, from Samuel to the close of the Old Testament, fall into six groups, namely, the group in which Samuel and Nathan and David were eminent, the Elijah and Elisha group, the Isaiah group, the Jeremiah group, the exilian prophets, and the postexilian prophets. Then any survey of these two great periods is incomplete unless supplemented by obtaining, in part from

[1] "Yea and all the prophets from Samuel and them that followed after . . . told of these days " (Acts iii. 24). It is easy to understand this as affirming that Samuel was the earliest prophet, but the immediate context shows that the writer intended no such meaning. Only a few sentences previously he has used this language : "The times of restoration of all things, whereof God spake by the mouth of his holy prophets which have been since the world began." Moses indeed said : "A prophet shall the Lord God raise up unto you . . . like unto me " (Acts iii. 21–22, cf. vii. 37; Lc. i. 70). With this agrees the New Testament mention of the prophetic gift in the times of Balaam and of Enoch (2 Pet. ii. 16; Jude 14).

extrabiblical sources, some account of the closing of the succession of the prophets.[1]

I. We take up the first great period. The Old Testament agrees with the New in representing that the patriarchs exercised prophetic gifts, that such gifts were abundant in the time of Moses, and that they continued during the time between Moses and Samuel.

Books on the subject have been very free in ascribing prophetic phenomena to the times before Abraham. Prophecy Jude says that Enoch prophesied (14), and in before Luke and the Acts it is affirmed that there Abraham have been holy prophets from the beginning of the world (Lc. i. 70; Acts iii. 21). Parts of the first eleven chapters of Genesis have figured largely in discussions concerning prophecy; for example, the protevangelium, the sacrifice of Abel, some of the experiences of Noah (Gen. iii. 15, iv, vi–ix, and New Testament parallels). Something very like prophetic character has been attributed to Adam, Seth, Enoch, Abel, Noah, and others. Any detailed consideration of these matters belongs to a later stage in our investigation. For the present it is sufficient to note that the various terms denoting prophetic function are not used in the accounts of the times before Abraham; but that there is nothing to forbid the opinion that the writers of these accounts

[1] The biblical account seems to be that with Samuel there began certain arrangements for cultivating the prophetic gift, which, thenceforward to the close of the Old Testament times, secured a more abundant succession of prophets than had previously existed. If we distinguish between prophets and prophetic men, applying the latter term to men who had prophetic gifts, but are better known in some other capacity, the great names before Samuel are of prophetic men only. It further happens to be true that the Old Testament books called the Prophets, in distinction from the Law and the Hagiographa, are ascribed in the traditions to the prophets of Samuel's time and later, while the Law and the Hagiographa are ascribed, in the main, to prophetic men.

thought of pre-Abrahamic men as possessing prophetic gifts.[1]

Old Testament history, however, properly begins with Abraham. From Abraham onward the Israelite literature is familiar with the distinctive titles and duties and powers that belong to a prophet.

It is represented that Abraham and Isaac and Jacob had prophetic gifts, though this representation is not very greatly emphasized. Abraham is once expressly called a prophet. In the time when he led a migratory life, going from one country to another, we are told that Abimelech took possession of Abraham's wife. To him a revelation was made : —

The patriarchs were prophets

. "And now, restore thou the wife of the man, for he is a prophet, that he may make his prayer in thy behalf," etc. (Gen. xx. 7 E).

One of the psalmists, centuries later, cites this incident in the following lines : —

"And they went about from nation unto nation,
    from one kingdom unto another people.
He suffered no man to wrong them,
    and he rebuked kings for their sakes :
Touch ye not mine anointed ones,
    and to my prophets do ye no harm."
            (Ps. cv. 14–15, repeated in 1 Chron. xvi. 20–22.)

In addition to this one instance in which the word "prophet" is used, it is represented that Abraham had visions, and that the word of Yahaweh came to him in

[1] One who accepts the Graf-Wellhausen analysis should observe that the passages which have commonly been cited as prophetic occur alike in the earlier and the later J and in P, though with characteristic differences. On any critical theory it is probable that all the authors of Genesis, earlier or later, thought of the prophetic gift as current among these predecessors of Abraham.

vision (Gen. xv. 1, 4 E).   A very prominent part of his experiences consists in those when Yahaweh "appeared" to him.[1]

"And Yahaweh appeared unto him at the oaks of Mamre," followed by extended details (xviii. 1 J).

It is further represented that Isaac and Jacob had similar experiences. Yahaweh appeared unto Isaac, forbidding him to go down into Egypt as Abraham had done; and again appeared to him, promising to bless and multiply him (Gen. xxvi. 2, 24 J). Jacob had a prophetic dream, wherein the Angel of God commanded him to return to Palestine (Gen. xxxi. 11, E). God appeared to him at Bethel, after his return from Paddan-aram (Gen. xxxv. 9 P). When he was about to go down into Egypt, —

"God spake unto Israel in the visions of the night" (Gen. xlvi. 2 E).

Look up these instances in detail, and it will be evident that the patriarchs are here represented as having personal interviews with the supreme Being, essentially the same as were enjoyed by the prophets of later times.

This is not a matter which depends wholly on the critical theories one may hold. If the hexateuch was written by Moses and Joshua and their associates, then we have the testimony of that generation to the facts in the case. But how is it on the theory of those who analyze Genesis into the three documents, J and E and P, dated respectively 800, 750, and 400 B.C. ? On the basis of their partition some of the passages that have

---

[1] For example, at his first coming to Palestine,

"Yahaweh appeared unto Abram, and said, To thy seed will I give this land.   And he built there an altar to Yahaweh that appeared unto him" (Gen. xii. 7 J).

"And Yahaweh appeared unto Abram, and said unto him, I am El-shaddai" (Gen. xvii. 1 P [RP?]).

been cited are taken from J, some from E, and some
from P.   That is, all three alike testify to the prophetic
gifts of Abraham and Isaac and Jacob.   It is not unimportant which theory of the hexateuch we hold ; but on
any theory the oldest Hebrew literature testifies to the
view we are advocating.

   In the records of the times of Moses and Joshua
the mention of prophecy is very abundant.   In the
account of the exodus, for example, the stem Prophecy in
nabha occurs seventeen times, and the other the time of Moses and
terms that denote prophetic phenomena are Joshua
much used.   Instances will presently be given.   Perhaps we habitually think of Moses as a statesman, a
warrior, a lawgiver ; but, none the less, the record says
that he was remarkably endowed with the prophetic
gift.   He is described as the greatest of prophets.[1]
He is frequently spoken of, both in the hexateuch and
elsewhere, as "the man of God" (*e.g.* Deut. xxxiii. 1 ;
Josh. xiv. 6 ; Ezra iii. 2 ; 1 Chron. xxiii. 14 ; 2 Chron. xxx.
16).   He has the various experiences that characterize
a prophet.   Habitually he has supernatural communication with God.   Yahaweh appeared unto him (Ex. iii. 2,
16, and many places).   Yahaweh caused him to see in
the prophetic sense (Ex. xxvii. 8 ; Num. viii. 4 et al.).
Using words of the stem *raah*, the beholding of visions
is attributed to Moses (Num. xii. 8 ; Ex. iii. 3).   In certain instances presently to be cited, he is the typical
prophet with whom others are compared.   The prophet
who is to be raised up he describes as "like unto me."
Yahaweh enables other men to prophesy by taking of

---

[1] "There arose not a prophet since in Israel, like unto Moses" (Deut.
xxxiv. 10).

   "And by a prophet Yahaweh brought up Israel out of Egypt, and by a
prophet he was guarded" (Hos. xii. 13 [14]).

the Spirit that was upon Moses and placing it upon
them. He is so superior to other prophets as to be
fairly in contrast with them.

The records represent that Moses was not the only
prophet of this period. We read that "Miriam the
prophetess took a timbrel in her hand," and celebrated
the overthrow of Pharaoh at the Red Sea (Ex. xv. 20 E).
Miriam appears again in the narrative in which she and
Aaron find fault with Moses on account of the Ethiopian
woman. Yahaweh rebukes them, in language that implies that Miriam is a prophet with whom Yahaweh
communicates in beholdings or in dreams, and that persons of this sort were not unfamiliar to that generation
of Israelites.[1] This same fact of the multiplication of
prophecy appears in the story of the prophesying of
Eldad and Medad and the seventy, and in the wish then
expressed by Moses that all Yahaweh's people were
prophets.[2]

[1] " If there be a prophet of you,
    I Yahaweh make myself known unto him in beholdings,
    in dreams I speak with him.
  Not so is my servant Moses,
    in all my house he is trustworthy.
  Mouth unto mouth I speak with him,
    even causing him to behold, and not enigmatically,
    and the likeness of Yahaweh he gazeth upon " (Num. xii. 6–8 E).
It is not implied here that Moses has a different gift from the prophetic
gift of Miriam and Aaron, but that he has prophetic seeing power in a
much higher degree than they.

[2] " And he gathered seventy men of the elders of the people, and made
them stand around the Tent. And Yahaweh came down in the cloud, and
spake unto him, and took of the Spirit which was upon him and gave it
upon seventy men, the elders. And it came to pass, as the Spirit rested
upon them, that they prophesied, and did no more. And there remained
two men in the camp, the name of the one being Eldad, and the name
of the second Medad ; and the Spirit rested upon them, they being among
those who were written, and they not having gone forth to the Tent ; and
they prophesied in the camp. And the young man ran and told Moses,

Besides these passages, in which certain persons are spoken of as prophets, there are others which make such mention of prophetic functions as to imply that prophets were something well known in that generation.

Words of the stem *hhazah* are less used in the records for this period than in those of later periods. But it is said of the elders of Israel : —

"They had vision of Deity, and did eat and drink" (Ex. xxiv. 11 J).

And it is represented that Balaam twice describes himself as —

" He that heareth the sayings of El,
   That seeth the vision of the Almighty,
   Having fallen, and his eyes having become uncovered" (Num. xxiv. 4, 16 JE).

Whatever the date of the book of Job, its action is located in the time of the exodus or earlier. It affords such instances as the following : —

" In thoughts from the visions of the night " (iv. 13).
" Thou scarest me with dreams, and terrifiest me with visions " (vii. 14).
" He shall be chased away as a vision of the night " (xx. 8).

Passing to the use of other terms, the relations of Aaron to Moses are defined in the words : —

"Behold I have given thee for a Deity unto Pharaoh, Aaron thy brother being thy prophet" (Ex. vii. 1 P).

Such language presupposes familiarity with the notion of a prophet, and of the relations he sustains to Deity. In Deuteronomy laws are given formally defining the

and said, Eldad and Medad are prophesying in the camp. And answered Joshua the son of Nun, the minister of Moses, of his choice young men, and said, My lord Moses, forbid them. And Moses said to him, Art thou jealous for me ? Would that all Yahaweh's people were prophets ! that Yahaweh would give his Spirit upon them ! " (Num. xi. 24–29 JE).

character of a prophet, prescribing how true prophets are to be distinguished from false, forecasting a line of prophets to come (xiii. 1, 3, 5 [2, 4, 6], xviii. 15, 18, 20, 22). There is no need here to consider these passages at length. They will be discussed when we reach the subjects of the functions of a prophet and of messianic prophecy.

In these several passages a prophet is defined, as we have seen, as a spokesman of Deity, divinely inspired through visions, dreams, trances, divine appearings. These affirmations are found not merely in the narrative portions of the books, but in the statements which the books say were made by the persons whose history they narrate. Their validity depends not at all, directly, on the question who wrote the pentateuchal books. If the books are historically true, then the statements are true, no matter when they were written in their present form. And even from the point of view of those who regard them as unhistorical, they testify to what their authors believed to be true of the times of Moses. Further, our citations have been made indifferently from sections which the critical hypotheses ascribe to J, E, JE, P, and D. If there were authors of all these classes, then all alike agree in affirming that prophecy was abundant in the days of Moses.

For the times from the settlement of Israel in Canaan to the birth of Samuel the mention of prophecy in the narratives is relatively unusual; but the stream of prophecy through this region of the history is perceptible though slender. Deborah is called a prophetess (Jud. iv. 4). Perhaps we may be at a loss whether to classify her as a statesman sometimes acting the part of a prophet, or as a prophet sometimes doing the duty of a statesman.

Prophecy in the times of the Judges

Gideon and others are occasionally represented as holding communication with God, such as a prophet might
hold.   We are told of a prophet whom Yahaweh sent
to Israel in the days of Gideon (Jud. vi. 8), and we
have a record in three verses of his prophecy.   We
are told of the appearing of the Angel of Yahaweh
to Gideon (Jud. vi. 12) and to Manoah and his wife
(Jud. xiii. 3, 10, 21).   Few instances of theophany in
the bible are presented with as much fulness of detail
as these two.   " The Angel," in the book of Judges,
is always a supernatural being, and not a prophet.
This is particularly the case with the Angel who appeared to the wife of Manoah, and afterward to her and
Manoah, announcing the birth of Samson.   But, four
times in the narrative, they speak of him as a "man of
God " (Jud. xiii. 6, 8, 10, 11).   Evidently a man of God,
a prophet, was a well-known fact within the range of
their experience.

In the time of Eli, just at the close of this period,
the dearth of prophecy was deepest.

" The word of Yahaweh being precious in those days, there being
no widespread vision " (1 Sam. iii. 1).

These words affirm that prophecy had then nearly dis-
appeared from Israel.   The same fact is implied in the
statement concerning the recognition of Samuel.

" And all Israel knew, from Dan and even unto Beer-sheba, that
Samuel was made sure for a prophet to Yahaweh.   And again
Yahaweh appeared in Shiloh ; for Yahaweh disclosed himself unto
Samuel in Shiloh in the word of Yahaweh " (1 Sam. iii. 20–21).

From these statements it has been inferred that there
was no prophecy in Israel before Samuel.   This inference differs from the representations of the In the time
bible.   If the passage last cited implies that of Eli
the wealth of prophecy which came in with Samuel was

in contrast with the poverty which directly preceded, it
equally implies that there had been an earlier time
when Yahaweh appeared in Shiloh by his prophetic
word. The other passage says that prophecy was at
that time a rare thing, not that it was nonexistent.
From the context we learn that it was not nonexistent.
We are told of a "man of God" who came to Eli with
just such a message as prophets are accustomed to
bring.[1] Further, we are told that Eli was sufficiently
familiar with the idea of prophetic function to recognize the nature of Samuel's call when it came to him.[2]
In fine, the history of the times of the Judges justifies
the assertion of Jeremiah : —

"Since the day that your fathers came forth out of the land of
Egypt unto this day, I have sent unto you all my servants the
prophets, daily rising up early and sending them" (vii. 25 RV).

So much for the first great period of the history of prophecy.   Besides other statements in other terms, the words
"prophet" and "prophesy" are applied not less than
twenty-four times, in the Old Testament, to the period
before the death of Eli.[3]   And let us once more remind
ourselves that this is the testimony of the records irrespective of the question when or by whom the records
were written.   Assuredly, if a person is in the habit

[1] "And there came a man of God unto Eli and said unto him, I surely
revealed myself unto the house of thy father when they were in Egypt,"
etc. (1 Sam. ii. 27–36).

[2] Of Samuel it is said that he, being an inexperienced boy, " did not yet
know," that "the word of Yahaweh was not yet disclosed unto him." But
Eli was older and more experienced.   "And Yahaweh again called Samuel the third time, and he arose and went unto Eli, and said, Here am I
for thou calledst me ; and Eli understood that Yahaweh was calling the
boy.   And Eli said to Samuel, Go, lie down, and it shall be, if he call unto
thee thou shalt say, Speak, Yahaweh, for thy servant is hearkening"
(1 Sam. iii. 7–9).

[3] As we shall presently see, there is in this nothing contradictory of
1 Sam. ix. 9.

of designating certain parts of the hexateuch and of Judges and Samuel as J and E, and of saying that J and E are "prophetic" narratives, that person is precluded from denying that these narratives recognize a prophetic element in the history.   And if he admits that these writings which he regards as the earliest testify to the existence of prophets in this part of the history, he must all the more admit that what he regards as the later parts of the record testify to the same fact.   Any one who reads the writings without thus dividing them into earlier and later sections, will find the same testimony there.   In other words, there is a consensus of testimony among the writers of the Old Testament, no matter how you regard them critically, to the effect that prophecy in Israel came down from the earliest times.

II. In the second great period of the history of the prophets, the first subordinate period is that in which Samuel and Nathan and David are promi- Prophecy in nent. Its natural limits are from the death of the times of Eli to the disruption of the kingdom after David, and Solomon. The chronology is in dispute, but Nathan the biblical numbers make it about one hundred and sixty years.

The distinguished prophets named in the record for this period are Samuel and Gad and Nathan, David and Solomon, Zadok, Asaph and Heman and Ethan or Jeduthun, Ahijah and Shemaiah and Jedo. The easiest and most effective way of obtaining information concerning these men would be to look them up, with the aid of a concordance, in the Old Testament. In this chapter we must dismiss them with just a few sentences.

Samuel is the earliest and, with the exception of David, the most distinguished great prophet of this

time. His career is too well known to need recapitulation here. Gad was associated with David from the time
when David first became an outlaw to near the close of
the reign. It was by his advice that David chose his
hiding places within the borders of Judah, and he was
the prophet consulted when Ornan's threshing floor
was purchased, and the temple site fixed (1 Sam.
xxii. 5; 2 Sam. xxiv. 11 ff.; 1 Chron. xxi. 9 ff.).
Nathan first appears in the middle years of David's
reign, rebuking him for his sin in the matter of Uriah;
and, later,[1] as the prophet through whom the great
promise was given to David, in response to David's dis-
position to build a temple (2 Sam. xii; Ps. li, title; 2
Sam. vii; 1 Chron. xvii). Still later Nathan figures as
the strong supporter of the claims of Solomon to the
throne (1 Ki. i). The Chronicler groups David and Gad
and Nathan, and refers to "the words" of Samuel and
of Gad and of Nathan as written sources for the history
of David and of the times before him (1 Chron. xxix. 29;
2 Chron. xxix. 25).

David is spoken of as a "man of God," upon whom
the Spirit came mightily, to whom Yahaweh appeared
(*e.g.* 2 Chron. viii. 14; Neh. xii. 24, 36; 1 Sam. xvi. 13,
etc.; 2 Chron. iii. 1. Also Acts ii. 30). In these and
other terms he is presented to us as richly endowed
with prophetic gifts. To Solomon also prophetic revelations are attributed.[2]

[1] The affair of Uriah occurred while the Ammonite war was in progress,
before David's conquests had brought him rest. The bringing up of the
ark to Jerusalem and the giving of the great promise occurred after Yahaweh had given David rest from all his enemies, and when his dominions
extended from Hamath to Shihor of Egypt (2 Sam. vii. 1; 1 Chron. xiii.
5). That is, the Uriah affair preceded the others, though it is narrated
after them.

[2] "In that night Deity appeared to Solomon." "In Gibeon Yahaweh

Zadok, afterward highpriest, is in one passage called a seer (2 Sam. xv. 27). In his detailed description of the large temple choirs organized by David, the Chronicler speaks of Asaph and Heman and Jeduthun as prophesying, and calls Heman the *hhozeh* of the king.[1] In his account of the last reigns in Judah he makes similar statements, speaking of Asaph as "the *hhozeh*," and of "Asaph and Heman and Jeduthun the *hhozeh* of the king" (2 Chron. xxix. 30, xxxv. 15).

Ahijah the Shilonite, we are told, in the later years of Solomon, promised the kingdom to Jeroboam, tearing his robe into twelve pieces, and giving Jeroboam ten. Later he gave a most uncomforting reply to Jeroboam's queen, who sought him in behalf of her sick son (1 Ki. xi. 29–39, xiv. 1–18). We are told of another prophet who came from Judah, when Jeroboam was king, and prophesied against the altar of Bethel, and of an old prophet who entertained him (1 Ki. xiii; 2 Ki. xxiii. 17–18). Josephus says that the prophet from Judah was named Jadon. In Chronicles, Jedo or Jedai is mentioned (2 Chron. ix. 29), along with Ahijah and Nathan, as a source for the history of Solomon. The name appears as Iddo in our English versions, but it is different from the name Iddo as elsewhere occurring, and Jedo is probably the Jadon of Josephus. Be-

appeared unto Solomon in a dream by night." "And the word of Yahaweh was to Solomon, saying" (2 Chron. i. 7–12; 1 Ki. iii. 5–15, vi. 11–13, *cf.* ix. 2).

[1] "And David and the captains of the host separated to the service the sons of Asaph and Heman and Jeduthun, who prophesied with lyres, with harps, and with cymbals . . . the sons of Asaph upon the hand of Asaph who prophesied upon the hands of the king. To Jeduthun; the sons of Jeduthun . . . upon the hands of their father Jeduthun, who prophesied with the lyre, to give thanks and to praise Yahaweh. To Heman; . . . all these were sons to Heman the *hhozeh* of the king in the words of God, to lift up horn" (1 Chron. xxv. 1–5).

longing to the same group of prophets is Shemaiah, who
forbade the attempt of Rehoboam to subdue the ten
tribes, and who encouraged Rehoboam against the invasion of Shishak (1 Ki. xii. 22; 2 Chron. xi. 2, xii. 7).
The Chronicler refers to him along with Iddo (probably
a much later writer) for the history of Rehoboam
(xii. 15).[1]

These distinguished prophets, with other great men,
constituted a brilliant circle around the thrones of David
Organiza-   and Solomon.   But besides these there were
tions   a large number of other prophets.   With
Samuel, prophecy had entered upon a brighter era.
There was a great revival of prophetism.   When the
writer of 1 Sam. iii. 1 says that during Samuel's child-
hood there was no widespread vision, he implies that
vision was widespread when he wrote.   That prophets
were numerous is suggested by Saul's complaint that
Yahaweh answered him not, either "by dreams or by
Urim, or by prophets" (1 Sam. xxviii. 6, 15).   Prominent among the evidences of the growing influence of
prophecy, at this time, are the organized bands of
prophets that present themselves to view.   We find a
procession of prophets meeting Saul when Samuel had
anointed him, and a body of them engaged in concerted
services at Naioth in Ramah when David fled thither
(1 Sam. x. 5 ff., xix. 18–24).   The nature of these organizations we are to consider later.   For the present we
simply note that they are characteristic of the period.
Through the influence of Samuel, prophecy so impressed
itself upon his generation, that the impression remained
to future generations.   There is no room for our being

---

[1] In the long addition after 1 Ki. xii. 24 in the Greek copies, Shemaiah
is said to be the prophet who tore his robe into twelve pieces and gave
Jeroboam ten.

surprised that he is commonly regarded as the father of prophecy.

In the literature concerning this period we find nearly all the different terms that are used in the bible to designate prophetic function, — "man of God," "word of Yahaweh," "Spirit of Yaha- weh," and the words of the stems *nabha* and *hhazah* and *raah*.[1] On the strength of 1 Sam. ix. 9 many affirm that the word "prophet" was new in Israel when this narrative in Samuel was written, and that neither the word nor the fact had ever before been known. The true inference from the biblical phenomena is that both the institution and the word had formerly been well known, but had temporarily faded from use, and now reappeared.[2] The statement in Samuel is: —

The terms that are used

" He that is to-day called a prophet was formerly called a seer."

But the writer of this statement says that the word "prophet" was in familiar use, and that prophets were well-known personages, not merely at the time when he

---

[1] Samuel and Zadok are called *roeh* (1 Sam. ix. 9, 11, 18, 19; 1 Chron. ix. 22, xxvi. 28, xxix. 29; 2 Sam. xv. 27). Samuel has vision, *mar'ah* (1 Sam. iii. 15). Theophany is frequent (*e.g.* 1 Ki. iii. 5, ix. 2, xi. 9).

The term *hhozeh* is applied to Gad, Asaph, Heman, Jeduthun, Jedo, Iddo (2 Sam. xxiv. 11; 1 Chron. xxi. 9, xxix. 29, xxv. 5; 2 Chron. xxxv. 15, xxix. 25, 30, ix. 29, xii. 15). Other nouns of the stem appear in 1 Sam. iii. 1; 2 Sam. vii. 17; 1 Chron. xvii. 15; Ps. lxxxix. 19 [20]; 2 Chron. ix. 29. The word *hhazon* first appears in 1 Sam. iii. 1, this being the word that is afterward mostly used in the literary titles of the prophetic writings.

[2] The disappearance of words from use, and their subsequent reappearance, is one of the familiar phenomena of language. For example, Mr. Leon Mead is quoted as saying in his book *Word Coinage* that such words as transcend, bland, sphere, blithe, franchise, carve, anthem, in good use in Chaucer, were regarded in the seventeenth century as obsolete, but have since been reinstated.

wrote, but at the time concerning which he makes the statement.[1]   On the very next day, this writer says, prophets were seen, mentioned, discussed, not by Samuel alone, but popularly.   The point which he makes is this : that though prophets and the name prophet were now familiar in Israel, Saul was one of a class who took no particular interest in them.   He still habitually used the term " seer," which had till recently displaced the term "prophet."   The writer contemplates prophecy, both the word and the fact, as a gift to Israel which had been interrupted but was now restored, and not at all as a new gift which had never till now been bestowed.   In this he agrees with the writers of the earlier history, who speak of prophets as existing at least from the times of Abraham.

[1] " And the young man . . . said, Behold there is found in my hand a quarter shekel of silver, and I will give [it] to the man of God, and he will tell us our way.   (Formerly in Israel thus said the man when he went to inquire of God, Come ye and let us go unto the seer.   For he that is to-day called the prophet was formerly called the seer.) . . .   And they went unto the city where was the man of God. . . .   And when they found young women coming forth to draw water, they said to them, Is the seer within ? . . .   And Saul approached Samuel, . . . and said, Tell me, pray, where is the house of the seer.   And Samuel answered Saul, and said, I am the seer."

The next day, when the two parted, Samuel gave Saul directions.

" Thou wilt come unto the hill of God, . . . and wilt fall in with a string of prophets coming down from the highplace, and before them psaltery and timbrel and pipe and harp, and they prophesying.   And the Spirit of Yahaweh will come mightily upon thee, and thou wilt prophesy with them, and wilt be turned to another man."

It happens as Samuel has said.   " And they came there to the hill, and behold a string of prophets meeting him, and the Spirit of God came mightily upon him and he prophesied in the midst of them.   And it happened in the case of any one who knew him formerly, that they looked, and behold he prophesied with prophets.   And the people said, each to his neighbor, What is it that has happened to the son of Kish ?   Is Saul also among the prophets ? " (1 Sam. ix. 8–11, 18–19, x. 5–6, 10–12).

The second subperiod may be designated by the names of its two great prophets, Elijah and Elisha. It extends from the disruption of the kingdom to the death of Elisha, about one hundred and thirty-five years by the biblical data. Its last fifty years correspond nearly to the earlier Assyrian period, when Shalmanezer II and Rimman-nirari III made most of Palestine tributary. Its distinguished prophets are Ahijah and Shemaiah and Jedo, who survive from the former period, Oded and Azariah and Hanani and Jehu, Elijah and Elisha, Micaiah and Jahaziel and Eliezer, Jehoiada and Zechariah.

Prophecy from the disruption to Elisha

Oded and Azariah his son urged Asa to reformation work, after his victory over Zerah the Ethiopian (2 Chron. xv. 1, 8). Hanani the *roeh* rebuked Asa for his intrigues with Ben-hadad, and was imprisoned (2 Chron. xvi. 7–10). "Jehu the son of Hanani the *hhozeh*," elsewhere described as "Jehu the prophet," prophesied against Baasha of Israel (1 Ki. xvi. 1, 7, 12). He met Jehoshaphat with rebuke and counsel, on his return from the Ramoth-gilead expedition, and his history of Jehoshaphat is said to have been "brought up upon the book of the kings of Israel" (2 Chron. xix. 2, xx. 34). His career was largely contemporary with that of Elijah the Tishbite. Elijah and Elisha are so well known that they may here be passed by. The picture of Micaiah the son of Imlah prophesying before Ahab and Jehoshaphat (1 Ki. xxii; 2 Chron. xviii) is a familiar one. A little later, when Jehoshaphat was preparing to meet the Moabite invasion, the Spirit of Yahaweh came upon Jahaziel the son of Zechariah, in the midst of the congregation (2 Chron. xx. 14). Just after the death of Ahab, when Jehoshaphat had joined with Ahab's son Ahaziah to build Tarshish-going ships,

Eliezer the son of Dodavah prophesied against the alliance (2 Chron. xx. 37). The long life of the prophetically gifted highpriest Jehoiada (2 Ki. xi–xii; 2 Chron. xxiii–xxiv, especially xxiv. 15) was nearly contemporary with this whole period of prophetic history. His death and that of his spirit-gifted son Zechariah (2 Chron. xxiv. 19–22) occurred not very long before that of Elisha.

In several instances prophets are individually mentioned, though their names are not given. Such, for example, is the prophet who announced to Ahab his victory over Syria (1 Ki. xx. 13). Later in the same chapter a prophet promises him another victory, and yet later a prophet, also spoken of as "of the sons of the prophets," rebukes Ahab for not securing the fruits of his victory. We have also an account of a person who is described as "a prophet," and as "one of the sons of the prophets" (2 Ki. ix), who anointed Jehu as king.

In the northern kingdom the organizations described as "the sons of the prophets" are, next to the personality of Elijah and Elisha, the characteristic feature of this period. Their character will be considered later. For the present we only note that they were under the supervision of Elijah and Elisha, and that they probably account for the very large number of the prophets at that time.

That the number was large the record clearly affirms. Of those in the northern kingdom, Elijah at Horeb says: "They have slain thy prophets with the sword" (1 Ki. xix. 10, 14). "When Jezebel slew the prophets of Yahaweh," Obadiah the steward of Ahab hid a hundred of them by fifties in a cave (1 Ki. xviii. 4, 13), and the account seems to suggest that this was but a fraction of the whole number.   The prophets of Baal and of the asherahs numbered eight hundred and fifty (1 Ki. xviii. 19), and it is possible that Yahaweh's prophets were as numerous.   Perhaps, however, there were not many prophets who were supernaturally gifted.   Most of those who are called prophets may have been "sons of the prophets" (see 1 Ki. xx. 35, 38, and 2 Ki. ix. 1, 4), that is, either pupils of some particular prophet, or members of the organizations.   Note that the community at Jericho was able to send out detachments of fifty (2 Ki. ii. 7, 16, 17).   For the southern kingdom the accounts are less explicit, but prophets were also numerous there. Jehoshaphat gives the exhortation : " Believe his prophets, so shall ye prosper " (2 Chron. xx. 20).   In the account of the defection of Joash of Judah we read : " He sent prophets to them to bring them again unto Yahaweh, and they testified with them, but they did not hear " (2 Chron. xxiv. 19).

A class of men make their appearance within this period whom the biblical writers regard as false prophets of Yahaweh, and from this time _{False} on they abound throughout the history. Of _{prophets} this class is the old prophet of Bethel (1 Ki. xiii). Apparently he has had genuine prophetic gifts, and has perverted them.   There were four hundred prophets, Zedekiah the son of Chenaanah being one of them who prophesied falsely in the name of Yahaweh to persuade Ahab and Jehoshaphat to go up to Ramoth-gilead (1 Ki. xxii. 6, 11 ; 2 Chron. xviii. 5).   The prophets had become so influential that there was a field of operations for counterfeit prophets.

Words of the stems *nabha, raah, hhazah,* and also the usual phrases descriptive of the prophet and of prophetic function, are current in the accounts of all parts of this

period.   In the latter part of the period, Jehu the king
is represented as using the word *massa*, "burden," in the
technical sense in which, from this time on, it denotes a
prophecy of a certain type (2 Ki. ix. 25–26).

The third subperiod is that of Isaiah and his near
predecessors and successors.   It extends from the death
of Elisha to the captivity of Manasseh, perhaps about two hundred years, but fifty years
less by the usual interpretation of the Assyrian chronology.   It covers the middle Assyrian period, that in which Tiglath-pilezer is prominent,
and the later Assyrian period, that of Sargon and his
dynasty.   To it belong the earlier group of the so-called
literary prophets.   The distinguished names for the
period are Joel, Obadiah, Jonah, the Zechariah of Uzziah's time, Amos, Hosea, Isaiah, the author or authors
of Zech. ix–xiv, Micah, the Oded of the time of Ahaz.
This is the most conspicuous time in the history of the
prophets, and the fullest in the materials it offers, but
we must deal with it only in the barest outline.

We have no information concerning the prophet Joel,
save as the author of the book of that name.   It is generally agreed that the book is either the earliest or the
latest of the fifteen known as the major and minor prophets.   I have no doubt that it is the earliest.   It presents a very distinct historical situation, which seems to
me to be that of the invasion when Hazael swept the
region and besieged Jerusalem (2 Ki. xii. 17–xiii. 9 and
2 Chron. xxiv. 23–25), the prophet being contemporary
with the event.   Perhaps the death of Elisha occurred
after this event, in the same year, so that Joel was in
early life a contemporary of the illustrious northern
prophet.   Joel teaches a doctrine of the Day of Yahaweh, on which the succeeding prophets build.   He prom-

Marginal note: Prophecy from the death of Elisha to Manasseh

ises an outpouring of the Spirit, which may be plausibly regarded as having its first fulfilment in the days of Isaiah and his contemporaries.

Obadiah takes up the great theme, the Day of Yahaweh, illustrating it by a single instance, Yahaweh's dealings with Edom. The brief prophecy pictures two historical situations, — that of Edom's offence, and that of Edom's punishment. The offence-situation, it seems to me, is the situation that had been outlined in Joel, the punishment being that inflicted in Amaziah's expedition (2 Ki. xiv. 7 and 2 Chron. xxv). There is an account of a man of God who persuaded Amaziah not to take Israelitish allies with him on this expedition, and an account of a prophet who rebuked him after his return for worshipping Edomite gods (2 Chron. xxv. 7–10, 15–16). Supposably this prophet and this man of God may be identical, and supposably one or both may be identical with Obadiah.

The prophet Jonah lived just before the conquests by Jeroboam II.[1] This historical prophet Jonah is the hero of the story in the book of Jonah, whatever one may think of the authorship or the character of the book.

The Chronicler tells us of one Zechariah, "who had discernment in beholding of the Deity" during those years of Uzziah in which that king was faithful and prosperous (2 Chron. xxvi. 5).

Concerning Amos we have no information except in the book of that name. He is represented as a Judæan prophet, not affiliated with the "sons of the prophets" of the northern kingdom (i. 1, vii. 14, etc.), though his

---

[1] "It was he who restored the coast of Israel, from the entering in of Hamath unto the sea of the Arabah, according to the word of Yahaweh the god of Israel, which he spake by the hand of his servant Jonah the son of Amittai, the prophet, who was from Gath-hepher" (2 Ki. xiv. 25).

extant prophecies concern mainly the northern kingdom.
The book has a title, dating it "two years before the
earthquake," at a point of time when Jeroboam was
king in Israel and Uzziah in Judah, perhaps making
Amos a boy when Joel was a man.   The several prophecies in the book seem to be of one date.   The book
opens with a motto cited from Joel (Am. i. 2 ; Joel iii.
16), and, apparently, it rebukes certain persons who are
taking unwarranted encouragement from what Joel has
prophesied concerning the Day of Yahaweh (v. 18 ff.).

What we know concerning Hosea comes from the
title and contents of his book.   He began prophesying
almost contemporaneously with Amos, but his career
extended through the reigns of Jotham and Ahaz, and
into that of Hezekiah, a period of several decades.   He
is a prophet of the northern kingdom, but his sympa-
thies are wholly with the house of David.

Isaiah is perhaps the greatest of all the prophets.
The title to his book mentions the same kings of Judah
with the title to Hosea.   Isaiah's career began later in
the reign of Uzziah than those of Amos and Hosea, and
may have extended into the reign of Manasseh.   In
more passages than one he perpetuates the preaching
of the Day of Yahaweh, which his predecessors had
inaugurated.   We cannot here consider the questions
that have been raised concerning the relations of Isaiah
the son of Amoz to our existing book of Isaiah.

The second part of our book of Zechariah consists of
two "burdens" (ix–xi, xii–xiv).   The first presents a
situation in which the separate kingdoms of Judah and
Ephraim are in existence, and in which Assyria is the
great world-power (ix. 10, 13, x. 6, 7, 10, 11).   The
second is addressed to persons who can remember the
earthquake in the time of Uzziah (xiv. 5).   Other marks

of like significance abound in both.   These marks seem to date these two Burdens during the time when Isaiah was contemporary with Hosea.

Micah, according to the title of the book, was the contemporary of Isaiah from some date in the reign of Jotham.   In later times Jeremiah's friends cite him as a precedent in favor of prophetic freedom of speech (Jer. xxvi. 17–19).   So far as appears, he was exclusively a prophet of Judah.

Early in the reign of Ahaz, in the midst of the careers of Hosea and Isaiah and Micah, we have a brief note concerning a prophet named Oded, a different man from the Oded of the time of Asa.   He secured the return of two hundred thousand women and children whom the Israelites under Pekah had carried captive from Judah (2 Chron. xxviii. 9).

Many allusions in the literature dealing with these times indicate that the prophet was a familiar figure,[1] and that prophets were numerous.[2]   This indication is reënforced by the very frequent mention of false prophets.[3]   The true prophets were numerous enough to have numerous counterfeits.   Perhaps the statement of Amos that he is not a son of a prophet implies that the prophetic organizations were still maintained in northern Israel (vii. 14), but this allusion stands alone.

[1] "The mighty man and the man of war, the judge and the prophet" (Isa. iii. 2).   "I raised up of your sons for prophets, and of your young men for Nazirites" (Am. ii. 11).

[2] "Yahaweh testified unto Israel and unto Judah by the hand of every prophet, and of every seer."   "As he spake by the hand of all his servants the prophets" (2 Ki. xvii. 13, 23).   "I have also spoken unto the prophets, and I have multiplied visions, and by the hand of the prophets have I used similitudes" (Hos. xii. 10 [11]).   See also, among other instances, 2 Ki. xxi. 10 and 2 Chron. xxxiii. 10; Isa. xxx. 10; Hos. vi. 5, iv. 5, ix. 7, 8; Am. ii. 12, iii. 7, 8, vii. 12, 13, 14, 15, 16; Mic. iii. 6, 7.

[3] Isaiah is emphatic concerning these.   "The prophet that giveth lies

Roeh, in the sense of seer, is employed for the last
time in the Old Testament in Isa. xxx. 10. The other
derivatives of *raah*, with those of *nabha* and *hhazah*,
continue to be used in this and the subsequent periods.
So do the phrases "man of God," "word of Yahaweh,"
"Spirit of Yahaweh." In Isa. xxx. 10 the English
versions render *hhazah* and its noun by "prophesy"
and "prophets," to distinguish them from *raah* and its
noun which they render "see" and "seer." *Massa*,
"burden," is much used in this period (*e.g.* Isa. xix. 1,
xxi. 1, xxii. 1). Twice (Prov. xxx. 1, xxxi. 1) the old
version renders it "prophecy" and the revised versions
"oracle." *Hittiph* and its noun are used of prophesying
only in this period (Am. vii. 16; Mic. ii. 6, 11) and in
two places in Ezekiel.

The fourth subperiod is that of the Palestinian
prophets of the time of Jeremiah, he himself being the
Prophecy   central figure. Counted from the captivity of
from
Manasseh to   Manasseh to the burning of the temple, the
the exile   time is perhaps about sixty years; counted
to the death of Jeremiah it is longer, perhaps by some
decades. The distinguished names are Nahum, Habakkuk, Zephaniah, Jeremiah, with three others that are
incidentally mentioned in the records. In the great
crisis of the reformation under Josiah, the prophet consulted was not Jeremiah or Zephaniah, but the prophetess Huldah, then living in Jerusalem (2 Ki. xxii. 14 and
2 Chron. xxxiv. 22). The narrative makes the impression
that she was a person of distinction and influence, and
highly gifted with prophetic power. In the book of

for *torah*, he is the tail" (ix. 15 [14]). "Priest and prophet have erred
through strong drink" (xxviii. 7). "Yahaweh . . . hath closed your eyes,
ye prophets, and hath covered your heads, ye seers; and to you vision
hath become wholly like the words of the book that is sealed" (xxix. 10).
And Isaiah is not alone in this (*e.g.* Mic. iii. 5, 11).

Jeremiah, Baruch the scribe appears with prominence (xxxii. 12–16, xxxvi, xliii, xlv), though it is not expressly said that he is a prophet. We have also an account of one Uriah the son of Shemaiah of Kiriath-jearim, who prophesied in the time of Jehoiakim, and who was brought by some form of extradition from Egypt and put to death (Jer. xxvi. 20–23).

Other prophets were numerous. The biblical writings concerning the time speak of them in more than thirty places. They speak thus of true prophets (*e.g.* 2 Ki. xxiii. 2 and 2 Chron. xxxvi. 16; Lam. ii. 9; Jer. vii. 25, xxvi. 5), and of false prophets as well (*e.g.* Zeph. iii. 4; Lam. iv. 13; Jer. ii. 8, 26, xiv. 18, xxiii. 9, 11). The false prophets are more to the front than the true. Not less than four are mentioned by name. In the fourth year of Zedekiah, the prophet Hananiah the son of Azzur broke the yoke from off the neck of Jeremiah, in token of the breaking of the yoke of Nebuchadnezzar. Jeremiah predicted his death in punishment for thus making the people trust in a lie ; and the prediction was fulfilled (Jer. xxviii). Ahab the son of Kolaiah and Zedekiah the son of Maaseiah prophesied a lie in the name of Yahaweh, and were roasted in the fire by the king of Babylon (Jer. xxix. 21–23). Shemaiah the Nehelamite prophesied, causing the people to trust in a lie, and sent letters to Jerusalem reviling Jeremiah as a madman, and was divinely punished (Jer. xxix. 24, 28, 31, 32). The last named and possibly some of the others prophesied in Babylonia among the exiles.

The fifth subperiod is that of the prophets in Babylonia during the seventy years of the exile. It begins with the earlier deportations by Nebuchadnezzar from Jerusalem, nearly twenty years before the burning of the temple, and thus overlaps the preceding subperiod, the

distinction between the two being in part geographical.
The two great names are Daniel and Ezekiel. On the
Prophecy in
Babylonia
among the
exiles basis of views concerning the book of Isaiah
that were held twenty years ago, many scholars
would add a yet greater name, that of the supposed second Isaiah. These prophets flourished in the
country of the Euphrates, and are thus placed in a different class from their contemporaries in Palestine,
whom we have assigned to the preceding period.

In the earlier part of this period, at least, we find
mention of numerous false prophets, male and female,
prophesying in the name of Yahaweh; men who daub
with untempered mortar, and women who sew pillows
upon all elbows (*e.g.* Ezek. xiii. 2, 3, 4, 9, 15–16, 17–18,
xiv. 4, 7, 9, 10). True prophets are not so much in
evidence, though there may have been numbers of them
also. Certain critical theories now current seem to
require the hypothesis that prophets now began to
multiply in the lands of the exile.

The last subperiod is that of the prophets after the
return from exile in the first year of Cyrus. The great
Prophecy in
the post-
exilian times names are those of Haggai, the Zechariah of
Zech. i–viii, Ezra, Nehemiah, the author of
Malachi. Daniel was still alive at the opening of the period. Haggai and Zechariah flourished
in the early years of it (Ezra v. 1, 2, vi. 14; Hag. i. 1;
Zech. i. 1, etc.). It is supposable that in early life they
may have known Jeremiah and Ezekiel. Ezra is chiefly
known as the scribe, and Nehemiah by his political
achievements; but there is no room to doubt that the
biblical narrators regard them as exercising prophetic
gifts. No one is qualified to say whether the book of
Malachi was written by a prophet of that name, or by
Ezra, or by some one else.

The period was not without its other prophets, true and false (Zech. vii. 3, viii. 9; Neh. vi. 7). Nehemiah speaks of Shemaiah the son of Delaiah, who had been hired to pronounce a false prophecy, and of "the prophetess Noadiah and the rest of the prophets" who sought to frighten him (vi. 10–14). These notices, with the analogy of the preceding periods, confirm the traditions concerning the Great Synagogue, which affirm that prophets were numerous at this time.

Nevertheless the time is priestly rather than prophetic. So far as the record shows, the prophetic organizations have vanished. In their stead we find the place Casiphia, for training men for the various duties of the temple service (Ezra viii. 17). A marked feature of the period is the habit of appeal to the prophets of earlier times (Zech. i. 4, 5, 6, vii. 7, 12; Mal. iv. 5; Ezra ix. 11; Neh. ix. 26, 30, 32). Evidently these earlier prophets are regarded as authoritative scriptures.

The question of the cessation of prophecy we must here dismiss with a few sentences. The period of the so-called men of the Great Synagogue covers the last two prophetic periods and the time following. With the exception of Ezekiel, who is probably included by implication, all the distinguished exilian and postexilian prophets are expressly named in the lists of the men of the Great Synagogue. Others besides prophets are also named, the number being one hundred and twenty in all, and the latest great name being that of the highpriest Simon the Just. The Talmuds say that Simon was highpriest in the time of Alexander the Great, and Josephus is clearly mistaken in assigning him to a later time.

Most statements that are made concerning the men of the Great Synagogue as an organization are insuffi-

ciently based—alike those that affirm and those that
deny. But there is no room for doubt that this succession of men existed historically, or that the traditions
apply this name to them, or that they did many of the
things which the traditions attribute to them. Among
the acts attributed to them are the writing of the latest
Old Testament books and the completion of the Old
Testament.

While the traditions say that many of the men of
the Great Synagogue were prophets up to the time of
Nehemiah and the writing of Malachi, they also say
that the men of the Great Synagogue as a whole are
later than the succession of the prophets taken as a
whole, that is, that the succession of prophets ceased at
some time before Simon the Just, and therefore before
the beginning of the Greek period. This finds confirmation in the phenomena of the latest narrative books of
the Old Testament. The latest events mentioned in
these occurred (many assertions to the contrary notwithstanding) some time before the death of Nehemiah.
Both in and out of the Old Testament, prophets are
abundantly mentioned as contemporaneous with Nehemiah, but none as living later. Josephus testifies (*Cont.
Ap.* I, 8) that the succession of the prophets ceased
with the reign of the Artaxerxes who reigned after
Xerxes. Of course he means that it ceased with the lives
of the prophets who were contemporary with Artaxerxes. Some of these, Nehemiah for example, may have
survived Artaxerxes by several decades.

There has been some dispute over the interpretation
of the Jewish traditions in this matter, and there is some
confusion in the traditions themselves, this last being in
part due to the inexplicable confusion of the rabbinical
chronology for the Persian period. But there are cer-

tain very solid facts which ought to interpret the facts that are less evident. Judas Maccabæus and his associates regarded themselves as under the influence of the divine Spirit, and claimed a certain power of making predictions and working miracles. It has been inferred that they counted themselves as prophets, but there is clear proof to the contrary. We are told that they were at a loss what to do with the altar of burnt offering which the heathen had profaned. So they pulled it down and laid away the stones "until there should come a prophet to give answer concerning them" (1 Mac. iv. 46). A few years later they decided "that Simon should be their prince and highpriest forever, until there arise a faithful prophet" (xiv. 41). We are told that under Bacchides "there arose a great affliction in Israel, such as had not occurred since the time that a prophet appeared not amongst them" (ix. 27). Such instances show that the Maccabees were consciously not prophets, however conscious they may have been of the possession of supernatural powers. In their time prophets in the proper sense were thought of as belonging to the past. Similar reasoning would apply to Simon the Just, or to Jesus the son of Sirach, or to others.

In fine, the Jewish tradition holds that the succession of the prophets ceased with the dying out of Nehemiah and his associates, about 400 B.C. There was an expectation that it would sometime be renewed, but it became at that time non-existent. From the Christian point of view it is plausible to affirm that the succession reappeared in the person of John the Baptist, followed by Jesus himself, and by the apostles and prophets of primitive Christianity.

CHAPTER IV

THE PROPHET.   A CITIZEN WITH A MESSAGE

WHAT manner of man was the prophet outwardly? What do we know concerning his personal appearance and the external insignia of his office and the visible life he lived among his fellow-citizens ?   In answer to these questions we will discuss mainly three topics : first, the outward presentment of the prophets ; second, their communal organizations ; third, the so-called prophetic order.

There is no reason why one's conclusions on these topics should be greatly affected by the critical position One's view as he occupies.   In regard to the external his-affected by tory of the prophets, as we ran it over in the his critical position   last chapter, the men of the Modern View differ widely with the older scholars ; though even here the difference is less over the question what the scriptures say than over the question how far what they say is to be believed.   But in the matter of the outward phenomena presented by the prophets there is less room for difference.   The prominent characteristics are the same at all dates in the history, however the prophets of the different periods may differ in matters of detail.   This fact the scholars of the Modern View might account for by regarding all the scriptural pictures of the prophet as late ; but however one accounts for it, it is a fact.   Owing to it, our conclusions on these points depend much less than in some other cases on

66

our opinions as to the dates of the writings. Some of the views presented in this chapter are unlike those that have been commonly held; but the differences are not along the lines of the controversy between the Modern View and the older views.

I. This preliminary being disposed of, we proceed to inquire as to the external appearance of the prophet of Israel.

In centuries past Christian people have been accustomed to think of him as though he were a Christian priest or monk. Painters have painted his picture with this idea in mind. In Christian art a prophet is hardly more or less than an ecclesiastic, barefoot, with a robe and a tonsure and a general air of unearthliness. This is a miracle equal to that by which art has transformed the angels of the bible, who are always either young men or old men, into stocking-less winged women. Far be it from me to make criticism upon this as art; I only remark that art isn't history. *Baseless current ideas*

With this idea of an ecclesiastical personage has been combined that of a revealer of hidden things. Certain lines of the picture have been modelled upon the mediæval astrologer, or the priest of a Greek oracle, as if the prophet were a weird, mysterious being who sits on a tripod in a cave, and gives other-world advice to such frightened souls as come to him.

Or one starts with the assumption that religion is developing from lower forms to higher, and that the earlier Hebrew prophets must have started at a pretty low degree. So he comes to the study of them with a mind preoccupied with African fetich-men, or voudou practitioners, or American Indian medicine-men. Looking through glasses of this color, he may see in Samuel's companies of prophets little else than medicine dances and powwow circles.

Or, taking his cue from the notion that the Orient never changes, that what now exists there is what always existed there, one may imagine the prophetic companies as bands of whirling dervishes.

Evidently we are in danger of being misled both by our preconceived notions and by our love of the picturesque, and we therefore especially need to be on our guard, attending with care to the evidence in the case. Let us do this. Let us examine what information we 'have, and base our pictures of the prophets upon that, instead of first forming our ideas concerning the prophets, and then manipulating the information to make it conform to the ideas.

A particularly significant thing in the biblical accounts is the absence of phenomena of this unearthly

Significant absence of unearthly phenomena

sort among the prophets as a class. On certain occasions particular prophets practised austerities for purposes of symbolical teaching. But ordinarily Moses or Samuel or Isaiah or David or Nathan or Daniel appear as men among men, citizens among citizens, and not at all like the frenzied seers or oracle priests of the heathen religions. To this even Ezekiel is not wholly an exception, though he comes near enough to it to be quite in contrast with the other prophets. An average Old Testament prophet is not weird or mysterious. He is not a recluse, but an active citizen. He is not picturesque through eccentric personal appearance or habits. Elijah, indeed, was a man of unusual personal appearance (2 Ki. i. 7–8), and for a time led the life of a recluse, but he is presented to us as being peculiar in these respects. He is as different from other prophets as he is from citizens of any

other class. We make a serious mistake if we count
him as typical, instead of counting him the exceptional
instance he purports to be.

The books of reference tell us that the prophets wore
a distinctive costume. In proof they cite what is said
in Zechariah (xiii. 2–6) concerning certain Was there a
prophets associated with idols, who "wear a prophetic
hairy mantle to deceive." It is inferred that costume?
Jehovah's prophets were accustomed to wear a hairy
mantle, and that these frauds adopted the usual prophetic garb, to give color to their pretences. It would
be exactly as logical to infer that they adopted an unusual garb in order to attract attention. Further, the
hairy mantle is here one of two devices by which these
idol prophets made themselves conspicuous. The other
was by cuts on their bodies.

"And one shall say unto him, What are these wounds between
thy hands ? And he shall say, Those with which I was wounded
in the house of my friends " (Zech. xiii. 6).

The cuts on the body are here on the same footing with
the hairy mantle. Clearly, the writer had no intention
of saying that either was a part of the regulation uniform of the prophets of Yahaweh.

Further, they cite the hairy mantle worn by Elijah
and inherited by Elisha, and in connection with this
they mention the hairy garment worn by John the
Baptist. But you will remember that when King
Ahaziah's messengers reported to him that the man
who had met them wore a hairy garment, he at once
knew that the man was Elijah (2 Ki. i. 8). Elijah's
mantle distinguished him from all other prophets, as
well as from citizens who were not prophets. This
clearly shows that the prophets in general did not
wear the hairy mantle as a uniform.

They cite also the statement that Isaiah once upon a time wore sackcloth, and put it off, going "naked and barefoot" (xx. 2). But Isaiah's wearing sackcloth exceptionally is no proof that all the prophets wore a uniform regularly. No more can the same inference be drawn from Samuel's being "covered with a robe" when the witch of Endor called him up. The word *me'il* is employed alike in describing the dress of kings and priests and private citizens and boys and girls.

This is all the testimony that is cited for the exist-ence of a distinctive prophetic costume. Evidently it has very little weight. And there are strong considera-tions on the other side. In the story that tells us how Saul and his servant sought the asses and found a king-dom (1 Sam. ix), we are informed that they met Samuel in the gate of the city, and asked him to tell them where the seer's house was (ver. 18). It is evident that there was nothing in his garb to indicate that he was himself the seer. But he was at that moment on his way to a public solemnity, and in those circumstances, if ever, he would have been officially attired. We have an account of a prophet who rebuked Ahab for suffering Benhadad to escape (1 Ki. xx. 38, 41). He disguised himself by pulling his headband over his face. The king knew him when he removed the headband. The king knew him by his face, and not by his costume. Similar statements would apply to the prophet who anointed Jehu for king (2 Ki. ix. 11). There is no sacred uniform to tell Jehu and his friends who the "mad fellow" is.

These are representative instances, and they seem to be decisive. The cases cited to prove the existence of a regulation prophetic costume are clearly exceptional, and, therefore, prove the contrary, so far as they prove anything. No article of prophetic apparel is ever spoken of as distinctive of the class. There is no trace of a special costume by which prophets were distinguished from men who were not prophets. Religious art has given to the prophet a monkish robe and tonsure; so far as the Old Testament accounts go, sober truth should give him the usual dress of a citizen of his time and nation. If we should picture him as wearing a sack coat and a Derby hat in the forenoon and a dress suit in the evening, our picture would be no more anachronistic than that of current art, and would be far truer in spirit.

Some one may rejoin that the Old Testament evidence in the case is negative rather than positive, and that we must still infer, from the analogy of other religions, that the Israelitish prophets had a peculiar dress of their own. Medicine-men and fetich-men, the prophets of savage religions, trick themselves out in grotesque dress. In higher civilizations the prophet makes himself impressive by the garb that indicates his profession. Is it possible that the prophets of Israel were an exception? *The fact significant, even if negative*

In reply to this, I should deny that the Old Testament evidence is a mere argument from silence. It seems to me positive and distinct. But if any one thinks otherwise, I should not take the trouble to argue the case with him. At all events, the biblical writers leave the question of a prophetic dress in the background. They describe in detail the costume of their priests, but not that of their prophets. The writers of other peoples make much of the garb of the men through whom they consult the unseen world; not so the writers of Israel. With them the man is everything, and his dress nothing.

The record is, therefore, unique at this point, whether

the fact recorded be unique or not. Why should we not hold that both are unique ?   Israel as existing to-day is unique. Jesus Christ, of the stock of Israel, is unique. These are unique, whether we look at them from the evangelical point of view or from the agnostic point of view. Unique results probably had unique antecedents. We should not be surprised if we find the uniqueness extending to many matters of detail. The fact that the biblical account of the prophets makes them in any particular different from the prophets of other religions is no argument against the truth of the account; for we ought to expect to find that they were different.

Some of the books of reference affirm that the prophets were addicted to habits of religious frenzy. In
Did the prophets rave ? proof is given an alleged derivation of the word *nabha*, from *nabhă*, " to boil up." But the derivation is at the strongest merely a conjecture; and it would not prove the point even if it were known to be correct.

Worldly men are twice spoken of as calling the prophets mad — that is, crazy. Shemaiah the Nehelamite wrote to the officials at Jerusalem, asking them why they had not rebuked Jeremiah, under the provision for putting " in the stocks and in shackles " " any man that is crazed, and maketh himself a prophet " (Jer. xxix. 26–27). This epithet, we learn from the context, was not called forth by crazy conduct on the part of Jeremiah, but by his writing a particularly sane letter to the exiles in Babylonia. The prophet who came to anoint Jehu, a quiet, secret errand, is called by Jehu's brother officers a " crazed fellow " (2 Ki. ix. 11). There is no trace of raving in either case. Worldly men called the prophets crazy, just as worldly men to-day call earnest preachers crazy.

In one place a prophet speaks of the prophets as
crazy.   Hosea says: —

"The prophet is a fool, the man that hath the spirit is crazed, for
the multitude of thine iniquity, and because the enmity is great "
(ix. 7).

Here, clearly, he represents himself and other prophets
as distracted under the strain of current evil; but he
does not attribute frenzied utterance to himself or to
them.

In one instance it is said that the evil spirit came upon
King Saul, "and he prophesied" (1 Sam. xviii. 10).
David played before him as usual, and he attempted to
kill David.   Doubtless this was an attack of mania, but
it does not follow that Saul's raving is called prophesying.   It is quite as easy to think that Saul talked on
religious subjects, and that this was a characteristic
symptom of his fits of insanity ; in other words, that
Saul's utterances are here called prophesying not
because they were crazy, but because they were religious.

In the account of Saul's pursuing David to Naioth in
Ramah (1 Sam. xix. 18–24) we have a similar connection between religious utterance on the part of Saul and
the insane attacks to which he was subject.   Excited
by his rage against David and the disobedience of his
messengers, and afterward by the prophesying as he
heard it, he himself prophesied, —

"And he went on and prophesied until he came to Naioth in
Ramah.   And he also stripped off his clothes, and he also prophesied before Samuel, and fell down naked all that day and all that
night."

Apparently Saul, in his prophesying, conducted himself
in an insane and indecorous manner.   But it does not

appear that any one else did so ; nor that Saul's conduct is called prophesying because of the craziness of it.

We have an account (1 Sam. x. 5–13) of the company of prophets that Saul met when he was first anointed king.

"A band of prophets coming down from the highplace, with psaltery and timbrel and pipe and harp before them ; and they shall be prophesying ; and the spirit of Yahaweh will come mightily upon thee, and thou shalt prophesy with them, and shalt be turned into another man."

We need not necessarily figure this as a company of dancing dervishes. It may equally well be a band of serious men, holding an outdoor religious meeting, with a procession and music and public speeches.

In all the instances of this kind the alleged prophetic frenzy is a matter of interpretation, and not of direct statement. If one comes to the passages with the idea that frenzied utterance lies at the root of the original notion of prophesying, he may find in the passages the outcropping of this underlying notion in the word ; but he will hardly find it without such assistance. This being the case, the passages should certainly be interpreted in the light of the habitual sanity that marks the conduct and the utterances of the prophets. The idea that Saul's attacks of mania made him very religious in his utterances is in accord with facts with which we are familiar. The idea that the prophets preached in the open air, attracting attention by means of a procession and a band, has in it no element of absurdity. If one starts by assuming that the prophet developed from a medicine-man or a voudou-man or a fetich-man, or that the prophet is of a piece with a Greek oracle priest, drunk with vapor, one may be able to stretch these texts so as to make them fit his assumption ; but that is not their natural meaning.

In short, the inference that the prophets were characterized by frenzy is baseless.   The statement that Jeremiah
was crazy is recorded as a slander, and not as a fact.
Religious talking was a symptom in Saul's periods of
insanity.   The prophets held religious meetings under
the excitement of which Saul conducted himself strangely.
But there is no proof that the prophets acted like crazy
men.

In one personal peculiarity the prophets are represented to have been remarkable, — their longevity.   As
a class, judging from the biographical notices The prophets
we have, they were unusually long-lived men.   long-lived
To say nothing of the patriarchs, Moses died at the age
of one hundred and twenty years, being till then vigorous (Deut. xxxi. 2, xxxiv. 7).   This is not to be explained
by saying that the term of human life has diminished
since then.   According to the priestly laws in Leviticus
(xxvii. 3, 7, etc.) the age of manly vigor was then from
twenty to sixty years.   Caleb regarded it as exceptional
that he was still a warrior at eighty-five (Josh. xiv. 10–11 ;
cf. Ps. xc. 10).   Moses had his successors in longevity.
Joshua reached the age of one hundred and ten years.
(Josh. xxiv. 29 ; Jud. ii. 8).   Jehoiada, the prophetically
gifted highpriest, lived to be one hundred and thirty
years old (2 Chron. xxiv. 15).   The public career of Elisha
extended through not less than sixty years, and that of
Isaiah was yet longer, and that of Daniel about seventy
years.   The list might be extended.   In a general way
art has good ground for its habit of picturing a prophet
as old and venerable ; though it happens that in many
particular instances art has given gray hairs to a
prophet who should have been pictured as a young
man.

So much for the prophets as they presented themselves

to the eyes of their contemporaries. Save in special
instances we are to think of their personal appearance
as simply that of respectable citizens.

II. Similar results await us as we turn to a second
topic, the arrangements for the communal organizations
of the prophets.

Of these we know but little, save what lies on the
surface of the biblical texts. It will help to a clear
understanding of what is said concerning these organizations if we begin by fixing firmly in our minds the
fact that they are mentioned in connection with two
periods, — the time of Samuel and the time of Elijah
and Elisha. Nothing is said concerning them in the
history of the other periods, the mention of "a son of a
prophet" in Amos (vii. 14) being properly no exception
to this statement.

In the King James version the phrase "company of
prophets" occurs in two connections, suggesting that
Prophetic   the prophets were organized and operated
organizations   in companies. The verbal statement of this
under
Samuel   fact vanishes when we examine the Hebrew;
but the fact itself remains, based on inference. The
account of it is given mainly in two passages.

The first of the two passages is the one cited above,
in which we are told of Saul's meeting the prophets
after Samuel had anointed him (1 Sam. x. 5–13). Saul
met what the old version calls a "company," and the
new version a "band" of prophets. "A string of
prophets" would be an exact rendering in vernacular
English, that is, a procession. They had a band of
music "before them," stringed instruments and drum
and fife. They were prophesying. After meeting them
Saul joined them in prophesying, the spirit of God coming "mightily" upon him. The change in him was so

remarkable that people noticed it, and asked: " Is Saul also among the prophets ? "

I have already indicated the opinion that we have here an account of outdoor religious services, differing, of course, from anything that could occur in our time, as that time differed from ours in everything, and yet properly analogous to such services as might now be held by a corps of the Salvation Army, or by the Young Men's Christian Association. The remarks that are represented to have been made by the people imply that they were familiar with such services by the prophets. They recognized the fact that Saul belonged to a worldly-minded family, not given to participating in evangelistic meetings. And whether you admit the correctness of these analogies or not, at least such movements as are here described must have had behind them some form of organization, looser or more compact.

The other passage in question has also been cited above, the one that describes Saul's pursuit of David to Naioth in Ramah (1 Sam. xix. 18–24). It is said of Saul's messengers that —

"They saw the company of the prophets prophesying, and Samuel standing as head over them."

The word here translated " company " occurs nowhere else. Evidently, however, the prophets were together in some sort of assembly, engaged in con- The Naioth certed action of some sort, Samuel being gathering of either the president or the conductor. The prophets atmosphere was charged with religious excitement. Saul's successive relays of messengers, as they came under the influence of the scene, joined in the prophesying, and so did even the king himself when he at last followed his messengers. Saul and possibly others divested themselves of part of their clothing. Saul seems to have had a fit that lasted several hours.

This incident, as well as the previous one, presupposes organization of some sort. Concerning the forms and the purposes of the organizing, we have little information. We cannot escape the conclusion, however, that an educational element was included. The instruments of music in the one incident, and the concerted prophesying under the conduct of Samuel in the other, suggest that training in orchestral and choral music was made prominent. We shall not be far out if we suppose that instruction was given in patriotic history, in theology, in literary practice, in whatever would fit the disciples of Samuel to be preachers of the religion of Yahaweh to their contemporaries. The remarkable blossoming out of Israel in the times of David and Solomon, in matters of literature and culture, was doubtless largely due to these prophetic organizations introduced by Samuel. It is probable, however, that these organizations were not merely schools, but were, like those of a later time, also centres of political and religious movements.

The mention of music as a part of the 'prophetic training under Samuel is in accord with those passages in the books of Chronicles which speak of Asaph, Heman and Jeduthun and their associates as prophesying in song or with instruments of music (*e.g.* 1 Chron. xxv), and with all the statements in the Old and New Testaments which represent the second half of the reign of David as resplendent with culture and music and psalmody. Before one rejects these traditions as unhistorical he should take into account, among other

things, their marked continuity with the recorded events
of the time of Samuel.   Supposing them to be historical, it was not by mere accident that the temple choirs
appeared in the generation following the death of
Samuel, or that Heman the grandson of Samuel was
one of their leaders.

So much for the organizations of Samuel's time.
The other type of prophetic organization is that described in the term "sons of the prophets."   "The sons of
So far as the records show, it belongs exclu- the prophets"
sively to the northern kingdom, and, save for general
mention in Amos (vii. 14), exclusively to the times of
Elijah and Elisha.   Groups of the sons of the prophets
existed at Bethel, Jericho, Gilgal (2 Ki. ii. 3, 5, iv. 38),
and presumably at other places.   We are accustomed
to call them the "schools of the prophets," but this
term is not biblical.   A good many details are given
concerning them.   In his lifetime Elijah was at the
head of them, and he left this office to Elisha (2 Ki. ii.
3, 15, etc.).   In studying them one should study the
entire biography of these two prophets.   We have a
story that one group of them found their home too narrow and went to cut timber for enlarging it, on which
occasion Elisha performed the miracle of causing an
iron axe to swim (2 Ki. vi. 1–7).   From this we learn that
in some cases the sons of the prophets were a community, living in a common house.   We also learn that they
were not afraid of manual labor.   They were numerous,
for the community at Jericho could send its fifty men to
search for Elijah (2 Ki. ii. 16, 17), and Obadiah hid a
hundred of Jehovah's prophets "by fifty in a cave"
(1 Ki. xviii. 4).   They were not mere lads, some of
them being married men, as we learn from Elisha's
miracle of the oil, wrought in behalf of the widow of

one of them. Kindly disposed people sometimes con-
tributed to their support. Witness Elisha's feeding a
hundred men with the twenty loaves of the man from
Baal-shalishah (iv. 42–44). Sometimes they eked out
their subsistence by gathering wild vegetation, as we
see in the incident when there was "death in the pot"
(iv. 38–41).

This system of communities was evidently widespread
and influential. Doubtless they had somewhat of the
character of schools for personal education ; but they
were rather houses of reform, centres of religious and
patriotic movement. Their members were especially
obnoxious to the Baalite party in Israelitish politics.
They promoted the overthrow of Joram and the accession of Jehu (2 Ki. ix. 1–12). Their political attitude is
one of the most significant things about them. We
shall return to this in another chapter. Meanwhile we
may fix in mind the fact that the work of the sons of the
prophets is represented to have been analogous to that
of our Young Men's Christian Associations, or of some
of our organizations for reform or for good citizenship,
rather than to that of our schools or colleges or semi-
naries.

The "college" in Jerusalem, where, according to the
King James translation, the prophetess Huldah dwelt
(2 Ki. xxii. 14 ; 2 Chron. xxxiv. 22), is simply an instance
of the uncertain meaning of a word.

III. We turn to a third topic, the so-called prophetic
order.

Much stress is laid on this by some writers. Most
denominations of Christians hold that the Christian
"Holy   ministry is an order of men who have "taken
orders"   orders" in the sense of being set apart by
ordination. The Anglican and Roman churches hold

that the ministry exists in three different orders ; namely, bishops and priests and deacons.   In a sense something like this many speak of the two orders of the ministry under the Old Covenant ; namely, the priestly order and the prophetic order.

Is this a proper use of language ?   Are we to think of the prophet as belonging to an order ?   Was he an ordained man, like a Jewish priest or a Christian minister ?   In other words, are we to think of the priests and the prophets as two orders of Israelitish clergymen ? These questions must be answered by examining the facts.

1.   First, it is probably true that there was an unbroken succession of prophets from Samuel to Malachi — perhaps from Abraham to Malachi — in The prophets the sense that Israel was never during that a succession time wholly without true living prophets or prophetic men.   This is probable, though it cannot at every point be proved.

2.   But, secondly, the prophets were not a sacerdotal order, holding definite relations to the priestly order. They were not a priesthood, or a section of The prophets the priesthood, or a body analogous to the not a sacer- priesthood.   In this the usage of Israel dif- dotal order fered from that of other peoples.   In Egypt, for example, the prophets were a class in the priesthood.   Mr. George Rawlinson tells us that they ranked next to the highpriests, and that they —

"were generally presidents of the temples, had the management of the sacred revenues, were bound to commit to memory the contents of the ten sacerdotal books " (*History of Egypt*, I, 447).

Similar representations are made in such a novel as the *Uarda* of Ebers ; and more minute and accurate statements may be found in later Egyptological works.

And what was true of the prophets of Egypt has been true of those of other countries. In Israel, however, the case was different. We have no account of any priestly functions regularly exercised by the prophets as prophets; and none of any official relations between the priestly body and the prophetic body.

It is true that some prophets were also priests, Zadok and Jeremiah and Ezra, for example. That is to say, a priest might become a prophet, as might any one else. Further, in certain instances, a prophet, without being a priest, may have been commissioned to perform priestly acts. We are told that Moses was so commissioned, officiating as priest in the original setting apart of Aaron to the priesthood (Lev. viii. 15–30). It is commonly alleged that Samuel performed priestly acts, but the records do not sustain the allegation.[1] There is no trace of any defined sacerdotal rights or duties regularly devolving upon the prophets. The prophet, as such, was not a priest. The two offices were entirely different.[2]

3. It is probable, thirdly, that the prophetic ranks

[1] Certainly, it is said that Samuel offered sacrifices (1 Sam. vii. 9, xvi. 2, and other places). But this would be said of any person who brought a sacrifice for offering, even if he employed a priest to sprinkle the blood and to perform all the other priestly functions in the case. In particular, a public man is said to offer sacrifices when he causes them to be offered by the proper officiating priests. The record is capable of this interpretation in every case where it speaks of an offering by Samuel. In one instance only we have a specific statement of the part personally taken by Samuel in a sacrifice (1 Sam. ix. 13); and in this instance he was to pronounce a blessing at the sacrificial meal, long after all the priestly rites had been completed.

[2] The priest must be from the tribe of Levi; the prophet might be from any tribe. The priest was selected according to descent and ceremonial condition; the prophet was directly and individually commissioned by Deity. The priest was accredited by solemn religious services and carefully kept genealogical registers, the prophet by the possession of the extraordinary powers that God gave him. The priests served in a yearly

were somewhat generally recruited from among men
who were disciples of the acknowledged _{Was the}
prophets, and had thus received special tui- prophet a
tion for the service. In the times of the ^{graduate?}
"sons of the prophets," for example, it is likely that
most men who became prophets were those who had
previously been connected with these so-called prophetic
schools (2 Ki. ix. 1, 4; Am. vii. 14–15). But there is
no trace of this having been done as a matter of regular
course. There is no evidence that most of these pupils
ever became prophets in the strict sense, much less that
they became so in a routine way, by graduating. Apparently, however, they were regarded as prophets in a
secondary sense, and were called by the name. In the
periods when prophets were very numerous, it is likely
that most of them were prophets only in this secondary
sense — sons of the prophets, followers of the great
prophets, rather than men who were believed to be
themselves highly endowed with prophetic gifts.

4. There is no indication, fourthly, that the prophets
were ordinarily set apart to their office by any ordaining
act. They were sometimes set apart to some
special work, but there is no instance in which _{Ordination}
any one is admitted to be a prophet by any such act.
The anointing of Elisha is the principal case in point
(1 Ki. xix. 16, 19). But the facts of Elisha's life show
that he was a distinguished prophet long before this
anointing. He was to be anointed, not to the prophetic

round, according to a minutely prescribed ritual; the prophets came and
went as God sent them. The priests administered and taught the divine
laws which the prophets brought and proclaimed. The priests ministered
at the altar; the prophets preached the word. The priests were the official clergy of the Israelitish church; the prophets, especially in the matter
of scripture-writing, "spake from God, being moved by the Holy Ghost,"
not to Israel only, but to all the ages.

office, but to be the successor of Elijah, in Elijah's
special work. It is a question whether there was any
ceremony of anointing save Elijah's casting his cloak
upon him.   And in any case the transaction is set forth
as exceptional and peculiar.   In the same breath in
which Elijah is directed to anoint Elisha he is also
directed to anoint Hazael and Jehu.   But the anointing
of Hazael king over Syria, by an Israelite prophet
(1 Ki. xix. 15), is evidently something exceptional.
Equally so is the anointing of Jehu over Israel, in a
private room at Ramoth-gilead (1 Ki. xix. 16; 2 Ki. ix.
1–13).   And not less exceptional is the setting apart of
Elisha that is mentioned along with these.   And with
this vanishes the last sign that any one ever entered
upon the prophetic office by taking orders.

5. In fine, every man or woman whom God endowed
with prophetic gifts thereby became a prophet. No
other door to the office is mentioned in the
scriptures. The law in Deut. xviii says: "A
prophet . . . will Yahaweh thy God *raise
up* to thee." The prophet becomes a prophet simply
by being raised up for that purpose. He becomes a
prophet, so far as the records show, solely by becoming
endowed with prophetic gifts. He becomes recognized
as a prophet through the exercise of his gifts among his
fellow-citizens. As people discovered that a person had
the gifts, they accepted him as a prophet, and that
irrespective of outward insignia or previous training
or ceremonies of ordination. If one claimed to be a
prophet of Yahaweh, his claims were to be tested not by
the clothes he wore, or by his ascetic mode of life, or
by appealing to a register of genealogy or of ordinations,
but by ascertaining whether he had the gifts of a prophet
— by observing, first, whether he spoke in Yahaweh's

*How one
became a
prophet*

name only, and, secondly, whether the signs which he
gave in Yahaweh's name came to pass.

This applies, of course, only to prophets who were
properly such. In the secondary sense of being a dis-
ciple, one of the sons of the prophets, one might become
a prophet merely by becoming connected with prophets
whose gifts were recognized.[1]

I have not the hardihood to expect that every one will
accept the opinion I am advocating as to the costume,
the freedom from excited conduct, the ordina- The prophet
tion, of the prophets; but every one will cer- especially a
tainly recognize the significant fact that these manly man
things are only slightly touched in the records; and this
fact constitutes nine-tenths of the value of the view I
offer. At least no stress is laid on matters of regulation
costume or of marvellous personal bearing or of ordination. In Deuteronomy the phrase, " of your brethren,
like unto me," stands in contrast to the characteristics
alike of the priests and of the heathen practitioners of
magic arts. Unlike these, the prophet is a man of the
same sort with other men. A distinguishing thing in
the religion of Israel is its proclamation *that a manly
man is the truest channel of communication between man
and God.* We cannot too strongly recognize the manliness and the manfulness of the prophets, as set forth in
the Old Testament, or of Jesus and the apostles as set
forth in the New.[2]

---

[1] Either in these organizations or in other forms and at other dates,
there is reason to hold that the prominent prophets had their disciples,
some of whom were permanently attached to them, looking to them for
instruction, and assisting them in their work. See such passages as Isa.
viii. 16, l. 4; Jer. li. 59–63. It may be assumed that literary and theological studies generally formed a part of the training of the disciples of the
prophets.

[2] I suppose that no careful student will hold that the positions which I

To repeat this once more. According to the records a prophet might be judge or king or priest or general or statesman or private person, in fine, might occupy any position in the commonwealth; as a prophet, he was simply a citizen with a special work to do. The prophets as such had no settled position in church or state. They were sent by God on individual missions, natural or supernatural, to supplement the routine administration of secular and religious affairs. The bible refuses to present any other picture of a prophet than that of a citizen, like other citizens, holding a commission from God, and endowed with the gifts requisite for accrediting his commission. This agrees with everything that we shall hereafter learn concerning the prophets. The human individuality of the prophet is emphasized, to the neglect of outward appearance, or official character, or other like things. In the scriptures as they stand, leaving out the exceptional instances that serve to emphasize the rule, our attention is withdrawn from external marks, and fixed upon the personal man or woman whom God has appointed to be prophet.

In this there is a significant contrast between the religion of Israel and other religions. The conception of religion which thus exalts manhood, when considering our relations to Deity, is a fine conception. Men sometimes speak of this conception as if it were the new product of the thinking of the last decades of the nineteenth century. When men exploit twentieth-century religious ideas, they give prominence to this : the recognition of

The absence of insignia noteworthy

maintain as to the absence of outward insignia can be positively disproved; and that no one will dispute that it is better to form our conceptions of the prophets more by the facts that are positively stated, and less by accessories that some suppose are alluded to, than many are in the habit of doing.

the truth that the most human man or woman is the person most suitable to be the prophet of the Lord. It is not a small thing among the glories of the religion of Yahaweh that it has recognized this truth from the beginning. This conception characterizes the monotheism of the worshippers of Yahaweh, as differing from all other religions. It characterizes this monotheism as expressed in the earliest records we have concerning the prophets, as well as in the latest. It is one of the phenomena which mark that religion as, among the religions, the one fittest to survive.

CHAPTER V

In the preceding chapter we have tried to answer the
question : How did the prophet look when you met him ?
and other affiliated questions. In the present chapter
the question becomes : How, in his character as prophet,
did the prophet occupy himself ? What did he do ?

We need from the outset to guard against two mistaken assumptions, — the assumption that the prophets
were merely or mainly predicters of events, and the re-
actionary assumption that they exercised no supernatural gifts.

No scholars hold that the prophets were mere givers
of oracles or predicters of the future ; and yet this phase
of their work has been so emphasized that
The assump-
tion that
prophecy is
prediction
wrong impressions are common. One needs
to reiterate the statement that a prophet is
not characteristically a person who foretells, but one
who speaks forth a message from Deity. To regard
him as mainly a foreteller involves a narrowing of the
idea of his mission that is all the more mischievous
because of its being popularly very common. The
argument from fulfilled prediction has been made so
prominent among the proofs of the divine origin of the
scriptures, and again in advocating the claim of Jesus
to be the Christ, that many have come to think of prediction as being substantially the whole of prophecy, and
even to interpret the prophetic writings as if they must

88

needs be regarded as predictive throughout.[1] This state of things renders it necessary to repeat the statement that prophecy and prediction are different terms. It greatly obscures the prophecies to count them as predictive only. In bulk, predictions constitute but a small part of them, and what predictions there are consist almost entirely of promises and threats.

This is one bad assumption. But we should not forget that the opposite assumption is as bad or worse. Prophecy is not prediction, but it does not follow that prophecy does not include prediction. The absence of supernatural endowment for the prophets is a thing to be proved, not a thing to be assumed. Prediction should neither be interpreted into the prophetic utterances, nor interpreted out of them. The predictive element in prophecy may be genuine and important, even if it is only a part and not the whole.

The worse contrary assumption

Taking the matter up positively, let us repeat once more that the functions of the prophet are correctly indicated by the etymology of the English word. A prophet is a person who speaks out the special message that God has given him. The priesthood, and, in a modified sense, the judge or king or other secular authorities, were, in their routine duties, the exponents of the will of Yahaweh in Israel. The prophets were his spokesmen for the purposes not covered by the routine administration of affairs.

The name indicates the function

---

[1] This is not confined to advocates of old-fashioned opinions. Several scholars have published, for example, arguments for the Maccabæan date of the book of Daniel, based on the assumption that prophecy and prediction are equivalent. They say that inasmuch as the book of Daniel is peculiarly predictive, the editors of the Hebrew bible would certainly have placed it among the prophets if it had been in existence when the writings of the prophets were collected.

In a general study of this topic very little depends on dates. In matters of detail, indeed, there is much difference between the earlier and the later prophets. The civilization of Israel was not stationary, and the training and the tasks of the prophets changed with their environment. But in its principal outlines their work was essentially the same at all periods.[1]

Principal functions the same at all dates

We will begin with passages which describe a prophet's duties in outline, and will afterward consider particulars.

In the narrative concerning Moses a prophet is thus defined : —

" And Yahaweh said unto Moses, See, I have given thee as a Deity to Pharaoh, Aaron thy brother being thy prophet " (Ex. vii. 1).

Aaron was to utter before Pharaoh the messages which Moses should commit to him for the purpose. In doing this, he sustained to Moses the relation which a prophet sustains to his God. Nothing could be more explicit. A prophet is a person who speaks forth the message that God has committed to him.

A prophet's functions outlined

Altogether the same is the definition of the function of a prophet as given in the twelfth chapter of Numbers : —

" If there be a prophet of you, I Yahaweh make myself known unto him in the vision, in a dream I speak with him. Not so is my servant Moses. In all my house he is faithful. Mouth unto mouth I speak with him " (vv. 6–8).

Here the prophet is described as one who receives mes-

---

[1] That the Old Testament writings declare this to have been the case is beyond dispute, though some critics may account for it by saying that the earlier writings have been reworked.

sages from God. That he utters the messages he receives is not affirmed, that being left to implication.

This idea that the prophets were revealing spokesmen for Deity is more fully defined in the eighteenth and the thirteenth chapters of Deuteronomy. First, the prophet is differentiated from the Levitical priest (Deut. xviii. 1–8), the ordinary spokesman of Yahaweh. The differentiation is none the less real for its being indirect and by suggestion only. The prophet's functions are unlike those of the priesthood in that they are special, rather than matters of routine. He is next distinguished from all practisers of occult arts (9–14). He is unlike these men to whom people are apt to go when they fancy themselves in need of supernatural information. The distinction in this case is made directly, and consists in the fact that the prophet has genuine revelations from Deity. Then (15–19) the prophet is positively described. He is a man, like other men, "of thy brethren, like unto me," raised up by Yahaweh for purposes of especial communication from him, so that men may not need to seek intercourse with the supernatural world through the magic arts just forbidden, or through any other channel. In the rest of the chapter and in the first verses of xiii, the test of a true prophet is declared.

The messianic bearings of this passage are reserved for future notice. It is enough for the present that they do not conflict with the interpretation just given. The word " prophet " in the passage, though not a collective noun, is distributively used. Yahaweh would raise up to Israel a prophet " from among their brethren," at his own pleasure, whenever he had a special revelation to make by one ; and that would be as often as they really needed communication with the unseen world. He promised that a prophet should appear on the arising

of any such need.   The New Testament writers correctly apply this to Jesus Christ, both because they
regard him as for his own time a prophet in this succession, and because they regard him as the great antitypal
prophet in whom the succession culminated.[1]

In our English version the last clause of the fourteenth verse reads : —

  " The Lord thy God hath not suffered thee so to do."

This translation is so inadequate as to be misleading.
Literally the clause is : —

  " And as for thee, not thus hath Yahaweh thy God given to thee."

That is, he has not given to thee the spurious and foolish modes of consulting with the unseen which are prac-

---

[1] " For these nations which thou art dispossessing hearken unto sorcerers and unto diviners; while as for thee, not thus hath Yahaweh thy Deity
given to thee.   A prophet, from the midst of thee, of thy brethren, like
me, will Yahaweh thy Deity raise up to thee; unto him shall ye hearken.
According to all which thou didst ask from with Yahaweh thy Deity in
Horeb, in the day of the Assembly, saying, Let me not again hear the
voice of Yahaweh my Deity, and this great fire I shall no longer see, lest I
die.   And Yahaweh said unto me, They have spoken well that which they
have spoken.   A prophet I will raise up for them from the midst of their
brethren, like thee, and will give my words in his mouth, and he shall
speak unto them all which I shall command him; and it shall be that the
man who will not hearken to my words which he shall speak in my name,
I myself will make inquiry from with him.

  "Only, the prophet who shall presume to speak a word in my name
which I have not commanded him to speak, or who shall speak in the
name of other Deities, that prophet shall die.   And inasmuch as thou wilt
say in thy heart, How shall we know the word which Yahaweh hath not
spoken?   The prophet who shall speak in the name of Yahaweh, and the
word shall not be, and shall not come to pass, that is the word which
Yahaweh hath not spoken " (Deut. xviii. 14–22).

  " When there shall arise in the midst of thee a prophet or a dreamer
of dreams, and shall give unto thee a sign or a miracle; and the sign or
the miracle come to pass, which he spake unto thee, saying, Let us go
after other Deities, . . . thou shalt not hearken to the words of that prophet
. . ." (Deut. xiii. 1–6).

tised by the augurs and diviners and sorcerers of other nations, but has given thee something immeasurably better, namely, his prophets; and he therefore forbids thy resorting to these other methods.   The words "not thus hath Yahaweh thy God given to thee," in mentioning what God has not given, call attention to the different thing which he has given.   He disallows the consulting of the invisible world through necromancers, because he has provided a glorious opening of communication with himself through the prophets.   The words of the verse distinctly contrast the forbidden looking into the unknown world, that by the practice of occult arts, with the revealing of the unknown which is promised in the following verse, in the office work of Yahaweh's prophet.   In fine, according to this chapter, the prophet is like the priest in that he is the authorized representative of Yahaweh, and unlike him in that his work is special.   He is like and unlike the magicians, in that he is genuinely the channel of especial communication with Deity, which they falsely pretend to be. To repeat this in other words, he is differentiated from the priest by the fact that his message is direct and special and from those who practise magic arts by the fact that his communication with Deity is real.

Having taken this general view, we are prepared to descend to particulars.   The functions which the records ascribe to the prophets may be arranged in two classes, — those which do not require the exercise of distinctly supernatural gifts, and those which require such gifts. For convenience let us designate these as their naturalistic and their supernaturalistic functions.

I. We begin with certain classes of their activities which presuppose no powers on their part but such as may be common to all gifted men.

1. They were prominent as the public men of their times ; they were statesmen, often political leaders.

When we find such men as Moses or Samuel or David or Daniel engaged in public affairs, we might perhaps explain it by saying that they occupy themselves thus, not in the character of prophet, but rather in that of law-giver or judge or king or prime minister. But even so, it seems to have been true that in times of crisis, when there were great deeds to do, the office of lawgiver or judge or prime minister was peculiarly apt to fall into the hands of a prophet.

But this way of accoun'ing for the matter will not apply in all the instances in which we find the prophets taking part in public affairs. So far as we are informed, Elijah or Elisha or Amos or Hosea or Isaiah or Jere-miah or Ezekiel were never officeholders, but they habit-ually deal with questions of state. Reflect on what you know concerning them, and you will see that a book which should contain their biographies in detail would also be a detailed history of national affairs. In the peculiar constitution of Israel, political and religious questions were so closely identified that the prophet could hardly be a religious teacher without being also a political leader.

Take Jeremiah as an illustration of this. In his time Judah has become a tributary kingdom, subject to Jeremiah as   Babylonia. The nobles are restive under the a statesman   yoke. They are constantly plotting to throw it off, are seeking to influence the king and the nation in that direction, are advocating alliances with Egypt. Jeremiah steadfastly opposes their policy. He con-trives to exert an influence over both Jehoiakim and Zedekiah, holding them back from revolt. He writes letters to the exiles in Babylonia, advising them to be

docile and make the best of their situation. Half of
his prophecies, as we have them, are attempts to convince the Jews that successful revolt is impossible, and
that attempted revolt can only bring additional miseries
upon them. He preaches a doctrine of restoration
after seventy years as a reason why they should cease
from their hopeless efforts for present independence.
Nebuchadnezzar recognizes the services of Jeremiah,
and shows him distinguished favors when Jerusalem is
at last destroyed.

But writers are unjust to Jeremiah when they simply
describe his political position as anti-Egyptian and pro-
Babylonian. He was not in any proper sense pro-Baby-
lonian. So far as appears he refused the Babylonian
king's invitation to go to Babylonia and be there treated
with honor. No prophet denounced Babylonia more se-
verely than he. His position is that of all the prophets,
opposed to all entangling alliances with foreign powers.
He wanted nothing to do with Babylonia any more
than with Egypt. But when his king had sworn alle-
giance to Babylonia, Jeremiah held that the oath should
be kept, that good policy as well as good faith forbade
the breaking of it. He would accept Babylonish
supremacy for the time being as an accomplished
fact, in opposition to those who advocated continued
resistance.

Similarly the career of Isaiah is throughout marked
by participation in national issues. In particular, he
works against the Assyrian alliance made by Isaiah and
Ahaz, and the opposing Babylonian or Egyp- Hosea as
tian alliances considered by Hezekiah. Hosea statesmen
is equally positive in denouncing intrigues with Assyria
or Egypt, and in advocating a policy of solidarity between
the northern and the southern kingdoms.

It was characteristic of the politics of the prophets that they were a bond of unity between the northern and the southern kingdoms. Judæan proph-ets such as Amos and Isaiah prophesied for Ephraim as well as for Judah, Isaiah dis-tinctly recognizing " both the houses of Israel" (viii. 14); and such northern prophets as Hosea and Elijah and Elisha prophesied for Judah as well as for Israel (Am. i. 1, iii. 1, 12, etc.; Isa. ix. 9, 21, xxviii. 1, 3, etc.; 2 Chron. xxi. 12; 2 Ki. iii. 14; Hos. i. 11, iii. 4-5, xi. 12, etc.). The northern prophets recognize some sort of alle-giance as due to Jerusalem and the house of David, as well as to their own kings. Those of both kingdoms earnestly seek to keep alive the consciousness of Israel-itish unity. They take pains to cultivate the fraternal spirit. Hosea, and Amos less obviously, had a definite programme for the reunion of the two kingdoms under a king of the line of David. The marriage of Jehoram and Athaliah probably indicates an earlier attempt in the same direction.[1]

Prophetic ideal of a united Israel

According to the record, Elijah and Elisha were party leaders, though their public policy is less obvious to a superficial reader than that of some of the other prophets. For two generations before the sudden coming of Elijah upon the scene, the false worship of Yahaweh through the calves of

Elijah and Elisha as statesmen

---

[1] It is obvious that this marriage might supposably have resulted in the acceptance of a prince of the house of David as heir to both the thrones. Supposably this was the intention in the negotiations for the marriage. Presumably the prophets favored it at the time, and built great hopes upon it. There is much plausibility in the hypothesis that the forty-fifth Psalm is a marriage song sung by a prophet of Judah on this occasion. On this hypothesis, the result was a grievous disappointment; but this would not be the only time in history when statesmen and prophets have been out-witted by a brilliant, wicked woman.

Bethel and Dan has been the state religion of northern Israel. But there have been nonconformists all the while. Lately, under Jezebel, the worship of Baal has been introduced, and the state church has largely gone over to the new cult. This has increased the numbers of the nonconformists, and their activity. Their ideal would be a participation in the sacrifices at the one place of national sacrifice in Jerusalem. But this is impracticable. As a protest against the false worship of the state church, they make offerings of certain kinds at many inconspicuous private altars. Unlike the adherents of the state religion, they are inflexible in their opposition to Baal, and thus draw upon themselves the horrible persecutions of Jezebel. This drove them to yet more desperate resistance. They formed the organizations known to us as the "sons of the prophets." Possibly the Tishbites, "the settlement men of Gilead" (1 Ki. xvii. 1), of whom Elijah was one, were another organization of the same sort. Elijah and Elisha were at the head of these organizations. We get glimpses of them going hither and thither, engaged in strenuous activities.

These people constituted in effect an ecclesiastical and political party, in opposition to the existing government. It is the familiar story of men professing to be loyal to a king, but in revolt and even in arms against his policy and his counsellors. John Knox and Mary queen of Scots have not a better parallel in history than that presented by Elijah in his relations with Ahab — Ahab, brilliant, impulsive, well-meaning, but weak when it came to resisting evil influences.[1]

---

[1] Sometimes Elijah and Elisha, the leaders of the opposition, are in a certain degree of favor at court. Their advice in public matters is sought, and in some instances followed. When Elisha offers to speak in behalf of the Shunamite to the king or the general of the army (2 Ki. iv. 13), it

In these several political affairs such prophets as Elijah and Elisha, Hosea, Isaiah, Jeremiah, are simply doing what other prophets of all dates were accustomed to do. The Israelitish prophet was a statesman. Most of the distinguished statesmen of Israel were prophets.

2. Apart from their political activities, the prophets were the reformers of their times.

Every age has need of men who shall lead in warfare against organized evils, or against evils that are otherwise rampant. Witness the efforts of John Howard in the cause of prison reform, of William Wilberforce in resistance to the slave trade and slavery, of John B. Gough against intemperance in drink, of Henry Bergh for the prevention of cruelty to animals, of Clara Barton for the more humane care of wounded soldiers and sailors. In matters analogous to these, the prophets were the leaders of reforms in Israel.

It is possible to mention here only a few of the many questions of public struggle against evils which, at different periods, engaged their activities, giving only a reference or two, out of many that might be given,

---

seems to be with confidence that his word will be influential. At other times the situation becomes strained, even to the extent of bloody hostility. When Elijah first appears in the narrative, he is in the act of presenting an ultimatum to Ahab. Then he withdraws from relations with him, and the rupture lasts three years, in spite of Ahab's strong efforts for resumption (1 Ki. xviii. 1, 10). When he at last meets the king, the slaughter of Baal's prophets at Mount Carmel follows. I suppose that this and, later, the destruction of Ahaziah's soldiers by fire from heaven may properly be counted as battles between the contending parties. The effect of them was salutary. The Baalites learned that Yahaweh's followers were not to be murdered with impunity, and the persecutions were relaxed. And so affairs moved on from year to year, until the prophets became convinced of the futility of their war against Jezebel so long as the existing dynasty remained in power, and consequently instigated Jehu to the revolution in which the house of Omri went down in blood.

under each question. In addition to matters of religious reform, such matters as idolatry, the high places, the support of the temple worship and the Some of the like, they advocated reforms in the matter reforms which the of divorce, of licentiousness, of usury, of prophets led land monopoly, of drunkenness and dissipation, of slavery (Mal. ii. 10–16; Jer. v. 7–9, etc.; Neh. v; Ezek. xviii. 8, etc.; Isa. v. 7–10, 11–22, etc.; Jer. xxxiv. 8–22). More prominently than anything else they rebuke unequal and unkind practices in the administration of justice, and inexorably demand reformation. It is largely for purposes of reform that they engage in public affairs. In the interests of reform we constantly find them rebuking kings and priests and people, teaching the populace, making public addresses, reading and expounding the scriptures, organizing the prophetic bands and other enginery for forming public opinion.

3. Again, the prophets were evangelistic preachers and organizers.

Their writings which we have show this. The historical books of the bible are narrative sermons. They so present history as to make it preach to us on the subject of our duties to God and men. Most of the other prophetic books are volumes either of sermons or of homiletical poems or tracts. In a good many instances a passage in the prophets becomes intelligible only when we recognize it as a syllabus or brief sketch of an address that was much longer when delivered orally.

In other ways than by their discourses they exerted an evangelistic influence. We have already had our attention called to the organizations of the times of Samuel and of Elijah and of Elisha. These were not mere literary institutions for giving instruction to young lads, but systematic arrangements for exerting an influence; as we should now say, arrangements for Christian work.

I have called this function evangelistic. It was something quite apart from the priestly function of maintaining ordinary services of public worship. It was aggressive and missionary in its character. But it would not be altogether amiss to say that it was also evangelistic in the sense of the proclamation of good news. Some of the distinctive doctrines taught by the prophets, particularly the doctrine of a Messiah, will be considered later. They came very much nearer than we sometimes imagine to possessing and preaching what we now call the gospel. At all events they urged the cardinal duties of repentance, faith, love, change of heart, the fear of God, public and private obedience to his requirements.

The work of the prophets as ethical and religious preachers is on the whole that which is most kept in the foreground in the descriptions given of them in the bible. What they did as public men or reformers or writers of literature might be said to be branches of their work as preachers.

4. Yet again, the prophets were the literary men of Israel.

It is fashionable in some quarters to assert that they did not become writers till the time of Amos and Isaiah; but by using a concordance of proper names any one can easily convince himself that the scriptures attribute literary authorship to prophets earlier than these. Express mention is made of it in the case of Moses, Joshua, Samuel, Gad, Nathan, David, Asaph, Heman, Ethan, Jeduthun, Solomon, Ahijah, Jedo, Iddo, Shemaiah, Jehu, Elijah, and this constitutes an implication that others also engaged in literary work. Such work is yet more prominently characteristic of the prophets of later times, whose names are attached to the books we now possess.

Whether Israel before Malachi had literary writers who were not prophets does not appear from the evidence; though it is natural to think that the men who are mentioned in connection with public affairs under the title of scribe or recorder were not in all cases prophets. That there was an extensive literature in addition to that now preserved in the bible appears from the references which the biblical writers make to books by their titles. We shall have occasion to speak more in full of the literary work of the prophets when we come to speak of them as the writers of the scriptures.

5. In connection with these naturalistic functions of the prophet there are two or three points which we ought not to neglect.

(a) The distinction between primary and secondary prophets here becomes important. In our study of the external history, our attention was called to the fact of the great numbers of the prophets at all periods between Samuel and Nehemiah. This may seem to be a strange fact, when one's attention is first called to it. Is it not inconsistent with the idea that the prophets are rare and special messengers from heaven?

Different kinds of prophets

In reply to this question it should be said that the prophets who were regarded as having supernatural gifts were probably more numerous than many suppose, though not so numerous but that they were always relatively rare. But the majority of those who are called prophets were doubtless secondary prophets, the " sons of the prophets," members of the prophetic organizations, or in some other capacity disciples of the prophets who were highly gifted. These secondary prophets were associated with the others in public or evangelistic or literary work. Most of the prophetic functions thus far enumerated were shared by them, and the term "prophet" was naturally extended to them.

Very likely a large proportion of the very numerous false prophets were secondary prophets who had become misled, though some of them were doubtless mere counterfeits. It is not necessary to think that the false prophets generally were men who were acknowledged as having supernatural gifts from Yahaweh.

(*b*) We should note, further, that a prophet, in virtue of his being a statesman or a reformer or a preacher or an author, is likely to have been at once a cosmopolitan man and a man who had local and temporary interests. While he was eminently one concerned with the whole world and with all future time, he was at the same time eminently practical, dealing with the concerns of his own locality and his own generation.

The prophet, both local and cosmopolitan

It hinders a correct understanding of the writings of the prophets to ignore the local and temporary element in them. In the main they are composed of the same sorts of material with sermons and reform addresses. They contain the truths with which the prophets tried to move the consciences of the men of their times and of all future time. Predictions, for example, were to them matters of supernatural revelation. They used them just as they and we use scripture texts, to enforce the practical message in hand. Isa. ii–iv, for example, is a sermon preached from the prediction, ii. 2–4, as a text, the sermon being of the nature of rebuke and counsel to the men of that generation.

Equally fatal, however, to correct interpretation, and now more widely prevalent, is the mistake of too much

restricting the prophecies to local and temporary meanings. Doubtless most of the prophetic discourses had
some specific local purpose to accomplish; but the discourse would seek its ends through those general appli-
cations of truth in which all men alike are capable of
being influenced, and not through those only which were
peculiar to their own times. The universalness that
differentiates literature is especially marked in these
writings.

In reading the prophecies we are to recognize a local
allusion or statement when we find one, just as we are
to recognize a prediction when we find one; but we are
not violently to give to any passage either a local character or a predictive character, as if the meaning of the
passage depended upon this. The Israelites of Isaiah's
time, for example, needed divine teaching because of
the peculiarities of the age and land in which they
lived. But they needed it yet more because they were
human sinners, like the men of all countries in all ages.

(c) Yet again, so far as the functions we have been
considering go, the Hebrew prophets have their counterparts both in the Christian church and elsewhere.
These counterparts are of two different kinds.

First, any adherent of the true religion may be said
to prophesy when the Spirit of God gives him a special
message for the edification of others. No A sense in
miracle is needed for this, but only that illu- which all devout persons
mination which devout persons sometimes are prophets
enjoy, and which God offers to all. In Paul's epistle
we have details concerning the gift of prophecy as
possessed by members of the Corinthian church (1 Cor.
xiv). The gift as described here and elsewhere in the
New Testament does not necessarily differ from that
set forth in the Old Testament. And, within limits,

prophesying still abounds among earnestly religious people. One who speaks for God in some special and marked message, in a Christian meeting, exercises so far forth the gift of prophecy.

But again, in a quite different sense, any gifted person, raised up by God for some marked and especial pur-

A sense in which great leaders are prophets

pose of reform or training for the age in which he lives, has some of the marks of a prophet. This is true if the man is earnestly religious, and it remains true even if he is irreligious or falsely religious. The New Testament goes so far as to say that Caiaphas prophesied (Jn. xi. 51), and its writers call Balaam a prophet, and the heathen poet of Crete a prophet.[1] Most believers in a personal God believe that God raises up the great men of history, the bad as well as the good, for the accomplishing of special purposes. To attribute to such men, within properly defined limits, the character of prophets is to say what is distinctly true.

There are reasons, perhaps decisive reasons, against ordinarily using the term "prophet" and the term "inspiration" in such ways as these. Unless carefully defined, the terms when so used are likely to be misunderstood and to be misleading; and if you delay every time for definition, the terms are liable to lose all their energy. But it is correct to illustrate the naturalistic functions of the prophets of Israel by applying the term "prophet" and the term "inspiration," so far forth, to men of all times and races; to say, for example, that Shakespeare

---

[1] " Balaam the son of Beor, who loved the hire of wrongdoing; . . . a dumb ass spake with man's voice and stayed the madness of the prophet " (2 Pet. ii. 15–16).

" One of themselves, a prophet of their own, said, Cretans are always liars, evil beasts, idle gluttons " (Tit. i. 12).

was a prophet of God, divinely inspired for the purpose of producing certain effects upon the literature and
culture and human character of England and of the
world.

There are disputants who say such things as these by
way of denying that the prophets had any divine message different from those of other leaders in human
thought.   One who opposes this denial will have a great
advantage if he fully acknowledges the reality and the
prominence of the naturalistic functions of the prophets,
such functions as we have thus far been considering.
Over a wide range their activities were like those of
other religious men at any time in history.   Again, over
a wide range their activities were like those of other
leaders of thought, at any date or of any blood.

II.   But an account of the prophets which should stop
at this point would be so incomplete as to be thoroughly
erroneous.   The scriptures affirm that the prophets, in
addition to these naturalistic activities, exercised distinctly supernatural powers.

The facts we have been looking at are genuine, and
are essential to an adequate view of the subject.   But
they are entirely subordinate as compared with certain
other facts.   The bible prophets also claim functions
that imply superhuman gifts — functions that differ in
kind, and not merely in degree, from those thus far
mentioned.   They claim an inspiration different from
that which they possess in common with other men.
And this higher inspiration they claim, not merely for
purposes of prediction, but for other activities as well.
Elisha working miracles, Daniel revealing the king's
dream, or any prophet uttering a rebuke that came by
revelation, lays claim to superhuman gifts as really as a
prophet who foretells the future.

These superhuman activities may be spoken of in five classes: the working of miracles, the disclosing of secrets, the foretelling of events, the revealing of Yahaweh's law, the teaching of the doctrine of the Messiah. The last two of these will be considered at length in subsequent chapters. The first three we will now discuss very briefly.

First, the prophets claim to have wrought miracles. We need not, in order to prove this, claim that every wonderful event narrated in the Old Testament is a miracle. Men of the past have mistakenly interpreted marvels into the bible. Perhaps it is true that even some of the most stupendous interpositions in which Yahaweh manifested himself to Israel were events which can be accounted for by known natural laws. There are those who think that the crossing of the Red Sea can be accounted for by an unusual combination of wind and tide, occurring at a certain juncture in the affairs of Israel; and that the rain of fire that destroyed Sodom can be accounted for by the sinking of a broken tract of ground into a deposit of bituminous products; and that Israel's crossing the Jordan dryshod can be accounted for by the hypothesis of a landslide above into the river; and that it was Arabs rather than ravens that brought bread and flesh to Elijah. We need not go into the discussion of such instances. The question in each case is a question as to the meaning of the testimony ; and the divine interposition is equally signal whether we can or cannot account for the events by the known laws of nature. But when we have gone as far as possible in accounting naturalistically for the deeds done by the prophets, it will still remain true that they claimed the ability sometimes to effect supernatural results. Familiar instances are the

The prophet a worker of miracles

wonders done by Moses in Egypt, Elijah's raising from
death the boy at Sarepta, and his calling down fire from
heaven, Elisha's multiplying the oil, causing the iron to
swim, raising to life the Shunamite's child.

Secondly, the prophets claimed to be able to disclose
secrets by supernatural help.   Instances of this, familiar
to all, are those of Joseph before Pharaoh, of   The prophet
Daniel before Nebuchadnezzar, of Elisha in   a discloser of
the matter of the raids planned by the king   secrets
of Syria (2 Ki. vi. 12).

Thirdly, the prophets claimed to predict the future.
In proof that they made this claim, and appealed to
fulfilled prediction as accrediting their com-   The prophet
mission from Yahaweh, one need only read   a predicter
such a passage as Isa. xli–xlv (especially xli.   of events
22–23, 26, xlii. 9, xliii. 9, 12, 18–19, etc.).   This claim
stands in the less need of being discussed, on account
of our being so familiar with it.   The predictions of the
prophets form the staple of one of the familiar arguments
for the divine origin of the religion of the bible.

Of course the validity of this argument depends in
each instance on the question whether the prediction is
specific enough to distinguish the case to which it refers from all other cases.   The threats of the prophets
against Tyre are different from those against Damascus.
Those against each of these are different from those
against Jerusalem ; and similarly with Babylon and
Nineveh and other cities and countries.   The strength
of the argument lies in the degree in which the differences in the fulfilments correspond with those in the
predictions.

Probably no one denies that the prophets made many
predictions that were remarkably fulfilled.   Certain
scholars affirm, however, that many of their predictions

are also shown by the events to have been false. Whether one accepts this charge as true will depend on his interpretations of the facts. Many predictions have been understood in senses in which they failed to conform to the events ; but against the charge that untruthful predictions abound in the utterances of the prophets of Israel, it is safe to enter a general denial.

I am not now concerned to prove that the prophets actually exercised these supernatural abilities — that At least they claimed these superhuman powers they wrought miracles, foretold the future, disclosed hidden things ; I am only concerned to call attention to the fact that they claimed to exercise them. Some proofs that their claim was well founded will come later. The fact now before us is that they make the claim, constantly appealing to these abilities as proving their divine commission. If one has convinced himself that miracles never occur, he will of course refuse even to consider this claim ; but if one's mind is open to conviction on this point, he must take these claims into the account. Indeed, they constitute a part of the phenomena of the case, even from the point of view of one who holds them to be false.

Without particularizing further, let us note that all the prophetic functions of every sort are capable of The monotheism of the religion of Yahaweh being generalized into a single statement. The religion of Israel is monotheism of a certain type, the monotheism of the worship of Yahaweh. Christianity and Mohammedanism, the two more bulky successors of the religion of Israel, preserve this same type of monotheism. We are all worshippers of Israel's God. This monotheism is the greatest factor in all Israelitish or Christian or Moslem civilizations. The great work of the prophets, the one essential work, was the giving of this type of monotheism to Israel and to mankind.

According to the claim of its adherents, Yahaweh revealed this monotheism to men by the process of first causing history to be transacted, and then causing a record of the transactions to be made. The prophets were the public men who had the greatest part in transacting the history. They were the literary men who made the record of the history. They were the preachers who interpreted to men the ethical and spiritual lessons of the history. They claim to have been the inspired seers who perceived and made known Yahaweh's purpose in the history. All their functions, natural and supernatural, may be summed up in this brief descriptive clause, the revealing of the monotheism of Yahaweh to Israel and to mankind.

CHAPTER VI

THE PROPHET'S MESSAGE — HOW GIVEN TO HIM, AND HOW UTTERED BY HIM

WE have found that the Israelitish sacred literature presents the prophet to us as a citizen like others, distinguished only by the fact that he has an especial message from Deity to his fellow-citizens. In the delivery of this message we have found him acting in the character of statesman, reformer, preacher, author, and claiming powers and authority from the realm of the supernatural. The question arises: Were there any distinctive peculiarities in the mode in which he received his message, and in the mode in which he uttered it? Our sources give us some detailed information on these points. We take up the two parts of the question in their order.

I. First, how the prophet's message was revealed to him. What was the source of his inspiration? What were the modes in which it made itself apparent?

1. The source of his inspiration is represented to be the Spirit of Yahaweh, variantly called also the Spirit of Elohim.

Save in exceptional instances the Hebrew word for spirit is feminine; but like the word for soul, also feminine, it may denote a masculine person. When personally used, its suggestions are masculine rather than feminine.[1] The prophetic gift is said to be by the Spirit

---

[1] The word denotes either spirit or wind. In both meanings it is regularly feminine. The lexicons give certain instances in which it is masculine when denoting wind (Ex. x. 13; 1 Ki. xix. 11; Jer. iv. 11; Job viii.

coming upon the prophet, coming mightily upon him, being put upon him or within him, being given, being poured out. This could best be studied by looking up all the numerous passages, with the aid of a concordance. We will recall a few of them, mostly those that are very familiar.

Every one remembers the instance when Moses, at Yahaweh's command, took the seventy elders to the tent of meeting outside the camp, and Yahaweh Prophets in-took of the Spirit which was upon Moses, spired by the and put it upon them, and they prophesied. speak Eldad and Medad, two of the men whose names were in the list, did not go with the others, and the Spirit came upon them where they were, and they prophesied in the camp. That the Spirit here spoken of is the Spirit of Yahaweh is throughout distinctly implied, and in one verse is explicitly stated (Num. xi. 16–17, 25–29).

In the passage from Joel, cited by Peter at the pentecost, we read : —

"I will pour out my Spirit upon all flesh ; and your sons and your daughters shall prophesy . . . And also upon the servants and upon the handmaids in those days will I pour out my Spirit" (RV of Joel ii. 28–29 ; *cf.* Acts ii. 16-18).

Samuel said to Saul: "The Spirit of Yahaweh will come mightily upon thee, and thou wilt prophesy." 2), but there is room for doubt. When used personally the word very naturally passes into a masculine.

"A spirit passed before my face" (Job iv. 15).

"Renew thou within me a spirit that is made ready" (Ps. li. 10).

"The Spirit of Yahaweh spake by me" (2 Sam. xxiii. 2).

"My Spirit shall not strive with man forever" (Gen. vi. 3).

"The Spirit of Yahaweh will take thee up" (1 Ki. xviii. 12).

"Lest the Spirit of Yahaweh hath taken him up" (2 Ki. ii. 16).

"And the Spirit came forth and stood before Yahaweh."

"Which way went the Spirit of Yahaweh from with me to speak with thee?" (1 Ki. xxii. 21, 24).

Accordingly, the narrator says, "the Spirit of Deity came mightily upon him, and he prophesied" (1 Sam. x. 6, 10). In a little prophetic song attributed to David the singer says : —

"The Spirit of Yahaweh spake by me" (2 Sam. xxiii. 2).

In the prayer in Nehemiah the worshippers say to Yahaweh : —

"And thou testifiedst against them by thy Spirit by the hand of the prophets" (Neh. ix. 30).

Micah says : —

"I truly am full of power by the Spirit of Yahaweh" (iii. 8, *cf.* ii. 7, 11).

Hosea uses the parallelism : —

"The prophet is a fool,
The man of the Spirit is made mad" (ix. 7).

Similar instances might be multiplied. In particular the book of Isaiah is full of them. It became customary to connect adjectives with the Spirit, describing him as Yahaweh's "good Spirit" (Neh. ix. 20 ; Ps. cxliii. 10), or his "holy Spirit" (Isa. lxiii. 10–11 ; *cf.* Ps. li. 11 [13]). If one should undertake to make a count of the instances, he ought not to omit those in which the divine name is represented by a pronoun (*e.g.* Gen. vi. 3 ; Pss. cvi. 33, cxxxix. 7 ; Isa. xxx. 1).

Our survey of the subject of the Spirit that inspired the prophets is not complete till we have looked at a very different class of manifestations of the Spirit of Yahaweh. In the narrative concerning Elijah we are told of the Spirit's carrying him away, rendering him invisible (1 Ki. xviii. 12 ; 2 Ki. ii. 16). Marvellous acts of this nature are not often attributed to the Spirit; but marvellous acts in the form of great achievements of men are as prominently so

Deeds of men inspired by the Spirit

attributed as even the inspiring of the messages of the prophets. Samson's exhibitions of wonderful strength, for example, were by " the Spirit of Yahaweh " coming " mightily " upon him (Jud. xiii. 25, xiv. 6, 19, xv. 14). It was when "the Spirit of Yahaweh " came upon Othniel and Gideon and Jephthah (Jud. iii. 10, vi. 34, xi. 29) and others, that they wrought the exploits by which they delivered Israel. When "the Spirit of Yahaweh came mightily unto David," its presence was probably manifested by David's achievements quite as much as by his words; and the removal of the Spirit from Saul was probably indicated by his failure in achievement (1 Sam. xvi. 13, 14). The Isaian singer says of Israel in the wilderness (Isa. lxiii. 10–11): —

" They rebelled, and grieved his holy Spirit." " Where is he that put his holy Spirit in the midst of them ? that caused his glorious arm to go at the right hand of Moses ? that divided the water before them ? "

In saying this he attributes to Moses the great deeds of the exodus, and not the great words only.

At first thought, the qualifying a man for war or statesmanship, and especially the qualifying a man for such athletic feats as those of Samson, by an inrush of spiritual influence, seems to be very different from the qualifying a prophet to utter a divine message; but certainly there is no incongruity between the two. Especially should this idea find a hospitable reception among us of the present generation, now that we have introduced athletics so prominently among our appliances for Christian service.

More difficult is the case where the four hundred prophets are prophesying in the name of Yahaweh before Ahab and Jehoshaphat, and Micaiah has his vision of "the Spirit" proposing to be a lying spirit in the mouths of the prophets, and finding his offer acceptable to Yahaweh (1 Ki. xxii. 21, 24); but we are Micaiah's not at liberty to evade the difficulty by omit-lying spirit ting this passage from our induction. This seems to me to be a truly oriental instance of extremism in the use of figure of speech. These prophets, professing to be moved by the Spirit of Yahaweh, were prophesying falsehood. Micaiah says that it is as if the Spirit of Yahaweh had become a lying spirit in them in order to deceive Ahab to his destruction. That is all that they understood him to mean. They did not understand that in fact the Spirit became a lying spirit.[1]

What is the Spirit of Yahaweh as delineated in the passages we have studied? To this question I give here no philosophical or theological answer. The answer The nature that lies verbally in the accounts is clear. of the Spirit The Spirit is effluent energy from Yahaweh of Yahaweh the infinite Spirit. But if we stop with this, the answer is incomplete. This effluent energy is spoken of in terms of personality. But the language used concerning the Spirit of Yahaweh is different from that used concerning the many personal spirits whom these writers conceive of as doing the errands of the supreme Spirit.[2] The inspiring Spirit is one, and is spoken of in terms that are definite. If we were confined to the instances in which other divine names than Yahaweh are used, there might be room for disput-

[1] The English versions try to solve the difficulty by translating, "a spirit," a translation that is within the limits of possibility. Other solutions have been proposed. In Deity's causing or permitting Ahab to be deceived, we have simply one more unsolved detail in the unsolved problem of the origin of evil.

[2] Of these Saul's evil spirit is a familiar instance (1 Sam. xvi. 14b, xix. 9). Job says: "A spirit passed before my face" (iv. 15). "He maketh his angels spirits" (Ps. civ. 4).

ing this, but concerning "the Spirit of Yahaweh" there
is no room for doubt.   And it is reasonably certain that
"the Spirit of Deity" in such cases as those of Bezalel,
Balaam, Azariah, Zechariah (Ex. xxxi. 3, xxxv. 31 ;
Num. xxiv. 2 ; 2 Chron. xv. 1, xxiv. 20), is the same
with "the Spirit of Yahaweh."   In fine, this Spirit that
inspires the prophets is presented to us as a unique
being, having personal characteristics, effluent from Yahaweh the supreme Spirit of the universe, at once identical with and different from Yahaweh.

2. We turn to the question of the modes in which
it is represented that the Spirit gave the prophet his
message.

In books of reference these are usually classified, I
believe, as three ; namely, by dreams, by visions, by direct
communication.   This classification seems to Modes of
me inadequate.   It is based in part on the revelation as
commonly
assumption that the words from the stem classified
raah, to see, are interchangeable with those from the
stem hhazah, to see.   This assumption, as we have seen
in Chapter II, is not confirmed by a close examination
of the instances.

Partly on the ground of the difference between these
two sets of terms, and partly on other grounds, it seems
to me that a better classification of the modes A better
of revelation to the prophets is the following : classification
first, dreams ; second, picture-visions ; third, visions of
insight ; fourth, theophanies.   The understanding of
this classification will be the vindication of it, provided
it is capable of being vindicated.   When we understand
it, we shall see that it is really the classification that is
implied in the statements of the bible.

(a) The first of these four modes of revelation is that
by dreams.   The number of passages in which this

mode is recognized is considerable, and the recognition is distinct; and yet the impression is made that this mode is regarded as of a lower type than the others.

General statements concerning revelation by dreams abound. In the thirteenth chapter of Deuteronomy, in

General mention of prophetic dreams the directions given for testing a prophet's claims, the phrase "a prophet or a dreamer of dreams" is three times repeated, as if one might be a prophet in virtue of his being a dreamer of dreams (Deut. xiii. 1, 3, 5 [2, 4, 6]). In the account of the incident when Miriam and Aaron "spake against Moses," Yahaweh says : —

"If there be a prophet among you, I . . . will make myself known unto him in a vision, I will speak with him in a dream" (Num. xii. 6).

We are told that King Saul resorted to the witch of Endor because Yahaweh did not answer him —

"by dreams, nor by Urim, nor by prophets" (1 Sam. xxviii. 6, 15).

Very familiar is the promise in Joel : —

"Your sons and your daughters shall prophesy, your old men shall dream dreams, your young men shall see visions" (ii. 28).

Job recognizes God's speaking "in a dream, in a vision of the night," and complains of God's scaring him with dreams, and terrifying him through visions (xxxiii. 15, vii. 14). Jeremiah lays down the following rule as applicable even when sham prophetic dreams abound : —

"The prophet that hath a dream, let him tell a dream, and he that hath my word, let him speak my word faithfully. What is the straw to the wheat ? saith Yahaweh" (xxiii. 28).

Observe, however, that it is possible, in each of these instances, so to interpret as to make the dream an inferior mode of revelation. I do not say that this is the true interpretation, but it is a possible one. And in other passages, considerable stress is laid on the deceiving dreams of some of the prophets. Speaking of "teraphim" and "diviners," the second **False** Zechariah says, "They have told false dreams" **prophetic** (x. 2). Jeremiah has a good deal to say of **dreams** the false dreaming of the prophets (xxiii. 25, 27, 32, xxvii. 9, xxix. 8).

"The prophets . . . that prophesy lies in my name, saying, I have dreamed, I have dreamed."

"Who think to cause my people to forget my name by their dreams which they tell."

"That prophesy by lying dreams."

"Hearken ye not to your prophets, nor to your diviners, nor to your dreams."

"Neither hearken ye to your dreams which ye cause to be dreamed."

There are about a dozen instances of significant dreams in the Old Testament ; Joseph's dreams concerning the sheaves, and concerning the **Instances of** sun and moon and stars ; Jacob's dreams **significant** at Bethel and in Paddan-aram ; Solomon's **dreams** dream ; Daniel's dream, with the vision of the four beasts ; the dreams of the chief butler and the chief baker and Pharaoh ; those of Nebuchadnezzar ; of Abimelech king of Gerar ; of Laban ; of a Midianite soldier in Gideon's time (Gen. xxxvii. 5–20, xxviii. 12, xxxi. 10–11 ; 1 Ki. iii. 5, 15 ; Dan. vii. 1 ; Gen. xl–xli ; Dan. ii, iv ; Gen. xx. 3, 6, xxxi. 24 ; Jud. vii. 12–15). In a majority of the instances the dreamers are heathen ; and in most of the instances where the dream is prophetic, it does not loom up very large.

Really the interpretation of dreams seems to be more honorably presented as a prophetic function than the dreaming of dreams. It is spoken of as especially distinguishing Daniel that he had "understanding in all

visions and dreams" (i. 17). His "excellent spirit"
manifested itself in the "interpreting of dreams" (v.

Prophets as 12), as well as in other ways. The inter-
interpreters pretations of the dreams of Nebuchadnezzar
of dreams and of Pharaoh by Daniel and Joseph are
certainly in the records on the ground of their being
notable achievements of men who had prophetic gifts.

(*b*) The second mode of revelation to the prophets
is that by visions that are conceived of as presented
to the physical eye. Not necessarily visions that are
actually perceived, notice, by the physical sight, but
visions that are thought of as so perceived.[1]

Instances of this mode of communication with Deity
are numerous in the Old Testament, and are familiar

Instances of to all readers. A few, taken at random, are
picture- Jeremiah's beholding the rod of almond, the
vision seething pot, the baskets of figs (Jer. i. 11, 13,
xxiv); Zechariah's beholding the lampbowl and olive
trees, the flying roll, the woman in the ephah, the
four chariots (Zech. iv, v. 1–4, 5–11, vi. 1–8); Ezekiel's
beholding the four living creatures, and the hand with
the book-roll (Ezek. i, ii. 9, etc.); Yahaweh's causing
Amos to behold the locusts devouring the latter
growth, the fire devouring the great deep, the plumbline, the basket of summer fruit (vii. 1–3, 4–6, 7–9, viii.
1–3); his causing Elisha to behold the approaching
death of Benhadad and the accession of Hazael (2 Ki.
viii. 10–13); the appearing to Ezekiel of the semblance

[1] These are the instances in which prophetic vision is described in terms
of the qal, the hiphil, the hophal, or the nouns of the stem *raah*, as distinguished from the stem *hhazah*. See Chapter II. In the remainder of this
chapter we will translate the words of this stem by such English terms as
"behold," "appearance," "picture-vision," reserving the words "see" and
"vision" to be used in translating from *hhazah*. The niphal of *raah* will
be considered later, when we reach the subject of theophany.

of a throne over his cherubim, and of a hand under their wings (x. 1, 8); and very many others.

(*c*) The third mode of revelation to the prophets may, in the lack of a better term, be said to be by visions of insight. It is expressed in the Hebrew by the words of the stem *hhazah*, when these are specifically used. It would include all methods of appeal to the mind except that by picture-vision.

We have already seen (Chapter II) that the verb *hhazah*, though it is in Aramaic the ordinary word for physical seeing, is in the Hebrew mainly con- *Hhazah* fined to the instances in which the seeing is versus prophetic, and in other instances the restric- *raah* tion of it to the idea of mental perception or thoughtful seeing is persistent. The *hhazah* words are used as literary terms in the titles of the prophecies and elsewhere, while the *raah* words are never so used. Even in the Aramaizing Hebrew of the book of Daniel the difference between the words of these two stems never quite fades out, and elsewhere it is very distinct.

The *hhazah* words sometimes denote a genus, under which the *raah* words designate a species. Every *raah* vision is a *hhazah* vision, but there may be *hhazah* visions which are not *raah* visions.[1] Again, the *hhazah* words are sometimes applied to the whole of some transaction, while the *raah* words are used to denote a picture-vision

[1] Speaking of his vision of the ram and the he-goat, Daniel says, "I Daniel had beheld the vision" (viii. 15). What he had beheld was an appearance presented to the eye, but it was also vision in the wider sense of prophetic revelation, and the speaker here prefers the generic word to the specific. In verse 16 the other term is used: "Make this man to understand the appearance." The phrase "whom I had beheld in the vision" is used in ix. 21. Similarly it is said in Joel (ii. 28) that the young men shall "behold visions." Amos is called a "seer" (vii. 12) in the midst of the account of the series of objects which Yahaweh "caused him to behold."

which constituted a part of the transaction.[1]   These uses
of the words of the two stems explain the phenomena
which have sometimes been mistakenly regarded as cases
of interchange.   Samuel and Zadok and Hanani are
doubtless called *roim* because they somehow came to be
thought of as receiving revelations in forms that appealed
to the senses.   Gad and Asaph and Heman and Jeduthun
and Iddo and Jehu the son of Hanani are called *hhozim*
because they were believed to have insight into the will
of Deity, without emphasizing the form of the revelations
made through them.

As the *hhazah* words may denote a genus under which
the *raah* words denote a species, so they may also denote
Vision other   another species of the same genus; namely,
than that by   mental vision in distinction from the actual or
sense-images   apparent presentation of objects to the senses.
This is apparently the meaning in a large proportion of
the instances in which a prophetic writing is spoken of
as a vision (*e.g.* Isa. i. 1; Na. i. 1; Hab. ii. 2), and in
those in which the word of Yahaweh is said to come to
some one in a vision, or in which some other like expression is used (*e.g.* Gen. xv. 1–6; 2 Sam. vii. 17; Nu. xxiv.
4, 16; Isa. ii. 1).

Obviously it is supposable that the prophet might
receive his message through other avenues than his
picture-making faculty.   Even if it were indispensable
that he be in a tranced or ecstatic condition, such a condition might supposably act upon his memory, his powers of perception or reasoning, his association of ideas,

---

[1] In Dan. viii–x *hhazon* (viii. 1, 2, 2, 13, 15a, 17, 26b, ix. 21, 24, x. 14)
denotes either the whole of a transaction, or some part of it thought of
generically as divine revelation; while *mar'eh* and *mar'ah* denote specifically objects that are thought of as presented to the eye (viii. 15b, 16, 26a,
27, ix. 23, x. 1, 6, 7, 7, 8, 16, 18).

and not exclusively upon his imagination. Through these other mental powers, without any intervention of sense-perceived images, he might be made to know things which he would not know in an ordinary state of mind. But the records do not say that the prophet was always in an ecstatic state when he received his message. In by far the larger number of the instances there is no mention of either dreams or apparitions or trances. It is possible to think of most of the communications to the prophets as reaching them through their aroused spiritual insight, unaccompanied by the consciousness of manifestations appealing to the senses. The revelation may have been the product of a sharpened intuition or a quickened intelligence, brought to bear upon the problem of the hour.

These things are supposable. That they are also matters of fact appear from the contents of the writings which have come down to us from the prophets under the title of visions. In these writings the prophets exhibit themselves as actively and consciously using all the faculties which a human mind possesses. Evidently they regarded themselves as guided by the Spirit in making investigations, in remembering, in judging of facts, in estimating persons, in making inductions and deductions, in mental processes of all sorts. The records specify dreams and appearance visions and other like modes, but they do not represent the prophet as restricted to these. The terms used have meanings wide enough to include any supposable influence exerted by the divine Spirit over the mind of the prophet. In many cases the language of the scriptures will justify no narrower interpretation than that Deity in some way made the prophet understand his will.

(*d*) The fourth mode of revelation to the prophets is

by theophany. It is superfluous to say that the word "theophany" is of Greek origin, and denotes an appearing of Deity in visible form.

The Hebrew expression for this fact is the Niphal of the verb *raah*, to see. It denotes the state of being The Niphal of *raah* seen, or the act of becoming visible. It is commonly translated by the English verb "appear." Not all the instances in which it is used are cases of theophany. For example, Yahaweh is said to have appeared to Solomon (1 Ki. iii. 5) in a dream. But the theophanic instances are easily distinguishable.

The cases of theophany may be described as those in which we find Yahaweh appearing in human form and conversing with the prophet, with or without additional miraculous manifestations ; or Yahaweh uttering audible words from the midst of miraculous manifestations.

Instances of theophany are given in passages that are those most familiar to us. Abraham is sitting at his tent Yahaweh in human semblance door, and suddenly becomes aware of three men standing near him. He talks with them, they eat with him ; one of them promises to Sarah a son ; he accompanies them on their way ; they part, two of them going toward Sodom. The one who remains with Abraham turns out to be Yahaweh, and he and Abraham have a memorable interview. The other two are the angels who rescue Lot when Sodom is destroyed (Gen. xviii. 1–2, 9–10, 13, 17, 20–21, 22, xix. 1).

This is, perhaps, the instance that is more explicit in its details than any other on record. In some of the Varying forms of theophany instances there is a miraculous manifestation in addition to the appearing in human form of the person who utters the message. A good example is that of Manoah and the Angel who talked with him, and the miraculous burning of the food which he placed before the Angel (Jud. xiii. 3, 6, 16, 19, 20–21, 22). In other cases, there is the miraculous manifestation and the uttering of audible words, without any human form being visible; for example, the giving of the ten words from Sinai, or the revelations from the pillar of cloud or of fire over the tent of meeting (Ex. xix–xx; Deut. v; Num. ix. 15–23). In some cases there may be a doubt as to whether the narrative represents that a human form appeared; for example, at the burning bush, or at the sacrifice of Isaac (Ex. iii. 2–3; Gen. xxii. 11–12, 14, 15–16).

The personage who is described as "the Angel" is prominent in most of the detailed instances of theophany. His presence is explicitly mentioned, I believe, in all the cases that have just been The Angel cited. Scholars have given much attention to this personage, and he deserves much. He appears in the Old Testament narrative, in nearly all its stages, not as some angel or other, but as the Angel, a distinct, separate being. In any particular case we are likely to find him presenting himself as a man, afterward spoken of as the Angel, and later in the narrative identified with Yahaweh himself. We must not delay to discuss the subject, but the Angel seems to be in some sense a temporary incarnation of Yahaweh.

From one point of view, theophany might be classed as a species of picture-vision. It is like picture-vision in that it presents Deity as assuming the Theophany form of a visible person, or as speaking from *versus* the midst of visible manifestations. It is picture-vision unlike picture-vision in that it is of the nature of a personal interview of a man with God, and not mainly of the nature of an object lesson taught by emblems. Genuine theophanies are regarded as something rare and precious, the highest form of divine communication with men. The difference between Moses and the less gifted prophets was that Yahaweh spoke with him in theophanic "picture-vision," mouth to mouth, and not merely in dreams or ordinary picture-vision (Num. xii. 6–8).[1]

(*e*) Very noteworthy in the biblical accounts of the prophets is the absence of the use of artificial parapher-
The absence of artificial excitation nalia or processes for exciting the prophetic mood. In one instance we are told that Elisha required the presence of a minstrel as the condition of his giving a message (2 Ki. iii. 15). This case is the only one of its kind. If we regard it as an instance in which external means were used to induce a suitable frame of mind in a prophet desiring a revelation, it is altogether exceptional.

In this the scriptures are in contrast with what we find elsewhere in all ages, in persons who profess to give supernatural revelations. The shaman has his snakeskin rattle, the conjurer has his strange-looking tools, the astrologer has his elaborate, scholarly-seeming apparatus; and they use these in compelling the other world to disclose its secrets or to bring help. The prophets of ancient Egypt had their magic formulas, the persons in the *Arabian Nights* pronounce the ineffable Name, Prospero compels the spirits by spells and charms. The Pythia at Delphi inhaled intoxicating vapor, the augurs consulted the flight of birds or the entrails of sacrificial victims, Ezra in the legend drinks a potion to enable him to reproduce the inspired scriptures, the witches

---

[1] It is surprising that the identifying of theophany with what is above described as mental vision has gained a good deal of currency, and along with it a theory that mental vision is presented in the Old Testament as the highest form of revelation. Linguistically, the descriptions of theophany are affiliated with the derivatives of *raah*, and not of *hhazah*.

in *Macbeth* dance around the caldron, the modern spiritualists have their seances.   In *Odd Craft*, the latest volume of stories, the fortune-teller burns something in a bowl, and he and the inquirers sit among the fumes. Other characters in recent novels consult the unseen by burning a hair, or by drawing blood, or by stirring the grounds in a teacup.   From the biblical narratives we learn that processes of these various sorts were in existence throughout the times covered by Israelitish history.[1]   In view of all this, it is a thing very remarkable that the prophets of Yahaweh are not represented as resorting to means of artificial excitation in order to stir up the spirit of revelation in them or for them.   In this, as in their being simply citizens with a message (Chapter IV), they are unique among the prophets of the nations.

II.   As our second principal topic we take up certain peculiarities which characterized the prophets in giving their messages to men.   As we should expect, these bear a certain correspondence to the modes in which revelation came from God to them.

1. They are noted, for example, for their very abundant use of symbols.   They delight in simple but striking object lessons, in which physical Prophetic objects or personal acts are employed to object represent truths.   Ahijah rends the garment lessons into twelve pieces and gives Jeroboam ten, in token that Jeroboam shall reign over ten tribes (1 Ki. xi. 30–31). Ezekiel inscribes one stick with the name Judah and another with the name Joseph, and puts the two together, in token of the union of the exiles from the

---

[1] Instance the witch of Endor, the prophets of Baal cutting themselves in their frantic efforts to obtain a revelation, and the derivations of the many different words that are used in speaking of practitioners of magic arts.

northern and the southern kingdoms (xxxvii. 15–25).
Isaiah went naked and barefoot, to indicate the way
in which the Assyrian would lead Egypt and Ethiopia
into exile (xx). Jeremiah wore a bar of wood as an
emblem of the subjugation of the nations to Nebuchadnezzar ; and when the false prophet Hananiah broke off
the bar, Jeremiah declared that Yahaweh would replace
it with a yoke of iron (Jer. xxvii, xxviii). Jeremiah
publicly broke the potter's vessel in the valley of the
son of Hinnom, to indicate Yahaweh's breaking of
Judah and Jerusalem (xix).

2. The teaching of the prophets by types should be
distinguished from their ordinary teaching by symbols.
The type is a higher form of symbolism, in which actual
persons or facts or events are used in setting forth
greater events or spiritual truths.

The older treatments of prophecy make much of the
doctrine of types. Extensive works have been written
A type   on Typology, and many of them. In some
defined   the doctrine has been mistakenly treated, but
it is nevertheless important. In actual use the word
"type" is applied to emblems or figures of speech of
all kinds, but it is better so to define it as to make it
distinctive. Perhaps the best definition for the purpose
is that which prevails in the sciences. A type is —

"one of a class or group of objects that embodies the characteristics
of the group or class"; or "the ideal representation combining essential characteristics, as of a species, genus, or family; an organism
exhibiting the essential characteristics of its group" (*Standard
Dictionary*).

Using this definition in connection with the phenomena
of prophecy, the most important form of type is that
in which a historical fact or person or event is used as
an example foreshadowing some other fact or event or

person. It is best to distinguish a type from all objects that are not thought of as historical, and from historical events that are used merely for purposes of illustration. A type is an emblem of a peculiar kind, a fact or a person embodying a truth, and used as a foreshadowing example of a greater manifestation of that truth.

The prophetic typology is mainly concerned with the messianic doctrine taught by the prophets, and will come before us again when we reach that subject. For the present it is sufficient to add that it is the characters and experiences and works of the prophets that are typical, rather than their utterances. They themselves claim to be a succession of types. The institutions of Israel as moulded by the prophets are typical of something higher to be unfolded in the future. Under their guidance much of the history has a typical value.

3. In considering the modes of utterance by the prophets, we cannot wholly ignore the questions that have been so often raised concerning a double sense and a manifold fulfilment.

(a) It is not to be admitted that any of the utterances of the true prophets of Yahaweh have a double sense, meaning thereby a deceitfully equivocal sense. The Greek oracle to Pyrrhus on his way to invade Italy is said to have been : —

Deceitfully equivocal meanings

> " I say that Rome
> Pyrrhus shall overcome."

When Pyrrhus failed to overcome Rome, and complained that the oracle had deceived him, he was told that the oracle was not to blame for his mistaken parsing. In 1 Ki. xxii. 12 the false prophets say : —

> "Go thou up to Ramoth-gilead and prosper, and Yahaweh will give it into the hand of the king."

They give the same equivocal message variantly in verse 6, and Micaiah repeats it ironically in verse 15. But among the recognized prophets of Yahaweh serious instances of this kind are conspicuous by their absence.

·Instances of alleged double sense of a different kind may be exemplified by the citation of Jeremiah (xxxi. 15) in Matthew (ii. 18) concerning Rachel weeping for her children. We read in Genesis that Rachel was buried in Ramah on the way from Bethel to Ephrath, known later as Bethlehem (Gen. xxxv. 19–20, xlviii. 7; *cf.* 1 Sam. x. 2). Jeremiah in a fine burst of figurative language represents Rachel in her grave as weeping over her children, who have vanished by slaughter and captivity from the depopulated region. Matthew quotes the language, with the formula: "Then was fulfilled that which was spoken by Jeremiah the prophet," and applies it to the slaughter of the infants by Herod. There are those who insist that Matthew says that the words of Jeremiah were a prediction of the slaughter by Herod, and were in that sense fulfilled. It would seem to follow that Jeremiah had two meanings in mind when he spoke the words, one meaning for his own time and another for the time of Jesus. Several of the places where the New Testament speaks of the words of a prophet as having been fulfilled are regarded as instances of this kind of alleged double sense. But it is not necessary to think that Matthew regarded the words of Jeremiah as a prediction of the cruelty of Herod. Probably he meant no more than that the words of the prophet are capable of being used as a vivid description of the affair under Herod. Nothing is more common than to apply familiar old diction to new situations. With this interpretation of instances of this sort every sign of a double sense vanishes.

(*b*) The question of manifold fulfilment is entirely different from that of an equivocal sense, and should be treated accordingly.

On this point the one most important consideration is that the idea of manifold fulfilment is not an afterthought, devised for the explaining of difficulties, but is a recognition of an essential part of the structure of biblical prophecy. The predic- tions found in the extant works of the prophets are almost exclusively either promises or threats. And they are not sporadic, but parts of a connected doctrine concerning the workings of a Deity whose plans are represented as extending through the ages. That his plans extend through the ages is a point much insisted upon.

Manifold fulfilment not an after- thought

In the very nature of things the execution of a threat may be accomplished in parts, and at different times. In the nature of things a promise, operative without limit of time, may begin to be fulfilled at once, and may also continue being fulfilled through future period after period. In the time of our civil war a soldier's life was saved by a comrade. He promised that he would always show himself grateful. After the war he came to possess wealth and influence. He kept his promise when his comrade was sick, by seeing that he was taken to a hospital and cared for. He kept it later by paying the expenses of his comrade's son through college. Year by year he insists upon a visit from his comrade and his comrade's family, and the two give themselves up to the good fellowship of the occasion. He has just presented his comrade's granddaughter with a handsome marriage portion. The prediction that he made when he promised to be grateful has naturally this manifold fulfilment. So a prediction that is in the form of a promise of never ending benefit from Deity has necessarily a manifold fulfilment. Most of the prophetic predictions are of this type. It is very clear that such a prophecy may have manifold application, manifold fulfilment, without having a double sense.

This matter is principally important in connection with the messianic forecast found in the prophets, and it will be abundantly illustrated when we reach that part of our subject. For the present we will only illustrate the principle in hand by barely mentioning a few of the different ways in which scholars have stated it.

Writers have applied the term "generic prophecy" in more ways than one. According to one idea a generic prediction is one which regards an event as occurring in a series of parts, separated by intervals, and expresses itself in language that may apply indifferently to the nearest part, or to the remoter parts, or to the whole — in other words, a prediction which, in applying to the whole of a complex event, also applies to some of the parts. A certain law of perspective has played a prominent part in this way of presenting the matter. It is as when a person looks out over a wide view made up of several parallel ranges of hills. The more distant ranges are much the grander; though to his eye the nearer look the larger, and the farther are blended with the nearer. Study, for example, the words of Jesus concerning the destruction of Jerusalem and his coming and the end of the age (Mat. xxiv–xxv).

Others speak of the successive or the progressive fulfilment of a prediction. An event is foretold which is to be brought about through previous events that in some particulars resemble it. The prediction is to be thought of as fulfilled, though inadequately, in the first event of the series, and as more or less adequately fulfilled in each succeeding event, but as completely fulfilled only in the final event in the series. Another form of statement is that only the final event is foretold, but that this incidentally includes the foretelling of some of the means by which it is accomplished, that is, of some of the intervening events that lead up to it.

With some a favorite way of presenting the case is to say that types and antitypes may exist in a series, one event being typical of a second, the second Series of being typical of a third, the third of a types and fourth, and so on. In such a case it is evi- antitypes dent that a prediction or other prophecy, applying to the first event in the series, may through it apply to the second, and so to each succeeding event till the antitype is reached. In foretelling parts of such a series the remaining parts are foretold.

When the point of a prophecy consists in its enunciating the principles on which God acts in dealing with individuals or communities, then the prophecy The may of course be so far forth applied to every principles of God's ad- instance that comes wholly or partly under ministration these principles. Especially is it true that if the prophets believed that Deity had some central plan in view in his management of the world, their teachings concerning that plan and its details would be thereby affected. Many of their statements would apply equally to the whole plan or to certain of its details. Some of their statements would apply equally to details which were in themselves very unlike. I have stated this hypothetically; but nothing is more certain than that the prophets had a theory of this kind, and that their utterances were greatly affected thereby.

4. In treating of the modes of utterance of the

prophets, we have considered mainly the points which seem most to call for remark.   But there is some danger that in doing this we may mistake exceptional things for the things that are essential.   Really the greatest quality in the modes of utterance of the prophets is that they were masters of the art of persuasive speech.   They were enabled to utter moral and religious truth so directly and incisively that the truth they uttered has lived ever since.

Masters of the art of persuasive speech

CHAPTER VII

AT the close of the fifth chapter our attention was called to the fact that the one great function of the prophets was the transmitting of monotheism in its Israelitish type to Israel, to mankind, and to future ages. The monotheism they transmitted may be looked at with respect to its contents or with respect to its form. As to its contents, the chief thing in it is its messianic doctrine. In its form it is an alleged revelation or series of revelations from God, commonly described by the prophets themselves as "law," *torah*. *Torah*, when written, becomes sacred scripture.

The discussion of the distinctive contents of the monotheism of this type, namely, its doctrine of the Messiah, will occupy the second part of this volume; the discussion of its form will occupy the present chapter. Nothing can be more important in this investigation than to get a clear idea of the relations of the prophets to *torah*, that is, directly or indirectly, to the written scripture.

Most students of the Bible, even if they do not understand Hebrew, are familiar with this word *torah*, commonly translated "law." From the careless use of it arise many errors. When one gets so far along as to know that the Old Testament consists of the Law and the Prophets and the Hagiographa, he is liable to assume that "law" and "pentateuch" are convertible terms. Even scholarly men have made this assumption, and with disastrous results. For this reason we need carefully to consider the term *torah* and its equivalents. We will study it, first, as used in writings later than the Old Testament; second, as used in the Old Testament; third, as indicating the character of the Old Testament.

I. First, the term is not restricted, in the literature that has been written since the Old Testament, to the denoting of the pentateuch. In particular, it is also employed to denote the entire bible, or to denote the Old Testament.

1. Certainly, we ourselves use the term "law" in this extended sense. If you heard some one speak of the written law of God, you might understand him to mean the pentateuch, but you would be more likely to understand him to mean the bible.

2. The same usage prevails among the Jewish scholars of past centuries. For example, one finds such a passage as the following : —

"This whole work is called *Mikra,* that is, Scripture or Bible. It is also often called Law, as R. Bechai teaches in *Chadh Hake-*
Rabbinical   *mach:* . . . 'The Law is divided into three parts, usage   into the Law, the Prophets and the Hagiographa'"
(*Ugolino,* Vol. I, Col. 226).

As another instance, Lightfoot (Pitman's ed., 1823, Vol. XII, p. 546) quotes from *Bab. Sanhedr.,* fol. 91, 2, a discussion in which three Old Testament passages are cited on the question : "Whence is the resurrection of the dead proved out of the law?" The passages are Josh. viii. 30; Ps. lxxxiv. 4; Isa. lii. 8. It is evident that the word "law" in this passage denotes the Old Testament, and not the pentateuch only.

These instances are relatively late. It is alleged that no such usage prevailed in the early Christian centuries, but this is a mistake. In the celebrated four- Usage in teenth chapter of 2 Esdras, for example, the 2 Esdras and things "which were written in thy law" in- Josephus clude, apparently, "the works that shall begin," and "all that hath taken place in the world since the beginning" (vv. 20–22), that is, the contents of the predictive and the historical parts of the Old Testament. Ezra is represented as saying: "The world therefore lieth in darkness . . . since thy law is burnt," and as asking for the gift of the Holy Spirit that he may write the things that had formerly been written in the law. Receiving the inspiration he sought, he writes, according to the most probable text, ninety-four books, the first twenty-four of which he is to publish openly (vv. 44–46). It is clear that these twenty-four books were, in the mind of the author of the story, the "law" of which he had been speaking, and it is equally clear that by them he intended the Old Testament.[1]

Josephus, like the author of 2 Esdras, wrote not far from the close of the first century A.D., a little later than the writers of the New Testament. In the third section of the Preface to his *Antiquities* he says, speaking of King Ptolemy and the Septuagint translation of the Old Testament : —

"For he did not obtain all the record, for those who were sent to Alexandria as interpreters gave him only the books of the law. But there is a vast number of other matters in the sacred literature." [2]

[1] If the expression "a law of life" in verse 30 refers especially to the pentateuch, that simply shows that this author, like others, used the term "law" in both senses. It should be noticed that the point here made depends solely on the author's use of language, and not at all on the truthfulness of his statements of fact.

[2] This translation is based on those of Whiston and Shilletto, but is

Josephus here distinguishes between "the books of the law" on the one hand and "the record," "the sacred literature," on the other. It is commonly assumed that by the first of these terms he means the pentateuch, and by the other two the rest of the Old Testament. But it is at least as plausible to say that by the first he means the Old Testament, and that in the other two he includes the body of secondary sacred literature which he uses so freely in the work that follows. The context proves that this latter statement is certainly the correct one. By "the books of the law" Josephus here means the aggregate of the Hebrew Old Testament writings. These had been for several generations accessible to Greeks, in the Septuagint translation. Josephus now proposes to render accessible a portion of the contents of the secondary sacred writings.

3. Not to consider other uses of the term "law" in the New Testament, its writers sometimes designate the New Testament usage pentateuch as the law, and sometimes include under this designation the whole body of the "scriptures" to which they are in the habit of referring. It is impossible to be sure which of these two meanings of the term was the more familiar to their minds.

A marked instance of the second of these two meanings is that in which Jesus asks the question : "Is it not written in your law, I said, Ye are Gods?"[1] Here the reference is not to a passage in the books of Moses,

changed to avoid their confusing of the literary terms used by Josephus. The plural γράμματα, letters, is rendered "literature," to distinguish it alike from γραφή, scripture, and βιβλία, books.

[1] "Jesus answered them, Is it not written in your law, I said, Ye are gods? If he called them gods, unto whom the word of God came (and the scripture cannot be broken), say ye of him whom the Father sanctified and sent into the world, Thou blasphemest; because I said, I am *the* Son of God?" (Jn. x. 34).

but to one of the psalms (lxxxii. 6). Jesus speaks of
this phrase from the psalm as "written in your law,"
and immediately afterward calls it "scripture." You
can only explain his use of words by saying that he and
those who heard him were alike in the habit of sometimes speaking of the whole body of the scriptures as
"the law." Similarly Jesus speaks of the sentence,
"They hated me without a cause" (Ps. xxxv. 19 or
lxix. 4), as "written in their law" (Jn. xv. 25). A
more general instance is the following (Jn. xii. 34) : —

"The multitude therefore answered him, We have heard out
of the law that the Christ abideth for ever : and how sayest
thou, The Son of man must be lifted up ? "

Here the reference may be to any one of several specific
passages, or it may be to the general spirit of the messianic passages; but in either case it is to the Old
Testament outside the Mosaic books.

John is not the only New Testament writer who employs language in this way. Paul says to the Corin-
thians (1 Cor. xiv. 21): —

"In the law it is written, By men of strange tongues and by
the lips of strangers will I speak unto this people ; and not even
thus will they hear me, saith the Lord."

This citation is from Isaiah (xxviii. 11, 12). Add to these
instances the series of citations in Rom. iii. 10–19 : —

"As it is written,
There is none righteous, no, not one ;
There is none that understandeth,
There is none that seeketh after God ;
They have all turned aside, they are together become unprofit-
    able ;
There is none that doeth good, no, not so much as one :
Their throat is an open sepulchre ;
With their tongues they have used deceit :
The poison of asps is under their lips :

Whose mouth is full of cursing and bitterness :
Their feet are swift to shed blood ;
Destruction and misery are in their ways ;
And the way of peace have they not known :
There is no fear of God before their eyes.

Now we know that what things soever the law saith, it speaketh to them that are under the law."

Here the marginal references are to the Psalms, Jeremiah, the Proverbs, and Isaiah. None of the sentences are from the pentateuch. Yet they are quoted as parts of what the law says to them that are under the law; and they are introduced by the formula, " It is written." No one can make the term " law " in this passage other than synonymous with the term " scripture."

These instances are conclusive to the effect that in the time of Jesus there was a distinct usage under which the whole body of the Old Testament scriptures was familiarly called " the law." [1]   And inasmuch as whatever is in the pentateuch is also in the Old Testament, these authors may sometimes have had the whole Old Testament in mind even when they cite the pentateuch. It follows that we cannot be certain which of the two meanings was the more prevalent.

4. Correct interpretation finds the same usage in the earlier extrabiblical literature. For example, the Usages of Ecclesiasticus, Baruch, etc. twenty-fourth chapter of the book of Ecclesiasticus, written either about 200 B.C. or about 300 B.C., is a part of a continuous series of citations, mostly from Job, Proverbs, and the scriptural books of that class, with enlargements taken in part from the pentateuch. This is followed by the affirmation : —

[1] There is a less distinct instance in Mt. xxii. 36, 40, where the question is asked concerning the law, but answered concerning " the whole law, and the prophets."

"All these are the book of the covenant of the most high God,
　The law which Moses commanded us
　As an heritage unto the congregations of Jacob" (ver. 23).

Apparently this author thinks of Moses as only the beginner of "the law which Moses commanded us," and thinks of that law as including the wisdom books of the Old Testament, as well as the pentateuch.

Precisely similar is the passage in the book of Baruch (iv. 1), where, after many lines made up from the books of Moses and from Proverbs and Job, the writer says: —

"This is the book of the commandments of God,
　And the law that endureth forever."

II. This glance at the later usage has prepared us for studying the term as it appears in the Hebrew of the Old Testament.

1. First, we look at its derivation.

The noun *torah* and its cognate verb *horah* are causatives from *yarah*, which denotes the act of shooting an arrow or hurling a javelin. The two have the same use, and should be studied together, the mechanical translation of the verb being "to give *torah*." The causative stem of *yarah* sometimes denotes shooting, like the simple stem. Its derivative *yoreh* (Deut. xi. 14; Jer. v. 24) is translated "former rain." The "arrows of the rain" afford a not unfamiliar figure of speech. But the causative verb of the stem nearly always, and the noun *torah* always, are used in the secondary sense in which the noun is translated "law" and the verb is translated "teach."[1]

Derived from yarah, "to shoot"

[1] The lexicons say that this secondary meaning comes through the notion of shooting out the hand by way of monitory gesture. Possibly a better conjecture is that the term is of military origin. An officer causes his men to shoot, when he gives the order for shooting. From such a beginning the noun might naturally come to denote an order given by com-

The usage of the word is abundant for the purpose of ascertaining its meaning. The noun occurs more than two hundred times, and the verb more than sixty times, in the different parts of the Old Testament.

2. Very important to the ascertaining of the signification of these words is the fact that the law or teaching they denote is divine. To this there are only a very few exceptions in the case of the verb, and probably none in the case of the noun.

In a few instances, as we have seen, *horah* retains the meaning "to shoot." Once it is used of Judah going *Horah* in advance of his father to Goshen, "to give *commonly torah*," that is, to give orders (Gen. xlvi. 28). *describes* In Proverbs (vi. 13) it is said concerning the *divine law or teaching* " man of iniquity " : —

> " He winketh with his eyes, he talketh with his feet,
> He giveth *torah* with his fingers."

But in most of the instances, the directions or teachings denoted by this verb are either given directly by Deity, or are given by one who speaks in the name of Deity.[1]

petent authority. This explanation, as we shall find, agrees with the usage of the word. In military usage, the " orders " given in a camp are sometimes of the nature of information rather than command, though the information so given is official and authoritative. If we could keep this in mind, we might translate *horah* by the English phrase " give orders," and *torah* by " an order " or " orders."

[1] In a few instances the subject of the verb is a false god, or simply some god or other. In Habakkuk the men are scathed who appeal to a molten image to give lying *torah*, or who look to a dumb stone to give *torah* (Hab. ii. 18, 19). In Isaiah (xxviii. 26) the husbandman's God is said to give him *torah*.

In perhaps one-third of the existing instances Elohim or Yahaweh is directly the subject. For example, Yahaweh gave Moses and Aaron *torah* as to what they should say and do before Pharaoh (Ex. iv. 12, 15). He gave Moses *torah* concerning a tree for healing the bitter fountain (Ex. xv. 25). He promised the tables of stone and the *torah* and the com-

So much for the verb. So generally does it denote requirement or teaching that is thought of as coming from Deity, that this is presumptively its meaning in all cases except where the context clearly shows the contrary. And if this is true of the verb, it is more decidedly true of the noun. There are probably no exceptions to the rule that the Old Testament men think of *torah* as of divine origin. If there are any exceptions, they are seven or eight of the thirteen instances in which the word is used in the book of Proverbs.[1] There are other Hebrew words

Torah means divine law or teaching

mandments, "to give them *torah*," or, "to give them as *torah*" (Ex. xxiv. 12). He is asked to give Israel *torah* concerning "the good way" (1 Ki. viii. 36). He is asked to give the Psalmist *torah* concerning "his way," "the way of his statutes" (Pss. xxvii. 11, lxxxvi. 11, cxix. 33). He gives different persons *torah* "in the way," "in that way thou shalt go," "in a way that he shall choose" (Pss. xxv. 8, 12, xxxii. 8). He gives the nations *torah* "out of his ways" (Mic. iv. 2; Isa. ii. 3). He gives Israel *torah* "unto the good way" (2 Chron. vi. 27). He gives *torah* (Ps. cxix. 102). Deity gives *torah* (Job xxxiv. 32, xxxvi. 22).

The most prominent use is that in which a prophet or a priest gives *torah* as the representative of Deity. Instances are needless, though many are given in the course of this chapter. In other instances the subject of the verb is indefinite, or is some person or thing, but the teaching given concerns divine matters, and has been received from Deity. Bezalel is to give *torah* concerning the tabernacle work (Ex. xxxv. 34). One of the *toroth* in Leviticus (xiv. 57) is for the purpose of giving *torah* concerning the clean and the unclean. In the forty-fifth Psalm (4) the king's right hand gives him *torah* in "terrible things." In various places in the Wisdom books, the fathers or the beasts or the earth or "my father" or Job's friends are said to give *torah*. In some of these places it is clear that the speaker has a divine revelation in mind, and in none of them is it clear that he has not.

[1] And these, although the revised versions annotate them with the alternative "or teaching," are not real exceptions. There is nothing to prevent the phrase "the law of thy mother" (Prov. i. 8, vi. 20) from meaning Yahaweh's law as taught thee by thy mother. Similar statements might be made concerning the phrases "my law" (iii. 1, iv. 2, vii. 2), "their law" (vi. 23, if one accepts the emendation), "a wise man's law" (xiii. 14), "a

which apply equally to human or divine laws or statements; but *torah*, unless in these passages, is always
divine.   Elsewhere, at least, the usage is uniform.

3. Another point follows from this; or it might be
independently made out by reëxamining the instances:
torah always denotes authoritative command or information.   The idea of authority is inseparable alike from
the noun and from the verb.

In the English versions the verb is commonly translated "teach."   In the revised versions the noun is
sometimes annotated with the phrase "or
teaching."   Some authors tell us that the
noun denotes instruction, and they draw important inferences from this weakened meaning of it.
This is commendable so far forth as it is an attempt to
disentangle the Old Testament term from misleading
associations with the English word " law," or its equivalents in other languages.   But we must limit the attempt
carefully, or, in rescuing the word from uncongenial
company, we shall lead it into company that is still less
congenial.   *Torah* and *horah* are never used of teaching or instruction merely in the sense of giving information.   Always they denote authoritative teaching.   With
the few exceptions already noted, they denote teaching
that is regarded as divinely authoritative.   Not that
they always express commands; the thing expressed by
them may be information, and not command; but it is
information that is thought of as authoritative, and,

(margin note) Always authoritative
teaching

law of loving kindness " (xxxi. 26).   It is easy to understand these to mean
simply thy mother's teachings, my teachings, the teachings of thy parents,
teachings of a wise man, teachings concerning loving kindness; but it is
quite as easy to understand them to mean God's revealed will as made known
to thee by thy mother, by me, by thy parents, by a wise man, by the " virtu-
ous woman."   Either we must thus interpret these phrases, following the
use of the word elsewhere, or we must regard them as a group of exceptions.

ordinarily, as of divine authority.[1]   In fine, the idea
they express is not far different from our current idea
of divine revelation, including God's commands, but
including also his promises and threats, and such
information or such inspiring truths as he may have
communicated to men.

4. Another point in the usage concerns the relation
of *torah* respectively to the prophets and the priests.

Since these were thought of as in a special sense the
representatives of Deity, we should expect that they
would be particularly concerned with *torah*.   This expectation is met in the record.   It represents the prophets as the medium through whom *torah* is given from
Deity; the priests as the official custodians and administrators of *torah;* and both as the expounders and
interpreters of *torah*.

(*a*) The prophet is the person through whom Yahaweh
reveals his *torah*.

There are general statements to this effect; for
example, the following from Daniel : —   General
                                                statements
   " His *toroth* which he gave before us by the hand of
his servants the prophets " (ix. 10).

---

[1] The English word "law" has connotations different from those of
torah, but it is relatively easy to set these aside so that they will not mislead us; much easier than in the case of the other English words that have
been suggested.   But "law" in English has no cognate by which to
translate the verb *horah*.   Such phrases as "give law," "lay down the
law," have some good points, but are impracticable.

When a government puts an officer in charge of an expedition, it gives
him "instructions," often written instructions, sometimes secret instructions
either oral or written, the instructions including information as well as
commands.   If we could confine our English words "instruct" and "instruction" to this meaning, they would fairly translate *horah* and *torah*.
But this we cannot do.   Similar statements might be made concerning the
English terms "orders," "give orders," and "direct," "directions," "give
directions."   For the purposes of this chapter we may transfer the words

Or this, from the record of the downfall of Samaria : —

" And Yahaweh testified with Israel and with Judah by the hand of every prophet of his, every seer, saying, Turn from your evil ways and keep my commandments, my statutes, according to all the *torah* which I commanded your fathers, and which I sent unto you by the hand of my servants the prophets " (2 Ki. xvii. 13).

Or this from Jeremiah : —

" Thus saith Yahaweh, If ye will not hearken unto me, to walk in my *torah* which I have given before you, to hearken unto the words of my servants the prophets whom I send unto you " (xxvi. 4–5).

General statements like these are frequent. They are supported by particular instances in abundance. Particular instances It was through Nathan the prophet that " the *torah* of mankind " was announced to David (2 Sam. vii. 19). Sealed written *torah* was given through Isaiah the prophet (viii. 16, 20). The various *toroth* of the pentateuch are represented to have been given by Moses the man of God, the greatest of the prophets.

Other passages teach the same by suggestion. In Nehemiah's time confession was made that Israel had " cast thy *torah* behind their back, and murdered thy prophets " (Neh. ix. 26), suggesting that the prophets were the givers of the *torah*. The writer of Lamentations says : —

" Her king and her captains are among the nations ; there is no *torah ;* also her prophets have not found vision from Yahaweh " (ii. 9).

And in Isaiah we read of —

"lying sons, sons that are not willing to hear the *torah* of Yahaweh ; who say to the seers, Ye shall not see ; and to them that have visions, Ye shall not for us have visions of things that are correct " (xxx. 9–11).

rather than translate them; but perhaps there is no translation that will be correct without careful definition.

It would be easy to multiply instances in which it is thus said or implied that the prophet is the man through whom Deity reveals his *torah* to men, but The act we will only add a few in which the verb is denoted by *horah* is used, not the noun.   Manoah desired that prophetic the Angel, whom he supposed to be a "man of God," might be sent again to give *torah* in regard to the son that was to be born (Jud. xiii. 8).   That is to say, he regarded the giving of *torah* as the function of a man of God.   Isaiah says that the prophet who gives false *torah* is the tail in Judah (ix. 15).   Samuel the prophet promised not to cease giving Israel *torah*, notwithstanding they had made a king (1 Sam. xii. 23).   The "teachers" — givers of *torah* — mentioned twice in Isa. xxx. 20 are probably prophets.[1]

(*b*) The priests are the guardians of the *torah*, but are not its revealing agents.

They are as prominently mentioned in connection with *torah* as are the prophets, but their functions are different.   In conjunction with the elders The priests' and with the judges or kings, they are the functions custodians and administrators of the *torah*, with *torah* but they are not law-bringers, like the prophets.   The conception is that as the successive parts of the *torah* were brought from Deity by men who had prophetic gifts, these *toroth* were placed in the hands of the priests for use.

What the priests had to do with *torah* in general is fairly represented by what they had to do with the so-called book of the *torah*.   The record is that this was written by the prophet Moses, and put into the keeping

---

[1] When Job (xxvii. 11) proposes to give his friends *torah* "at the hand of God," we probably ought to understand him as claiming prophetic gifts. Those whom the outcast (Prov. v. 13 RV) calls "my teachers" may have been prophets. There is nothing to indicate that they were not.

of the priests and elders.   They were to guard it safe,
and once in seven years were to teach it by public reading (Deut. xxxi. 9–13).   They were to have charge of
the *torah* in the place which Yahaweh should choose,
and were to administer it in cases of appeal.   The king
was to have a copy of the *torah* made from the one that
was before "the priests the Levites" (Deut. xvii. 8–12,
18).   We are told that Jehoshaphat had priests who
went through the land on a mission of instruction and
reform, carrying with them "the book of the *torah* of
Yahaweh" (2 Chron. xvii. 9).   The prophet Haggai
sends men to the priests to ask questions as to a point
in the ceremonial law (ii. 11, 12, 13).

In these passages the noun is used, some of them
using the verb also; the following may indicate the
usage of the verb when priests are in question.   The
priests are to "teach" the people, give the people
torah, concerning leprosy (Deut. xxiv. 8).   That is, they
are to make known and enforce the law on this subject,
as it has been committed to them.   Aaron and his
sons are to teach the sons of Israel, to give the sons of
Israel *torah*, all the statutes which God gave by Moses
(Lev. x. 11).   Here their *torah* is the statutes which
have already been given through the prophet Moses.
Ezekiel says of the priests (xliv. 23) : —

"And they shall give *torah* to my people between holy and profane,
    And between clean and unclean they shall give knowledge to them."

We are told that the king of Assyria sent the Israelite
priest to the foreign populations which he had placed
in Samaria, —

"that he might give them *torah*, the usages of the god of the land,
. . . how they might fear Yahaweh " (2 Ki. xvii. 27–28).[1]

------

[1] Study also the following additional passages.   In Asa's time Israel is
said to have long been " without a *torah*-giving priest, and without *torah* "

(*c*) The prophets and the priests were alike the expounders and the interpreters of the *torah*, but with a difference.

Some scholars are accustomed to speak of a priestly *torah* and a prophetic *torah*, as if the two differed in their contents. There is no ground for this. No separate priestly *torah* There may be passages that are capable of being understood in this way, but there are none that necessarily give this meaning, and none that with any strong probability imply it. The representation is rather that the prophets and the priests had a common body of *torah*, to which they stood in differing relations. They were both teachers of *torah*, but the prophet was, in addition, the revealing agent through whom the *torah* was given.

We have examined a good many passages in which this is explicitly said, and others in which it is implied.

(2 Chron. xv. 3). Jeremiah calls the priests "the handlers of the *torah*" (ii. 8), and censures his opponents for saying that "*torah* shall not perish from priest" (xviii. 18). Zephaniah complains that "her priests have profaned sanctuary, have done violence to *torah*" (iii. 4). In the "Blessing wherewith Moses the man of God blessed Israel," the function of Levi is thus stated: —

> "They shall give as *torah* thy judgments to Jacob,
>   and thy *torah* to Israel" (Deut. xxxiii. 10).

Micah makes it a matter of rebuke that "her priests give *torah* for hire" (iii. 11). The relations of the priests to the law are magnified in the second chapter of Malachi: —

> "A true *torah* was in his mouth" (6).
> "For a priest's lips keep knowledge,
>   and *torah* they seek at his mouth,
>   because he is the angel of Yahaweh of hosts.
> While ye, ye have removed from the way,
>   ye have caused many to stumble in the *torah*,
>   ye have corrupted the covenant of Levi,
>   saith Yahaweh of hosts" (7–8).
> "And ye are lifting up faces in the *torah*" (9).

The priest does not, like the prophet, receive *torah* by direct revelation from Deity ; but he has charge of *torah* which has already been revealed, to administer and interpret it. The only way in which he gives additional *torah* is by interpreting that already given, answering questions concerning it, making decisions upon it, establishing precedents and usages from it. Functions of this sort belonged to both prophets and priests, and rendered them both, in a sense, sources of *torah*. But in the prophet's gift of revelation the priest, as such, had no share. Of course both functions might be combined in one person, as in Jehoiada the prophet-priest, the *torah*-teacher of King Joash (2 Ki. xii. 2).[1]

5. Having in mind this conception of *torah* as a body of divine revelation given through the prophets, and administered and expounded by them and the priests, we are ready to take up another point,— the different forms which *torah* assumed, as indicated by the variant uses of the word.

(*a*) *Torah* was sometimes oral and sometimes written. To prove that the prophets gave *torah* orally, or that they and the priests gave oral interpretations, and oral decisions on points that arose, would be a work of supererogation. It is equally needless to prove the existence of written *torah*. But we have to note that at this point

[1] Some one may raise the objection that the respective relations of the priests and the prophets to the law probably differed in different periods of the history. The reply is that the passages that have been cited cover all the periods. If they tell the truth, that settles the question, no matter when or by whom they were written. And even critics who dispute their truth will nevertheless concede that they present correctly the situation that existed in the later times when these critics allege that they were written, and that their writers believed that the same situation existed in the earlier times. It would not be easy to find sufficient reason for denying that these writers were correct in their opinion. Reasons for affirming that they were correct will appear as we proceed with our investigation.

the element of time becomes more important than it has been in the matters thus far discussed.

Written *torah* began at an early date. In Isaiah we have an account of *torah* written and sealed Early written (viii. 16, 20). Hosea, in a passage that has *torah* been much discussed, says of Ephraim : —

> " I write for him the ten thousand, my *torah*
> As a stranger they are accounted " (viii. 12).

That there was written *torah* from the time of Moses is the testimony of all the numerous passages that speak of Moses writing the law, or of the book of Moses, or of the book of the law. These affirm that Moses wrote *torah* (*e.g.* Deut. xxxi. 9, 11, 24, 26, xxviii. 58, 61, xxix. 21, 29, xxx. 10), and that Joshua wrote *torah* (Josh. xxiv. 26). Of course there are scholars who assign a late date to these passages,[1] and count their testimony as either false-hood or fiction. But these scholars themselves hold that the writing of *torah* was a part of the earliest literary writing in Israel, though they date this earliest writing many centuries after Moses. The passages cited in this chapter abundantly indicate that the Old Testament writ-ers lay especial emphasis on the idea of written *torah*.

(*b*) Again, the noun *torah* is subject to the various modes of use which we should expect in the case of a term that was so frequently employed. These throw light on its meaning.

It is used in the singular number, in the plural, col-lectively, abstractly. In other words, we find mention of a law, laws, law as an aggregate, law as an abstract conception. It is used definitely or indefinitely, with a subject genitive, with an object genitive. Certain par-ticulars in its use are especially significant.

---

[1] *The Hexateuch* regards Josh. xxiv. 26 as a late addition to E.

First, the term *torah* is applied to any particular divine requirement or other message. It is thus used indefi-

Torah denoting a particular revelation

nitely in the singular, both indefinitely and definitely in the plural, definitely in the singular with an object genitive, and perhaps also with a subject genitive.[1] This usage is found in the records concerning the exodus and concerning Abraham, in the writings which the older tradition attributes to Moses, and in the sections which the analytical critics assign to E and to J. That is, you find it, no matter to what critical school you belong, in the earliest extant Hebrew literature, and in every subsequent period.

[1] As *torah* comes from Deity, the subject genitive is invariably a noun or pronoun denoting Deity; for example, "the *torah* of Yahaweh," or "my *torah*," in the passages cited above. The object genitive denotes the matter with which the *torah* concerns itself, *e.g.* "a *torah* of loving kindness" (Prov. xxxi. 26). Whenever the word is used, the subject genitive is implied, and there may be in addition a second subject genitive. For example, in the instance just given one might speak of the worthy woman's Yahaweh's law of loving kindness, that is, Yahaweh's *torah* concerning loving kindness as presented by the worthy woman.

A reader is not likely to master these distinctions sharply except by the process of actually examining instances. The following will serve for this purpose.

Torah is used indefinitely in the singular: "Bind thou up a testimony, seal a *torah*, among my disciples" (Isa. viii. 16). The context shows that by *torah* the prophet here means a particular message in writing. In the balancing statement (ver. 20) the term *torah* is perhaps used abstractly.

The term is also used indefinitely in the plural: "They have transgressed laws" (Isa. xxiv. 5).

Oftener the plural is used definitely. In connection with the visit of Jethro, Moses is spoken of as making the people to know the *toroth* of Deity (Ex. xviii. 16, 20 E), apparently in judicial matters. Abraham is commended for keeping Yahaweh's *toroth* (Gen. xxvi. 5 J or J[s]). At the giving of the manna, Yahaweh rebukes Israel for not keeping his *toroth* (Ex. xvi. 28 J or P[s]). Later instances of the word in the plural are Neh. ix. 13; Ps. cv. 45; Lev. xxvi. 46; Ezek. xliv. 24 and perhaps xliii. 11, xliv. 5.

For this purpose of denoting a particular message the word is also used definitely in the singular with an object genitive. This is frequent in literary titles or subscriptions. "Moses began to declare this *torah*" (Deut.

Second, the word *torah* in the singular is employed to denote an aggregate of divine messages or requirements. A more specific use with the article or with a defining subject genitive will be considered later. For the present, we note that this use occurs when the word has no article, or when the article only indicates that the *torah* spoken of has been defined by the context. An instance without the article occurs in the prayer of Nehemiah : —

Torah as an aggregate of *toroth*

"And commandedst them commandments and statutes and a *torah*, by the hand of Moses thy servant" (Neh. ix. 14).

Here, clearly, *torah* denotes the aggregate of the Mosaic requirements or revelation. There are enough similar instances, some of them referring to Moses and some not, to make out a clear case.[1] Instances with the article will be found below, especially in connection with

i. 5), the *torah* referred to being the address that occupies the four following chapters. "This is the *torah* of the burnt-offering" (Lev. vii. 37–38). "This is the *torah* of the plague of leprosy in a garment" (Lev. xiii. 59). *Cf.* Lev. vii. 1, 11, xi. 46–47; Num. v. 29–30, etc.

Possibly the term denotes a particular message in some cases where it is definite with only a subject genitive.

"Hear ye the word of Yahaweh, ye officials of Sodom!

Give ear to the *torah* of our God, ye people of Gomorrah!" (Isa. i. 10).
Here it is possible to hold that the *torah* to which the prophet refers is merely the message which he is in the act of uttering; though the context shows that the term may equally well have a wider meaning.

[1] "A true *torah* was in his mouth" (Mal. ii. 6).
"A law Moses gave in charge to us,
   A possession for the assembly of Jacob" (Deut. xxxiii. 4).
"And he established a testimony in Jacob,
   And a law he placed in Israel" (Ps. lxxviii. 5).
"A wise man's *torah* is a fountain of life" (Prov. xiii. 14).
"A *torah* of loving kindness is on her tongue" (Prov. xxxi. 26).
"A commandment is a lamp, and a *torah* is a light" (Prov. vi. 23).
The requiring "one law" for the stranger and the homeborn, or for the sin-offering and the guilt-offering (Ex. xii. 49; Num. xv. 16, 29; Lev. vii. 7), may perhaps be regarded as a variant of this usage.

what is said concerning the book of the law. Some of
the instances with the article are of early date.

Third, this indefinite general use easily passes over
into an abstract use. This is mainly concealed in the
Torah used English versions, which translate in such
as an abstract cases with the article, but the usage is very
noun abundant. It occurs sometimes in plain prose.
In Asa's time Judah was "without law-expounding
priest, and without law"; and Jehoshaphat's judges
were to be faithful "between law and commandment"
(2 Chron. xv. 3, xix. 10). But the usage is more frequent in poetry, and is to some extent a matter of
poetic diction. In the only place where the word *torah*
occurs in the book of Job, Job's friends are exhorting
him to submit to the divine will : —

"Receive, pray, law from his mouth " (xxii. 22).

In the glowing description common to Isaiah and Micah
we read : —

"For out of Zion law shall go forth,
    and the word of Yahaweh out of Jerusalem" (Isa. ii. 3 ; Mic. iv. 2).

It is not "the law," but "law," which Yahaweh — or
his Servant — magnifies and makes honorable (Isa. xlii.
21). And so in other instances.[1] Such use as this of
such a term presupposes that the term has long been

[1] Additional instances are : —
"Forsakers of law praise a wicked person,
    While keepers of law contend with them."
"He that guardeth law is a discerning son."
"He turneth away his ear from hearing law,
    Also his prayer is an abomination" (Prov. xxviii. 4, 7, 9).
"Where there is no vision a people is to be shunned,
    But one that keepeth law, happy is it" (Prov. xxix. 18).
"Law will go forth . . . for a light of peoples" (Isa. li. 4).
"Law is slackened" (Hab. i. 4).
"Her priests . . . have done violence to law" (Zeph. iii. 4).
"Law is not" (Lam. ii. 9).

familiar, and we are therefore not surprised at finding this use absent from the earlier writings.

Fourth, among the uses of the word *torah* one in particular is significant — that in which the definite phrase "the *torah*" designates a certain definite and recognized aggregate. The phrase may of course appear in variant forms: "the *torah* of Yahaweh," "the *torah* of our God," "my *torah*," "thy *torah*," "his *torah*," "the *torah*," "this *torah*." We must presently consider this somewhat in detail, but it is more convenient to complete first our classification of the uses of the term. The definite aggregate known as the *torah*

Fifth, there remains one more use to be noted. It is a matter of natural variation that any part of the *torah*-aggregate may sometimes be called by the name that properly belongs to the whole. A conspicuous instance is that of "the law," which Joshua is said to have inscribed on the altar at Mount Ebal. As this was written not on fine-grained stone but on plaster, it must have been in coarse script, and therefore cannot have been a very long piece of literature. Yet it is described as "all the words of this law" (Deut. xxvii. 3, 8).[1] "The *torah*" as some part of the aggregate

"Law shall perish from priest" (Ezek. vii. 26).

"Pray, ask the priests for law" (Hag. ii. 11).

"And law they seek from his mouth" (Mal. ii. 7).

[1] This appears more specifically in the statements in Joshua: —

"And he wrote there upon the stones the duplicate of the law of Moses which he had written before the sons of Israel." "And afterward he read all the words of the law, the blessing and the cursing" (Josh. viii. 32, 34).

This altar inscription must have been a good deal briefer than the whole book of Deuteronomy, and much more must it have been briefer than "the book of the law" taken in any wider meaning. Perhaps it was that part of Deuteronomy that contains the blessings and the curses, say xxvii–xxviii or xxvii–xxx (Josh. viii. 33–34; Deut. xi. 26–29, xxvii. 2 sqq.). Perhaps it had the same limits with "the covenant" of "the land of Moab" (Deut. xxix. 1 [xxviii. 69]). It may perhaps be identical with "the book of the

Such are the five uses of the term. It is used of a
single divine requirement or other message; it is used
of an undefined aggregate; it is used abstractly; it is
used of *the* recognized definite aggregate; it is used by
synecdoche of the parts of this aggregate.[1]

covenant" (2 Ki. xxiii. 2) which, in Josiah's time, was read entire at one
public meeting, and which is clearly identical with either the whole or a
part of the book of the law that was found at that time.

We should be careful not to confuse the phraseology in Josh. viii. 30–
35. Verses 30–34 describe the solemnities of the altar, with the accom-
panying blessing and cursing. Verse 35 seems to describe a different solemnity as occurring at the same time — that of the public septennial reading
of the law, as required in Deut. xxxi. 10–13. This appears from the mention of "all the assembly of Israel, and the women and the little ones, and
the sojourner that walketh in the midst of them."

In the account of the altar solemnity we are told that they acted "according to that which is written in the book of the law of Moses" (31),
and that one read the blessings and cursings "according to all that is
written in the book of the law" (34). In these two places "the book of
the law" is the book which Deuteronomy says that Moses wrote. From
this book they took "the duplicate of the law of Moses" which was inscribed on the altar, and "all the words of the law, the blessing and the
cursing" which were read. The passage that was inscribed is probably
also the one that is here said to have been read. It was both read and
copied from the book of the law, but the question whether it was the whole
of that book is left open.

[1] There can be no dispute, I think, that these five categories are distinct,
or that they include all the instances that occur, though there may occasionally be room for difference of opinion as to the category to which a
particular instance should be assigned. Above we have cited, for example,
the Levitical " *torah* of the burnt-offering" as one of the particular *toroth*
which have been combined into the *torah*-aggregate; it would be equally
possible to regard it as merely a section of that aggregate. Or how is it
with the *torah* introduced in Deut. iv. 44? Did the writer conceive of what
follows as a single prophetic message? or as a relatively brief aggregate of
such messages? or as a section of the well-known *torah*-aggregate?
When David speaks of the message which Nathan has just brought him as
"the *torah* of mankind" (2 Sam. vii. 19; 1 Chron. xvii. 17), he seems to
be thinking of it not as a separate message, but as the significant repetition
of something in the *torah*-aggregate. Such differences in detail do not
affect the validity of the classification itself.

6. What we have learned concerning the five uses of the term will help us as we now inquire into the nature of the *torah*-aggregate.

(*a*) The word *torah* might supposably denote the formally recognized aggregate of the *toroth* received from Deity whenever the word has the definite Limitations article, or is made definite by some designa- of the term tion of Yahaweh or Elohim used as a subject genitive. In fact, however, there are important limitations to this, both those drawn from the several contexts and those drawn from other sources. It seems best to examine some of the limitations before we look at instances.

First, as we have already seen, the term "the *torah*" may denote some particular *torah* made definite by the context, instead of denoting the one recognized *torah*-aggregate.[1] Or second, the definite phrase may be used of some lesser aggregate, and, in particular, of some section of the great aggregate.[2] Third, there may be instances in which the definite phrase is used in a vague and general way. One cannot with perfect sharpness draw the line between the use in which *torah* is an undefined aggregate and that in which the aggregate is perfectly defined. Fourth, it will not do to assume that the phrase is always the equivalent of written scripture. "The *torah*" is wide enough to

---

[1] For example, "the law of our God" (Isa. i. 10) is capable of being understood as denoting the message which the prophet is uttering at the time.

[2] For example, the entity that in Deuteronomy is called "the book of the law" seems to be also called "the law" (Deut. xvii. 18, 11, iv. 8). The long discourse in Deuteronomy (iv. 44–xxvi) is in its title called "the *torah*." It is possible to regard an instance of this kind as a particular *torah*, or as a lesser aggregate of *torah*, or as a section of the one *torah*-aggregate; it is not imperative, and in some cases is impossible, to regard it as the one *torah*-aggregate.

include oral as well as written *torah*.[1] And, fifth, if
the *torah*-aggregate existed at all, it was as a growing
A growing   aggregate.   It was a body of literature when
aggregate   the term first began to be applied to writings,
and it enlarged its boundaries afterward.[2]

Remembering these points, as we examine the instances, we shall find them yielding the conception that
all *torah*, oral or written, is a unit.   There are plenty of

[1] Nevertheless it is in fact applied mainly to written *torah*, which offered
especial facilities for being aggregated.   The phrase is not tied up to any
particular theory of the collecting of the writings; they might supposably
be thought of as an aggregate without any collection being physically made,
or prior to the making of a collection.   But certain passages inform us
that there was a custom of laying up writings " before Yahaweh," and the
existence of this custom is affirmed even by scholars who reject as unhistorical the particular accounts we have of it.   It seems certain that written
torah was aggregated physically, as well as in thought.

It was in the temple that the men of Josiah's time found "the book of
the law" (2 Ki. xxii. 8).   The accounts say that the priests of Jehoshaphat's time had in their charge "the law of Yahaweh" in writing (2 Chron.
xvii. 9).   The book of Deuteronomy is very explicit in its account of the
written law placed by Moses in the charge of the priests and the civil authorities (Deut. xxxi. 25–26), and touching their use of the written law for
the guidance of the king, when there should be a king (xvii. 18).   In view
of these instances we cannot resist the conclusion that the author of 1 Samuel regarded "the book" (x. 25, not "a book") in which Samuel wrote
"the manner of the kingdom" and "laid it up before Yahaweh" as a recognized aggregate of *torah*.   On the same footing is "the book" (Ex.
xvii. 14) in which Moses wrote "for a memorial" concerning Amalek.
"The *torah*" in writing is said to have been accessible to Joshua "at the
sanctuary of Yahaweh" (Josh. xxiv. 26).

[2] This conception is not necessarily excluded by the views of any school
of criticism, though the different schools would picture the details differently.   The view properly to be inferred from the phenomena is not that
there came to be in Israel a heterogeneous accumulation of writings, from
which ecclesiastical authority at length made a selection, the selection
thereby acquiring the character of *torah*.   On the contrary, all *torah*,
whether oral or written, was regarded as sacred from the moment when it
came from the tongue or the pen of the prophet.   The writings testify to
this, and it is also independently proved by the phenomena they present.

instances that are not vague, but clear and distinct. There are plenty of instances that are not limited to some particular *torah*, or to some lesser aggregate. We shall find that this conception implies a general aggregate of written *torah*. Not all the *toroth* given through the prophets were preserved, but some of them were. They were regarded as an accumulating sacred literature, God-given and authoritative; and this growing aggregate was, while it was yet growing, called "the *torah*."

(*b*) We proceed to examine some of the instances.

Look first at a group of instances from the records of the early part of the public career of Moses, in writings which the older tradition ascribes to Moses, Instances and which the analysis now current ascribes from the ear-lier Mosaic to J and E. Above, we have found these records writings mentioning *toroth* in the plural. They also use the definite singular phrases, "the *torah* of Yahaweh," "my *torah*," "the *torah*."[1] The instances prove at least that in that generation men thought of Yahaweh's requirements not merely as so many *toroth*, but as a unit, *torah*. Of course the unit is here not the pentateuch, for the passages represent that most of the pentateuchal events were then still in the future. But the habit of thinking of Yahaweh's communications as aggregated in a unit was already a mental habit in Israel. And we

---

[1] The Israelites are to teach their children concerning the passover "that the *torah* of Yahaweh may be in thy mouth" (Ex. xiii. 9 J). When he gives the manna he chides Israel for not keeping his *toroth*, but he also tests them "whether they will walk in my *torah*" (Ex. xvi. 28, 4 J). And at Sinai he says: "And I will give thee the tables of stone and the *torah* and the commandment which I have written" (Ex. xxiv. 12 E or E³).

In the first two of these instances, and probably in the third also, "the *torah*" is an aggregate. In the third, and possibly in the other two, "the *torah*" is in writing.

may be sure that people who had this habit did not exempt from its operation any written *torah* which they might possess. The testimony of the passages is that this habit dates as far back as the beginning of the forty years of the exodus; and even one who disbelieves the testimony of these writers must see that the writers themselves have the habit. Whatever be one's critical point of view, one is compelled to hold that this way of thinking was prevalent in Israel from the times of the earliest records.

Second, the conception of "the *torah*" as an aggregate is frequent in Deuteronomy, and in the scriptures which presuppose Deuteronomy.

Conspicuous here are the passages that speak of the "book of the *torah*." The account specifies portions of "The book its contents (Deut. xxxii. 44–46, xxvii, xxviii of the *torah*" especially 58, 61, xxix especially 21, 29, xxx especially 10). It says that Moses wrote this book and laid it up by the side of the ark, in the custody of the priests and of the civil authorities (Deut. xxxi. 9–13, 24–26). It says that the book was to be publicly read every seventh year; was to be kept by the priests at the capital, and the king furnished with a copy (xvii. 18–19); and, by inference, that the priests shall use it in deciding appealed cases (xvii. 11). The biblical narratives further say that this book of the law was handed to Joshua, and used by him (Josh. i. 7, 8, viii. 31, xxiii. 6), and was an important factor in all the subsequent history.[1]

[1] It is represented to have been so when David charged Solomon, in language strongly Deuteronomic, to act "according to that which is written in the law of Moses" (1 Ki. ii. 3); and when it is recorded of Amaziah that "the children of the murderers he put not to death, according to that which is written in the book of the law of Moses" (2 Ki. xiv. 6; *cf.* Deut. xxiv. 16); and in the days of Josiah, when the highpriest "found the book

What was this "book of the law"? Supposably it might be a general name for the aggregate of all recognized written *toroth*, or supposably it might denote some section of this aggregate, or some lesser aggregate, or supposably it may be used sometimes in one of these senses and sometimes in another.[1] In its wider use it expresses the conception of a growing body of sacred literature, which was regarded as having begun with Moses, and as having been carried forward by his successors. As the wider aggregate included such narrower aggregates as might exist, any speaker may have had the wider in mind even when he refers to the contents of the narrower.

But whatever else the book of the law may be, it is a unique, explicitly recognized aggregate of written *toroth*. It is conclusive proof that this concept existed in the Deuteronomic and post-Deuteronomic times. This concept is presupposed even in the instances in which the book of the law itself is something less than the great aggregate.

The same concept appears in many instances that mention the law without mentioning the book. Witness the following: —

of the law in the house of Yahaweh" (2 Ki. xxii. 8); and in the days of Nehemiah, when they read in "the book of the law of Moses," "the book of the law of Deity," "the book of the law of Yahaweh" (Neh. viii. 1, 18, ix. 3).

[1] In some instances the most natural inference from the context is that the book is the whole or a part of our Deuteronomy, and that the record says that it was completed by Moses; but other instances give a different view, making "the book of the law" a wider body of literature, one in which Joshua wrote after the death of Moses (Josh. xxiv. 26). In Josiah's time the most influential statements that were read were certainly from Deuteronomy, but that does not decide the question whether "the book of the law" from which they were read was Deuteronomy or merely included Deuteronomy.

Other Deu-
teronomic
instances

"And what great nation is there that hath statutes and judgments so righteous as all this law which I set before you this day?" (Deut. iv. 8).

The term "this law" here clearly denotes an aggregate of "statutes and judgments," a recognizable, well-known aggregate. The same definite use abounds in the later history and in the psalms and the prophets.[1]

The basal conception in these Deuteronomic and post-Deuteronomic utterances is that of "the *torah*" as the aggregate of the *toroth* that have been revealed from Deity. In many of the instances the term has literary implications, and the aggregate it denotes either is or includes an aggregate in writing. It would be less easy to prove that this aggregate was a canon, or even physically a collection; but it is recognized, in thought at least, as a known unit. If one accepts these writings as credible testimony, he is convinced of the existence of the *torah*-aggregate in Israel from the time of Moses. And even if one thinks that the testimony is false, and that Deuteronomy was written about 620 B.C., or a century earlier, or some centuries later, he must still find that Israel had an aggregate of written *torah* from the time when Deuteronomy was written, and no one knows how much earlier. And from the historico-critical viewpoint of such an one, even this makes the conception prevalent at a relatively early period in the history.

[1] Witness "the law . . . which Yahaweh commanded the sons of Jacob" (2 Ki. xvii. 34); "the law . . . which he wrote for you" (37); "the law of Yahaweh" in which Jehu failed to walk (x. 31), in which the sons of Israel were to walk (2 Chron. vi. 16), which Rehoboam forsook (xii. 1), in which the perfect man meditates day and night (Ps. i), which is perfect (xix. 7), which is better than thousands of gold and silver (cxix. 72), which Yahaweh will write within his servants (Jer. xxxi. 33), which Judah has despised, but for which the coastlands wait (Isa. xlii. 24, 4), which is in the heart of those who know righteousness (li. 7); "the law of Moses my servant" (Mal. iv. 4 [iii. 22]).

And thus a third and much smaller group of instances becomes of especial importance for determining the date when this conception of *torah* as a single aggregate became current. *Torah* is mentioned many times in Amos and Hosea and the first half of Isaiah, and the definite phrase occurs not less than seven times in these writings.[1] In one or two of these seven instances "the *torah*" may possibly be something less than the recognized *torah*-aggregate; but in most of them it is clearly that aggregate, more or less definitely conceived. In one of them the aggregate is described as an existing body of literature, and this one must needs have weight in interpreting the others.

Instances from the earlier prophetic books

In these instances, when compared with those of the other two groups, we have proof — proof from phenomena as well as from testimony — of the early prevalence of this concept of the divine *torah* as a known aggregate. Whatever your critical position, instances of this emerge in the earliest Israelite literature. At the beginnings of the authentic history, no matter when one dates these, we have glimpses of "the *torah*" as an aggregate of some sort, and glimpses of literary *torah*. The concept of "the *torah*" as a literary aggregate cannot have been long delayed.

---

1 " I write for him the ten thousands of my law."

" And thou hast forgotten the law of thy God."

" They have transgressed my covenant and trespassed against my law" (Hos. viii. 12, iv. 6, viii. 1).

>" Because they have rejected the law of Yahaweh,
>   and have not kept his statutes,
>And their lies have led them astray,
>   after which their fathers walked " (Am. ii. 4).

" The law of our God," " the law of Yahaweh of hosts," " the law of Yahaweh " (Isa. i. 10, v. 24, xxx. 9).

In order to reach these conclusions we have not had to press doubtful instances. In most of the actual The instances instances there is no ambiguity ; in them the clear conception of a single recognized aggregate is clear, and these instances have value for interpreting the others. We have pursued the safe course of leaving each instance to its own natural implications. If we accept the testimony of the Old Testament, what we have found is the aggregate of written *torah* beginning with Moses, and growing, after his time, by additions made to it at different periods, the later as well as the earlier parts being sometimes called by his name. And if we reject the testimony, and accept the currently assigned late dates for the writings, we still find that this conception of Yahaweh's *torah* as a unit is one of the earliest of the phenomena, and that at a relatively early time it had become a conception of the *torah* as a known body of literature.

(*c*) It remains for us to discuss the relations between " the *torah* " and our present pentateuch, or our present Old Testament.

First, the aggregate we have been considering is not primarily the pentateuch, although, necessarily, the pentateuch has from its first existence been included in the *torah*.

" The *torah* " is rather, at any date, a general name for the aggregate of the *toroth* as then recognized. When-The law, ever men began to think of the written *torah* the prophets, and the as an aggregate, they would naturally apply hagiographa to it the three names that now describe the three divisions of the Old Testament. They would think of the aggregate as " the law," the body of *torah* which Deity had given. They would think of it as " the prophets," because they regarded it as given through the prophets. They would think of it as "the writings," distinguishing it from the *toroth* that were given orally. They would think thus of the aggregate, even if no collection of it were made ; much more would they think thus of it if they possessed it in collected form. It was doubtless the law and the prophets and the writings during the time when additions were being made to it. And when at length it ceased to grow, and thereby became the fixed body of writings which we now call the Old Testament, it was still the law, and was still also the law and the prophets and the writings.

We have found the definite phrases in the pentateuch itself, applied to situations of a date long before the pentateuch as a whole existed. In these instances the aggregate intended is of course something different from the pentateuch. The *torah* not the pentateuch

Many of the passages we have examined speak of *torah* as commensurate with the authoritative teaching of the prophets, and these indicate that the *torah* is something wider than the pentateuch. The same view appears in such a statement as that Joshua wrote "in the book of the law" after the death of Moses (Josh. xxiv. 26). When one reads with care he sees that "the law" so much emphasized in the books of Ezra and Nehemiah and Daniel is a body of writings differing from the pentateuch, though implying the pentateuch. The institutions presented in these books are quite as much those that are attributed to David as to Moses. And even such phrases as "the law of Moses" or "the book of Moses" are not restricted to the designating of the pentateuch.[1]

---

[1] The enemies of Daniel sought occasion against him in his obedience to "the law of his God" (vi. 5). That the Aramaic word is here used as the equivalent of *torah* is evident by comparison with Ezra (vii. 12, 14, 25,

If one holds that the pentateuch was completed in Mosaic times, and also holds that the pentateuch and not the hexateuch is the literary unit, he will find room in his theory for a time when the pentateuch constituted the aggregate of existing written *toroth ;* but otherwise this is logically impossible.

It is even doubtful whether the Old Testament anywhere recognizes any separation between the penta-

Is the pentateuch recognized as separate ? teuch and the other writings to which it attributes prophetic authorship. There are several passages that use the terms "law" and "prophets" in such proximity that we might interpret them as distinguishing between the two, after the fashion of the later times. There are other passages which emphasize the Mosaic character of the law in a

---

26). But the law-keeping for which Daniel was accused consisted in his praying toward Jerusalem three times a day. Praying toward Jerusalem is not mentioned in the pentateuch, but appears elsewhere (1 Ki. viii. 29, 30, 44, 48; Ps. v. 7; Jon. ii. 4). Praying three times a day is not found in the pentateuch, and is found elsewhere (Ps. lv. 17). It is evident that the writer and the first readers of the book of Daniel thought of the law as including matters now found in the prophets and the hagiographa.

We are told that in Zerubbabel's time —

"they set the priests in their divisions, and the Levites in their courses, for the service of God which is at Jerusalem, as it is written in the book of Moses" (Ezra vi. 18).

The matters touching the divisions and courses of the priests and Levites, here said to be written in the book of Moses, are to be found in 1 Chronicles (xxiii, xxiv), and not in the pentateuch. In the prayer in Nehemiah, based on "the law" that has been read, the historical recapitulation passes without a break from the contents of the pentateuch to those of the other Old Testament books (ix, especially 3, 13, 14, 26, 29, 34, etc.). Similar statements would be true of the several psalms that recapitulate the early history. "The *torah*" which Ezra and Nehemiah put in force included matters concerning the singers and gatekeepers and Nethinim, and concerning choral and orchestral worship, and fasting and public prayer, all of which belong to the other parts of the Old Testament, and not to the pentateuch.

way which has been understood as implying the same distinction. But in none of them is this a necessary interpretation.[1] The passages intermingle the pentateuchal requirements with those of other writings. They

[1] The more important of these passages are the following: —

"And their heart they set as adamant not to hear the law and the words which Yahaweh of hosts sent by his Spirit by the hand of the first prophets" (Zech. vii. 12).

"And we hearkened not to the voice of Yahaweh our God, to walk in his laws which he gave before us by the hand of his servants the prophets. And all Israel having transgressed thy law, . . . thou hast poured out upon us the curse and the oath which is written in the law of Moses the servant of God." Then follow allusions to Deuteronomy, and then: "According as it is written in the law of Moses there came in all this great evil upon us" (Dan. ix. 10–13).

"If ye will not hearken unto me to walk in my law which I have given before you, to hearken upon the words of my servants the prophets whom I send unto you, even rising early and sending and ye have not hearkened, I will give this house as Shiloh" (Jer. xxvi. 4–6).

"And Yahaweh testified with Israel and with Judah by the hand of every prophet of his, every seer, saying, Turn from your evil ways and keep my commandments, my statutes, according to all the law which I commanded your fathers and which I sent unto you by the hand of my servants the prophets" (2 Ki. xvii. 13).

In the case of Manasseh, king of Judah, the narratives emphasize the statement that God's promises to Israel were conditional. "If they will observe to do according to all that I have commanded them, and to all the law that my servant Moses commanded them" (2 Ki. xxi. 8). "If they will observe to do all that I have commanded them, to all the law and the statutes and the judgments by the hand of Moses" (2 Chron. xxxiii. 8). At the first glance one might say that "the law" here spoken of is clearly the pentateuch. But the charge against Manasseh is that he failed to comply with the condition; and the point in his failure that is emphasized is that "he set the carved image . . . in the house of God, concerning which God had said to David and to Solomon his son, In this house and in Jerusalem, which I have chosen from all the tribes of Israel, will I put my name forever" (2 Chron. xxxiii. 7; 2 Ki. xxi. 7). This is an abridgment of such statements as those in 1 Ki. ix. 3–7, ii. 3–4; 2 Sam. vii; 1 Chron. xxii. 6–13. The writer was thinking of the times of David and Solomon as well as of the times of Moses, and he apparently thinks of the record of both periods alike as included in what he calls the law of Moses.

evidently use the name of Moses when they mean
Moses and those who followed him in the giving of
torah. And a good deal of weight is to be allowed to
the fact that the Old Testament recapitulations of the
history regularly pass without a break from the pentateuchal events to those recorded in the other books (*e.g.*
Neh. ix; Pss. lxxviii, cv, cvi).

Did this recognized aggregate consist, at every stage,
of those parts of our present Old Testament which had
The *torah* then been written? The two are certainly in
and our pres- a general way identifiable, but beyond this
ent Old Tes-
tament the question is not to be answered without
definitions. That "the *torah*" contained matters not
now in the Old Testament is a proposition which it
would be difficult either to prove or disprove. In the
sense in which the Old Testament is of the nature of
torah, its authors were by the very fact of their writing
it writers of *torah*. It is clear that they used as sources
earlier writings that were of the nature of *torah;* and
equally clear that they drew from sources that were
not *torah*. What they drew from profane sources only
became *torah* through the process of incorporation.
One cannot always be sure as to which parts they drew
from sources that were already authoritative, and which
parts from other sources. And we have no adequate
means of deciding how far the earlier *torah* was abridged
or amplified or otherwise changed in their hands. This,
however, can be safely said : the existing Old Testament
is "the *torah*" in the sense of its being the aggregate in
the form which it finally assumed.

In this treatment "the *torah*" has several times been
spoken of as a growing aggregate. This is proved
both by the phenomena we have been examining and
by the oldest traditions. But the growth indicated by

the evidence is not strictly uniform, little by little, each
generation having its *torah*-writing prophets; rather
there were five periods that were especially   Five *torah-*
fruitful in the production of written *torah.*   producing
The first period is that of Moses and his con-   periods
temporaries who survived him, the latter best represented by Phinehas the grandson of Aaron. The second
is that of Samuel, Gad, David, and Nathan. The third
is that of Isaiah and "the men of Hezekiah" (Prov.
xxv. 1). The fourth is that of Jeremiah and his disciples who survived him. The fifth is that of Ezra and
Nehemiah.

These results do not favor the commonly accepted
notion that the *torah* is primarily the pentateuch, and is
made to include the prophets and the hagi-   Not three
ographa only by a process of extension. On   canons
the contrary, they indicate that the three terms were
originally applied alike to the whole aggregate, both
while it was growing and after it became complete.
The restrictions of meaning by which each of the three
terms became the name of one division belongs to a
later and secondary use. The idea of three successively
formed canons — the idea that the pentateuch was first
selected from other literature and segregated as sacred,
the prophets being segregated later, and the hagiographa still later — is not necessarily inconsistent with
the conception of the *torah* as a growing aggregate;
but there is a hypothesis which is at once simpler and
more adequate; namely, the hypothesis that the Old
Testament as a whole was differentiated first, and the
three divisions adopted later as matters of classification.
The order of succession was clearly this: first, concrete
toroth, regarded as messages from Deity; at a very early
date some of these *toroth* in writing; also, from an early

date, the habit of thinking of Yahaweh's *torah* as an aggregated unit; this habit fixing itself especially upon the written *toroth*, and leading to the use of means for collecting and authenticating these; the written aggregate coming to be known as *par excellence* the *torah*, and also coming to be known as the *torah* and the prophets and the writings; and these terms acquiring later the secondary sense in which they denote respectively the three divisions of the aggregate. Whenever the Old Testament came into existence, it was the aggregate of the written *toroth* as then extant, and was therefore the *torah*; and this remains true even if the pentateuch had then already come to be known as "the *torah*," in the sense of being the part of it which was most emphasized.[1]

III. From our study of the term *torah* certain corollaries follow touching the character of the prophets as writers of scripture. Only a summary statement of these is here possible.

First, the Old Testament scriptures are the extant

[1] The postbiblical facts fit in continuously with these phenomena. The author of Ecclesiasticus possessed a body of writings that were nearly or exactly the same with our Old Testament. We know this from his list of worthies, from Adam to Nehemiah, which is virtually a table of contents. It presents the books in an order which is mainly that of the events of which they treat, and which gives no hint of a division into the pentateuch and the prophets and the hagiographa. He has something to say concerning the law of Moses, but his law of Moses apparently included more than the pentateuch, and in particular it included the wisdom books. Two generations later his grandson emphasizes some sort of a division between the law and the prophets and the other books, but leaves the matter indefinite. Some generations after him Philo at last sharply marks off the pentateuch as the law, and perhaps hints at a line between the prophets and the other writings. A century after Philo we first find a mention of our present masoretic threefold division; and this was contemporaneous with the entirely different threefold division mentioned by Josephus. It is not till some time after this that our present division can be counted as a settled fact.

aggregate of the prophetic *toroth*. No one disputes that the prophets were, in general, in some sense the authors of these scriptures. Our investigation shows that they wrote them in their capacity of bringers of *torah* from Yahaweh. The revelation they brought, so far as it is now discernible, has become aggregated in this familiar body of writings.

Second, they make the claim, and it is supported by the New Testament and by the secondary Israelitish literature, that the word of a supernaturally endowed prophet is, next to God himself, the ultimate source of authority in Israel.

Torah is binding, they say, because it comes through a prophet. Whenever Deity sends a great prophet properly accredited, then kings and priests Other author-
and governors are alike subordinate to him. ity subordi-
nate to the
Moses the prophet outranks Aaron the priest. prophetic
Whatever difference they make between the Mosaic part of the *torah* and the other parts, they insist that the authority of Moses was simply that of a great prophet. This has been discussed in our earlier chapters, but it is in place to add here a citation or two. Hosea says : —

"Meanwhile I am Yahaweh thy God from the land of Egypt ; I yet cause thee to dwell in tents as in tabernacle days ; and I speak upon the prophets, it being I that have multiplied vision, and I give similitudes by the hand of the prophets." "And by a prophet Yaha- weh brought up Israel from Egypt, and by a prophet he was kept " (Hos. xii. 9, 10, 13 [10, 11, 14]).

This represents a claim which the prophets steadily made. It was under prophetic guidance, they say, that God brought up Israel from Egypt, sending before them " Moses, Aaron, and Miriam " (Mic. vi. 4). God gave Moses his Holy Spirit, they affirm, as he gave it to the

prophets who succeeded Moses (Isa. lxiii. 11, 12, 14).
Next to Deity, they say, supreme authority is ultimately
lodged, not in the priesthood, nor in civil rulers, nor in
written or oral legislation, but in the supernaturally
endowed prophets and prophetic men.

The same view prevailed, as we have seen, in the
times of the Maccabees, and, later, in the times of Josephus and of the New Testament. The books of Moses
and the Psalms are quoted as authoritative on the
ground that Moses and David were prophets (*e.g.* Acts
iii. 22, vii. 37, ii. 30). Up to the time of the destruction
of Jerusalem this was certainly the accepted view.

Third, what was the authority of the living prophet
as compared with that of *torah* that had already become
The living prophet *versus* the written *torah* accepted in writing? Of course he might
interpret or supplement the written precept;
but might he repeal or suspend or supersede
it? Inasmuch as *torah* originally depends on the word of
the living prophet, there is no absurdity in supposing
that it may always have been given subject to modification at the word of some later prophet. If it were true
that Samuel and Elijah and Elisha are represented as
sanctioning acts inconsistent with the pentateuch, this
might be explained as the superseding or suspending
of an earlier prophetic word by a later. But if such
instances occur, they are exceptional. The respect of
the prophet for the prophets who had preceded him was
a marked characteristic.

Fourth, the facts we have been examining forbid
Are the scriptures unequal in their authority? certain assumptions which, unfortunately,
are often made, as to the unequal authority
of the different parts of the Old Testament.
Professor W. Robertson Smith makes an as-
sertion that is not peculiar to his school when he says : —

"What place, then, was left for the prophets, the psalms, and the other books? They were inspired and authoritative interpretations and·applications of the law of Moses, and nothing more" (*Old Testament*, Lect. VI).

In the context he intimates that the Jews were accustomed to regard all the books except the pentateuch as on the same footing with the oral tradition.

This representation differs radically from those which we have been considering. The latter regard all the books of the Old Testament as alike the prophetic word of God, and as having, in that sense, equal divine authority. Some were better known and more prominently cited than others. The books of Moses, as treating of the oldest events, and as containing the received directory for worship, had the place of honor and were mentioned first. But the most obscure scriptural book was regarded as the prophetic word of God; while the pentateuch itself could not possibly be anything more than the prophetic word of God.

It would be out of place to discuss here the nature of the divine authority thus attributed to the scriptures, or the inspiration that was the basis of it. Certainly the different parts of the scriptures are very unlike in the matter of the mental processes through which they came into existence, and in their applicability as a rule of conduct. And there is a sense in which the entire Old Testament is the unfolding of certain original germs of revealed truth. In this sense one might regard all the other books as an enlargement of the first five. Jesus and his disciples and the scribes alike held that both the pentateuch and the entire scripture is summed up in the precepts of love to God and to man (Rom. xiii. 9 and parallel passages). In a parallel sense they may have regarded the pentateuch as comprehend-

ing all the scriptures.   But this is different from counting the other scriptures as of a secondary and inferior
grade.

Certain relatively late Jewish rabbis are cited as holding opinions concerning the superiority of the pentateuch which may be transposed into affirmations of the
inferiority of the other scriptures.   But can any one
produce a particle of proof of the prevalence of such
opinions prior to the destruction of Jerusalem by Titus ?
What evidence we have examined is clearly to the
opposite effect.   The New Testament is for this purpose typical.   It contains about two hundred formal
controversial appeals to the Old Testament.   These are
almost evenly distributed between the pentateuch, the
prophets, and the hagiographa, though a majority of the
hagiographic citations are from the psalms, and a majority of the prophetic are from Isaiah.   With this wide
field before us it is incredible that we should find no
hint of the fact, if either Jesus or his opponents regarded the other scriptures as less binding than the
pentateuch.   But is there a single New Testament
instance in which a disputant, on either side, replies, or
could naturally be thought of as replying : "Oh, your
citation is from one of the other books, and is therefore
not as authoritative as if it were from one of the five
books of Moses ?"   Jesus rebuked the scribes, not for
making the other books and the oral tradition alike inferior to the five books of Moses ; but for exalting the
oral tradition at the expense of the books of Moses and
of the other books.   In his view the word of God was
equally incapable of being broken, whether found in the
Mosaic books or the psalms or Isaiah or Daniel.

PART II

THE PROMISE. MESSIANIC PROPHECY

CHAPTER VIII

THE PROMISE-DOCTRINE AS TAUGHT IN THE NEW TESTAMENT

In the preceding chapters it has been asserted that the thing which differentiates the monotheism of Yahaweh from other religions is its doctrine of the Messiah. Other religions, it may be, have their Messiahs, but ours is different from the others, and this difference is the really distinctive element. Of this assertion I offer no proof except our examination of this same doctrine of the Messiah, but we shall find, I think, that this is sufficient.

For clearness of thought we need to begin by sharply perceiving the differences of meaning among the three terms, "messianic prediction," "messianic prophecy," "messianic doctrine" taught by the prophets. The first of these terms is narrower than the other two. The second and third really describe different aspects of the same fact.

Provided we remember this, messianic prediction is a good term. We have been taught that the prophets uttered predictions of a coming Deliverer; that these were fulfilled in the events of the life and mission of Jesus; and that this proves, first, that the prophets were divinely inspired, and second, that the mission of Jesus was divine. All this is true if rightly understood, but full of difficulty if we stop here. It is correct procedure, when correctly carried out, to select passages

from the Old Testament in which specific facts are foretold concerning the Messiah, and then show, from the
history, that these marks characterized Jesus, that he is
therefore the Christ, and that prediction, thus made and
fulfilled, is a mark of supernatural knowledge, authenticating revealed religion.   But if we go at it in this way
we are liable to misconceive the terms we use in our
reasoning.   And we mislead ourselves if we imagine
this to be an exhaustive study of messianic prophecy,
or even of the much narrower subject, messianic prediction.

Some persons, pursuing these studies, have been
struck with the great variety and the apparently disconnected character of what are commonly regarded as
messianic predictions, coupled with the remarkable fact
that, diverse as they are, they all meet in the history of
Jesus, so that what would otherwise be heterogeneous
and unintelligible is thus seen to have a common end,
and becomes intelligible.   Thus, it is said, the gospels
become the key to the prophecies, opening the meaning
of things that were otherwise obscure.   Considerations
of this kind are regarded as giving especial strength to
the argument from messianic predictions.

This reasoning is valid within its own proper limits.
But it suggests another point.   If we really have here
a wide and varied body of instances, capable of being
shown by induction to have a common value, then the suggestion is that as they thus converge toward a single fact,
so they may originally have diverged from a single fact.
If further study shall thus discover in them a unity at
the beginning, as well as at the end, their value as evidence will thereby be increased.   And this is what
further study actually discovers.   The more adequate
idea is not that of many predictions meeting in one ful-

filment, but that of one prediction, repeated and unfolded through successive centuries, with many specifications, and in many forms; always the same in essential character, no matter how it may vary in its outward presentation or in the illustrations through which it is presented.

Messianic prophecy is doctrine rather than prediction. The prophets were preachers. If there was some one messianic prediction which they repeated and unfolded from age to age, we should expect that they would present it in the form of a religious doctrine, for the practical benefit of the men of their times. We Christians preach the facts concerning Jesus Christ. On the basis of these facts we ask men to repent of sin, to obey God, to seek their own highest good, to receive help against temptation, and comfort in distress. Had the prophets any doctrine that they could preach for the accomplishment of these and other like ends? There can be no doubt that they had. Their foretelling of the Christ stands on a different footing from all their other predictions, just as the biography of Jesus, in the New Testament, is on a different footing from all other matters of fact there recorded. As the biography of Jesus is really doctrine rather than biography, and is the heart of the apostolic Christian doctrine, so the prophetic forecast of the Messiah is doctrine rather than prediction, and is the heart of the religious teachings of the prophets.

Certainly we should treat their utterances as predictive; but this by itself is inadequate. They teach a doctrine concerning God's purposes with Israel, intelligible in each stage of Israel's history, so as to be the basis of religious and moral appeal for that age, but growing in fulness from age to age until it becomes the completed doctrine of the Messiah.

In other words, we are accustomed to a generalization of what the prophets say concerning the Messiah which

A scriptural generaliza- tion

was devised to meet the needs of our theological systems.   One need find no fault with this.   But if we could substitute for it a strictly scriptural formula of generalization, there would at least be a gain in the way of freshness of statement.   Is there a scriptural way of stating this matter ? and if so, what is it ?

The proposition that the Old Testament contains a large number of predictions concerning the Messiah to come, and that these are fulfilled in Jesus Christ, may be scriptural in substance, but it is hardly so in form. The bible offers very few predictions save in the form of promises or threatenings.   It differs from the systemized theologies in its not disconnecting prediction from promise or threatening.   We shall find that it also differs from some of them in emphasizing one promise rather than many predictions.   This is the prevailing note in both Testaments — a multitude of specifications unfolding a single promise, the promise serving as a central religious doctrine.

This biblical generalization of the matter may be thus formulated : *God gave a promise to Abraham, and through him to mankind; a promise eternally fulfilled and fulfilling in the history of Israel ; and chiefly fulfilled in Jesus Christ, he being that which is principal in the history of Israel.*   In the present chapter we are to consider this doctrine as taught in the New Testament.

The most prominent thing in the New Testament is its proclamation of the kingdom and its anointed king. But it is on the basis of the divine promise that its preachers proclaim the kingdom, and when they appeal to the Old Testament in proof of Christian doctrine, they make the promise more prominent than the king-dom itself.

I. First, the men of the New Testament hold that a doctrine of the Messiah, the Anointed one, in the form of a record of a promise made by Deity, appears in all parts of the Old Testament scriptures.

They say that this doctrine is taught not in selected passages only, but throughout the scriptures. Jesus in the Emmaus incident reminded his disciples that all things must needs be fulfilled which were written con-cerning him " in the law of Moses and the prophets and the psalms." In the same passage it is said of him : —

" And beginning from Moses and from all the prophets, he inter-preted to them in all the scriptures the things concerning himself" (Lc. xxiv. 44, 27).

That this statement is typical no one will dispute. Under the general fact which it affirms, we note a few specifications.

1. In the first place, the New Testament men regard the messianic teaching of the Old Testament as mainly the unfolding of a single promise ($\epsilon\pi\alpha\gamma\gamma\epsilon\lambda\iota\alpha$). How-ever scholars may have neglected this aspect of the view they present, it is the one which they themselves bring to the front.

Paul, on trial for preaching Jesus as the Messiah, risen from the dead, said to Agrippa : —

" And now I stand to be judged for the hope of the promise made of God unto our fathers ; whereunto our twelvetribe nation, strenu-ously serving night and day, hopeth to attain ; and concerning this hope I am accused by the Jews, O King " (Acts xxvi. 6–7).

It was on such an occasion as this, if ever, that Paul would formulate most carefully the central article of his creed. Evidently he has weighed his words and made them exact. The messianic hope, he says, is based on the promise; not some promise or other, but the promise. He founds his appeal to Agrippa not on a good many Paul before scattered predictions, but on the one prom- Agrippa ise; and he expects Agrippa to understand him. Speaking of his hope as a Christian, he describes it as "the hope of the promise made of God unto our fathers," and he speaks of the twelvetribe Jewish nation as hoping to attain to this promise. The thing he is speaking of he calls, not prediction, but promise; not promises, but promise; not a promise, but the promise. The word he uses is singular and definite. The whole essential messianic truth, as he knows it, he sums up in this one formula, "the promise made of God unto our fathers."

The context here sufficiently indicates what promise is meant; and Paul's words are to be interpreted by the fact that the offence for which he stood accused was his teaching that the promise was for the gentiles as well as the Jews. But, waiving these points, we just now only note that Paul here speaks of "the promise." Similar phraseology abounds in the New Testament appeal to the Old Testament. Nearly forty passages that contain this word "promise" might be cited, besides many that touch the matter in other ways. And these passages in which the doctrine of the one promise is found are the central, conspicuous passages of the New Testament. They affirm that all revelation concerning the Messiah is the unfolding of the one promise. Into this mould all the New Testament teaching on the subject may readily be cast. This is the way in which the men of the New Testament themselves generalize the messianic statements they make, this in distinction from all the other ways that have been devised.

2. In the second place, the New Testament writers

do not leave us in doubt as to the identity of the one
promise which they regard as summing up the hope
of those who believe in Christ.   They iden-   The one
tify it for us as the promise that was made   promise
to Abraham when God called him, the prom-   identified
ise that in him all the nations of the earth should be
blessed.   With this transaction in mind the writer of
the Epistle to the Hebrews speaks of God's having
"made promise to Abraham," says of Abraham that
"having patiently endured, he obtained the promise,"
and that God's oath was given to show "unto the heirs
of the promise the immutability of his counsel " (vi.
13–15, 17).   He speaks of Isaac and Jacob as "heirs
with him of the same promise."   And of "these all " he
says that they —

"received not the promise, God having provided some better thing
concerning us " (Heb. xi. 9, 39–40).[1]

In a similar strain Paul says to the Romans that "the
promise to Abraham or to his seed " was "not through
the law," "but through the righteousness of faith," and
that unless this is so "the promise is made of none
effect." He adds concerning Abraham, that "looking
unto the promise of God, he wavered not through
unbelief " (iv. 13–14, 20).[2]

[1] "For when God made promise to Abraham, . . . he sware, . . .
Surely, blessing I will bless thee, and multiplying I will multiply thee.
And thus, having patiently endured, he obtained the promise. . . . God,
being minded to show more abundantly unto the heirs of the promise the
immutability of his counsel, interposed with an oath " (Heb. vi. 13–15, 17).

" By faith he became a sojourner in the land of promise, as in a land
not his own, dwelling in tents, with Isaac and Jacob, the heirs with him of
the same promise " (Heb. xi. 9).

[2] " For not through the law was the promise to Abraham or to his seed,
that he should be heir of the world, but through the righteousness of faith.
For if they which are of the law be heirs, faith is made void, and the promise is made of none effect " (Rom. iv. 13–14).

3. In the third place, the New Testament writers speak of promises, using the word in the plural, but not in such a way as to weaken what has just been said concerning their doctrine of the one promise.

Very rarely they use the word without the article. For example, certain worthies are spoken of " who "Promises" through faith . . . obtained promises," that and "the is, promises of some sort or other (Heb. promises" xi. 33). But most of the instances are in contrast with this, the definite article being used — for example, the following from Romans : —

"Who are Israelites ; whose is the adoption, and the glory, and the covenants, and the giving of the law, and the service, and the promises " (Rom. ix. 4).

"Christ hath been made a minister of the circumcision for the truth of God, that he might confirm the promises [given] unto the fathers, and that the Gentiles might glorify God for his mercy ; as it is written " (Rom. xv. 8–9, followed by four quotations in succession, in reference to the Gentiles).

Here the thing spoken of is not promises in general, but "the promises." The definite article is used. A recognized specific group of promises is indicated, and it is identified as the Abrahamic group. That is, "the promises " here intended are precisely the same thing that we have heretofore found spoken of in the singular as "the promise." The one promise is capable of being thought of as divided into specifications, and when so thought of, the plural number is used.

Similar instances are frequent in the book of Hebrews. We are exhorted to "be not sluggish, but imitators of them who through faith and patience inherit the prom-

---

" For this cause it is of faith, that it may be according to grace; to the end that the promise may be sure to all the seed; not to that only which is of the law, but to that also which is of the faith of Abraham (16)."

ises " (vi. 12). It is said that Melchizedek blessed
" Abraham . . . him that hath the promises " (vii. 6).
We read : —

"Yea, he that had gladly received the promises was offering up
his only begotten [son] " (xi. 17).

It it said of Abraham and Sarah and their predecessors : —

"These all died in faith, not having received the promises "
(xi. 13).

The new covenant is called, in contrast with the old, —

"a better covenant . . . enacted upon better promises " (viii. 6).

In these and like instances the use of the plural is
simply a recognition of the fact that the one promise
includes many specifications.

4. In the fourth place, this one promise, with its
specifications, the New Testament men regard as the
theme of the whole Old Testament.

They trace the unfolding of it throughout the history of Abraham's descendants, identify it with the
promise made later to Israel, and still later to David,
and regard it as having been continually fulfilled, but
likewise as always moving forward to larger fulfilment.

Stephen is represented as beginning his oration before
his accusers with the statement : —

"The God of glory appeared unto our father Abraham, when he
was in Mesopotamia, before he dwelt in Haran, and Stephen's
said unto him, Get thee out of thy land, and from thy view of the
kindred, and come into the land which I shall shew matter
thee " (Acts vii. 2).

From this beginning Stephen traces down through the
events recorded in the Old Testament a doctrine which
he evidently intends to identify with the doctrine of the

Messiah as held by Christians. When he reaches the period of the exodus, he says : —

"But as the time of the promise drew nigh, which God vouch-safed unto Abraham, the people grew and multiplied in Egypt" (17).

That is to say, he represents the promise made to Abraham as being fulfilled, in its proper time, in the events of the exodus; though he regards it as still holding on, after the exodus, for further fulfilment

Paul, in his speech in Antioch of Pisidia, adopts the same method, beginning, however, with the exodus. Following the history down, he comes to the time of Saul the king of Israel, and adds : —

Paul's view

"And when he had removed him, he raised up David to be their king; . . . Of this man's seed hath God according to promise brought unto Israel a Saviour, Jesus" (Acts xiii. 22–23).

Evidently Paul, like Stephen, regards the messianic revelation as a process extending through the history of Israel, so that it is proper to cite the facts of that history in explaining how it came about that Jesus is the Messiah.

The hymns cited in the first two chapters of the Gospel according to Luke are saturated with the same idea. They speak of the events connected with the births of John the Baptist and Jesus as proving that the Lord remembers —

The Lucan hymns

"his holy covenant;
The oath which he sware unto Abraham our father" (i. 72–73).

But they also speak of the same events as the Lord's having —

"raised up a horn of salvation for us
In the house of his servant David" (69).

In doing this they identify the promise made to and

through Abraham with the promise made later to and through David.

If additional instances were needful, we might add all the numerous New Testament passages in which the Christ is directly or indirectly spoken of as the son of David.

5. In the fifth place, they not only trace the promise through the Old Testament, but make the Old Testament phraseology a part of their own diction.

In their teachings concerning the promise they employ peculiar terms brought over from the Old Testament, in some cases modifying the terms by the use they make of them; for example, kingdom, Messiah, servant, son, mine elect, holy one, and the like. They also bring over a good many peculiar forms of representation: the last days, the day of the Lord, my messenger, the Spirit, ceremonial types, biographical types, the prophet as a type, Jehovah's day of judgment, and the like. Most of these will be discussed in subsequent chapters. At present we only note that such phraseology exists. *Special terms and forms of representation*

II. If now we have firmly grasped the idea that the men of the New Testament base everything on the one great promise which they found in the beginning of the old scriptures, and which they regarded as radiating thence all through those scriptures, we are prepared to proceed to a study of the use they make of this promise.

1. First of all, they regard the promise as eternally operative, and as irrevocable, and they emphasize this. The author of the book of Hebrews says : —

"For when God made promise to Abraham, since he could swear by none greater he sware by himself."

"Wherein God, being minded to shew more abundantly unto the heirs of the promise the immutability of his counsel, interposed with an oath ; that by two immutable things, in which it is impossible for God to lie, we may have a strong encouragement " (Heb. vi. 13, 17–18).

Note how strongly the eternal operativeness of the ancient promise is here affirmed. In the eleventh chapter of Romans, the chapter in which Paul affirms that though "a hardening in part hath befallen Israel " (25), yet God has not cast off his people, the irrevocability of the old promise is presupposed throughout,[1] and is explicitly stated in the words : —

" For the gifts and the calling of God are not repented of " (Rom. xi. 29, marg. of RV).

And yet more forcible, if such a thing can be, is Paul's language to the Galatians : —

" Though it be but a man's covenant, yet when it hath been confirmed no one maketh it void, or addeth thereto. Now to Abraham were the promises spoken, and to his seed. . . . A covenant confirmed beforehand by God the law, which came four hundred and thirty years after, doth not disannul, so as to make the promise of none effect. For if the inheritance is of the law, it is no more of promise ; but God hath granted it to Abraham by promise " (Gal. iii. 15–18).

And in a score of passages which I have cited or shall cite to prove other points, this same thought of the eternity and immutability of the promise is magnified.

2. As a second point, the men of the New Testament claim that Jesus Christ is the culminating fulfilment of

---

[1] In particular, one does not completely understand the allusion to Isaiah (Rom. xi. 26–27), unless he has in mind the clauses which in Isaiah follow the ones cited : —

" This is my covenant with them, saith Yahaweh : My Spirit that is upon thee, and my words which I have put in thy mouth, shall not depart out of thy mouth, nor out of the mouth of thy seed, nor out of the mouth of thy seed's seed, saith Yahaweh, from henceforth and forever " (Isa. lix. 21).

the ancient promise, so that, in preaching him, they are preaching the promise.

We have noticed above that Paul, in his address at Antioch, follows down the history of the promise from the times of the exodus; and we have found him reaching the point where David appears in the history, and then speaking of "a saviour, Jesus," as coming from Israel, from the seed of David : —

"Of this man's seed hath God according to promise brought unto Israel a saviour, Jesus " (Acts xiii. 23).

He makes this lead up to another statement : —

"And we bring you good tidings of the promise made unto the fathers, how that God hath fulfilled the same unto our children, in that he raised up Jesus " (32–33).

That is, Jesus is the fulfilment of the promise made to the patriarchs and to David.

We have just considered the statement made to the Galatians concerning the promise-covenant that cannot be disannulled.   Paul insists upon that, not on account of its abstract importance, but because, as he says, he and his fellow-believers have a direct interest in it. And here again he leads up to a specific statement : —

"The scripture hath shut up all things under sin, that the promise by faith in Jesus Christ might be given to them that believe " (Gal. iii. 22).

Here Paul speaks of the Abrahamic promise as "the promise by faith in Jesus Christ."

With the apostles this is a common way of speaking. The whole eleventh chapter of Hebrews might be cited in proof of this assertion.   We cited from the sixth of Hebrews, a moment ago, certain words concerning God's oath to Abraham, and the two immutable things in which it is impossible for God to lie.   The author is insistent

upon the promise thus authenticated, in order that he
and his fellow-Christians may claim a share in it.   He
makes the statement for the purpose of enforcing the
exhortation —

"that each of you may show the same diligence unto the fulness of
hope even to the end; that ye be not sluggish, but imitators of
them who through faith and patience inherit the promises " (Heb.
vi. 11–12).

He carries his thought forward to the conclusion that —

"we may have a strong encouragement, who have fled for refuge
to lay hold of the hope set before us; . . . that which is within the
veil; whither as a forerunner Jesus entered for us " (Heb. vi. 18–20).

We might quote in addition a long list of passages
(*e.g.* Gal. iii. 6–9, 26–29).   The more one studies such
utterances in their contexts, the more he sees the reason
for the intense interest which the men of the New Testament take in the eternity and the immutability of the
promise.   They regard it as the charter of all the rights
which they and their successors may possess as Christians.

3.   Further, they claim especially that the salvation of
the gentiles through Christ comes under the promise.
They make it emphatic that God's promise to Abraham
was for the nations, and therefore conveys title to the
gentiles, under which they may receive the gospel.   Paul
says to the Galatians : —

"And the scripture, foreseeing that God would justify the Gentiles
by faith, gave the gospel beforehand[1] unto Abraham, [saying], In
thee shall all the nations be blessed" (iii. 8).

In this sentence Paul affirms three things : that the giving of the gospel to Abraham was a giving of it before-

[1] The versions translate " preached beforehand." The word is προευαγ-
γελίζομαι, not προκηρύσσω. The statement that the scripture *evangelized*
Abraham beforehand means, I suppose, that it preserves the record of the
gospel as announced to him. But in any case the contents of the Old
Testament are here described as a giving of the gospel.

hand; that the substance of the gospel thus given was in the words, "In thee shall all the nations be blessed"; that this promise, given to Abraham, is the same gospel by which the nations are saved in Jesus Christ.

Paul says further to these gentile Christians:—

"And if ye are Christ's, then are ye Abraham's seed, heirs according to promise" (iii. 29).

And again:—

"That upon the Gentiles might come the blessing of Abraham in Christ Jesus; that we might receive the promise of the Spirit through faith" (iii. 14).

He makes the same claim, in different language, in the fourth chapter of Galatians:—

"The [son] by the handmaid is born after the flesh; but the [son] by the freewoman through promise." "Now we, brethren, as Isaac was, are children of promise" (iv. 23, 28).

And to the Ephesians Paul says that "the gentiles are . . . fellow-partakers of the promise"; that the Ephesian gentile converts have ceased to be "strangers from the covenants of the promise"; that they "were sealed with the holy Spirit of promise."[1]

4. Yet further, the men of the New Testament trace a connection between the promise and the several great doctrines of the gospel.

(a) They connect it with their proclamation of the kingdom of God, on earth and in heaven, and so with the universal and eternal reign of Christ as prince of

---

[1] "In whom, having also believed, ye were sealed with the holy Spirit of promise" (i. 13).

"Ye, the Gentiles . . . were . . . alienated from the commonwealth of Israel, and strangers from the covenants of the promise" (ii. 11–12).

"That the Gentiles are fellow-heirs, and fellow-members of the body, and fellow-partakers of the promise in Christ Jesus through the gospel" (iii. 6).

peace. This statement scarcely needs proof. Any one can verify it by means of a concordance.

(*b*) In view of the eternal and irrevocable character of the promise, their doctrine of the kingdom easily carries the promise idea with it as it passes into the eschatological teachings of the New Testament.

In many passages, both those which mention the coming of the Lord and others, they closely connect the promise with the doctrine of the resurrection and of future reward. The second Epistle to Timothy opens with these words : —

"Paul, an apostle of Christ Jesus by the will of God, according to the promise of the life which is in Christ Jesus."

In 2 Peter we are told that—

"the Lord is not slack concerning his promise, . . . the day of the Lord will come as a thief" (iii. 9–10).

And we are warned against those who say —

"Where is the promise of his coming ? " (iii. 4).

Paul before Agrippa, arguing the promise given to the fathers, asks the question : —

"Why is it judged incredible with you, if God doth raise the dead ? " (Acts xxvi. 8).

In 1 John we read : —

"Ye also shall abide in the Son and in the Father. And this is the promise which he promised us [even] the life eternal " (ii. 24–25).

And in Hebrews : —

"He is the mediator of a new covenant, that . . . they that have been called may receive the promise of the eternal inheritance " (ix. 15).

And again : —

" For ye have need of patience, that, having done the will of God, ye may receive the promise " (x. 36).

(*c*) They connect the promise with the gift of the Holy Ghost that marks the new dispensation.

Paul writes to the Galatians : —

" That upon the Gentiles might come the blessing of Abraham in Christ Jesus ; that we might receive the promise of the Spirit through faith " (iii. 14).

Peter is reported to have said on the day of Pentecost : —

" Repent ye, and be baptized . . . ; and ye shall receive the gift of the Holy Ghost. For to you is the promise, and to your children, and to all that are afar off " (Acts ii. 38–39).

Peter is here speaking of the ancient promise, though he does not explicitly connect it with Abraham.

These two instances will serve to interpret others. It is not necessary to think that the speaker is always thinking of Abraham when he uses the word "promise." This mode of conception and of diction, once established, would maintain itself. But the reference to the ancient record is real, whether direct or indirect. When Jesus was about to part from his disciples at his ascension, he said : —

" And behold I send forth the promise of my Father upon you ; but tarry ye in the city until ye be clothed with power from on high " (Lc. xxiv. 49).

" He charged them not to depart from Jerusalem, but to wait for the promise of the Father," adding, " But ye shall be baptized with the Holy Ghost not many days hence " (Acts i. 4–5).

Peter refers to this in the words : —

" Being therefore by the right hand of God exalted, and having received of the Father the promise of the Holy Ghost, he hath poured forth this which ye see and hear " (Acts ii. 33).

(*d*) Finally, they connect Abraham, the recipient of the promise, with what they have to say concerning redemption from sin ; and in particular with their doctrine of justification by free grace, through faith.

In Genesis we are told that Abraham " was wont to believe God, and he counted it righteousness to him." This utterance is made central by the apostles, not merely in their theology, but in their messianic theology. Paul and James alike cite the words, and insist upon them (Jas. ii. 21–23; Rom. iv. 2–5, 9, 10). Paul declares that —

"it was not written for his sake alone, . . . but for our sake also, . . . who believe on him that raised Jesus our Lord from the dead, who was delivered up for our trespasses, and was raised for our justification " (Rom. iv. 23–25).

He draws the inference : —

" Even as Abraham believed God, and it was reckoned unto him for righteousness. Know therefore that they which be of faith, the same are sons of Abraham." " So then they which be of faith are blessed with the faithful Abraham." " If ye are Christ's, then are ye Abraham's seed, heirs according to promise " (Gal. iii. 6–7, 9, 29, and the whole chapter).

We have thus seen that the men of the New Testament find a messianic doctrine pervading every part of the Old Testament. In their minds it takes Recapitulation the form of the one promise. They identify it as the promise made to Abraham for the nations. They recognize the particulars included in it as "the promises." They trace it throughout the Old Testament. They appropriate the phraseology in which the Old Testament speaks of it. Further, they preach this promise as the one great thing they have to preach ; emphasizing its irrevocability, claiming that Jesus Christ is the culminating fulfilment of it, basing upon it the hope of salvation for the gentiles, connecting it with the whole body of the doctrines of the gospel.

The passages which describe the promise to Abraham, his faith as related thereto, the experiences that arose from it, are those which the men of the New Testament cite more prominently than any others as sources concerning the Messiah. In these recent centuries Christian scholars have busied themselves with the important doctrines of justification and election as taught in the New Testament comment on these passages, and have largely overlooked the messianic part of it. What the New Testament here principally teaches is that Christ is the perfect realization of this promise as made to the patriarchs, and as renewed to Israel later, particularly in the times of Moses and of David. The Christ is the goal of the mission of Israel. In him the line of David is eternal. His kingdom is David's everlasting kingdom.

We cannot dismiss this survey of the facts without calling attention to one very important bearing of it. It offers the basis for a genuine Christocentric theology. As men employ this term, it is sometimes a mere euphemism for a theology *A Christo-centric theology* from which everything has been omitted save a few glittering generalities concerning Christ. I for one have no use for such a theology as that. But the apostolic world-view that has been traversed in this chapter is certainly Christocentric. It is Christ to whom the promise points forward. It is on account of its containing Christ that the promise is cited with so much reiteration, and not for anything it contains apart from Christ. The promise passages connect themselves with everything that is essential in Christian doctrine. They outline the nature and the person of Christ. The theology of the Holy Spirit is in them, he being the divine Agent in carrying out the promise. They are a study in the doctrine of the divine decree, that decree having Christ as its determinative point. The whole of this

line of teaching is true to the summary of it given in
the Epistle to the Ephesians : —

"Having made known unto us the mystery of his will, according
to his good pleasure which he purposed in him unto a dispensation
of the fulness of the times, to sum up all things in Christ, the things
in the heavens, and the things upon the earth " (i. 9–10).

The Calvinistic theology is Christocentric in fact,
even if not in form. Perhaps some theologian will arise
who shall succeed in discovering a dogmatical rearrange-
ment into a system that shall be Christocentric in form
as well as in fact. At all events, the theology of the
promise, as it appears in the New Testament, is Christocentric.

CHAPTER IX

In the last chapter we examined the doctrine of Yahaweh's promise to mankind through Israel, as that doctrine is formulated in the New Testament. The men of the New Testament say that Yahaweh, when he called Abraham, announced a promise given through him to the human race; that the history of Israel is the unfolding of this promise; that the promise was renewed with David, and preached by all the prophets; that it began to be fulfilled directly after it was made, and has been fulfilling ever since; that its greatest fulfilment is in the person and work of Jesus Christ; that it will never cease being in process of fulfilment; and that this promise-doctrine is the sum of what the prophets teach in the scriptures.

We are now to inquire whether the New Testament writers are correct in their exegesis of the Old Testament. An adequate answer would require an examination of all the teachings of the prophets, and would fill a series of volumes rather than a couple of chapters. All that can be here attempted is an informal study of the situation at four periods in the history; namely, the times of the patriarchs, of the exodus, of David, of the post-Davidic prophets. The present chapter deals with the patriarchal times.

The main line of the Old Testament record, for any purpose, is that which presents the history of Israel. Properly this begins with the account of the calling of

Abraham from Ur of the Chaldees, as found in the twelfth chapter of Genesis, the contents of the preceding eleven chapters being preliminary.

But these preliminary sections are of prophetic authorship, and were written from prophetic points of view. It is therefore not surprising that interpreters have found in them abundant traces of the prophetic doctrine of the Messiah.   Much stress has been laid on Yahaweh's relations with Adam, including the protevangelium (Gen. iii. 15); on the sacrifice made by Abel (Gen. iv; Matt. xxiii. 35; Lc. xi. 51; Heb. xi. 4, xii. 24; 1 Jn. iii. 12; Jude 11); on the experiences of Noah, especially the covenant (Gen. vi. 18, ix. 9, 11, 12, 13, 15, 16, 17).   The messianic subject-matter includes whatever indications there may be of God's plan of redeeming blessing for mankind, as found in the accounts of the creation, the fall, or the flood. The instances are very fully treated in current works, but I do not purpose to discuss them here ; not even to argue the question in case any one shall think that they belong to the main line of Old Testament messianic teaching, that line beginning with Adam rather than with Abraham.   In any case, the record of these pre-Abrahamic events supplements the messianic teaching found elsewhere, especially in such important matters as sin and redemption, and God's purpose for mankind.

Pre-Abrahamic messianic passages

Dismissing these preliminary chapters, we turn to the calling of Abraham, and there begin our search for the main line of messianic doctrine.   Both at the beginning and afterward, we shall find it to be the principal thing in the Old Testament.   Luthardt well says (*Bremen Lectures*, p. 195) that the whole history of Israel is prophetic of Christ.   We will first examine the presentation of the case as made in Genesis, and will afterward look at certain problems which arise from this presentation.

I. We have seen in the preceding chapter that the Old Testament passage more emphasized in the New than any other is the promise made to Abraham. Let us study this promise.

1. The earliest account of it is as follows : —

> "And Yahaweh said unto Abraham, Get thee out from thy land, and from thy native place, and from the house of thy father, unto the land that I shall cause thee to see; that I may make thee a great nation, and may bless thee, and may make thy name great; and be thou a blessing; and I will bless those who bless thee, and curse those who make light of thee, and in thee shall all the families of the ground be blessed" (Gen. xii. 1–3 J).

The promise is in two parts : first, a promise to Abraham that he shall have the land of Canaan, shall become a great nation, shall have a distinguished name, and shall have the divine favor for his friends and disfavor for his enemies ; second, a promise to him and all mankind that he shall be the channel of Yahaweh's blessing to the human race. The second part comes last, the order being apparently climacteric. Abraham is represented as chosen to be the recipient of peculiar favors, not for his own sake, but that through him all the families of the ground may receive blessing. This is the supreme thing in the promise as given, all the other specifications being subordinate to it.

The subordinate items reappear in many places in Genesis. A glance at them will help us in our understanding of the principal promise. Subordinate items in the promise

First, a "seed," that is a posterity, is promised to Abraham, Sarah, Isaac, Jacob (xiii. 14 ff., xv, xvii. 6–7, 15–16, etc., xxvi. 3, 4, xxviii. 3, 4, xxxv. 11, 12, xlviii. 3, 4).

Second, this seed shall be or shall include persons countless as the stars, as the dust of the earth, as the sand on the seashore (*ib.*).

Third, it shall be or shall include a great nation (xviii. 18, xxxv. 11, xlvi. 3).

Fourth, it shall be or shall include what is called "an assembly of nations," "an assembly of peoples" (xxviii. 3, xxxv. 11, xlviii. 4). In xvii. 6, 16, the meaning is the same, though the phrase is simply "nations." The nation intended is Israel, and the federated parts of Israel are the assembly of nations or of peoples, though confused translation has sometimes led to other conclusions.[1]

Fifth, in these same passages it is promised that kings

[1] It is a pity that the versions, in rendering these passages, have made them unlike, as they should not be, and have also confused them with other passages that are very unlike them. For example, the versions make it that Ephraim's seed (xlviii. 19) shall become "a multitude of nations"; its distinctive meaning is that his seed "shall fill the nations." The meaning of Gen. xvii. 4–5 will be considered below. It is entirely different from that of the passages just cited. It is often assumed that the "nations" of Gen. xvii. 6 include the Ishmaelites and Edomites and other Abrahamic descendants; and it is true that Ishmael and Esau are elsewhere spoken of as nations, and as having promises through Abraham (xvii. 20, xxi. 13, 18, xxv. 23, etc.); but xvii. 6 is to be grouped with xvii. 16, as referring to Sarah's descendants only, and these two passages belong with the other three in which the "assembly of peoples" or of "nations" are derived from Jacob.

The Hebrew word in these three places is *qāhāl*, sometimes translated in the Septuagint by ἐκκλησία. Stephen (Acts vii. 38), alluding to this word as found in Deuteronomy (xviii. 16), says: "the church in the wilderness." The word properly denotes the officially convened assembly of the twelve tribes, called to order for important business (*e.g.* Jud. xx. 2, xxi. 5–8). It appears scores of times in this use, and seldom, if ever, save in this use or some natural modification of it.

The meaning, therefore, is definite and clear, though much ignored. Abraham was to be the ancestor of a nation, Israel, which would exist in the form of an assembly of nations; namely, the federated tribes and families of Israel.

shall spring from Abraham, from Sarah, from Jacob (xvii. 6, 16, xxxv. 11). The kings that spring from Jacob can be no other than the line of the monarchs of Israel. Whether the promise to Abraham should be interpreted as also including the kings of the Ishmaelites, Edomites, Midianites, etc., may be a question.

Sixth, in many of the passages cited and in other passages it is promised that Abraham's posterity, in the line of Isaac and Jacob, shall inherit the land of Canaan, sometimes called "this land," or "these countries."

Seventh, there are other items. Abraham's name shall be made great; his friends are to be blessed, and those who contemn him are to be cursed (xii. 2–3). His seed shall take possession of the gates of their enemies (xxii. 17).

2. Among these various aspects of the promise, where does the emphasis lie? The answer is clear. The principal thing is that all mankind shall be blessed in Abraham and his seed. In the narratives concerning the patriarchs this is emphasized beyond all else.

With slight variations in phraseology this statement is five times repeated in Genesis. Besides its first occurrence, already noticed, it is uttered by Five times Yahaweh to Abraham at the time of his inter- repeated cession for Sodom,[1] and at the time when he has been commanded to sacrifice Isaac.[2] After the death of

[1] "Seeing Abraham shall surely become a great and strong nation, and all the nations of the earth shall be blessed in him" (Gen. xviii. 18 JE²). Note how formally the two separate parts of the promise are here distinguished.

[2] "I will greatly bless thee, and will greatly multiply thy seed, as the stars of the heaven, and as the sand that is upon the edge of the sea; and thy seed shall take possession of the gate of his enemies; and in thy seed shall all the nations of the earth bless themselves" (Gen. xxii. 17–18 JE²).

Abraham it is repeated to Isaac.[1]   Finally, we are told
that when Jacob started for Paddan-aram, Yahaweh repeated it to him at Bethel, where he saw the angels
ascending and descending.[2]   In these passages the difference between "nations of the earth" and "families
of the ground" seems to be unimportant.   The presence
of the "seed" in some of the passages, and its absence
from the others, makes no real difference in the meaning.   The difference between the variant phrases "be
blessed" and "bless themselves" is not significant.
What is significant is the fact that the promise is thus
five times repeated, the clause concerning the nations
being each time in the climacteric position.   Irrespective of position, its more noble meaning would give it
superiority to the other specifications, but it has the
dignity of position also.   As the whole promise to
Abraham and his seed is the central fact in our record
of the patriarchs, so the clause of blessing to mankind
is set forth as central in the promise itself.   That is the
heart of the heart of the book of Genesis.

In a form quite different the promise to mankind is
Father of a   emphasized in the transaction in which
multitude of   Abram's name is changed to Abraham, at
nations   the time when the covenant of circumcision
was made : —

"Behold my covenant is with thee, and thou shalt become father
of a multitude of nations. . . .   And thy name shall be Abraham,

[1] "Sojourn in this land, and I will be with thee . . . ; because to thee and
to thy seed I will give all these countries; and I will establish my oath
which I sware to Abraham thy father; and will multiply thy seed as the
stars of heaven, and will give to thy seed all these countries; and in thy
seed shall all the nations of the earth bless themselves" (Gen. xxvi. 3–4
JE⁸).

[2] "The earth upon which thou art lying, I will give it to thee and to thy
seed.   And thy seed shall be as the dust of the earth, . . . and in thee

because I have given thee to be father of a multitude of nations"
(Gen. xvii. 4, 5 P).

The phrase, "multitude of nations," here used, is entirely
different from "assembly of nations," "assembly of peoples," used elsewhere to denote the federated tribes of
Israel, springing from Abraham; and is analogous to
"all the nations of the earth" in the form of the promise
which we have been considering. Paul is correct when
he cites this passage in proof that the Gentile Christians
are children of Abraham (Rom. iv. 16–18, 11–12).[1]

shall all the families of the ground be blessed, and in thy seed" (Gen.
xxviii. 13–14 J).

[1] The old version does not distinguish the phrase here used from
Ephraim's filling the nations (Gen. xlviii. 19), or from the phrases concerning the federated Israel (xxviii. 3, xxxv. 11, xlviii. 4), but the word used is
entirely different. "Assembly" is a limited word. Some populations
have a right to be represented in any given assembly, and others have
not. "Multitude" is an unlimited word.

It is through their failure to discriminate that some have here charged
Paul with an accommodating interpretation. Paul is arguing to prove that
Abraham is —
"the father of all of them that believe, though they be in uncircumcision"
(Rom. iv. 11).
His argument is: —
"To the end that the promise may be sure to all the seed; not to that
only which is of the law, but to that also which is of the faith of Abraham,
who is the father of us all (as it is written, A father of many nations have
I made thee) before him whom he believed, even God, . . . Who in hope
believed against hope to the end that he might become a father of many
nations, according to that which had been spoken, So shall thy seed be"
(Rom. iv. 16–18).

At first blush one might say that Abraham's being made father of a multitude of nations must have the same meaning with the clause, "I will make
nations of thee," which occurs in the next verse in Genesis. But it is more
reasonable to regard the latter as a specification under the former. As in
the five passages in which the promise is verbally repeated, the statement
of Abraham's relation to the nations is accompanied by specifications subordinate to it. One of these is that nations will descend from him. But
his being father of a multitude of nations is parallel with all the nations

The promise for the nations is further emphasized by what the narrative says concerning the seed of Abraham. Among the subordinate items, those touching the seed are especially connected with the principal item, and are especially emphasized. The " seed " appears in a twofold character : it is associated with Abraham as the recipient of the promise, and is itself a crowning part of the promised blessing ; [1] and in both these characters it is the indispensable link for the transmission of the promise. Abraham's anxieties and trials are mostly concerning his seed. It is through his seed that the nations are to be blessed (xxii. 18, xxvi. 4, xxviii. 14).[2]

The prom-ised " seed "

---

being blessed in him, and not with his being the progenitor of numerous descendants.

[1] Paul in the New Testament keeps up this distinction. Sometimes he uses the term " the seed " to denote the Christ, the great benefit promised, and sometimes to denote the beneficiaries, those whom he calls " the heirs of the promise," whether Jews or believing gentiles.

[2] It may be assumed that Abraham at first thought of Lot as his heir, and thus as the seed that had been promised. From the time when Lot left him he is anxious concerning the seed. Directly after that, his seed is associated with him in the promise : —

" All the land which thou seest, to thee will I give it, and to thy seed forever " (xiii. 15).

When Lot remained separate from Abraham, after he had been rescued from the four kings, we find the following record (Gen. xv. 2–6) : —

" And Abraham said, O Lord Yahaweh, what dost thou give me, as long as I am going childless, while the son of possession of my house is Damascus Eliezer? And Abraham said, Behold to me thou hast not given seed, and behold the son of my house is my heir. And behold the word of Yahaweh was unto him, saying, This one will not be thine heir, but one who will come forth from thy bowels will be thine heir. And he made him go forth out of doors, and said, Look, pray, toward the heaven, and count the stars, if thou art able to count them. And he said to him, So shall thy seed be. And he was wont to believe in Yahaweh, and he counted it righteousness to him."

So the promise to Abraham becomes one that is to be fulfilled through his

The promise of the nations is emphasized in what is said concerning the covenants between Deity and Abraham. Two formal covenant transactions are described, — that in which Yahaweh's symbol of fire passed between the parts of the sacrifice (xv), and that when circumcision was instituted (xvii). In each the covenant is in confirmation of the promise, and with especial reference to the "seed." The connection with the promise is implied in the narrative of the covenant of the parts; the covenant of circumcision is explicitly connected with Abraham's change of name, and so with his relations to the multitude of the nations. Clearly the covenants are concerned with the larger purpose of Deity to bless mankind through Abraham, and not exclusively with his narrower and subordinate purposes.

The covenants and the promise

The one especially condensed and comprehensive statement of the substance of the covenant, as the matter appears in the records of the later history, is that Israel is to be to Yahaweh for a people, and Yahaweh to Israel for God; in other words, that Israel is Yahaweh's peculiar people. Perhaps it is not, though it ought to be, superfluous to say that the word "peculiar" in this familiar phrase denotes, not a people different from other peoples, but God's own people. In the patriarchal times, when Israel had not yet become a people, this formula appears seldom, and only in part; but a part of it appears in con-

The peculiar people and the promise

posterity, and here the faith of Abraham centres. In the subsequent record the birth of Ishmael, the promise of Isaac, his birth, the plan to offer him as a burnt-offering, all emphasize this idea of the seed of Abraham as connected with the promise. It is the seed that shall constitute the promised nation of federated nations. In a meaning considerably different, though not inconsistent, Paul argues that the believers from the "multitude of nations" are also Abraham's seed, since they have him for father.

nection with the covenant of circumcision, and at the renewal of the covenant with Jacob.[1]

The covenant is simply the promise in a different form. Yahaweh constitutes himself the God of Abraham and Israel, their God in a peculiar sense, not for their sakes alone, but for the sake of mankind. It is thus that the seed of Abraham is to be the channel of the divine blessing to all the nations.

3. We do not properly understand the bearings of the promise as thus emphasized, unless we note with care the fact that it is declared to be eternally operative. We have seen that the New Testament lays great stress on this. In so doing, it merely echoes the representations found in Genesis. According to both alike, the promise and the covenant and the seed are eternal.[2]

The promise eternally operative

[1] "That I may give my covenant between me and thee, and may multiply thee very exceedingly, . . . Behold my covenant is with thee, and thou shalt be father of a multitude of nations, . . . And I will establish my covenant between me and thee and thy seed after thee, to their generations, for an eternal covenant, to be to thee for God, and to thy seed after thee. . . . And I will be to them for God" (Gen. xvii. 2, 4, 7, 8). After this follows, with much reiteration of similar language, the establishing of circumcision, with the promise that Isaac shall be born, and that —

"I will establish my covenant with him, for an eternal covenant to his seed after him" (xvii. 19).

See also Jacob's vow at Bethel : —

"If God will be with me, and will keep me in this way that I go, . . . and Yahaweh will be to me for God, then this stone which I have set up for a pillar shall be God's house" (xxviii. 20–22).

[2] "For all this land which thou art beholding, to thee I give it, and to thy seed, unto eternity" (Gen. xiii. 15).

"And I will establish my covenant between me and thee and thy seed after thee, to their generations, for a covenant of eternity, to be to thee for God, and to thy seed after thee" (xvii. 7).

"And I will give to thee and to thy seed . . . all the land of Canaan, for a possession of eternity, and I will be to them for God" (xvii. 8).

Observe that the promise does not mean precisely the same that it would if this idea of eternity were not connected with it.   If Abraham's retainers and Therefore of friends thought that this promise had been progressive made to him, they thought that it was fulfilled fulfilment when Isaac was born.   But inasmuch as they were informed that the fulfilment was to be eternal and cosmopolitan, they must have regarded the birth of Isaac as only the beginning of it.   They looked forward, far forward, to additional fulfilment.   The promise would be operative in the future in a never ending line of descendants ; it would be operative in ever widening limits till the blessing had reached all nations.   The idea of a progressive fulfilment is inherent in the promise itself ; it is not the afterthought of a later time, contrived for the obviating of difficulties.   Whoever at the outset understood the promise at all must necessarily have understood it in this way.

It might occur to any one as significant that these passages employ the word " seed," a collective noun in the singular, to denote Abraham's descendants for the never ending time to come — never any plural noun, such as "sons," for example.[1]   Presumably this is not

" The one born in thy house or bought with thy money shall surely be circumcised, and my covenant shall be in your flesh for a covenant of eternity " (xvii. 13).

" And thou shalt call his name Isaac, and I will establish my covenant with him, for a covenant of eternity to his seed after him " (xvii. 19).

" And I will give this land to thy seed after thee, a holding of eternity " (xlviii. 4).

" And he called there on the name of Yahaweh, God Eternal " (xxi. 33).

[1] In the Hebrew the word is never used in the plural in the sense of posterity.   The Aramaic sometimes pluralizes it when used in this sense (e.g. Targ. of Gen. iv. 10), but in the promise passages follows the Hebrew usage, and uses the singular only.   Sometimes, however, in the Aramæan dialects, the word "son" is used instead of seed in translating these passages.

accidental.   The word thus chosen designates the whole line of Abraham's descendants as a unit, and marks their whole future history, without limit of time, as a single movement.   The expression is elastic, and not rigid.   It is flexible for denoting either one person or many persons, and it represents Abraham's posterity as a unit, whether the thought be concerning one or concerning many.   If the record had used the phrase, "the sons" of Abraham, that phrase would not have been thus flexible.

The seed a continuing unit

As this view might naturally suggest itself to any one, so it actually suggested itself to the apostle Paul.   His argument in Galatians is to the effect that the word used in Genesis contemplates the descendants of Abraham as a unit, the Christ being the dominant part of the unit. His reasoning is scholarly and correct, though it is not what a good many understand it to be.[1]

[1] "To Abraham were the promises spoken, and to his seed. He saith not, And to seeds, as of many ; but as of one, And to thy seed — which is Christ."   "What then is the law ?   It was added because of transgressions, till the seed should come to whom the promise hath been made" (Gal. iii. 16, 19).

These words are often cited as an instance of rabbinical misinterpretation by Paul.   They would be so if his argument were that the word is in the singular number, and therefore refers to the one person Christ, to the exclusion of the descendants of Abraham in general.   But, as we have seen, this is not the nature of Paul's argument.   He argues from the fact that the scriptural author uses a collective noun in the singular, instead of some plural noun which he might have used, to designate the descendants of Abraham, and thus indicates that the "seed," from Isaac to the end, is to be thought of as a unit.   Then Paul counts Jesus Christ as preëminently this unit, but not to the exclusion of the other members of it.   And of course Paul is correct, provided his estimate of the greatness of Jesus is correct.

Note that Paul here presents the dual relation of the seed to the promise, as we have above alluded to it.   In this passage, Christ the seed is the benefit promised ; while the descendants of Abraham, both lineal and spiritual, are the seed to whom the benefit is promised.   And

II. Two particularly important problems connect themselves with this presentation as made in Genesis. The first of these concerns the critical character of the presentation itself. The second concerns the contemporary understanding of it.

1. In the first place, whatever may be one's personal point of view in a matter like this, one needs to look at it from the different points of view held by others. And on any critical theory now held, the views just stated as to the presentation made of the promise in Genesis have in them at least an important residuum of truth.

The older view is, of course, that the accounts in Genesis are at least virtually of Mosaic authorship, and that whatever they affirm as historical fact is something that actually occurred. On this theory the statements in Genesis concerning the promise-doctrine have the simplicity and strength of pure fact. Certain critical theories now prevalent teach that Moses wrote nothing that has come down to us; that our book of Genesis is a conglomeration, produced in different centuries long after Moses; that the earliest parts of it were based on oral legends, and confuse fact with fiction; that the writers of the later parts deliberately imported into the narrative the ideas of their own times.

The old view versus the Modern View

The difference between these two views is not unimportant. It is especially to be considered because of the attitude of the men of the New Testament. No one doubts that they held essentially to what has just been described as the older view. I know of no sufficient reason for thinking that they were mistaken. Nevertheless

if any one finds in this a confusion of thought, at least the thought is intelligible when we recall Paul's habit of mystically identifying Christ with believers.

it is worth while to inquire what the promise-doctrine in Genesis becomes on the basis of the other view. The question is not, notice, what the scholars of the so-called Modern View teach concerning the promise, or whether they have taken enough interest in it to formulate a doctrine. We ask, rather : What is the logical bearing of the recent critical theories on the promise-doctrine as presented in Genesis ?

Our conclusions as above reached do not depend entirely on any one view as to the inspiration or the critical or historical character of the penta- teuch. If one holds that this literature is ancient and is genuinely historical, these are propositions to be affirmed on their own merits ; but we are not compelled to argue them as preliminary to our study of the messianic doctrine in Genesis. Our interpretation is not tied by any logical necessity to this view of the case. The most important elements in it stand unimpeached even if one goes far in accepting the opinion that the book of Genesis is of late origin and of doubtful historicity. On this basis the Genesis presentation of the promise becomes greatly emaciated, but that in it which is most essential survives.

These con- clusions in the light of recent criticism

It is obvious that the view we have taken of the promise depends not at all on the question of author- ship, provided the recorded facts are correct. Suppos- ing the record to be true, it is so whether made by Moses or by others. If any one holds that it was written after the exile, but that it is authentic history, we have no need, for our present purpose, to argue the matter with him. If the history of the promise given to Abra- ham and repeated to Isaac and Jacob be authentic, that is all we need. So far as our present use of it is con- cerned, it makes no difference when the history was written, provided only it is true history. The argument depends on the facts, and not on the person who recorded them.

This point, however, is not very important, because most persons who deny the early origin of Genesis deny also its historical truthfulness. A more important thing is that we may in thought separate this theological doctrine concerning the promise from the external details which the narrative connects with it. I do not care to make the obvious point that one might find the doctrine to be theologically true, even though he regarded its literary setting as fiction. A different point is that the fact of this doctrine being known and taught in Israel in the earliest times does not necessarily depend on the historicity of the details. It follows that the most important parts of our position might remain intact, even if one held that there are such uncertainties concerning the authorship of Genesis as to cast doubt upon the facts there recorded. Suppose one should even go to the extreme in this, counting the narratives in Genesis as not history at all, but as fiction written for the purpose of theological teaching; at least, the theological doctrine is there — the doctrine that Yahaweh anciently chose Israel to himself for his own people, that Israel might be his channel of blessing to all the populations of the earth. Even those who question the historicity of the records cannot question the fact that this teaching concerning the promise is one of the ancient doctrines of the religion of Yahaweh, dating as far back as that religion can be traced.

The doctrine *versus* the details of it

The scholars who analyze the hexateuch into documents hold that a good deal of the matter in Genesis concerning the promise, including one or more of the five repetitions of it, are from the writings which they designate J or E, that is, from the very earliest of the written sources of the Old Testament.[1] From their point of view it may not be a fact that the ancestor of the Israelitish nation actually received a divine call with this promise to mankind in it, but it is a fact that the earliest prophets whose teachings are now extant taught that he received such a call. That is, this idea of the matter was in existence in Israel from the earliest times concerning which we have information.

It was known in the earliest times

Other parts of the matter connected with the promise, these scholars attribute to the sections of Genesis which they regard as of later authorship. The logical inference from this is that when the alleged later writers in Genesis came to deal with the writings of their predecessors, they were so impressed with this promise-doctrine, as they found it there, that they enlarged upon it, and emphasized it by much repetition.

Whatever critical view we take, therefore, we are confronted with this immensely important fact, — that at the very beginning of the recorded history of the religion of Israel the prophets were teaching this promise-doctrine, the doctrine that Yahaweh was in communication with mankind through Abraham and his seed, and that through them he had promised distinguished blessing to all nations. They were teaching that this had been the supreme fact in Israel from the

---

[1] These scholars differ much as to matters of detail. The *Hexateuch* attributes Gen. xii. 3 and xxviii. 14 to J ; and xxii. 18, xxvi. 4 to a supplementer of JE ; and xviii. 18 to a J supplementer later than JE. Driver everywhere assigns more to J and E without qualification than do the critics who analyze more minutely than he. Ball, in the Polychrome Bible, shows a tendency to assign the promise passages to late supplementers.

time when Israel had his beginning in Abraham. They were teaching that this was what the seed of Abraham was for, that it was for this that Yahaweh had made them his own people.

2. In the second place, we ask the question : What was the contemporary understanding of this doctrine ?

We have gone over the record of the patriarchal times. It is the record of an eternal covenant, made by an eternal God with Abraham and his seed to eternity, signalized by the change of name from Abram to Abraham, having the nature of a promise, and having its principal force in the statement that in the seed of Abraham all mankind is to be blessed. The passages that give this record are not one or a few, but many. The book of Genesis so persists in repeating declarations of this sort as to make it evident that they are regarded as the utterance of a political and religious doctrine of the highest importance. This doctrine is reiterated at every turn of the narrative. It is brought into connection with each stage of the lives of the patriarchs. It is treated as the key to all the historical and biographical statements that are made.

This is the record of that which, in the New Testament and in Christian tradition, is referred to as messianic prediction, or, to speak more correctly, as messianic doctrine. How was this doctrine understood by the men to whom it first came ? As the knowledge of it existed in their minds, what did it mean ?

Assuming that the history is authentic, what did the contemporaries of Abraham understand to be the meaning of the promise ? Or, assuming the standpoint of the so-called Modern View, what did the Israelites of the century before Hosea understand to be the meaning of the promise ?

We do not ask, observe, how Abraham or Jacob or others who may have had prophetic gifts understood the matter; whether they saw all that we think we see in the revelation that was made through them. As men commonly estimate the prophets, we have no means of knowing to what extent their knowledge may have been modified by special inspiration. It has been generally believed that Deity may have given them a far-reaching foresight of the future. It was not beyond the power of the divine Spirit to enable Abraham to look forward and see every incident in the personal life of Jesus. But we have no information as to how far such inspiration was granted to the patriarchs and prophets, and it is better not to let such an uncertain element enter into our study. And on the other hand it would be of no account to ask how the promise seemed to unsympathetic persons, who took no interest in it. The proper question to ask is how it seemed (or, if you hold the other view, how the prophets who first taught it thought it seemed) to uninspired but devout and intelligent persons of the patriarchal times. How did it seem, for example, to Eliezer of Damascus, or to some other circumcised servant of Abraham, who had received just such information as we now find in Genesis and no more?

The proper form of the question

Necessarily, he found in it an element of prediction. In the uttering of it something was foretold. Every promise is a prediction. This promise was the foretelling of something that should happen to the posterity of Abraham and to mankind for ages to come, to time unlimited. From the time when it was first given it was doubtless thought of as something by which future ages would

Contemporaries understood the promise as a prediction

be able to test God's ability to reveal coming events. Those who first heard it might reflect that in no long time men would begin to verify this miracle of fulfilled prediction, and that the verifications would thereafter continue to be made, eternally. This would make the promise the greater in their estimation. In this aspect of it, it would stir their imaginations, and set them to looking forward.

The fulfilment of the promise hitherto, if it has had one, has been accomplished in the history of Israel; and, according to the claim of the men of the New Testament, that which is greatest in the history is that which has entered in and through Jesus Christ. Apart from miraculous inspiration, however, there is no reason to think that a contemporary of Abraham would form in his mind a distinct picture of the details that have entered into the history. He would have no detailed expectation, for example, of a person living and dying in Palestine, many centuries in the future, and doing there the things that Jesus did. His thought would contain no materials for constructing beforehand personal biographies of Moses or David or Jesus, or for constructing accounts of Israel's ancient conquests, or of the dispersion among the nations, or of Israel's modern glories won in finance and art and learning and statesmanship. If this is what you mean by prediction, or by messianic prediction, then there is none of it in Genesis.

Nevertheless the promise is essentially and necessarily predictive. Its devout though uninspired contemporary could not help seeing it to be so. As it was for eternity, he would expect that the events included under it would still be in progress, whatever their nature, hundreds of years in the future. If he happened to fix his mind on the date that we now designate as 28 A.D., he would be certain that the descendants of Abraham would then be living, would be in relations with the land of promise, would be in some form carrying forward God's plan of blessing for men.   There would be nothing to exclude from his conception such facts as those concerning Jesus.   We need not take the trouble to say how far the first promulgators of the promise understood the contents of the messianic doctrine that was revealed through them ; how far they had foresight of the future, or knew the ways in which Yahaweh's plan for the nations was to be carried out.   At least they regarded themselves as cognizant of the fact in general; they understood enough to make them see that Yahaweh's choice of Israel brought responsibilities upon themselves and their generation.

It is worth while to note, at this point, that the men of the New Testament, in all that they say concerning the promise to Abraham, do not claim that it was predictive in any other sense than that just indicated.

Probably, however, the predictive aspect of the promise-doctrine was not greatly emphasized by the earliest teachers and recipients of it.   In the main, the promise was to them of the nature of religious doctrine.   The book of Genesis presents it as a matter of practical preaching, rather than as prediction.   The ostensible purpose is to give information bearing on conduct, rather than to make known things to come.   As the teachings of the New Testament give the promise a central position, so it is in Genesis the central and commanding article of theological dogma.   Its earliest student found in it a great religious fact, holding the same place in his theology that the fact of Christ holds in ours, something to be believed and taught and practised for purposes of cur-

But rather as a practical religious doctrine

rent living; a doctrine that could be preached, and made pivotal in all attempts at religious persuasion.

The thought of sin and of redemption is basal in all religions. In both the New Testament and the Old it underlies messianic doctrine at every point. It characterizes the narratives in Genesis, and it connects itself with the promise; though perhaps by implication rather than by direct statement. The men to whom it first came were conscious of being sinners. However crude their ideas of sin may or may not have been, they had this consciousness. To them the promise was something that looked forward into the future, and was for eternity; but it was also for the present. They themselves were of the tribe of Abraham, and they were entitled to their present share in that which had been promised. In short, the promise constituted for them just such a basis for faith and for moral and spiritual character as the Christian of to-day claims that he possesses in Christ.

As thus explained, the promise was to these earliest recipients and teachers of it something immeasurably more than mere prediction, though its predictive value is not thereby diminished. It was spiritual bread for them to feed upon. Accepting the promise for just what lies in its terms, irrespective of the contents with which future history might fill it, it would serve the purposes of practical faith and spiritual nourishment. A person who had some idea of the infinite personality of God; who held that God had purposes of blessing to the whole human race, and had laid upon himself and the family to which he belonged both the honor and the responsibility of guarding and transmitting this grace, had a theology that would serve the purposes of an evangelical faith. Independently of the question how minutely he understood the details of God's plan, he had a good intellectual basis for moral and spiritual character.

How could one better influence Abraham's tribe and their descendants than by indoctrinating them with this truth? by making them feel that they were God's chosen people, chosen for the benefit of all the nations? by awakening within them the religious experiences which this truth ought to awaken? They might thus be led to faith and repentance and hope and love and obedience; might be so brought under the power of these gracious truths that they should thereby be comforted in sorrow, restrained from yielding to temptation, nerved to fidelity in times of testing.

What is said in the book of Genesis concerning the blessing of Abraham certainly includes prediction; but it is essentially not prediction but instruction. The very core of the book is the affirmation that Abraham and his posterity are eternally God's peculiar people, not for their own sake, but for the sake of the nations. This teaching is ethically lofty, but it is not recondite nor obscure. It is level to the comprehension of even a barbarous intellect. Any man who wanted to do right could understand what it meant, and could feel the persuasive power of it. It was the heart of the theology of Israel from the time of the earliest recorded doings of the prophets. The New Testament writers are correct in finding it in the old record, and correct in identifying it with the gospel which they themselves preached. Paul made no mistake when he spoke of the gospel "given beforehand to Abraham."

CHAPTER X

In tracing the history of the promise-doctrine in the Old Testament, we have already recognized the necessity of confining ourselves to relatively a few instances, belonging to the great representative periods. In the preceding chapter we have covered briefly the times of the patriarchs. The present chapter must be made to cover, however inadequately, the times of the exodus and of David.

I. We begin with the time of the exodus. Do we find that the promise through Abraham and Israel to the nations is made conspicuous in the record of this period?

1. The promise to Israel, constituting Israel Yahaweh's peculiar people, is much emphasized for the times of the exodus.

The covenant formula, " Ye shall be to me for a people, and I will be to you for God," of which we found barely a hint in Genesis, is very abundant in "To me for a the writings that treat of the exodus. Take people" an example or two: —

" And I will take you to me for a people, and will be to you for God, and ye shall know that I am Yahaweh your God, the one bringing you out from beneath the burdens of Egypt " (Ex. vi. 7).

" For thy passing into the covenant of Yahaweh thy God and into his oath which Yahaweh thy God is making with thee to-day; in order to establish thee to-day to him for a people, while he shall be to thee for God, according as he hath spoken to thee, and according as he sware to thy fathers, to Abraham, to Isaac, and to Jacob" (Deut. xxix. 12–13).[1]

In the accounts of the exodus a new form of statement appears for indicating this relation between Yahaweh and Israel. They are said to be father Yahaweh's and son. The phrase is used sparingly. son Israel's peculiar relation of sonship is not made very prominent. The matter is significant chiefly for its foreshadowing the diction of the history of the later times. Nevertheless it is distinct, and should not escape notice.[2]

To the same effect might be cited all those hexateuchal institutions which have it for their purpose to keep Israel separate from the other nations. I ab-Hexateuchal separative stain from specifying. No fact is more famil-institutions iar than that a large part of the hexateuch is made up of legislation of this sort. A full treatment of this point would require us to go through the six books.

---

[1] Other instances may be found in Deut. xxvi. 17–19; Lev. xxvi. 12, etc. Instances which offer the first half of the formula, without the second, are Deut. iv. 20, etc. Instances which offer the second half of the formula only are Ex. xxix. 45 ; Lev. xi. 45, xxii. 33, xxv. 38, xxvi. 45 ; Num. xv. 41, etc. The instances here cited are all from sections which are assigned to either P or D.

[2] The following are the instances : —

"And thou shalt say unto Pharaoh, Thus saith Yahaweh, Israel is my son, my firstborn ; and I have said unto thee, Let my son go, that he may serve me ; and thou hast refused to let him go ; behold I will slay thy son, thy firstborn" (Ex. iv. 22–23 J).

"Thou hast seen how that Yahaweh thy God carried thee, as a man carrieth his son, in all the way that ye went" (Deut. i. 31).

"Do ye thus requite Yahaweh,
O people foolish and not wise ?
Is not he thy father that bought thee ?
Himself made thee and prepared thee" (Deut. xxxii. 6).

For the times of the exodus, as for the patriarchal times, much stress is laid on the assertion that Yahaweh's promise and covenant are in force to eternity.[1] In the records of these times this assertion takes on a new form; namely, that the benefits of the promise are irrevocable even for sin. This is a fresh way of affirming that it will be forever operative.

The promise for eternity, and irrevocable

Ordinarily Yahaweh's promises to men are conditioned on obedience. Even the promises of eternal blessing to Israel are thus conditioned (*e.g.* Deut. iv. 40, xii. 28). In some passages it is perhaps fairly implied that the

---

[1] "To the end that it may be well to thee, and to thy sons after thee, unto eternity" (Deut. xii. 28).

"That it may be well to thee, and to thy sons after thee, and that thou mayest prolong thy days upon the ground which Yahaweh thy God giveth thee, all the days" (Deut. iv. 40).

At the burning bush : "I AM THAT I AM. . . . Yahaweh the God of your fathers . . . hath sent me unto you : this is my name to eternity, and this is my memorial to generation and generation" (Ex. iii. 14-15).

The requirement upon Israel concerning the sabbath is : —

"To observe the sabbath throughout their generations for a covenant of eternity ; it is a sign between me and the sons of Israel to eternity" (Ex. xxxi. 16-17). Here observe the threefold repetition of expressions for eternity.

It is to the same effect that a large proportion of the Levitical ordinances are said to be eternal. "It shall be a statute of eternity to you : in the seventh month, on the tenth day of the month, ye shall afflict your souls." "It is a statute of eternity." "This shall be a statute of eternity to you" (Lev. xvi. 29, 31, 34). These words are spoken of the great annual sin offering. Similar statements are made in regard to the ordinary sin offering, the wave breast and the heave thigh, the single place of sacrifice, the ceremonies connected with the firstfruits (Lev. vi. 18, vii. 34, 36, xvii. 7, xxiii. 14, 21).

These are but instances. Like instances are very numerous. Make whatever allowance may be due for any supposed modifying of the idea of eternity, and it still remains true that the record insists on future time without limit as characterizing the covenant and the promise and the laws based thereupon.

promise to Abraham and Israel for the nations is conditioned on Israel's obedience. However this may be, there are a few remarkable passages in which the promise is expressly declared to be unconditional — not to be forfeited even by disobedience. In Leviticus, for example, we find a series of terrible denunciations of punishment upon Israel in retribution for sin, and this is followed by these words : —

> " And yet for all that, when they be in the land of their enemies, I will not reject them, neither will I abhor them, to destroy them completely, and to break my covenant with them ; for I am Yahaweh their God. And I will remember for them a covenant of first things, how I brought them out from the land of Egypt in the eyes of the nations, that I might be to them for God " (Lev. xxvi. 44–45).[1]

It is not difficult to solve the verbal paradox involved in thus declaring this promise to be both conditional and unconditional. So far forth as its benefits accrue to any particular person or generation in Israel, it is conditioned on their obedience. But in its character as expressing God's purpose of blessing for the human race, we should not expect it to depend on the obedience or disobedience of a few. So we are not surprised to find passages in which the other aspect of the case appears. Israel may sin, and may suffer grievous punishment ; but Israel shall not become extinct, like other sinning peoples. The promise is for eternity, and Israel shall be maintained in existence, that the promise may not fail.

---

[1] Perhaps certain passages in the parallel series of threatenings in Deuteronomy (xxix–xxx) should be also so construed as to make them unconditional. The following passage certainly should be so construed, though the old version and the margin of the revised version make it conditional : —

" When thou art in tribulation, and all these things are come upon thee, in the latter days thou shalt return to Yahaweh thy God, . . . he will not fail thee, neither destroy thee, nor forget the covenant of thy fathers, which he sware unto them " (Deut. iv. 30–31 RV).

Incidentally but importantly connected with the great promise, as it appears in the records of the exodus, is the subsidiary promise that Yahaweh will give The rest-Israel rest, and will choose a place for his name promise to dwell in.[1] This promise is reiterated in the records, making it conspicuous. It constitutes a significant matter of detail under the great promise. But it becomes especially significant later as a link of connection between the time of the exodus and the time of David.

2. In all this we find a record of a great promise to Israel; but is it also taught that Israel's vocation is for the benefit of mankind? The answer to this question must be that this is taught in these records, though less persistently than in the history of the patriarchs.

In Deuteronomy occurs the following representative statement : —

"Yahaweh will establish thee to him for a holy people, according as he hath sworn to thee; for thou shalt keep the com- That man-mandments of Yahaweh thy God, and walk in his ways, kind may and all the peoples of the earth will see that the name know of of Yahaweh hath been called upon thee, and will be Yahaweh afraid from thee" (Deut. xxviii. 9–10).

In explicitness such a statement as this falls far behind the patriarchal statement that in the seed of Abraham all the nations shall be blessed ; and yet it implies relations between Deity and Israel and the nations. At least, the

---

[1] "And he said, My presence shall go, and I will give thee rest" (Ex. xxxiii. 14). Driver is in doubt whether to assign this to J, with Dillmann, or, with Wellhausen, to the compiler of JE.

"For ye have not as yet come in unto the rest and unto the inheritance which Yahaweh thy God is giving thee; and ye shall cross the Jordan, . . . and he will give you rest from all your enemies from round about, . . . and there shall be the place which Yahaweh your God shall choose to cause his name to dwell there" (Deut. xii. 9–11). Add Deut. xii. 14, 21, xxv. 19, etc., and Deut. iii. 20; Josh. i. 13, 15, xxi. 44, xxii. 4, xxiii. 1. Cf. Ps. xcv. 11; Heb. iii–iv. The passages in Joshua the critics assign to D.

nations shall recognize Yahaweh's name as "called upon" Israel.   They shall do this so distinctly that they will be filled with wholesome fear.   To this extent, at least, Israel is to transmit to the nations the monotheism of the religion of Yahaweh.

Another group of passages is represented by the following : —

> "For thou art a holy people to Yahaweh thy God.
> His own, out Yahaweh thy God hath chosen thee to him to be his
> of all the
> peoples own people more than all the peoples that are upon the
> face of the ground" (Deut. vii. 6, repeated without
> essential variation in xiv. 2).

In a moment we will pay some attention to the meaning of the phrase "his own" as here used.   We now only attend to the fact that Yahaweh is here represented as having relations with all mankind, and as having mankind in view when he separates Israel to himself to be his in a peculiar sense.   This is equally the meaning of the words, whether you translate "more than all the peoples," or "out of all the peoples."

The same is taught yet more distinctly in an earlier passage.   In the account of the transactions which A kingdom preceded the giving of the "ten words" on of priests Mount Sinai is a brief message which stands by itself, being in the form of thirteen short balanced lines of verse.   The consideration of this belongs in our chapter on the Kingdom, but we may now attend to one phrase in the message.   Yahaweh is represented as saying : —

> "Ye shall be mine, my own, out of all the peoples.
> For mine is all the earth,
> While ye yourselves shall be mine —
> A kingdom of priests and an holy nation" (Ex. xix. 5–6).[1]

[1] Driver regards this as from E "in the main."   Others make it to be late matter, supplementary to JE.

In thus proposing to adopt Israel as his own, Yahaweh has all the nations in mind, so he says.   This does not utterly differ from saying that he chooses Israel for the benefit of all the nations.   Further, he has his covenant in mind, the covenant with Abraham, of course, in virtue of which all the families of the ground are to be blessed eternally.   Yet further, Israel, in being a separate nation, is to be a "kingdom of priests."   The function of a priest is to mediate between a people and the God they worship ; that is, Israel is to be a mediatorial nation.

Of course this interpretation will be disputed.   It follows, however, the natural meanings of the words ; and it is the interpretation which we accept in the four places in the New Testament in which our Exodus text is cited (Rev. i. 6, v. 9, 10 ; 1 Pet. ii. 5, 9).   These passages regard Christian believers as inheriting this promise.   They teach that we are " unto our God a kingdom and priests," that we "are an elect race, a royal priesthood, a holy nation, a people for God's own possession," to the end that we may transmit the divine blessing to others.   And there is no reason for saying that in

The word here translated " my own," *s' gullah,* is an unusual word, occurring eight times only in the Old Testament.   David is represented as using it when he says that he has given of his own, that is, of his private property, for the building of the temple (1 Chron. xxix. 3).   It is used in Ecclesiastes to denote that which is so fine that only kings have it for their own (ii. 8).   The other five instances are repeated from this place in Exodus.   Four times Yahaweh is spoken of as having chosen Israel " to be to him for a people, his own " (Deut. vii. 6, xiv. 2, xxvi. 18 [19]; Ps. cxxxv, 4).   In Malachi is a promise to faithful Israelites : —

" And they shall be mine, saith Yahaweh of hosts, for the day which I am making, my own, and I will have compassion upon them as a man hath compassion upon his son that serveth him " (iii. 17).

In this last passage the King James version renders " my jewels."   Elsewhere the English versions render " peculiar people," " special people," " peculiar treasure," " mine own possession."

this they are guilty of either misquotation or misinterpretation.

This view of the case is strongly confirmed by the fact that the promise made at the exodus is regarded as a continuation of that made to the patriarchs.   This warrants the inference that it was not thought of as radically changed in character.

Whatever is done for Israel in the time of Moses and Joshua is represented as in continuity with what was done in the earlier time.   Moses comes with the words : " The God of your fathers hath sent me unto you " (Ex. iii. 13).   This idea and this phraseology are repeated at every turn of the narrative.[1]   Already we find in the recorded history of Israel this peculiarity, that it is simply the unfolding of the promise made to Abraham.

Continuity with patriarchal times

The continuity becomes the more marked when we observe the stress that is laid in this history on the statement that the covenant made with the patriarchs is still in existence.   At the outset it is said of the oppressed Israelites in Egypt : —

A continuous covenant

" And God heard their groaning ; and God remembered his covenant with Abraham, with Isaac, and with Jacob " (Ex. ii. 24 P).[2]

It is true that Yahaweh represents himself as publicly entering into a fresh covenant, at the bringing of Israel

[1] " Yahaweh the God of your fathers, the God of Abraham, the God of Isaac, and the God of Jacob hath sent me unto you : this is my name forever, and this is my memorial unto all generations."

" Yahaweh the God of your fathers, the God of Abraham, of Isaac and of Jacob, hath appeared unto me, saying, I have surely visited you " (Ex. iii. 15, 16).

Driver assigns these sections to E, but verse 16 to J.

[2] As additional instances note Deut. xxix. 12–15, 25, and the following : —

" I am Yahaweh.   And I appeared unto Abraham, unto Isaac, and unto Jacob, as El-Shaddai, and by my name Yahaweh I was not known to them.   And I also established my covenant with them, to give them the

out of Egypt; indeed, as making more than one such covenant; but it is possible to understand these transactions as the renewal and perpetuation of the covenant with Abraham; and this is clearly the intended understanding.

That the supreme end of Israel's mission is his being the channel of Yahaweh's blessing to all peoples is persistently repeated in Genesis, both in the covenant passages and elsewhere. That this idea is present in the transactions of the exodus is an inference demanded by the continuity of the transactions, unless there be something in the records to exclude it. As we have seen, there is nothing to exclude it, and there is much to confirm it. Israel's separation to Yahaweh is for the benefit of the nations. If this is not here so insisted on as in Genesis, it is at least entirely clear. The God of all mankind takes thought for the interests of mankind, in what he does for Israel. If this is not here so much reiterated as in Genesis, it is at all events not left entirely in the background.

To this it might be objected that it supposes in Israel a benevolent feeling toward the nations quite inconsistent with the harshness he was required to show to the Canaanites and Amalekites, and in some cases to other peoples. We cannot now stop to discuss this problem on its merits. For the purposes of the present argument it *The harshness toward the Canaanite and Amalekite, etc.* is sufficient to say that the alleged instances of harshness are exceptional. It was to be exercised toward a

land of Canaan, the land of their sojournings, wherein they sojourned. And also, I have heard the groaning of the sons of Israel, . . . and have remembered my covenant " (Ex. vi. 3–5 P).

"For Yahaweh thy God is El, a compassionate one ; he will not fail thee, and will not destroy thee, and will not forget the covenant of thy fathers, which he sware to them " (Deut. iv. 31).

few only of the many peoples known to Israel. As
a rule the international policy of Israel was to be liberal
and generous, even while it involved religious separation.
The laws for the stranger and the sojourner, and the
provisions for incorporating foreigners into Israel by
the rite of circumcision, are familiar instances. Even
in the cutting off of the condemned nations, Israel
might supposably be rendering a service to the human
race.

It might be further objected that Israel never during
his history appears to have been actuated by the high
Only the few   ideal of having a mission to mankind. The
have the   reply is obvious. Only a few, relatively, of
highest ideals the hundreds of millions of Christians now
living give evidence of being greatly under the control
of the ideals set forth by Jesus. There is no difficulty
in supposing that the cosmopolitan promise-idea may
have been known and accepted by the devout few in
Israel, even in the times when its absence from the
thinking of the majority was most conspicuous.

3. As in the case of the preceding period, we meet
here the two questions: How must these statements of
fact be modified if one would make them fit current
critical theories? What was the contemporary understanding of the statements?

The scholars of the Modern View hold that all statements of fact in the bible in regard to the times of the
The case   exodus are untrustworthy. The history we
according to   have represents, they say, not the actual facts,
the Modern
View   but the ideas concerning the exodus which
were held by certain Jewish writers, some of them as
early as Hezekiah, others of Josiah's time, others still
later. It gives us, however, the earliest ideas concerning these times that have been anywhere preserved, the

oldest known conception of this part of the history of the religion of Israel. On the basis of this critical view, therefore, we are not entitled to say that the promise-doctrine was actually dominant in the minds of Israel's leaders when they came from Egypt, but only that this is the idea of the matter that appears earliest in Israelitish literature.

This view of the case is starved and meagre, but even this ought to count for something. These earliest writers on the subject, whoever they were, thought that Moses and his contemporaries thought that the covenant with Abraham and his seed was then still in existence; that in virtue of that covenant Israel was Yahaweh's peculiar people; that he was so in the line of Yahaweh's purposes for mankind; that he was thus Yahaweh's son; that this covenant and promise are eternal, irrevocable even if Israel is to the last degree disobedient. It is the same religious idea which we found dominating the history of the patriarchs; somewhat unfolded, indeed, with the progress of the centuries; less insistently cosmopolitan by reason of the existing situation; but still the same idea.

How did men then living understand this idea? How did they interpret the body of sacrifices and other institutions to which the idea gave shape? The The contemporary interquestion is not how it was understood by pretation Moses, for example, or by some other inspired man, who might supposably have all the details of the future history of redemption miraculously revealed to him. And the question is not how it was understood by one whose religious instincts had become atrophied, or by depraved or stupid or excessively ignorant persons. But how was it understood by an uninspired, though intelligent and devout, Israelite of the period? There is no reason to think that such an one saw in the covenant revelations of his time any premonition of a man who would some time live and be crucified in Palestine, to be the Saviour of men; what he saw in them was a religious doctrine, in the form of a promise from God, already for some hundreds of years in process of fulfilment, and to remain in process of fulfilment forever.

On any tenable theory of the rise and progress of civilization, such a doctrine was easily intelligible to persons of that period, and capable of influencing such of them as were open to ethical influences. And it appealed to the imagination. Yahaweh's covenant was for eternity. It was not to fail, no matter how perversely Israel might disobey, or how grievously he might be punished. Other races might be annihilated, but this race would not be. It should be perpetuated, that through it God's purpose of blessing for mankind might be unfolded. All this is prediction. It is an exhibition of divine foreknowledge in the making known of future events. It was so understood by those who first understood it. But it was more than prediction. It was doctrine, doctrine effectively preachable, for the guiding of the conduct of those to whom it came, for the awakening of their patriotism and their moral virtues, for the building up of their spiritual character.

II. Similar things are to be said concerning the promise as entering into the history of the time of David.

Next to the promise made to Abraham the New Testament magnifies as messianic doctrine the promise made to David. This needs no proof. Nothing is more familiar to readers of the New Testament than the idea that the Christ is the son of David.

The classical Old Testament passage concerning this is the seventh chapter of 2 Samuel, with its duplicate, the seventeenth chapter of 1 Chronicles.   It The classical is the account of David's proposing to build passage a temple to Yahaweh, and the message he received concerning it through Nathan the prophet.   Few Old Testament incidents are more familiar.   Nathan at first acceded to the king's suggestion, but afterward brought a message from Yahaweh forbidding David to build the temple.   No reason for the prohibition is given in this passage, though elsewhere (1 Chron. xxii. 8) David's being a man of battles is mentioned as a reason.   Along with the prohibition Nathan brought to David a promise, which is spread out in several verses, and which so affected David that he " went in and remained before Yahaweh," with adoration and with supplications in view of the wonderful honor conferred upon him.

What was this honor?   An average reader of the bible would probably say that it consisted in David's being told that his son should build the David's temple which he himself was forbidden to house which Yahaweh build.   But to say this is to substitute a sub- will build ordinate matter of detail for the principal fact. him The central thing is this : that in response to David's thought to build Yahaweh a house (5b), Yahaweh will make David a house.   This is emphasized by reiteration, the house that Yahaweh will make for David being eight times mentioned in this short passage.[1]   Its nature is indicated in the context.

[1] " And Yahaweh telleth thee that Yahaweh will make to thee a house " (11b).

" For thou, Yahaweh of hosts, the God of Israel hast uncovered the ear of thy servant, saying, A house will I build for thee " (27).

" Thy house and thy kingdom shall be made sure forever before thee " (16).

1. It is explained that David's "house" is the line of descendants which Yahaweh will give to him (12, 16, David's 19, 26, 29). The promise to David, like the "seed" promise to Abraham, is a promise of a "seed," though this word is used but once in the chapter (12). That the seed is not one person only, but a line of descendants, appears from the eternal duration assigned to him and his activities. This line of descendants is the essential feature of the promise.

(*a*) Incidentally it is said that the "seed" shall build the proposed temple (13), that is, that it shall be built The temple by some member of the house of David, by builder some one of his eternal line of descendants. We naturally and correctly infer that the temple builder is to be the first successor in the line. But this becomes merely incidental; the main thing is the eternally enduring house and throne promised to David. The temple building is mentioned only once in Nathan's message, and not at all in David's utterances before Yahaweh. Although the project for building the house furnishes the occasion for the giving of this promise, David has not a word to say about temple building, when he goes in before Yahaweh. Evidently the other parts of the promise seemed to him so important as to throw this into the background. Temple building, important as it was, was eclipsed by the larger thought that had suddenly come to fill David's mind.

"Thou hast spoken also concerning thy servant's house for a far time" (19).

"The word which thou hast spoken concerning thy servant, and concerning his house, cause thou it to stand forever" (25).

"The house of thy servant David being made ready before thee" (26).

"And bless thou the house of thy servant . . . may the house of thy servant be blessed forever" (29).

Besides these eight instances, the idea is repeated in other language.

(*b*) The thing emphasized in regard to the line of David's descendants is that they shall be kings, having a kingdom, sitting on a throne (12, 13, 16, 16). A line of One item of the promise for the times of the kings patriarchs and of the exodus was, as we have seen, that Israel should be a kingdom, and should have kings (Gen. xvii. 6, 16, xxxv. 11, *cf.* xxxvi. 31 ; Ex. xix. 6; Num. xxiv. 7, 7), and it is clear that the kingdom here assigned to David's family is the kingdom of Israel (23, 24, 26, 27). The Chronicler calls it Yahaweh's kingdom (1 Chron. xvii. 14).

(*c*) Equal stress is laid — and here again the promise to David parallels that to the patriarchs and to Israel of the exodus — on the affirmation that David's line the Davidic line of kings and their kingdom and kingdom are eternal, this being an irrevocable divine eternal purpose.   Besides other ways of expressing this, the word "forever" is used three times in the message of Nathan, and five times in the utterances of David before Yahaweh, being applied six times directly to David or to his seed.[1]

In the record of the times of the exodus we have found certain passages in which Yahaweh's great promise is declared to be irrevocable even for sin. The same phenomenon appears in the accounts of the

---

[1] "I will establish the throne of his kingdom forever" (13).

"Thy house and thy kingdom shall be made sure forever before thee ; thy throne shall be established forever" (16).

"Thou hast established to thee thy people Israel, to thee for a people forever" (24).

"And now, Yahaweh God, the word which thou hast spoken concerning thy servant and concerning his house, establish thou forever, . . . that thy name may be great forever" (25, 26).

"Bless the house of thy servant that it be forever before thee, . . . and out of thy blessing let the house of thy servant be blessed forever" (29).

promise to David.   Although it is sometimes presented
as conditioned on obedience (*e.g.* 1 Chron. xxviii. 7 ; Ps.

The promise irrevocable even for sin
cxxxii), it is also, in other places, declared to
be beyond recall even in case of disobedience.   In the original narrative, for example,
Yahaweh is represented as saying : —

> "And I will establish the throne of his kingdom forever. I will
> be to him for a father, and he shall be to me for a son ; in whose
> being perverse I will correct him with a rod of men, and with stripes
> of sons of man, while my loving kindness shall not remove from
> him, as I removed it from with Saul, whom I removed from before
> thee. And thy house and thy kingdom shall be made sure forever
> before thee " (13b–16a).

The explanation of the paradox is doubtless the same as
in the earlier instance : any member of the line of David
may by sin forfeit his own share in the promise, but he
may not forfeit that which belongs to his successors to
eternity.

2. But is there anything to indicate that the promise
to David is for mankind, like the promise to Abraham
and to Israel ?

In answering this question much depends on the
closeness of the identification we make between this
transaction and the earlier promise-transactions.   If
the promise to David be a renewal, with further unfolding, of the promise made to Abraham and renewed
at the exodus, then we naturally infer that it has
the same scope as they in its relations to mankind.
There is nothing in its terms to exclude the nations.
Their right to a share in it is therefore proved, provided
it is the continuation of the older promise.

At the outset we must notice the fact that this chapter does not explicitly mention Abraham, as do the
records of the time of the exodus.   There is no sharp

statement to the effect that Deity called Abraham to the end that all families of mankind might be blessed in him, and that he now extends the same call to David. Nevertheless the promise to David abundantly identifies itself with that to Israel, and therefore with that to Abraham, since these last two are identical.

We have already noted certain points of identification. The seed of David is the seed of Abraham and of Jacob. It is a royal seed as Yahaweh had promised that theirs should be. We have again the great characteristic of the promise, that it is for eternity and irrevocable. But there are yet other points of identification more specific than these, and on that account perhaps even more convincing.

The account in the seventh chapter of 2 Samuel begins with the implication that David was familiar with the line of hexateuchal passages which say that Yahaweh would give Israel rest from his enemies round about (Deut. xii. 10, 9, xxv. 19, etc.). This is repeated a few verses further on, in the same Deuteronomic phrase,[1] with the additional Deuteronomic statement that the rest has come through Yahaweh's cutting off of Israel's enemies (Deut. xii. 29, etc.), this being elaborately connected with the situation existing when the promise was given.[2] In the

The Deuteronomic rest-promise

---

[1] " The king dwelt in his house, Yahaweh having given him rest from round about from all his enemies."

" I am giving thee rest from all thine enemies " (1, 11).

[2] " And I have been with thee whithersoever thou hast gone, and have cut off all thine enemies from before thee, and am making for thee a great name, as the name of the great ones who are in the earth, and am setting a place for my people Israel, and am planting them, and making them to dwell in their place, and they no longer tremble, nor do sons of mischief continue to afflict them as formerly, even to from the day when I put judges in charge over my people Israel" (9–11, cf. 1 Chron. xxii. 9, 18, xxiii. 25, xxviii. 2; 1 Ki. v. 4 [18]; 2 Chron. vi. 41; Ps. cxxxii. 8, 14, etc.).

Deuteronomic passages it has been promised that when
Yahaweh has thus cut off Israel's enemies and given
him rest, then Yahaweh will choose a place where his
name shall dwell (Deut. xii. 11, 14, 21, etc.). Evidently
the record gives us to understand that David believed
that Yahaweh had now at length chosen Jerusalem as
the place where his name should dwell, this being the
circumstance that led David to think that the time was
come for the building of a permanent temple (2 Sam.
vii. 13 ; 1 Ki. viii. 16; 2 Chron. vi. 4–7, etc.).

Further, as the phrases "to be to thee for God, and
to thy seed after thee," "and I will be to them for
God," first appearing in the promise to Abraham (Gen. xvii. 7, 8), are expanded for the
time of the exodus into a more complete formula (*e.g.*
Deut. xxvi. 17–18), and are much used, so we find this
formula prominent in the account of the Davidic promise.
The formula appears here in direct terms,[1] and the idea
appears several times in phraseology that is less technical. It is Israel's God that David finds himself dealing
with in this matter. We are told that it is "Yahaweh
of hosts, the God of Israel," that has uncovered David's
ear (27). Other like phrases are used.[2] And indeed,
even without these specific phrases, any one can see
that the promise to David concerns his kingdom, and
that his kingdom is Israel.

Among the clauses that mention Israel as Yahaweh's

The peculiar
people idea

---

[1] " And thou wilt confirm to thee thy people Israel, to thee for a people
forever, thou Yahaweh being to them for God " (24).

" Like thy people, like Israel, . . . to ransom to himself for a people,
. . . thy people which thou didst ransom to thee from Egypt " (23).

[2] " I am setting a place for my people Israel " (10).

" And may thy name be great forever, to say, Yahaweh of hosts, God
over Israel; the house of thy servant David being meanwhile established
before thee " (26).

peculiar people, those in the twenty-second and twenty-third verses are especially marked in their "One nation hexateuchal phraseology.   The statements in the earth" are not entirely clear, but the verses are evidently made up of phrases taken from the accounts of the exodus.[1]   At the opening of the twenty-third verse the English versions translate, "What one nation in the earth is like thy people Israel?"   This fails to convey the true meaning.   The question, "Who are like thy people, like Israel, one nation in the earth?" is odd in form, whether in Hebrew or in English, and its oddity identifies it as a quotation.   The plural verb in the clause "whom Elohim have gone" presents a construction that is unusual.   Clearly the sentence is based on a passage in Deuteronomy that offers the same two peculiarities : —

"For who are a great nation which hath Elohim that draw near unto it like Yahaweh our Elohim in all our calling unto him?   And who are a great nation that hath righteous statutes and judgments like all this *torah* which I am giving before you to-day?" (Deut. iv. 7–8).

The writer here represents David as echoing the peculiar diction of Deuteronomy.   The clauses that follow can best be made intelligible by regarding them as similar echoes, and filling out the meaning by the aid of the contexts from which they were taken.

In these various ways David is evidently represented as thinking of the time of the exodus, and of Israel's being constituted Yahaweh's people in a peculiar sense,

[1] "For there is none like thee, and there is no Elohim besides thee, altogether as we have heard with our ears.   And who are like thy people, like Israel, one nation in the earth whom Elohim have gone to ransom to him for a people, and to set for him a name, and to do for you that which is great, and terrible things for thy land, from before thy people which thou didst ransom to thee from Egypt?"

and is identifying the promise to himself with that transaction.

In the records of the promise at the exodus, as we have seen, Israel is sparingly called the son of Yahaweh. This form of expression comes into prominence in the record of the time of David : —

David's seed Yahaweh's son

"I will be to him for a father, and he shall be to me for a son " (14).

This statement is made emphatic by the clauses which follow, telling how Yahaweh will treat David's son, in view of their paternal and filial relation.

In the respects thus far mentioned the promise to David is clearly in continuation of that to Abraham and Israel, both in its contents and its dic- tion.   An additional instance of parallel dic- tion occurs in the twelfth verse : —

Other mat- ters of diction

"Thy seed after thee, which shall come forth from thy bowels."

The first half of this expression is not very common in the bible, but it occurs five times in one of the promise chapters in Genesis (xvii. 7, 8, 9, 10, 19).   The second half occurs only here and in the Abrahamic promise (Gen. xv. 4), and twice elsewhere (2 Sam. xvi. 11 ; 2 Chron. xxxii. 21).   It would not be safe to build upon such an item as this, if it were unsupported ; but, taken in connection with the rest of the case, we may infer that these two phrases in Samuel were borrowed from Genesis.   Not to delay for other instances, the passage in Samuel is throughout by its diction brought into continuity with the record of the times of Abra- ham and of the exodus.   Its echoes of the penta- teuchal phraseology are not much less numerous than its verses.

We look at one more phrase. By position it is the climacteric clause of David's statement of the case when he went in before Yahaweh. Its meaning is The *torah* of concealed in the English versions by impos- mankind sible translation. Rendered with strict literalness this clause and its duplicate in Chronicles read as follows : —

"This being the *torah* of mankind, O Lord Yahaweh!" (2 Sam. vii. 19).

"And thou art regarding me according to the upbringing *torah* of mankind, O Yahaweh God!" (1 Chron. xvii. 17).[1]

In these texts "this" ought logically to mean the revelation recorded in the context concerning the "seed" of David, who is to exist and reign forever, Yahaweh's son, Yahaweh's king. "The *torah* of mankind" naturally denotes a well-known revelation which Yahaweh has made concerning mankind. "The upbringing *torah* of mankind" can only mean Yahaweh's *torah* for the uplifting or exalting of mankind. It is presupposed that David has a knowledge of something which he describes in this phrase — something so great as to be the crowning fact in the honor Yahaweh is bestowing upon him.

[1] The following are the current renderings : —

"And *is* this the manner of man, O Lord GOD?" (Old Ver.).

"And this *too* after the manner of men, O Lord GOD!" (Rev. Ver.).

"And is this the law of man, O Lord GOD?" (Rev. Ver., Marg.).

"And hast regarded me according to the estate of a man of high degree, O LORD God."

None of these renderings are of the nature of simple translation. Each includes an explanation, and one that is conjectural instead of being drawn from the context. All are false in syntax. Three of them give to the word *torah* the absolutely anomalous rendering "manner," "estate." All neglect the fact that the law denoted by *torah* is regularly divine law. The verb in Chronicles is not a present-perfect, but is either a future or a continuative present.

See *Journal of Biblical Literature*, VIII, 137.

What is this "*torah* of mankind," this "elevating *torah* of mankind"? Was David thinking of some matter of petty personal exaltation? The context shows that his mind was fixed, with deep emotion, on the thought of Yahaweh's having chosen Israel to be his peculiar people; and that it was more or less occupied at the moment with the phraseology in which the ancient promises had been given. In the circumstances, the expression "the *torah* of mankind" must have a broad and high meaning. The most natural understanding is that David recognizes in the promise just made to him a renewal of the ancient promise of blessing for mankind. His eternally reigning line of descendants, Yahaweh's king, Yahaweh's son, is to be also Yahaweh's channel of benefit to all the nations. For this fact we are not left to mere inference; it is explicitly affirmed in this clause concerning the *torah* of mankind. The mere process of putting together the logical elements of the clause gives us a meaning so simple and so rich that its very simplicity and richness cause some natural hesitation about accepting it. There is no sufficient reason, however, for not accepting it. There is no escaping the conclusion that the narrative represents that David recognized in the promise made to him a renewal of the promise made of old that all the nations should be blessed in Abraham and his seed.

As in the treatment of the earlier periods, we pause for an instant to inquire what this record becomes on the basis of certain theories of criticism now prevalent. Stenning (*Dic. of the Bib.*) assigns 2 Sam. vii to a writer of the E school, living about 700 B.C., but also assigns it to a much later Deuteronomistic editor. Kuenen and Well-

What this becomes on the basis of certain critical views

hausen both regard it as preëxilian.   Stade (*Encyc. Bib.*) is sure that the Deuteronomist who wrote it was postexilian.   The men of this school would agree that the statements of fact made in this chapter are untrue, whether they date from about 700 or 600 or 400 B.C.   But there still remains this remarkable phenomenon : that the prophets or scribes, whatever their date, who wrote the history of David, had this idea of David's relations to the promise.   The idea either is or is not true to fact. If not true to fact, then it is a product of imagination so wonderful as to demand careful study.

Such, then, is the promise for the time of David, as the records describe it.   Had this promise any clear meaning to an Israelite of the time when it was given, supposing that Israelite to be uninspired but intelligent, and a devout believer in the idea that Yahaweh makes promises and afterward fulfils them?   If it had a meaning, what did it mean?   The meaning can be nothing else than that David would have as his posterity an unending succession of kings, one of whom, presumptively the first, would build the temple, while through the whole line would be fulfilled eternally the promise made of old to Abraham and Israel.   This meaning is simple, is as comprehensible to men of one age as to men of another, and is required by the words as recorded.

Contemporary interpretation

In other words, this man of the time of David, or, if you will, of the later time when some unknown scribe invented the account, understood that the promise made to Abraham was still in existence, and that Israel was still entitled to its benefits, but that henceforth its central fulfilment was to be along the line of the royal descendants of David.

He would understand that it was of the nature of pre-

diction, prediction that had already been gloriously verified, especially in the then recent conquests made by
David, but looking forward to still more glorious fulfilments in the future. He would understand that the
future glorious events which were to occur under it
would be events in which all mankind would have an
interest. He would doubtless infer a divine foreknowledge, made manifest through the prophets. If we may
suppose him to be asked concerning affairs in Palestine
at the then future date which we now designate 28 A.D.,
we should hardly expect him to be able to narrate details concerning Jesus ; but we should expect him to
reply that the great promise would at that date still be
working itself out, in Palestine, and especially through
the line of David.

Nevertheless it must have been true that the contemporaries of the first publication of the promise to
David, while they regarded the promise as a genuine
prediction, yet mainly looked upon it as religious teaching rather than as a foretelling of the future. Here
was a great fact concerning God's relations to men —
a truth for the prophets to teach and for the people to
feed upon ; a truth suitable for purifying and stimulat-
ing their loyalty, for controlling their conduct, for the
building of character.

CHAPTER XI

THE PROMISE-DOCTRINE OF THE PROPHETS AND
PSALMISTS

WE have found that the narratives of Genesis include an account of the revealing of a divine promise to Abraham and Isaac and Jacob. The narra- Recapitula-tives of the exodus describe a renewal and tion continuation of that revelation. They declare Israel to be Yahaweh's son, his own people, a kingdom of priests and a holy nation. In this Yahaweh claims the whole earth, and makes Israel a priestly nation, thus declaring afresh that the election of Israel is for the benefit of mankind. To David the promise is again renewed, and especially vested in his seed, the interest of mankind in it being again affirmed.

We are now to inquire how these traditions concerning the promise were regarded by the prophets of David's time and later — the prophets who A new phase wrote the Psalms and the historical books and of the subject the wisdom books, as well as those who wrote the so-called prophetic books. In their writings the covenant promise to Abraham, to Israel, to David, is perpetually insisted upon. The prophets who were David's contemporaries or successors constantly appeal to the promise as made to him, interchangeably with the promise as made to Abraham and to Israel. To such an extent does this teaching affect the Psalms, the prophetic addresses, and even the historical statements, that there is no way of considering it more briefly than by studying the Old Testament through.

The messianic material in these writings is so abundant that it could be exhausted only by a treatment that should cover the entire writings. Directly or indirectly, nearly all that they say is somehow connected with the promise.

As with the contemporaries of Abraham and Moses and David, so with the successive generations of prophets that followed them, in the matter of the use they made of the promise: it had at any given time a twofold character; it was a standing prediction of the time to come, and it was an available religious doctrine for the time being. In their hands the messianic teaching was always anticipative, always looking forward, always not yet fulfilled, though it had been fulfilling for ages. Yahaweh's purpose in it was for eternity, with unfoldings that reached endlessly into the future. But the promise, to the Israel of David's time and later, as to their predecessors, was after all religious doctrine rather than prediction. It was a dogma which they had inherited from the past. If we have thus far rightly understood the matter, we should expect to find these prophets using this dogma, very prominently, in religious instruction and appeal, for the temporal and spiritual benefit of their contemporaries. Precisely this is what we actually find. Their theology centres in the promise. This is the spiritual bread with which they feed the souls of the men of their day.

Both a prediction and a dogma

They had this as the great doctrine of their religion: that Yahaweh had made Israel to be peculiarly his people; had vested this relation centrally in the royal line of David; had done this for purposes of blessing to mankind — purposes that had already been unfolding for centuries, and were on the way to an ever larger unfolding. Henceforth this messianic doctrine, preached by the prophets, sung in the Psalms, built into the temple, rising with the smoke of every sacrifice, the great quickener of Israel's conscience, the bulwark against idolatry, the protection of patriotism from despair, the comfort under affliction, the warning against temptation, the recall to the wandering; in short, a doctrine of salvation offered to Israel and every Israelite; more than this, Israel's missionary call to the nations, inviting all without exception to turn to the service of Yahaweh — is this doctrine of the promise of blessing, made to Abraham and Israel, renewed in David and his seed, to be eternally without recall, and including the human race in its scope.

The messianic passages in the writings of the prophets are mostly the repetition, the unfolding, the supplementing, or the homiletic use of the promise, as given either to Abraham, to Israel, or to David. This is their gospel, as the same *The messianic passages homiletic* promise in a more advanced stage of fulfilment is the gospel that we preach in the twentieth century. It varies in the different stages through which revelation passes, and yet is uniform in its essential character throughout the Old Testament.

Descending to particulars, we will consider some of the modes in which the prophets present this doctrine, and some of the points in it which they principally emphasize.

I. First, their modes of presentation are such as we should expect in a homiletical literature that preserves, in prose or poetry, the substance of sermons actually preached.

In this literature there are a large number of passages which are capable of being understood as disconnected predictions of the experiences of a Person who was to appear at a certain time in the future, for the Predictive passages redemption of Israel and mankind. Instances of these, in very large number, are given and argued in the older works that treat of the argument from prophecy (*e.g.* Pss. ii, xvi, xxii, cx). It may be that some of these are genuine instances of disconnected prediction, though most of them, when studied in their contexts, appear to the mind in new aspects. Most of them should not be regarded as disconnected predictions, but as shoots from a common stem — the common stem being the body of connected messianic promise-history which we have been examining. Very many of them have a certain quality of universalness, in virtue of which they are capable of being understood as direct forecasts of a coming personal Messiah. That is to say, they are so constructed that their original setting may be left out of the account without the effect of perverting their meaning. In a large proportion of its conclusions the older apologetic is virtually correct, in spite of its neglect of the local elements of the problem. But even the instances of this kind yield more satisfactory meanings when examined in connection with their relations to the central promise.

In some cases the so-called prediction occurs in a continuous discourse, but loosely connected with it. The promise as a sermon-text or a proof-text The messianic statement may be used as a text on which the contiguous discourse is based. Isa. ii–iv, for example, is a sermon, based on the messianic prevision of ii. 2–4 as a text. Or the promise-passage is used as we use a proof-text, for illustrating or confirming something in the discourse. For example, an Israelite bard sings (Ps. xvi. 10) : —

" For thou wilt not abandon my soul to sheol,
  Thou wilt not permit thy *hhasidh* to see corruption. "

For the meaning of the term *hhasidh*, see Chapter XIV. In this passage the singer assumes that it is a well-known truth that Yahaweh's *hhasidh* will not see corruption, will never cease to be; and so, identifying himself with the *hhasidh*, he expects immortality.   He cites this well-known truth for confirming his own faith in Yahaweh.[1]   To mention but one more instance, the promise to David is called to mind to emphasize Manasseh's wickedness in using the temple for idolatrous purposes (2 Chron. xxxiii. 7).

To a limited extent the preachers and singers of Israel repeat the formulated phrases that accompanied the original giving of the promise.   Jeremiah promises that if Israel will return and be faithful, " then nations shall bless themselves in him " (iv. 1–2).   The forecast of the future of David's dynasty, as found in the seventy-second psalm, culminates in the words : —

Repetitions of the old phrases

" Yea, all nations shall bless themselves in him,
  Shall call him happy " (17).[2]

[1] This view is entirely consistent with the use made of the psalm in Acts ii. 25, 27, 31, and xiii. 34–37.

[2] Whatever differences of opinion there may be concerning this psalm, no one doubts that it is a song concerning the seed of David.   The versions translate the cited couplet thus : —
  " And [men] shall be blessed in him,
    All nations shall call him happy."
But " nations " is placed where the subject of the first of the two verbs ought to be placed ; and the structure of the psalm, as found throughout, requires that the two verbs have the same subject, and that it be expressed with one, and implied with the other.
  The fact that these passages echo the phraseology of Genesis is not changed even if one regards the phrase " bless themselves " as here indicating merely a recognition of Israel or of the Davidic king, rather than an expectation of receiving a blessing.

With these two passages compare a third, in which the same diction is echoed, though with a different idea.

"So that he who blesseth himself in the earth shall bless himself in the God of truth" (Isa. lxv. 16).

And in changed form we find the Abrahamic phrase in the twenty-first psalm : —

"Thou settest him to be blessings forever" (ver. 6, marg. of RV).[1]

These instances of the use of the promise phraseology will serve for illustration. Others will be found abundantly in what is said in this chapter concerning the interest of the nations in the promise, and in what is said in future chapters concerning the messianic terminology.

A more conspicuous mode of use appears in passages or complete poems which take the promise made to David as a theme, amplifying parts of it, and making variations upon it. In these cases the treatment is sometimes very formal.

Amplifica-
tions

Take, for example, the accounts of the preparation for the building of the temple. A single passage must suffice, though similar marks characterize the records throughout.

"Behold a son born to thee. He it is that will be a man of rest, and 'I will give rest to him from all his enemies round about.' For Solomon shall be his name, and I will give peace and quiet upon

[1] The prophets often refer to the call of Abraham without expressly mentioning the blessing for the nations. Note an instance or two.

"Look unto Abraham your father . . . for ·when he was but one I called him, that I might bless him, and make him many" (Isa. li. 2).

"And their seed shall be known among the nations,
    and their offspring in the midst of the peoples,
All that see them shall recognize them,
    that they are a seed that Yahaweh hath blessed" (Isa. lxi. 9).

Israel in his days. 'It is he who shall build a house to my name.'
'And he shall be to me for a son, and I to him for a father.'   'And
I will establish the throne of his kingdom' over Israel 'forever'"
(1 Chron. xxii. 9–10).

The clauses here included in single commas are quoted,
with slight variations and transpositions, from the language of the promise to David as recorded in 2 Sam. vii.

The same method appears in the account of the dedication services of the temple, in Solomon's address and
prayer on that occasion (1 Ki. viii. 15–21, 24–26, and
2 Chron. vi. 4–11, 15–17).   In the prayer, Solomon
pleads God's faithfulness in the temple-building item
of the promise as an earnest that God will equally
accomplish the wider promise of the perpetuity of the
royal line of David.

The eighty-ninth psalm is perhaps the most notable
instance of this habit of amplification.   This poem mentions the promise to David through Nathan, Ps. lxxxix as
with extensive verbal citations, insists espe- an instance
cially upon its being a promise which is to of amplifica-
endure forever, and makes it the basis of expostulation tion
with Yahaweh concerning the misfortunes that had
befallen the king then on the throne of David.   In its
middle section the psalm takes four or five clauses
from the narrative in 2 Sam. vii, and expands them into
stanzas aggregating thirty or forty lines.[1] Ps. cxxxii
might also be cited as affording a notable instance of
similar amplification.

The promise-doctrine appears in poems and addresses

[1] In this psalm the singer first states and expounds his theme (1–4).
The theme is stated in the first verse, The Faithful Lovingkindness of
Yahaweh.   In the third verse it is narrowed to the specific topic, Yahaweh's
Oath to David to make his Throne Eternal.

Having thus stated his theme, the singer abandons himself to a burst
of praiseful song in view of it (5–18), coming back in the eighteenth verse

that celebrate events.   The second psalm, for example,

celebrates a futile attempt of kings and nations to break away from the dominion of a king reigning in Zion.   The singer designates this king in terms of the promise.   He is Yaha-weh's Anointed, Yahaweh's Son, to whom the uttermost

to the thought of " our shield," that is, " our king," and his relations to Yahaweh.

Then, in verses 19–37, the singer takes up in detail the account of the giving of the promise to David.

19. " AT THAT TIME thou spakest in vision to thy kindly loved ones,
        and saidst : —
    I have laid help upon a mighty one,
    I have exalted one chosen out of the people,
20. I have found David my Servant,
    With my holy oil have I anointed him.
21. With whom my hand shall be kept ready,
    Yea, mine arm shall make him strong.

22. No enemy shall harass him,
    Nor son of mischief afflict him.
23. And I will beat down his adversaries from before him,
    And them that hate him will I defeat.

24. And my faithfulness and my lovingkindness being with him,
    And his horn being exalted in my name,
25. I will place his hand at the sea,
    And his right hand at the rivers.

26. He for his part shall call me, Thou art my father,
    My God, and the rock of my salvation.
27. Yea I for my part will give him to be firstborn,
    A most high one to the kings of earth.

28. To eternity will I keep for him my lovingkindness,
    My covenant being made faithful to him.
29. And I will place his seed for everlastingness,
    And his throne as the days of heaven.

30. If his sons forsake my law,
    And go not in my judgments,
31. If they profane my statutes,
    And keep not my commandments,

parts of the earth have been given.   Apparently it was originally written of a situation in the reign of David himself.   But it has that character of universalness of

32. Then will I visit their transgression with a rod,
    And their iniquity with stripes,
33. And my lovingkindness I will not break off from with him,
    And I will not be false in my faithfulness.

34. I will not profane my covenant,
    And the outgo of my lips I will not change,
35. Once have I sworn by my holiness:
    If I will be deceitful to David!

36. His seed shall be to eternity,
    And his throne as the sun in my presence;
37. As the moon that is made ready forever,
    And a witness that is faithful in the sky.

The remainder of the psalm is an expostulatory prayer to Yahaweh in behalf of the then reigning king of the line of David.   The singer says that Yahaweh, so far as appearances go, is not keeping this great promise made to David and his seed.   The living representative of David's blood, whom the promise entitles to be regarded as Yahaweh's Anointed, Yahaweh's Servant, has been cast off by Yahaweh.   His fortresses are broken down. He is a failure in war.   He is helpless.   His only recourse is to plead Yahaweh's " first lovingkindnesses " as expressed in his oath to David.

The thing to be here observed is, first, that every part of this psalm is based on the promise to David, and second, that the details of the quoted section of it are those of the passage recording the promise.

" At that time," *az*, verse 19, points to a definite occasion which the singer has in mind.   " Thou spakest in vision " is an echo of 2 Sam. vii. 17.   " Nor son of mischief afflict him," is copied from a clause in 2 Sam. vii. 10, while verses 20-25 of the psalm give the same situation with verses 9-11 in Samuel, and verse 19bc is simply a variant of verse 8 in Samuel.   In the following verses the phenomena are still more marked.

In the fourteenth verse in Samuel we find : " I will be to him for a father, and he shall be to me for a son."   This is expanded in the psalm into the four lines of verses 26-27.   In Samuel it is promised that if David's sons are perverse, Yahaweh will chastise them, but will not remove his lovingkindness from them.   The psalm enlarges this into eight lines (30-33).   And in verses 28-37 the eternalness of the transaction, so insisted upon in Samuel, is repeated in line after line, with the heavens and sun and moon and sky cited for illustration.

diction that marks so many of these messianic passages. The language might plausibly be applied to the reigning king of the line of David in any one of several different generations, with no need to change the phraseology to fit the situation. The apostles make no change in the words when they apply them directly to him whom they regard as preëminently Yahaweh's Anointed Son (Acts iv. 25–26, etc.).

The forty-fifth psalm is primarily a marriage song. In it the singer addresses the bride (10–12), and addresses three different kings (2–7, 8–9, 13–17). The king to whom the principal address is made (2–7) is presumably the reigning king of Judah. The singer thinks of him as the living representative of the promise, the contemporary occupant of the throne of David, which has been declared to be Yahaweh's throne (1 Chron. xvii. 14, xxix. 23 ; 2 Chron. ix. 8, xiii. 8). So the singer makes his climax in the form of a direct address to Deity : —

"Thy throne, O God, is for ever and ever " (6a).

The singer does not here address the Davidic king as God, but he speaks of him as of unique character in that the throne he occupies is God's throne on earth.[1] Whoever this king was, the singer's soul is filled with the thought of the eternal promise to David, and from this comes the great undertone of his song.

Two celebrated brief prophecies in which the prophet takes the promise to David as a theme, and works it out into glowing terms of encouragement for Israel, are those in Isa. ix. 1–7 and xi. 1–10.

Other modes of the teaching of the promise-doctrine by the prophets were through the originating of a some-

---

[1] This interpretation offers as perfect a logical basis for the reasoning of Heb. i. 8–9 as if the singer addressed the king as God.

what extended vocabulary of special terms, used in setting forth the doctrine, and collaterally through the institutions of Israel, including the prophets themselves as an institution.   To the special terminology we shall devote several chapters, and a chapter to the collateral lines of teaching.   *A technical vocabulary. Collateral presentations*

In regard to their modes of presenting the doctrine it remains to be said that they everywhere teach it more by presupposition than by express statement.   They take the promise for granted, as some-thing with which their hearers are acquainted, on which they may build at any time.   They regard it as public property.   The singer of the eighty-ninth psalm counts the vision as given not to Nathan or David alone, but to Yahaweh's *hhasidhim* in general.   *By presupposition more than by open statement*

"Thou spakest in vision to thy saints " (Ps. lxxxix. 19 RV).[1]

The promise idea is evidently thought of as to some extent familiar and well known.   This doubtless implies that the doctrine was more widely taught and under-stood than many suppose.   The prophets certainly used it just as we use religious dogma, for enforcing public and private duties.   The messianic passages commonly occur in the midst of connected discourse on current subjects.   Oftenest the messianic utterance is within some continuous treatment concerning Israel or Israel's king, and is itself an interwoven part of the treatment. Instead of mentioning the great promise, the prophets take it for granted as well known and needing no expla-nation.   Just as Christian ministers assume that their hearers are acquainted with the facts stated in the

[1] The King James version, following the Hebrew bibles that have been most in use, makes the noun singular, but there seems to be no room for doubt that the true reading is that in which it is plural.

gospels, so the preachers of the older Israel assumed that their hearers had some degree of familiarity with the promise that had been made to Israel, and they based their appeals on the knowledge which they thus presupposed in the minds of their countrymen. In all the variety of forms known to literature, the prophets presuppose and use the theme offered them in the doctrine of the promise made to Abraham, to Israel, to David.

II. To complete our view of their presentation of the doctrine, we need to glance at some of the points which they most emphasize. In doing this we shall have to take for granted some things that are reserved for fuller treatment in the next four chapters.

1. They identify the promise made to David with that made to Israel and that made to Abraham, some-
The three
promises
identical
times blending the characteristics of the three in a single presentation, passing without apparent consciousness of change from the promise in one form to the promise in another form. We have already passed under review several instances of this, and we shall find other instances. So, though we need just here to state the point by itself, we may dismiss it with the cursory mention of an illustration or two. We have found the seventy-second psalm, for example, bringing its panegyric on the line of David to a close by quoting the words of Genesis: "All nations shall bless themselves in him," in other words, by representing that the promise in and to the seed of Abraham is fulfilled in and to the seed of David. In the eighty-ninth psalm we have found the term "servant" applied to David. Elsewhere it is a few times applied to Abraham, but most commonly to Israel. This psalm contemplates David and his seed as a single

object of thought, and identifies this, in interest at least, with Israel. The writer in 2 Samuel says of Israel that sons of mischief no longer afflict him (vii. 10), and the psalm quotes this, applying it to the line of David (22). The psalm, in citing the passage in Samuel concerning sonship, mingles with it the Deuteronomic phraseology concerning the exaltation of Israel (Ps. lxxxix. 27; *cf.* 2 Sam. vii. 14; Deut. xxviii, 1, xxvi. 18, 19): —

> " Yea I for my part will give him to be firstborn,
> A most high one to the kings of earth."

2. The prophets and psalmists sufficiently recognize the cosmopolitan character of the promise.

That they habitually thought of the promise interests of Israel as centring in the line of David needs no further proof. That they habitually regarded the promise interest as something in which the nations were concerned is equally true, though less attention has been paid to it. The dogma which they inherited included the specification that Yahaweh's purpose was not for Israel alone, but for mankind. *[margin: They teach that the promise is cosmo-politan]*

This appears significantly enough in the passages cited above (Ps. lxxii. 17; Jer. iv. 1–2; Ps. xxi. 6a, marg. of RV; Isa. lxv. 16), in which the Abrahamic promise of blessing to the nations is connected with the destinies of Israel and of the house of David.

The cosmopolitan idea is elaborately wrought into the services that followed the completion of Solomon's temple. The fifth of the seven supplications in the dedicatory prayer on that occasion is as follows: — *[margin: The share of the nations in the temple]*

> " And also concerning the foreigner, who is not of thy people Israel, and shall come from a far land for the sake of thy name; for they will hear of thy great name and thy strong hand and thy

stretched out arm, and will come in and pray toward this house ; do thou thyself hear in the heaven, thy prepared dwelling-place, and do according to all which the foreigner shall call unto thee for, to the end that all the peoples of the earth may know thy name, for fearing thee as thy people Israel, and for knowing that thy name is called upon this house which I have builded " (1 Ki. viii. 41–43 ; *cf.* 2 Chron. vi. 32–33).

In verse 60 the plea is made : —

" To the end that all the peoples of the earth may know that Yahaweh is the God, there is none else."

This language is rendered the more significant by the fact that the plea is in the following verse transformed into a reason why Israel's heart should be perfect with Yahaweh, to walk in his statutes. This is what Israel is for, this extending of the knowledge and the fear of Yahaweh to the nations. These dedicatory utterances emphasize throughout the idea that Israel is Yahaweh's peculiar people. A dozen excerpts to this effect might be made, for example : —

" For they are thy people and thine inheritance, whom thou didst bring out of Egypt " (51).

The doctrine here taught is distinctly that which we have found at all points in our investigation; namely, that Israel, and centrally, Israel in the line of David, is Yahaweh's chosen eternal channel of blessing to man-kind. It is here taught that this is the divine plan, the plea of the Israelite when he approaches Yahaweh in prayer, his motive for fidelity to his God, his inspiration for achievements, his hope in the midst of calamities.

The interest of the nations in the temple is very strikingly presented in the passage from Isaiah which the gospels (Matt. xxi. 13 ; Mc. xi. 17 ; Lc. xix. 46) represent Jesus as citing : —

" Ho every one that thirsteth, come ye to the waters." " And let me make for you an eternal covenant, the assured lovingkindnesses of David." " And let not the son of the foreigner who hath joined himself unto Yahaweh say, Yahaweh hath utterly separated me from his people." " And I will bring them in unto my holy mountain, and will make them glad in my house of prayer, their burnt offerings and their sacrifices will be for acceptance upon my altar; for my house shall be called a house of prayer for all the peoples " (Isa. lv. 1, 3, lvi. 3, 7, and the whole context).

This is in accord with what is said about the nations going up to Jerusalem to worship at the feast of tabernacles (Zech. xiv. 16–21), and with other utterances which represent the nations as coming to worship, or as having the privileges of Yahaweh's people extended to them.[1]   In such utterances as these we have full proof that the prophets, with those of their auditors who were most in sympathy with them, were aware that the

---

[1] For example : —

" All nations whom thou hast made shall come in that they may worship before thee, O Lord, that they may do honor to thy name " (Ps. lxxxvi. 9).

" In that day shall Israel be a third country to Egypt and to Assyria, a blessing in the midst of the earth; whom Yahaweh of hosts hath blessed, saying, Blessed be my people Egypt, and Assyria the work of my hands, and Israel my inheritance " (Isa. xix. 24–25).

Cyrus is called " for Jacob my Servant's sake," but also " that they may know from the rising of the sun and from the west that there is none beside me."   In the same passage it is said that " in Yahaweh shall all the seed of Israel be justified, and shall glory "; and this is balanced by " Look unto me and be ye saved, all ye ends of the earth."   " By myself have I sworn . . . that unto me every knee shall bow, every tongue shall swear." " Even to him shall men come, and all that are incensed against him shall be ashamed " (Isa. xlv. 4, 6, 25, 22, 23, 24).   Here we have very emphatically the double truth that Israel is Yahaweh's own people and that Israel's greatness is for " all the ends of the earth."

In many other passages, in exceedingly varied phraseology, Israel is represented as destined to judge the nations, to give *torah* to the nations, to be the light of the nations, to accomplish other like offices (*e.g.* Isa. ii. 2–4, xlii. 1, 4, 6, xliii. 9, xlix. 6–7, lvi. 6, 8b).   Specific instances in abundance will come up for discussion in subsequent chapters.

nations had a share in the benefits of the promise as it was preached in Israel.

3. Further, the preachers and poets of Israel do not fail to recognize the eternal and irrevocable character of The promise the benefit promised. We have found the suc-
for eternity,
and irrevo- cessive narratives strongly characterized by
cable this, and the characteristic runs through to the close of the Old Testament. In proof, one might adduce most of the passages that have been cited in this chapter, and very many others. The biblical writers magnify the claim that the promise is for eternity. At every date their language implies that the promise has been fulfilled in the past, is in process of fulfilment in the present, and is on the way to larger fulfilment in the future.

Notice a few instances taken at random, most of them from passages already cited. The seed of David is to reign eternally (1 Chron. xxii. 10). The twenty-first psalm is an exultation in the mouth of an Israelitish king, who is represented as living and conferring blessings forever (RV of 4 and 6 marg.). In the various passages based on 2 Sam. vii, scores of instances might be gathered where the eternity of the promise to David is spoken of. In the eighty-ninth psalm, for example, the word *olam* is six times thus used, and other expressions for eternity still oftener. The comparisons with the sun and moon and sky, as the most durable objects known to men, are especially notable.[1]

In these writings, as in the narratives of the earlier

[1] " And I will place his seed for everlasting,
And his throne as the days of heaven " (29).
" His seed shall be forever,
And his throne as the sun in my presence,
As the moon that is made ready forever,
And a witness that is faithful in the sky " (36–37).

times, stress is laid on the statement, many times repeated, that, although the interest of individuals in it is
conditioned on obedience, the promise itself is irrevocable, even for the sins of its beneficiaries.   We have
already noted this in the eighty-ninth psalm : —

" If his sons forsake my law,
   And go not in my judgments,
   If they profane my statutes,
   And keep not my commandments,
   Then will I visit their transgression with a rod,
   And their iniquity with stripes,
   And my lovingkindness I will not break off from with him " (30–33).

Other instances, a few out of many, may be found in
1 Ki. xi. 36, 39; 2 Chron. xxi. 7 ; 2 Ki. xiii. 23 ; Isa.
lix. 20–21.

4. Very notable in the presentation of this matter by
the prophets is the habit which they formed of looking
upon Israel as the people of the promise.

In the circumstances such a habit was inevitable.
When one devotes much of his mental activity to some
one group of ideas, his ways of thinking and   Our objects
of expressing himself are affected thereby.   of thought
affect our
In particular, religious people come to have   forms of
their peculiar forms of thought, and their   thought
consequent peculiar uses of language.   We ourselves
ask in song : —

   " Are your windows open toward Jerusalem ? "

We sing : —

   " The hill of Zion yields
     A thousand sacred sweets."

We say of one who has a happy way of uttering his
religious experiences, that he speaks the language of
Canaan.   A member of a local congregation speaks of
a revival there as " God's blessing upon our Israel."

In particular, we, whose religion comes by ancestral descent from the Old Testament, use the proper name Israel with wide variations of meaning. By it we mean, sometimes the Israelitish race ; sometimes their ancient political organization ; sometimes their country ; sometimes their religious organization ; sometimes the spiritually minded among them ; sometimes the religious or social forces which they embody ; sometimes the Christian church ; sometimes the true church within the visible church ; sometimes the spiritual forces of Christianity ; sometimes a local congregation ; with a long list of other possible variations.   In any of these meanings we apply the term sometimes to the whole indicated by it, and sometimes to any part.   And all this variety indicates, not that we employ the term unintelligently, but rather that we treat it as a term widely used and familiar.   Our minds herein simply follow certain natural laws of human thinking.

These same natural laws of thinking were in operation in millenniums past as now.   In the Old Testament teaching of messianic doctrine there is this same assumption that the principal terms used are so familiar that they will be intelligible through a wide range of variation of meaning.   For example, the human channel through which the blessing is conveyed is sometimes spoken of as the person Abraham ; sometimes as the person Jacob or Israel ; sometimes as the person David ; sometimes as the progeny of Abraham and Israel taken collectively ; sometimes as the line of David's descendants ; sometimes as any one person in that line ; sometimes as Israel enlarged by the promised ingathering of the nations ; sometimes as the aggregate of the true believers within Israel ; and not seldom in terms that may

The same law in the thinking of the prophets

be applied to a coming Person of the stock of Israel and
of David. These writers count the promise to Abraham
as germinal. They find its unfolding in the history of
Israel and of the nations. In this unfolding it comes
perpetually into new historical relations. New portions
of its meaning are constantly opening to the light.
Some of the assertions they make concerning it apply
equally to its whole extent or to any part of it, while
others apply only to the particular part that is under
consideration at the moment. Certain statements are
true alike of Israel, of any true Israelite, of a personal
Messiah, of the church universal, of any believer; while
other statements are more restricted in their application.

There is one conception which existed in the minds
of the prophets, which we need to recognize with especial distinctness, because of its importance in $\quad$ Israel as the
the understanding of their utterances. They $\quad$ people of the
habitually thought of Israel as not merely the $\quad$ promise
population of their fatherland, but as Yahaweh's promise-
people; not merely from the point of view of patriotism,
but from that of religious doctrine. This fact is evident,
however it may have been overlooked. And the distinction is vital.

The mother of a certain distinguished man is said to
have been a woman of remarkable insight. The man
had an unpromising boyhood; but through all the
stupidity and wickedness of it, the mother recognized
the potentialities of greatness and goodness, and was
able to guide her son to their ultimate realization. All
the while she had in her thought two sons, — the actual,
unregenerate youth that he was, and the ideal person
who had in him the making of what she meant that
he should come to be. So to the prophet, the existing
ethnical aggregate known as Israel was, in reality, two

Israels. Israel looked at in his actual faultiness was one entity, while Israel as the embodiment of Yahaweh's promise was a different entity.

This is nowhere more marked than in the passages that use personal terms concerning future manifestations of the promise. Some of these passages we shall, later, consider more in detail. For the present we only note that while they sometimes speak of the Coming one as the chief product of Yahaweh's dealings with Israel, they quite as often make him to be Israel himself. Oftenest they use language which explicitly designates Israel as a race or people or nation. But in such utterances they always refer to Israel in his especial character of the nation of the promise. Israel, when thought of as representing Yahaweh's promise, is always glorious, no matter how inglorious he may be in himself.

It is not only true that the prophets have this conception of the promise-Israel, but that in virtue of this conception they make the existing Israel a witness against himself, and a teacher to himself. As we have seen, the great bulk of messianic prophecy is not the mere foretelling of facts, but the preaching of religious doctrine for the securing of public and private conversion and growth in grace. The prophets regard the promise as made for the sake of the nations, and Israel as God's peculiar people for the manifestation of the divine lovingkindness to the world. Because Israel is thus the divinely appointed hope of mankind; because Israel's monarch is Yahaweh's anointed Servant, in a kingdom that is to be universal and eternal; because this, while already true, is to become more grandly true in the future; Israel is exhorted to turn from idols, to purify himself, to repent, to take comfort in the midst of affliction; in short, to act as becomes the people whom

God has made the channel of his grace. In other words, the existing Israel is exhorted to conform himself to the ideal Israel as defined by the conditions of the promise.

5. It could not escape the notice of the prophets that the various calamities which befell Israel had their connection with his mission as the people of the Mediatorial promise. Though he is for a blessing to the suffering nations, the nations bring suffering upon him. He cannot escape by becoming annihilated, for his mission is eternal. He must be preserved in existence and made to suffer, that the nations may be benefited. In some of the prophetic writings this idea of suffering for the benefit of others becomes very prominent (*e.g.* Pss. xxii, xl; Isa. liii). This point needs to be mentioned here; it will be more fully discussed in our study concerning the Servant, in the next chapter.

This chapter has been prepared from the critical point of view which assumes that the several Old Testament books were written at the dates Critical assigned to them in the Old Testament itself. questions From this point of view the doctrine taught by the prophets presents an orderly unfolding and progress from David to Malachi, though the main points in it are the same throughout. From a different point of view, the unfolding and the progress would look differently, and there would be modifications in many of the details. In particular, the criticism that puts over more and more of the writings into the postexilian times would transfer a large part of the messianic utterances to those times; and that would change their setting, and to some extent their meaning. But I think that the results would not be greatly changed so far as the main points are concerned, provided we allow the utterances of the biblical writers to mean what by their words they naturally mean. A vast number of questions have arisen as to the date and the authorship of these writings; but whatever their date or origin, they certainly contain these strains of thought concerning the promise and the mission of Israel.

CHAPTER XII

As we have seen, the prophetic literature says that the calling of Abraham from Ur of the Chaldees was the beginning of Israelitish history.   At that time, these writings say, Yahaweh made a promise to Abraham, the benefits of which extend to all mankind.   This promise was the heart of the creed of what the prophets regard as the true religion of Yahaweh in Abraham's time. This literature further affirms that the promise was renewed to Israel when Israel became a nation, still with the necessary implication that it constituted the heart of the creed of those who most truly worshipped Israel's God.   There was another distinguished renewal of it, these writings say, to David the king, making his line central in Israel in the fulfilment of the promise. In David's time and the centuries that followed, they say, there arose in Israel a large number of singers and other prophets, and these generally made this promise, already well known, the basis of their religious and political teachings; and in doing this they unfolded and illuminated the promise itself.

Now if this is true, we should expect to find in the writings of these singers and other prophets a considerable number of technical terms, set apart to _{Rise of technical terms} the uses of this teaching.   The evolution of such terms would in the circumstances be inevitable, under the known laws of human speech.   Similar phe-

263

nomena mark our own habits of thinking and utterance.
A dictionary which should include all our technical religious terms and phrases, with an exhaustive classification of the uses of each term, would be a large volume.
It is incredible that the teaching of the prophets concerning the promise should have been maintained generation after generation without giving rise to such terms.
As a matter of fact, the literature is marked by them.
In the course of time certain words came to have a
partly technical sense when used in the treatments of the
promise-doctrine.   Especially do we find personal terms
denoting the "seed" through whom the promise and its
benefits are transmitted, — for example, Servant, Son,
Chosen one, Branch, Holy one, Messiah; and other
terms denoting his relations to human history, — for
example, the kingdom, the last days, the day of Yahaweh.   In most instances the roots of this use are pre-
Davidic.   There is a strong development of it in the
Psalms that are assigned to the times of David.   The
use remains to the close of the Old Testament.

Taking up these terms in the order of their conspicu-
ousness, we should perhaps expect that "Messiah"
"Servant" is would come first; but that is not the case.
the most con-
spicuous   On the whole, the term "Servant" is the most
term   prominent and is the best fitted to stand as a
representative of the rest in any brief statement of the
matter.   In the King James version this term is occult in
the New Testament, but it appears in the revised version.[1]
Aside from its use elsewhere in the Old Testament, it

---

[1] For example, Peter says: "Ye are the sons of the prophets, and of
the covenant which God made with your fathers, saying unto Abraham,
And in thy seed shall all the families of the earth be blessed.   Unto you
first God, having raised up his Servant, sent him to bless you" (Acts iii.
25–26.   See also iii. 13, iv. 27, 30, etc.).

characterizes the last twenty-seven chapters of Isaiah, and in our consideration of it we will mainly confine ourselves to these chapters. They are more cited in the New Testament as messianic than any other scriptures except those that contain the promises to Abraham and to David.[1] I should say that there is no room for dispute over the use of the term "Servant" in these chapters were it not for the fact that it is actually very much in dispute. Owing to this we shall have to make a study of the term, though necessarily an incomplete one.

I. We shall simplify the study if we begin with two auxiliary points.

1. First, the author of these chapters of Isaiah, being a Hebrew-speaking person, follows the Hebrew idiom when he applies a personal name to a nation. That is, he thinks of the nation as a personality rather than as personified. In English we think of a business corporation as an artificial person, created by law. There is a Hebrew conception of a nation that is as personal as our idea of a corporation.

National personality in Hebrew

We personify a country in the feminine. We say America expects her sons to be loyal. The Hebrew

---

[1] As the word "servant" is one of the words most frequently used in the Hebrew literature, we cannot always easily differentiate its technical use, that is, its use as a messianic term. It is used untechnically of the patriarchs and of Moses, Caleb, Samson, David, and others (see concordance). In the later prophetic books the word "servant" is used in the singular of such men as Moses and Daniel and Nebuchadnezzar, and in the plural of the prophets. But these facts do not disturb the fact of the technical use. Something like the technical use occurs in personal references to David and to the patriarchs (*e.g.* Acts iii. 26 RV, perhaps Gen. xxvi. 24, and concordance of both Testaments). It is used of Israel and of the house of David in other prophetic writings than the last twenty-seven chapters of Isaiah (*e.g.* Jer. xxx. 10, xxxiii. 21, 22, 26, xlvi. 27, 28; Ezek. xxviii. 25, xxxiv. 23, 24, xxxvii. 24, 25, 25; Hag. ii. 23; Zech. iii. 8).

does the same. Our prophet might speak of Judah as
expecting the return of her sons. In mentioning national characteristics, we speak of a typical individual.
We say, The Spaniard is proud, or, The German is plod-
ding. The Hebrew uses the same form of expression,
but rather with the conception of a national personality
than of an individual typifying a nation. In Hebrew
one would say, in the masculine singular, the Canaanite,
or, the Moabite, meaning thereby the collective body
of the Canaanites or Moabites, speaking of them as if
they constituted a single person.

But the Hebrew carries this a step farther. In
Hebrew one speaks of a nation precisely as of a person,
using the name itself, and not merely its gentile adjective. When one says Asshur or Mitsrayim, you have to
look at the context to see whether he means the founder
or the country or the nation or the persons who compose the nation. If the agreeing words are feminine
singular, he means the country. If they are masculine
plural, he means the persons who compose the nation.
If they are masculine singular, he may mean either the
founder or the nation. He talks of the nation as a person precisely as he talks of the founder as a person.

This point in Hebrew diction is important in the study
of these twenty-seven chapters. Through inattention to
it, wrong inferences have been drawn from the strongly
personal way in which these chapters speak of "the
servant of Yahaweh."

2. Second, these chapters are saturated with the ideas
and the diction of Genesis and of the other parts of the
Old Testament where the promise-doctrine is taught.

They are familiar with the creation story, using the
word "create" twenty times, about as many as all the
rest of the Old Testament together, leaving out the nar-

ratives in Genesis. They make much of Abraham (xli. 8, li. 2, lxiii. 16). They magnify the covenant (xlii. 6, xlix. 8, liv. 10, lv. 3, lvi. 4, 6, lix. 21, lxi. 8).

They refer repeatedly to the incidents of the exodus: the crossing of the sea, the passage through the wilderness, the water from the rock, Yahaweh's Spirit with Moses, and the like. They lay stress upon Yahaweh's choosing of Israel.[1]

While Abraham and Israel are thus to the front in these chapters, David is not neglected. Mention is made of "the sure mercies of David " (lv. 3). The promise to David, —

"There shall not be cut off to thee a man from upon the throne of Israel" (1 Ki. ii. 4, viii. 25, ix. 5),

finds its echo in the passages that speak of the everlasting name that shall not be cut off (xlviii. 19, lv. 13, lvi. 5).

Just as the pentateuch and 2 Samuel emphasize the thought of the " seed " of Abraham, of Jacob, of David, so the second part of Isaiah emphasizes the same term.[2]

---

[1] "Jacob whom I have chosen; " "I have chosen thee, and not cast thee off; " "my Servant whom I have chosen; " "Israel whom I have chosen; " "Jeshurun whom I have chosen; " "I chose thee in the furnace of affliction; " "my Chosen one in whom my soul delighteth; " "to give drink to my people, my Chosen one; " "and Israel my Chosen one" (xli. 8, 9, xliii. 10, xliv. 1, 2, xlviii. 10, xlii. 1, xliii. 20, xlv. 4). In the later chapters, where the word "servants" is used in the plural, we also find this other word used in the plural: "My chosen ones shall inherit it;" "for an oath for my chosen ones; " "my chosen ones shall long enjoy" (lxv. 9, 15, 22).

[2] "Seed of Abraham my friend " (xli. 8).
"I will bring thy seed from the east " (xliii. 5).
"I will pour out my Spirit upon thy seed " (xliv. 3).
"I have not said in vain to Jacob's seed, Seek ye me " (xlv. 19).
"In Yahaweh all the seed of Israel shall be righteous, and shall glory for themselves " (xlv. 25).

The second part of Isaiah, like the other writings that emphasize the promise, lays especial stress on the point that the promise is to be eternally operative.   To say nothing of other phraseology in which eternity is mentioned (*e.g.* xlv. 17, liv. 8–9, lxv. 18, 22), the word *olam* occurs thirty-four times in these chapters.[1]

These chapters, like the other scriptures that treat of the promise, make much of the fact that the promise is for the nations.   The word "nation" occurs thirty-six times in these twenty-seven chapters.[2]

"Thy seed also had been as the sand" (xlviii. 19).

"He shall see seed" (liii. 10).

"And thy seed shall possess nations" (liv. 3).

"The seed of the adulterer."   "A seed of falsehood" (lvii. 3, 4).

"Out of the mouth of thy seed, or . . . of thy seed's seed" (lix. 21).

"And their seed shall be known among the nations . . . for they are a seed that Yahaweh hath blessed" (lxi. 9).

"And I will bring out from Jacob a seed" (lxv. 9).

"For they are a seed of those blessed of Yahaweh" (lxv. 23).

"For as the new heavens . . . stand before me . . . so shall your seed and your name stand" (lxvi. 22).

[1] For example, the following : —

"The word of our God shall stand to eternity" (xl. 8).

"Israel hath been saved in Yahaweh a salvation of eternities; ye shall not be ashamed and shall not be confounded unto eternities of endlessness" (xlv. 17).

"While my salvation is to eternity; and my righteousness shall not go to pieces" (li. 6).

"In an outpouring of wrath I hid my face an instant from thee; and in lovingkindness of eternity I have compassion upon thee" (liv. 8).

"Yahaweh to thee a light of eternity" (lx. 19, 20).

"Inherit the land to eternity" (lx. 21).

"A covenant of eternity" (lv. 3, lxi. 8).

"Joy of eternity" (li. 11, lxi. 7).

"For a sign of eternity" (lv. 13).

"A name of eternity" (lvi. 5).

"For an excellency of eternity" (lx. 15).

[2] The Servant shall "bring out judgment to the nations" (xlii. 1).

He shall be "for a light of the nations" (xlii. 6, xlix. 6).

He shall "startle many nations" (lii. 15).

In Exodus xix we are told that Israel was to be " a kingdom of priests," thus sustaining a peculiar relation to Yahaweh, the owner of all the earth. This priestly character of Israel as compared with the other nations appears in the last chapters of Isaiah.[1]

And in many other matters of detail these chapters are full of the promise made by Yahaweh to the nations through Abraham and Israel and David. The one supreme, ever recurring idea is that Israel, however unworthy he may be, or however desperate his condition, is nevertheless Yahaweh's Chosen one, chosen for a purpose, a purpose that will surely be accomplished.

" In the eyes of all the nations " (lii. 10).

" Thy seed shall inherit the nations " (liv. 3).

" Behold thou shalt call a nation thou knowest not; and a nation that have not known thee shall run unto thee" (lv. 5).

" And nations shall come to thy light " (lx. 3).

" A power of nations shall come in to thee " (lx. 5).

" To bring in unto thee a power of nations " (lx. 11).

" For the nation or kingdom that serveth thee not shall perish, the nations being utterly brought to waste " (lx. 12).

" Suck the milk of the nations " (lx. 16).

" Giveth nations before him, and maketh him subdue kings " (xli. 2).

[1] " And strangers shall stand in waiting,
    and shall shepherd your flock,
Sons of a foreigner being
    your husbandmen and your vineyardmen ;
While ye yourselves shall be called
    the priests of Yahaweh.
'The ministers of our God ! '
    shall be said to you " (lxi. 5–6).

" A robe of righteousness hath he made me wear,
    as when the bridegroom acteth the priest, garlanded " (lxi. 10).

" And they will bring in all your brethren
    out of all the nations " (lxvi. 20).

" And I will also take of them for the priests,
    for the Levites, saith Yahaweh " (lxvi. 21).

II. From the point of view thus gained we approach the main question, the question of the use of the term " Servant " in these chapters.

With all the differences of opinion that exist, I suppose that the following statements of fact would be accepted by all who have studied the subject. The word " servant " occurs 20 times in the first 14 of these 27 chapters, always in the singular number, and 11 times in the last 13 of the chapters, always in the plural.   In but one of these 31 places is it used as an ordinary common noun.[1]   In 12 of the 20 instances in which it is used in the singular it is defined in the context as denoting Israel.   In all the cases in which it is used in the plural it denotes Israelites, though in some of the cases those who are Israelites by adoption (*e.g.* lvi. 6).

Outline statement

1. From this general survey we turn to details.   We look first at instances in which the Servant is expressly said to be Israel,

(*a*) The twelve instances occur in the following eight passages : —

> " And thou Israel my Servant,
>   Jacob whom I have chosen,
>   seed of Abraham my friend!
> Whom I firmly laid hold of from the ends of the earth,
>   and called from the distant parts of it,
> And to whom I said, Thou art my Servant,
>   I have chosen thee, and have not cast thee off ;
> Fear not, for I am with thee!
>   be not dismayed, for I am thy God! " (xli. 8–10).

---

[1] " Servant of rulers " (xlix. 7).   But even this is hardly an exception, for the meaning is determined by the implied contrast of " servant of rulers " with " Servant of Yahaweh."   The instances in xliv. 26 and l. 10 are not exceptions, even if any one thinks that the Servant in these verses is the prophet.

"And now hear thou, Jacob my Servant,
 even Israel whom I have chosen:
Thus saith Yahaweh thy maker,
 even thy fashioner from the womb, who helpeth thee,
Fear thou not, my Servant Jacob,
 even Jeshurun whom I have chosen.
For I will pour water upon a thirsty [field],
 and streams upon dry land;
I will pour my Spirit upon thy seed,
 and my blessing upon thy offspring" (xliv. 1-3).

"Remember these things, O Jacob,
 and Israel, for thou art my Servant.
I fashioned thee, Servant to me thou art,
 thou, Israel, wilt not be forgotten of me" (xliv. 21).

"For the sake of my Servant Jacob,
 and Israel my Chosen one,
I have called thee by thy name,
 I surname thee though thou hast not known me" (xlv. 4).

This is spoken to Cyrus, who is in the context called
Yahaweh's "anointed," but is distinguished from the
Servant.

"Yahaweh hath redeemed his Servant Jacob" (xlviii. 20).
"And he said to me, Thou art my Servant,
 O Israel, in whom I glorify myself" (xlix. 3).

In the instances thus far cited the defining context is
separated from the word "Servant" by only a few clauses
at most; in the two following instances the defining context is a little more remote, but it is unmistakable.

"Hear, ye that are deaf,
 and look, ye blind, that ye may see!
Who is blind as my Servant,
 and deaf as my Messenger whom I am wont to send?
Who is blind as the Perfected one,
 and blind as the Servant of Yahaweh?" (xlii. 18-19).

" Let them give their witnesses, that they may be justified,
　　that men may hear and may say, Truth.
Yourselves are my witnesses, saith Yahaweh,
　　and my Servant whom I have chosen,
To the end that ye may know, and may believe me,
　　and may discern that I am he " (xliii. 9–10).

(*b*) To appreciate the full force of these instances one needs to read carefully the whole context.   Israel is in deep trouble.   The purpose of the poem is to bring consolation (xl. 1), and thereby to awaken courage and conscience and aspiration in Israel.   To this end, the formally stated subject of the poem is "The Word of Our God Standeth Forever" (xl. 8).   The poet's thought is that Yahaweh has made utterances concerning Israel, and that these will not fail.   In his estimation this fact overbalances all possible discouraging facts.   This one comforting fact he urges and illustrates, with wonderful fertility of resource and variety of treatment, in every sentence of the entire poem.   The Servant passages are those in which the poet is especially felicitous in presenting his thought.   Many scholars regard some of them as lyrical excerpts, but their meaning does not depend upon this.   Read again the instances, and see how this meaning stands out in them.   Israel is presented as blind and deaf and disheartened and obstinate and abused, but he is nevertheless Yahaweh's Chosen, the "seed of my friend Abraham," Yahaweh's dear little Jeshurun, his Messenger, his Meshullam the complete, his Called one, and above all his Servant. Yahaweh has brought him with firm grasp from the ends of the earth, and called him, and made him promises, and said encouraging words to him, and redeemed him; is his maker and his helper; will not

(marginal note) The instances should be studied in their context

cast him off or forget him; gives him the Spirit, glorifies himself in him, manages such world movements as that of Cyrus in his interest. All this the poet brings in for the consolation of Israel, as a part of the riches included in his great theme, "The word of our God standeth forever."

We fail, however, of rightly understanding this, if we neglect to notice that the poet is here looking at Israel from the point of view of the promise. The point of In the last chapter our attention was called view of the to the prophetic habit of observing things promise from this point of view. This is an important matter, and one that has been too much neglected. Neither in the instances just cited nor elsewhere in these twenty-seven chapters is the term "Servant" ever applied to Israel considered merely as an ethnical aggregation of persons. It implies, indeed, that Israel is an ethnical aggregation, but also that he is something more. When the prophet uses the term, he is invariably thinking of Israel as Yahaweh's own people. We have already seen that these chapters are saturated with the idea — the same idea that appears in the pentateuch and in 2 Samuel — that Yahaweh has made an eternally operative covenant with Abraham, Israel, David, in virtue of which he will bless all nations through them. It is in this character of promise-people, covenant-people, that the chapters speak of Israel as the Servant, not in the character of a mere political aggregation.[1]

This distinction is not in all respects new. Paul long ago wrote : —

" For they are not all Israel which are of Israel ; neither, because they are Abraham's seed, are they all children ; but, In Isaac shall

[1] This might be illustrated at length from the cases of peculiar phraseology with which these chapters abound. Take, for example, the verb *paar*

thy seed be called." "It is not the children of the flesh that are children of God, but the children of the promise are reckoned for a seed " (Rom. ix. 6–8).

As interpretations of Paul's word, we are familiar with such phrases as "the Israel within Israel," "the ideal Israel," "the spiritual Israel." Whatever phrase you use for it, the distinction is genuine. I think that the best of these phrases is "the Israel of the promise," or, "Israel regarded as the promise-people." This corresponds most closely to the facts, and to the phraseology of the Old Testament, and to Paul's term " the children of the promise."

Israel the Servant is therefore Israel regarded as the promise-people, Israel regarded as Yahaweh's Chosen one. From one point of view he is identical with the political aggregation known as Israel, while from other points of view he is something entirely different. It should not surprise us if we find Israel the Servant and Israel the political aggregation sometimes spoken of as two, or even as having relations one with the other.

in the Piel or Hithpael. It occurs eight times in Isaiah II, and six times in all in Ezra, Deuteronomy, Psalm cxlix, Exodus, Judges, and Isaiah x.

"And to the Holy one of Israel, for he hath glorified thee" (lv. 5, lx. 9).

"To glorify the place of my sanctuary " (lx. 13).

"I will glorify the house of my glory " (lx. 7).

"And glorifieth himself in Israel " (xliv. 23).

"O Israel in whom I glorify myself " (xlix. 3).

"Thy people, being all of them righteous,
    shall possess earth forever,
  The flower of my planting,
    the deed of my hands for glorifying myself" (lx. 21).

. . . "glory instead of ashes . . .

And they shall be called, The trees of righteousness,
    the planting of Yahaweh for glorifying himself " (lxi. 3).

Obviously it is not Israel as a mere mass of persons in whom the prophet is interested ; but Israel as the one whom Yahaweh glorifies because of a certain relation of identity with himself which he has established.

2. We turn to a second class of passages, those in which the word "servant" is used or implied without an explicit contextual identification with Israel.

At the outset we may lay aside all anxiety as to the bearings of these passages on the claims of the New Testament. If the passages represent the Servant to be a person different from Israel, then the New Testament claims that what is said concerning that person is fulfilled in Jesus. If on the other hand we find that the Servant, in these passages, is still Israel, we shall also find that the New Testament claim is that Jesus Christ is Israel the Servant in his highest manifestation. In either case the passages are messianic, and in either case the New Testament claims that they are fulfilled in Jesus the Messiah.

(a) Study first a group of two passages. The first consists of the lines that introduce the mention of Cyrus (xliv. 25–26).

> "He breaketh impostors' signs,
>   and maketh diviners mad.
> He maketh wise men return backward.
>   and maketh their knowledge folly.
> He raiseth up the word of his Servant,
>   and fully performeth the counsel of his messengers.
>
> "That saith to Jerusalem, She shall be made to abide ;
>   and to the cities of Judah, They shall be builded ;
>   and, Her ruinous places I will rear up."

At a superficial glance it is natural to say that "the word of his servant," here placed parallel with "the counsel of his messengers," must of course be the word uttered by the prophet, the prophet being here the servant. This will afford a passable interpretation of the whole passage. But it is not a necessary interpretation. It is possible to regard the genitive as objective, so that

"the word of his Servant" will be Yahaweh's word concerning his Servant.   This makes good parallelism with
"the counsel of his messengers," for Yahaweh's word
concerning his Servant is an important part of his counsel as transmitted through his prophetic messengers.
So far, therefore, as parallelism and syntax are concerned, we may translate —

"He establisheth his word concerning his Servant,
　　and fully performeth the counsel announced by his messengers."

This is clearly the meaning that best fits the logical and
poetic requirements of the whole context.   The writer
uses the word " Servant " here in the same sense in which
we have found him using it elsewhere.[1]

The same peculiarities appear in the remaining instance.

　　" Who is there among you fearing Yahaweh,
　　　　hearkening to the voice of his Servant,
　　That hath gone in darknesses,
　　　　there being no brightness for him ?
　　Let him trust in the name of Yahaweh,
　　　　that he may stay himself in his God " (l. 10).

We have here again the objective genitive.   " The voice
of his Servant " is the voice concerning his Servant, the
word "voice" being used as in Isa. xl. 3, 6.   Cheyne is
correct in regarding the preceding verses as spoken by
the Servant, and is therefore wrong in thinking that
there is here an arbitrary break, and that the tenth verse
is perhaps spoken by the prophet in his own person.

(b) Taking the passages in the order of the obvious-
ness of their meaning, we notice next those in which the
word "servant" is used in the plural.

[1] Some have held that the Servant is here the prophet, but the prophet
as the representative of the true Israel, who is properly the Servant.   This
gives in part the same result as the interpretation I have proposed, but it
seems to me less feasible.

We have already touched the fact that this word occurs only in the singular in these chapters up to the fifty-third, and only in the plural from the fifty-fourth onward. Of course scholars who regard the later chapters as written at a dif- ferent period from the earlier, and from a different view-point, will count these plural instances as irrelevant ; but at all events they will not prejudice the argument. The instances are as follows. Observe that in each case the servants are Israelites either by birth or by adoption.

The plural instances not irrelevant

> " Return thou for the sake of thy servants,
>   the tribes of thine inheritance " (lxiii. 17).

> " And the sons of the foreigner that join themselves
>   upon Yahaweh, to minister to him,
> And to love the name of Yahaweh,
>   to be to him for servants " (lvi. 6).

> " So will I do for the sake of my servants,
>   in order not to destroy the whole ;
> And I will bring out from Jacob a seed,
>   and from Judah one possessing my mountains,
> That my chosen ones may possess it,
>   while my servants have their dwelling there.
>   *   *   *   *   *   *
> And you, ye forsakers of Yahaweh,
>   those forgetting my holy mountain,
>   *   *   *   *   *   *
> Behold my servants shall eat,
>   and ye shall be hungry ;
> Behold my servants shall drink,
>   and ye shall be thirsty ;
> Behold my servants shall be glad,
>   and ye shall be ashamed ;
> Behold my servants shall sing aloud
>   from gladness of heart,
> And ye for your part shall cry out
>   from sorrow of heart,

> And from breaking of spirit ye shall wail.
> And ye shall deposit your name
>   for an oath to my chosen ones ;
> And the Lord Yahaweh will slay thee,
>   and will call his servants by another name " (lxv. 8–15).

The two remaining instances are like the others, though less marked.

> " This is the heritage of the servants of Yahaweh,
>   their righteousness being from with me,
>   saith Yahaweh " (liv. 17).

> " And Yahaweh's hand with his servants shall be known,
>   and he will spurn his enemies " (lxvi. 14).

Whatever one may hold as to the unity of the twenty-seven chapters, it is clear, at least, that the " servants " mentioned in the later chapters are the individual Israelites who compose Israel the Servant as mentioned in the earlier chapters. They are Israelites, either native or adopted, regarded as sharing in the promise, and not merely Israelites in an ethnical sense.

This is in itself an indication that the later chapters are a part of the same unit with the earlier. This unity is disputed, but really there is no room for dispute. The twenty-seven chapters, however they originated, are a single poem. They are so, whether they became so by processes of original composition or by combining processes. The action of the poem is homiletic rather than dramatic or epic. In point of sublimity of thought and strength of conception, the climacteric passages are in the earlier or middle sections ; but in point of practical urgency, pressure upon the conscience of individuals, the poem grows more and more intense to the end. Having aroused the thought and the imagination of his audience by his picturing of the lofty character and mission of Israel as the Servant, the poet treats each Israelite as himself a servant, and presses home upon him his failings and his obligations.

In this second group of instances, therefore, the servants are Israelites, regarded as the persons in whom the promise stands firm. This is not quite the same as to say that they are the faithful in Israel, though perhaps the difference after all is not very great.

(c) We will take next the instances in which the Servant is presented as speaking in the first person. In these instances it is quite generally true that the Servant is differentiated from the actually existing Israel, and is represented as having a mission to Israel. The most distinct instance is that in the forty-ninth chapter (1–7).

" Hearken ye coastlands unto me,
　　and be attentive ye peoples from afar.
　He that called me from the belly is Yahaweh;
　　from the bowels of my mother he made mention of my name.
　And he placed my mouth as a sharp sword,
　　in the shadow of his hand he hid me,
　And he placed me as a polished arrow,
　　in his quiver he concealed me.
　And he said to me, Thou art my Servant,
　　thou, Israel, in whom I glorify myself.

" And I, I said, Vainly have I toiled,
　　for nought and vanity have I used up my strength.
　Verily, my judgment is with Yahaweh,
　　and that which I have wrought is with my God.
　And now [be ye attentive] : Yahaweh hath said —
　　he that formed me from the womb for a Servant to him,
　For bringing back Jacob unto him,
　　and that Israel may be gathered to him,
　So that I might be honored in the eyes of Yahaweh,
　　my God being my strength —
　He hath said, It is too light a thing,
　　thy being Servant to me
　To raise up the tribes of Jacob,
　　and to restore the preserved of Israel;

And I will give thee for a light of nations,
    that my salvation may be unto the end of the earth.
" Thus saith Yahaweh,
    Israel's redeemer, his holy one,
To one despised of soul, to one abhorred
    of a nation, to a slave of tyrants :
Kings shall see and arise,
    captains, and they shall worship,
For the sake of Yahaweh who is faithful,
    the Holy One of Israel who hath chosen thee."

In the beginning of this passage Israel is the Servant.
Farther on the Servant has a mission to Israel. The
Servant is to be honored for bringing back Jacob and
gathering Israel to Yahaweh. What he is Servant for
is in part the raising up of the tribes, and the restoring
of such Israelites as have been preserved.

Who is this Servant that has a mission to Israel ? Is
he the same who has just been called Israel ? Verbally
Israel he is presented as different from Israel, and
thought of as a person doing personal acts rather than
as having a as a personification. Does this prove that
mission to himself he cannot possibly be Israel ? Who is he ?
Is he a new character introduced here without warning ?
or is he the Israel of the promise, differentiated in
thought from the merely ethnical Israel, and conceived
of as having relations with him ?

The second of these alternatives is the true one.
Israel is here represented as having relations with himself. There is nothing strained in this way of stating
things. Even those who do not accept it must at least
admit that it is free from absurdity. The American
church has duties to its own membership. The French
nation has obligations to its own citizens. We can
easily imagine Mr. Booker T. Washington or Professor
DuBois or some other colored citizen of the United

States as saying to his compatriots that the African race in America has its work not for negroes and mulattoes merely, but for men of all races everywhere. In each of these cases the church or the nation or the race, when conceived of as a divine agency, has a mission to the persons who compose it, as well as to others. So Israel the Servant may be conceived of as having a mission to Israel the aggregation of persons.[1]

This one clear instance in which the Servant is introduced as speaking in the first person, and as having a mission to Israel, though also he himself is Other Israel, may serve to interpret four other in- instances stances, and may in turn be interpreted by them. In these four other instances the word "Servant" is not used; but a character, not Yahaweh, is introduced speaking in the first person.[2] In each of them the speaker is in commission from Yahaweh. One of them is

[1] Some say that the Servant who is here mentioned as having relations with Israel is the prophet speaking in his own person, or is some typical Israelite. This is not so different from the view I have given as one might at first think. When the prophet thinks of Israel the chosen people as differentiated from the political Israel, he of course identifies himself and men of like spirit with Israel the chosen people. It would not be surprising if he should sometimes speak of himself or some other representative Israelite as typically the Servant. But any interpretation is untenable that does not directly or indirectly identify the Servant of the fifth and sixth verses with the Israel-Servant of the third verse.

[2] One of these instances is the sixty-first chapter, read by Jesus in the synagogue of Nazareth, with the comment: "To-day hath this scripture been fulfilled in your ears" (Lc. iv. 16–21), the section that begins: —

"The Spirit of the Lord Yahaweh is upon me;
Because Yahaweh hath anointed me
    to bring good tidings to the meek.
He hath sent me to bind up the brokenhearted,
To proclaim liberty to captives,
    and recovery of senses to the imprisoned" (*cf.* ver. 10).

Cheyne regards this as a soliloquy of the Servant. The section in its whole

very brief; in each of the others the speaker identifies himself with Israel, but may be differentiated from Israel. In each it is plausible to say that the speaker is the personified Israel of the promise, as in the forty-ninth chapter.

(*d*) One group more remains. It consists of three instances, in two passages which are very prominently quoted in the New Testament.

The first is found in Isa. xlii. 1–4.

"Behold my Servant whom I uphold,
 my Chosen one in whom my soul delighteth.
I have given my Spirit upon him,
 he will bring out judgment to the nations.

"He maketh no outcry, nor lifteth up
 nor publisheth his voice in the street.
A bruised reed he breaketh not,
 and a flickering wick he quencheth not.

extent is an address to Israel rather than a soliloquy, but the suggestion that it is uttered by the Servant is natural and plausible.

The instance in Isa. l. 4–9 is briefer, but is almost equally familiar.

"The Lord Yahaweh hath given me a tongue of learned ones . . . I gave my back to the smiters, and my cheeks to them that plucked off the hair," etc.

This might more properly than the other be called a soliloquy. It pictures the abuse the speaker suffers, his trust in God, his tactful, courageous, persistent service. Many attribute it to the Servant.

The third instance is brief. It occurs in the midst of an address by Yahaweh, and can be understood only by supplying a clause.

"And now [I remind thee that thou art able to say],
It is the Lord Yahaweh that hath sent me,
 and his Spirit" (Isa. xlviii. 16).

Scholars differ concerning this passage. But, like the two preceding instances, it employs the rather unusual divine name "the Lord Yahaweh."

The remaining instance (Isa. lxiii. 7–lxiv) is much fuller, but less differentiated. The speaker is engaged in earnest prayer to Yahaweh in behalf of Israel, using part of the time the first person singular, and part of the time the first person plural.

" Of a truth he will bring out judgment,
    he will not flicker nor be broken,
Until he put judgment in the earth ;
    meanwhile coastlands wait for his law."

This is quoted somewhat in full and applied to Jesus, in the gospel by Matthew (xii. 18–21). Notice that the emphatic statement in these three stanzas is that the Servant shall be the supreme judge of the nations. This is spoken of in the first stanza ; its inconsistency with the manifested meekness of the Servant is suggested in the second stanza ; and the third stanza four times affirms that it is nevertheless a fact. The point illustrated in Matthew is the meekness of the person spoken of, in contrast with his victoriousness and his being the hope of the nations.

The Servant supreme over the nations

The other passage is the complete section concerning the humiliated Servant (Isa. lii. 13–liii). It occupied a remarkably large place in the thinking of the first preachers of Christianity.[1] Its full messianic significance cannot be appreciated except through a thorough study of the entire passage. But we must be content with citing briefly the two places in which it uses the word " Servant."

" Behold my Servant dealeth wisely,
    Is high and exalted and lofty exceedingly " (Isa. lii. 13).

" It being Yahaweh's will to bruise him, making him sick ;
    even if thou regard his soul as a trespass-offering,
He shall behold a seed, shall prolong days,
    the will of Yahaweh prospering in his hand.

[1] It is formally cited at least nine times, in at least the six books Luke, John, Acts, Romans, Galatians, 1 Peter ; and is informally cited much oftener. See the reference bibles. Probably the most familiar instance is that it was the passage which the Ethiopian eunuch was reading when Philip joined him (Acts viii. 32–33).

Of the toil of his soul he shall behold, shall be sated ;
in knowing him shall my Servant, righteous,
Give righteousness to the many,
and their iniquities himself shall bear as a load " (liii. 10–11).

In this passage Yahaweh represents the Servant's being stricken as the result of the transgression of "my
people" (liii. 8). That is, this section, like the forty-
ninth chapter, makes a distinction between Yahaweh's
people and the Servant, that is, between Israel the
Servant and Israel the aggregation of persons. But it
goes farther in this direction than the forty-ninth chapter. It distinguishes the Servant from his generation,
his unspeakable generation, and represents him as cut
off from the earth, as having a grave, as experiencing
"deaths" (vv. 8–9). So far as these representations
go, he is not an unending succession of persons, but is
one Person. Later we shall meet again this figure of
the Person of the promise, wonderful both in his sorrows and his exaltation.

This passage brings out into strong relief an experience of the Servant that is also much emphasized
The Servant's   elsewhere, namely, his humiliations and suffer-
sufferings   ings ; but it brings out an aspect of this expe-
mediatorial   rience that is presented in other places only
by allusion or implication. The sufferings of the Servant are vicarious and mediatorial in their character.
In many of the passages heretofore cited we find Israel
suffering for his own misdoings, and this is the case
in some of the passages in which he is called the Servant. But in this fifty-third chapter we find a different
view. Over and over the passage reiterates that the
Servant is blameless. It is not as the result of his
own sins that he suffers, but of those of his people
and of the many nations. The result shall be their

being made righteous from their sins, and this shall
eventuate in such victory and glory and joy for the
Servant as shall more than compensate him for all his
sorrows.

III. We must not dismiss the term " Servant " without
recurring to the point that this is the one messianic
term that is best fitted to stand as representative. What
is true of the term " Servant " in its messianic use is typically true of the other terms that have the same signification.   For this reason let us ask here, in regard to
the Servant, two or three questions which we shall have
to repeat, later, in regard to the whole body of messianic prediction. It is no reason against this procedure that we thus catch a glimpse of certain still distant
goals toward which our study is moving.

Who is the Servant spoken of in these Isaiah chapters? A certain interpretation replies that the Servant
clearly is the people of Israel, and therefore Two one-
is not Jesus of Nazareth. It is Israel, this sided inter-
interpretation affirms, whom Yahaweh chose, pretations
separated from the peoples, led through a career of
mingled suffering and victory, set for a light to the
nations, and made to be, in very important senses, the
world's redeemer. It is Israel whose mission of good
to mankind has so largely resulted from his sufferings,
from his being scattered among the peoples, and subjected to undeserved contempt and ill treatment. This
is not an ignoble interpretation, and it agrees with most
of the facts as we have been studying them. But it
does not, unless supplemented by something else, account
for some of the personal experiences attributed to the
Servant, nor for the degree of the exaltation ascribed to
him.

This interpretation is contradicted by another which

affirms that the Servant is Jesus Christ, and therefore is not Israel. This view fully accounts for the personal terms, the exaltation of the Servant, his being sometimes separate from Israel and in relations with Israel, and the wonderfully minute identity between the characteristics and experiences of Jesus and those of the Servant ; but it necessitates a dreadful amount of difficult explanation when it is called upon to account for the passages which explicitly declare that the Servant is Israel.

The truth is, that both interpretations are correct in what they affirm, and incorrect in what they deny. If the Servant is Israel, that does not prove that the Servant is not Christ. If he is Israel, then he is Israel thought of as the promise-people, Israel in all the fulness of his mission to the world, and not in some relatively narrow and circumscribed portion of it. The prophet was dealing with what he regarded as the eternally operative promise of Yahaweh. He is speaking constantly of the future of Israel the Servant, though of course not to the exclusion of the past or the present. He holds that the promise has been fulfilling in the past, is at present in process of fulfilment, and will continue to be fulfilled in the future, without limit of time. He holds this as an article of religious doctrine, independent of any power which he may possess of miraculously foretelling the future. The statements he makes concerning Israel the Servant do not terminate their effect with the Israel of his own time. By their very terms they look forward. They apply especially to any future portion of Israel's history which shall be especially the manifestation of God's purpose toward mankind through Israel. They so apply if the prophet had a definite knowledge as to the events in which the manifestation

The true interpretation

would be made; and equally they so apply if his knowledge of the coming events was vague — merely a conviction that Yahaweh would somehow accomplish the word he had spoken.

It follows that there is no contradiction between the statement that the Servant is Israel and the statement that the servant is Jesus Christ, provided Jesus Christ is the most significant fact in the history of Israel as the people of the promise; and this Christianity claims that he is.

This may be variantly stated. The prophetic use of the term "Servant" has such a character of universalness that really it might be applied to any person of any race or time, provided he is characteristically the agent of the divine purpose for mankind. It might be applied to the personified aggregate of all such persons, or to any lesser aggregate. In the Old Testament, as a matter of fact, it denotes Israel regarded as such an aggregate. It might be properly applied to any Israelite who is in this respect typical, and it is so applied to Moses and Caleb and David and others, though perhaps not in all cases in its full meaning. In particular, the Servant might be any priest or prophet or other public man, brought into such relations with Yahaweh that he is the representative of the Israel of his generation. If the New Testament writers are correct in regarding Jesus as preëminently the representative Israelite, as the antitype of all types, then they are correct in applying directly to him what the prophets say concerning Israel the Servant. *[Universalness of the term "Servant"]*

It will help to give us a steady grasp of these facts if we take a glance forward to our own times, and the fulfilment now in progress of the things that are said concerning the Servant. Israel the Servant is now in very important senses the light of the nations, as the prophet said he would be. His being so consists in three things, and it is a mistake to omit any one of the three from our con- sideration. First, the promise-people is in a unique degree a blessing to mankind if we consider only what Israel the race has accomplished and is accom- plishing in business and commerce and governmental administration and learning and literature and art. If Israel's contributions of this kind to the civilization of the twentieth century could be suddenly obliterated, the world of mankind would come to a standstill. Second, the work of the promise-people for mankind is being wrought in what the religion of Israel and its daughter religions, Christianity and Islam, are ac- complishing. And third, these two great things be- come insignificant when compared with the person and work of Jesus, provided Jesus is the Son of God that we Christians believe him to be. The career of Israel the Servant includes all the beneficent things that God has wrought through him, including God's supreme manifestation through him in the person of Christ the Lord. Defining thus, we Christians should accept, instead of rejecting, the statement that in all the instances Isaiah's Servant of Yahaweh is Israel.

A glimpse of the later fulfilments

CHAPTER XIII

In the last chapter we studied the term the " Servant" as being the most nearly representative among the
special terms created by the teaching of the promise-
doctrine in Israel. We now take up the pair of terms
which are on the whole the most significant. The fact
that the kingdom and the Messiah are cognate terms,
that they go together, is better understood now among
Christians than it was a generation ago. So far as
words are concerned, the Messiah is simply the anointed
king of the kingdom. Conspicuous in the New Testament is this " kingdom of God," this " kingdom of
heaven," with its sphere of operations in the present
world of men, but extending into the world to come.
In this kingdom the Christ is the royal judge both
here and hereafter.

Three topics especially claim our attention : first, the
Old Testament presentation concerning the kingdom ;
second, its presentation concerning the king, the
Anointed one, the Messiah ; third, the eschatological
trend of the doctrine of the kingdom and the king.

I. First, the doctrine of the kingdom is a part of the
promise-doctrine of the Old Testament.

In the record for the times of the patriarchs the kingdom is not at all in the foreground. It only comes in
incidentally that kings shall descend from Abraham,

from Sarah, from Jacob (Gen. xvii. 6, 16, xxxv. 11).
Doctrine of the kingdom in the earlier times   Among the kings descended from Abraham might perhaps be included Ishmaelites and Midianites and Edomites, but the royal line descending from Jacob is necessarily Israelite.

In the records for the time of the exodus the kingdom idea is not presented often or at large, but it is somewhat conspicuous by reason of the importance of the passages where it appears. Not wholly insignificant is the representation that Moses was looking forward to a king in Israel (Deut. xvii. 14–20), or that a writer in Genesis is impressed with the fact that there has been a line of kings among Abraham's Edomite descendants before there were any in Israel (Gen. xxxvi. 31). A much more important record, however, is found in the account of the happenings at Mount Sinai. The heart of the whole is the message from the mountain, arranged in symmetrically balanced short lines.

" Thus say thou to the house of Jacob,
And tell thou to the sons of Israel :

"Yourselves saw what I did to Egypt;
And I lifted you on wings of eagles,
And brought you in unto me.

" And now if ye will thoroughly hearken
To my voice, and keep my covenant,
Ye shall be mine, my own, out of all the peoples.

"For mine is all the earth,
While ye yourselves shall be mine —
A kingdom of priests and a holy nation.

" These are the words
Which thou shalt speak unto the sons of Israel "
(Ex. xix. 3b-6).

This purports to be the original communication from Yahaweh, constituting Israel differentially his own people.[1] The New Testament writers claim, as we have had occasion to see, that under its provisions believers in Christ are God's own people. A part of this communication is to the effect that Israel is to be "a kingdom of priests and a holy nation." This phraseology in particular the New Testament men eagerly quote and appropriate, though their doing this is not apparent in the King James version, and has therefore been ignored by English-speaking students.[2]

The first book of Samuel testifies to the existence before the monarchy of this idea of Israel as Yahaweh's holy kingdom. For example, the song of Hannah over the birth of Samuel, whether composed by Hannah herself or by some prophet speaking in her person, testifies that she had in mind a lofty conception of this sort.

> " It is Yahaweh that judgeth earth's uttermost parts,
> That he may give strength to his king,
> and exalt the horn of his Anointed " (1 Sam. ii. 10).

Samuel's objection to the setting up of the monarchy was that this would tend to obscure the fact that Israel

---

[1] See above, tenth chapter, I. 2, especially the foot-notes.

[2] " But ye are an elect race, a royal priesthood, a holy nation, a people of [God's] own " (1 Pet. ii. 9).

In the same context it is said that Christians are "to be a holy priesthood, to offer up spiritual sacrifices " (5).

In the book of Revelation it is said of Jesus that he "loosed us from our sins by his blood ; and he made us [to be] a kingdom, [to be] priests unto his God and Father " (i. 6 RV).

" Didst purchase unto God with thy blood [men] of every tribe, and tongue, and people, and nation, and madest them [to be] unto our God a kingdom and priests ; and they reign upon the earth " (v. 9–10 RV).

" Over these the second death hath no authority ; but they shall be priests of God and of Christ, and shall reign with him a thousand years " (xx. 6 RV).

was Yahaweh's kingdom (1 Sam. viii. 7, x. 19, xii. 12). From the time of the anointing of Saul the conception appears more prominently that the kingdom of Israel is in peculiar relations with Yahaweh, and that its king is Yahaweh's Anointed (see concordance).

From the time of the making of the great promise to David, the records give a central and emphatic place The king- to the kingdom. The kingdom, they say, is dom in and from David's God's kingdom among men, it is Israelite, time its kings are of the line of David, it is to be eternal, its sway is to be worldwide. Already in Chapter X we have examined a good many passages that affirm these points. We will look again at some of these, and will look at some others. We cannot make the survey exhaustive, because the passages are too numerous ; we can only look at specimens.

In the original record of the promise to David the throne and the kingdom are conspicuous.[1] Here the kingdom is Israel. The king is of the line of David. Both are to be eternal. The same points appear with much reiteration in the eighty-ninth psalm, which we have already quoted so much. In this psalm the kingdom (ver. 25) is said to be widespread. In many of the passages it is declared to be universal as well as eternal.

Take, for example, the seventy-second psalm. Whatever its date or author, it is a glowing supplicatory The king- description of Solomon and his reign, with dom in a presentation that is accurately the same Ps. lxxii with that in the books of Kings and Chronicles. The leading verbs should be translated either as present or as precative; by making them future the

---

[1] For example : "I will establish his kingdom." "I will establish the throne of his kingdom for ever." "And thy house and thy kingdom shall be made sure for ever before thee " (2 Sam. vii. 12, 13, 16 RV).

English versions obscure the meaning, though they do not utterly hide it. First, the subject is stated — not "the king," but "a king," who is also a king's son (1). His administrative and judicial abilities are commemorated (2, 4, 7, 12–14), and the peace that characterizes his reign (3, 7). His wide dominion is mentioned (8), and especially his commercial victory over the desert.[1] The tribute paid by many kings is spoken of — Tarshish and the coastlands and Sheba and Seba (10, 15). In such details we find Solomon in the psalm from beginning to end, but Solomon as the representative of the promised line of David. The singer knows that Solomon is mortal; but David's royal line is immortal, and in this sense the king whom he sings will live "while the sun endureth, and before the moon, throughout all generations," "till the moon be no more," "as long as the sun" (5, 7, 17). His kingdom is worldwide as well as everlasting.

"Yea, all kings shall do obeisance to him,
    all nations shall serve him" (11).

"And let him be conqueror from sea as far as to sea,
    and from the River as far as to earth's uttermost parts" (8).[2]

And this culminates, as we have seen in a preceding chapter, by vesting in this king the Abrahamic promise : —

"Yea, all nations shall bless themselves in him,
    shall call him happy" (17).

[1] "Before him deserts bow" (9), not "they that dwell in the wilderness" (*cf.* 1 Ki. ix. 18 ; 2 Chron. viii. 4).

[2] Compare Zech. ix. 10 : —

"He shall speak peace to the nations, and his dominion shall be 'from sea as far as to sea, and from the River as far as to earth's uttermost parts.'"

Study carefully this conception of a universal and eternal kingdom, represented, however, for the time contemplated in the song, by the Davidic king then reigning over Yahaweh's chosen people.

An equally explicit example is the second psalm, so extensively quoted in the New Testament. In this The second psalm we find a character who is variously psalm described as Yahaweh's "anointed," Yahaweh's "king," Yahaweh's "son." The powers of earth are in revolt against him, and God sees the ridiculousness of their setting up their puny might against his. In this psalm the eternalness of the kingdom is left to implication, but its cosmopolitan character is made explicit.

> " Ask thou of me,
>   And I will give nations as thine inheritance,
>   and earth's uttermost parts as thy possession " (8).

Additional instances are given below for various specific purposes. Or one might use a concordance, and look up all the post-Davidic passages which mention a king or a kingdom. It should be noted, however, that this conception of universal dominion for Yahaweh's promise-people, for the purposes of the promise, is not confined to the passages that use these specific words.[1]

---

[1] Note, for example, statements like the following concerning the Servant: " He shall bring out judgment to the nations." " In truth he shall bring out judgment." " He shall not fail . . . till he have set judgment in the earth." "The coastlands wait for his law" (Isa. xlii. 1–4).

Or such passages as the following : —

" And it shall come to pass in future days that the mountain of Yahaweh's house shall be made ready at the head of the mountains, and shall be exalted above the hills ; and all the nations shall flow unto it. And many peoples shall go and say, Come ye and let us go up unto the mountain of Yahaweh, unto the house of the God of Jacob ; that he may give us *torah* out of his

There is a line of passages in the books of Chronicles which speak of Israel under the reign of a king of David's family as "the kingdom of Yahaweh." Whether _{Yahaweh's} this is to be regarded as a late expression orig- _{kingdom} inating with the Chronicler, or as taken by him from some earlier source, at all events it has significance as interpreting the conception of the kingdom that was prevalent.[1] The same mode of expression appears in the forty-fifth psalm, which I believe to have been written some centuries earlier than the Chronicler. When the singer says (ver. 6), —

"Thy throne, O God, is for ever and ever,"

he refers not to God's throne in heaven, but to God's throne on earth — the eternal throne promised to the seed of David, and at the time occupied by the Davidic king whom the singer is praising. And the glory and the everlastingness of Yahaweh's kingdom are

ways, and that we may go in his paths. For out of Zion *torah* shall go forth, and the word of Yahaweh out of Jerusalem. And he shall judge between the nations, and reprove many peoples" (Isa. ii. 2–4).

[1] One of these passages is in the Chronicler's duplicate of the narrative in 2 Sam. vii: "I will settle him in my house and in my kingdom for ever" (1 Chron. xvii. 14 RV).

Elsewhere David is represented as saying: "Yahaweh . . . hath chosen Solomon my son to sit upon the throne of the kingdom of Yahaweh over Israel" (1 Chron. xxviii. 5).

In another place David says: —

"For all that is in the heaven and in the earth [is thine]; thine is the kingdom, O Yahaweh, and thou art exalted as head above all" (1 Chron. xxix. 11).

The queen of Sheba is represented as saying to Solomon: —

"Blessed be Yahaweh thy God who hath taken pleasure in thee to set thee on his throne, to be king for Yahaweh thy God; because thy God loved Israel, to establish them for ever" (2 Chron. ix. 8).

And Abijah king of Judah accuses Jeroboam and his associates of arraying themselves against "the kingdom of Yahaweh in the hand of the sons of David" (2 Chron. xiii. 8).

nowhere more enthusiastically mentioned than in another
psalm : —

> " They shall speak of the glory of thy kingdom,
> And talk of thy power;
> To make known to the sons of men his mighty acts,
> And the glory of the majesty of his kingdom.
> Thy kingdom is an everlasting kingdom,
> And thy dominion [endureth] throughout all generations "
> (Ps. cxlv. 11–13 RV).

Very prominently the idea of the dominion of Israel
and the Anointed one takes on the form of glowing descriptions of a good time coming — a reign
of universal peace and happiness. We have
just cited in a foot-note the passage concerning the mountain of Yahaweh's house fixed at the head
of the mountains (Isa. ii. 2–4 ; Mic. iv. 1–5). As given
in Isaiah, that passage terminates with a picture of
swords beaten into ploughshares and spears into prun-
inghooks, and the nations learning war no more. To
this, in Micah, is added : —

A reign of universal peace

> " But they shall sit every man under his vine and under his fig
> tree, and none shall make them afraid."

In the ninth chapter of Isaiah the names attributed to
the child that is to be born reach their climax in "God
all-victorious, Father of eternity, Captain of peace," with
the statement added : —

> " Of the increase of his government and of peace there shall be no
> end, upon the throne of David, and upon his kingdom, to establish
> it, and to uphold it with judgment and with righteousness from hence-
> forth even for ever " (Isa. ix. 7 RV).

Few passages in the Old Testament are more familiar
than the one concerning the " shoot out of the stock of
Jesse," through whose wise and just administration of
affairs —

"wolf shall sojourn with lamb, and leopard shall lie down with kid,
. . . They shall not hurt nor destroy in all my holy mountain; for
the earth shall be full of knowing Yahaweh, as the waters cover the
sea" (Isa. xi. 6–9).

This is directly followed by the assertion that "the
nations shall seek" unto "the root of Jesse, which
standeth for an ensign of the peoples." With this compare the following : —

"Wolf and lamb shall pasture together, and the lion shall eat straw
like the ox, and dust shall be the serpent's bread. They shall not
hurt nor destroy in all my holy mountain, saith Yahaweh" (Isa. lxv.
25).

And with these compare Ezek. xxxiv. 24–31 ; Isa. iv.
2–6, etc.

In the latest Old Testament books the kingdom-doc-
trine is as explicit as in any of their predecessors. We
have already noticed the definiteness with which First
and Second Chronicles specify that the Davidic kingdom is Yahaweh's kingdom on earth. In Daniel we
find the idea of "an Anointed one, a Regent" (ix. 24,
25, 26), and also, in passages that are very familiar to
us, the writer's expectation of the renewed manifestation
of the kingdom. Of the stone cut out of the mountain
without hands he says : —

"And in the days of those kings shall the God of heaven set up a
kingdom, which shall never be destroyed, nor shall the sovereignty
thereof be left to another people ; but it shall break in pieces and
consume all these kingdoms, and it shall stand for ever" (Dan. ii.
44–45 RV).

And in Daniel's vision of the four beasts it is said : —

"And the kingdom and the dominion and the greatness of the
kingdoms under the whole heaven shall be given to the people of the
saints of the Most High ; his kingdom is an everlasting kingdom,
and all dominions shall serve and obey him" (Dan. vii. 27 RV).

My personal opinion is that the Old Testament gives us approximate dates for most of these utterances, and that when we arrange them in chronological order, that brings out their meaning more explicitly and strongly.   But others dispute the dates.   Without delaying to settle all questions, this at least is true : that these utterances concerning the kingdom are numerous, and that there is no large section of the literature as it has come down to us which is not in some way marked by them.

Independent of disputed dates

It should be noted, however, that in the latest biblical times the utterances concerning the kingdom take on a new color.   When Nebuchadnezzar had destroyed Jerusalem, and there was no longer, politically, a descendant of David reigning there, this did not interfere with the confidence of the prophets in the reality and the perpetuity of the kingdom.   From the first the prophets had presented their doctrine of the kingdom in two aspects, — that of a personal sovereign reigning in Zion, and that of a beneficent influence going out through the nations.   As long as Judah had a personal sovereign, the prophets regarded that sovereign as Yahaweh's Anointed, in and for the generation to which he belonged.   When for generation after generation Judah was no longer a monarchy, the prophets still taught that the kingdom and the line of David were eternal, but the emphasis fell more and more on the idea of the kingdom as a cosmopolitan influence which the God of Israel has established in the world.   It is an easy transition from this to the New Testament idea of the kingdom as a body of spiritual forces for the social and ethical elevation of men.

A kingdom of influence

II. We turn from the kingdom to the king.

It is perhaps needless to say that our English word

"Messiah" is transferred from the Hebrew, and that our English word "Christ" is the Greek translation of the Hebrew word. The Hebrew word is a passive verbal of the stem which signifies to anoint with oil. Physically, it denotes a person who has been anointed with oil.

The verb of the stem is used in connection with the promise quite as prominently as the noun.[1] But a sufficient study of the meaning can be made from the noun alone.

Most readers of the Old Testament would probably accept offhand the statement that the prophets foretell the coming of a person whom they most com- The usual monly designate as the Messiah. This state- statement ment is inaccurate rather than untrue. One might make it, having a meaning that is true. But, first, the prophets use this word less than some other words as a messianic term. And, second, in most of the instances in which they use it, it does not directly and exclusively denote a coming person.

The noun occurs thirty-nine times in the Old Testament. Four times, all in Leviticus (iv. 3, 5, 16, vi. 22 [15]), the anointed one is the Levitical priest. Analysis of Twenty-three times the word is unmistak- the usage ably the official title of the reigning king of Israel. Among the instances are those in which Saul was in David's power, and David would not put forth his hand

---

[1] For example : —
"Thou hast loved righteousness, and hated wickedness :
  Therefore God, thy God, hath anointed thee
  With the oil of gladness above thy fellows" (Ps. xlv. 7 RV).

"I have found David my servant,
  With my holy oil have I anointed him" (Ps. lxxxix. 20).
"Because Yahaweh hath anointed me to bring good tidings to the meek" (Isa. lxi. 1).

against Yahaweh's anointed ; or when Samuel went to
Jesse's house to anoint a king in place of Saul, and saw
Eliab and said : " Surely Yahaweh's anointed is before
him ; " or when Abishai said that Shimei ought to be
put to death for cursing Yahaweh's anointed (1 Sam.
xxvi. 9, 11, 16, xvi. 6 ; 2 Sam. xix. 21 [22]).   The word
is thus used ten times of Saul, ten times expressly of
David or the kings of his line and in three other instances.   Further, it is once applied to Cyrus (Isa. xlv.
1); and in two passages, or rather in one repeated passage, to the patriarchs, with " my prophets " in the
parallel line.[1]   In none of these thirty passages, certainly, is the term Messiah, "anointed one," applied exclusively to a great coming person, who is to be the
deliverer of the nation or of mankind.

There remain nine instances in which one might claim
that the word denotes a coming person, but in every
one of them this is disputed.   One of these is the prayer
of Hannah (1 Sam. ii. 10) : —

> " It is Yahaweh that judgeth earth's uttermost parts,
>   That he may give strength to his king,
>   and may exalt the horn of his Anointed."

Another is in the prophecy against Eli (1 Sam. ii. 35) : —

> " Hophni and Phinehas,
> In one day they shall die, both of them.
> And I will raise me up a priest that is made sure,
> According to that which is in my heart and in my soul he shall do.
> And I will build him a house that is made sure,
> And he shall walk before mine Anointed all the days."

[1] " Touch ye not mine anointed ones,
        and do my prophets no harm " (1 Chron. xvi. 22; Ps. cv. 15).
Here the allusion is to Gen. xx. 7 and its context, where Abraham is
spoken of as a prophet.

Other instances are the following : —

" Kings of earth set themselves,
    and rulers take counsel together,
    against Yahaweh and against his Anointed " (Ps. ii. 2).

" Now know I that Yahaweh saveth his Anointed " (Ps. xx. 6).

" Yahaweh is strength to them,
    And he is the stronghold of the salvations of his Anointed "
                                        (Ps. xxviii. 8).
" Behold thou our Shield, O God,
    and gaze upon the face of thine Anointed " (Ps. lxxxiv. 9).

" Thou wentest forth for the salvation of thy people,
    for salvation with thine Anointed " (Hab. iii. 13).

" From the going forth of the word to restore and to build Jerusalem up to an Anointed one, a Regent, shall be seven weeks ; and
threescore and two weeks, it shall be built again, street and moat,
even in troublous times. And after the threescore and two weeks
shall Anointed one be cut off, and shall have nothing " (Dan. ix.
25–26).

In this passage in Daniel the syntax of the word
" Anointed " is practically that of a proper name. The
words " Anointed " and " Regent," (*nagidh*, regent, viceroy, primate, see concordance) are used as synonyms.

We need not spend time discussing these nine instances. Any one who will carefully examine them
will see that in most of them the Anointed one is primarily the actual or supposed reigning king of the line
of David. The margin left for the use of the word for
denoting simply a coming person is very small.

If we ask the question in this form, therefore : What
do the prophets say concerning a coming person called
the Messiah ? — we shall not obtain a satis- The correct
factory answer. But the answer will be form of the
satisfactory if we ask the question in the question
different and better form : What do the prophets say

concerning the Messiah, the Anointed one? They
say that the Anointed one is Yahaweh's regent, his
primate, his king, over his eternal kingdom on the
earth. He is at any moment the man who is entitled
to sit as Yahaweh's representative on the imperishable
throne over Israel. To the prophets of David's time,
David is the Anointed one, especially when they think
of David as the depositary of the promise. To each
succeeding prophet the reigning Davidic king of his
own time is the Anointed, especially when thought of
as the representative of the promise. After the exile
a like character was attributed to Zerubbabel, and
possibly to others.

There came a time, however, when for generation
after generation there was no recognized living repre-
The Messiah sentative of the blood of David who could be
as a coming regarded as the promised king, occupying the
person promised eternal throne. The Anointed one
had ceased to be a manifested fact among men. But if
one believed the promise, he believed that the imperishable kingdom was still in existence, and that in coming
time it would again be manifested. He believed that
the line of David still survived, and that a time would
come when a king of that blood would be manifestly on
the throne. Those who thus believed were watching for
this manifestation; and thus they came to think of the
Anointed one as he that should come. Usage fixed
upon this term, in preference to all the others, as the
fittest to describe the expected king of the kingdom, in
its new manifestation; and the selection was a happy one.

To repeat this, in part. The prophets count the fulfilment of the promise to David, Yahaweh's Anointed,
as beginning at once in his lifetime. They find it in
the preparations for building and in the building and

dedication of the temple. And each prophet recognizes in the events of his own time a double embodiment of the promise. It is embodied in the people Israel, Yahaweh's Servant, and in the living representative of the line of David, the reigning king of Judah, Yahaweh's Anointed. To each prophet the people and the king alike have a dual character. No matter how unworthy either may actually be, each stands on a lofty pedestal when thought of in the character of the representative of the promise. By their teachings the prophets aroused expectations that endured long after their own succèssion ceased. As the generations passed, the character of the expectation was affected by the historical events. From a time as early as the temporary political independence under the Maccabees, the characteristic form of the expectation was that the kingdom and its Anointed king would again become visible realities.

We have glanced at the passages in which the noun "messiah" is used in the Old Testament. We might gather a much larger number in which the personality denoted by the noun is mentioned, but in which the noun itself is not used. We might, for example, group the places in which other derivatives of the stem are used, or those in which the messianic person is called king, or by some other official name. But the result would be simply to lay additional emphasis on the points already gained. *Other terms for the messianic person*

Obviously there is nothing violent in the transition from the Old Testament conception of the kingdom, with its world-wide and unending reign of righteousness and peace and happiness, and with its king who is one in an eternal succession, to the New Testament idea of the spiritual king- *Transition to the New Testament idea* dom of Christ, including in its domain all the kingdoms of the world, with a son of David as king. The most marked difference between the two conceptions is that Christians regard Jesus as the eternal king, not merely in the sense of being one person of an eternal succession, but also in the sense of being himself an eternal person.

In the time of Jesus the messianic hope included with much prominence the expectation of a coming person (Matt. xi. 3, xxi. 9, xxiii. 39; Lc. vii. 19, 20, xix. 38; Jn. vi. 14, xi. 27, xii. 13; Acts xix. 4, etc.). His coming was to be the revival of God's kingdom on earth, and so he was called the Anointed one, the king. In their own times the prophets had used a variety of terms, and this term among others. It was simply one of several terms which they were accustomed to employ. In the time of Jesus it had come to be the one preferred term, and it would not be easy to say how long before his time it became so.

III. There remain to be considered certain expressions concerning the regnal and judicial acts of Yahaweh, in their relations to his kingdom and its Anointed king.

These expressions are the ones translated "the latter days," "the day of Yahaweh," with certain variants, and, as interpreting these, certain representations of Yahaweh as coming to judgment. It is the New Testament rather than the Old which connects these expressions specifically with the messianic "kingdom of heaven"; but even in the Old Testament they connect themselves not merely with the universal sovereignty of Yahaweh, but also with his particular sovereignty in the promise-kingdom.

The phrase *ahharith hayyamin,* translated "latter

days," "last days," in the English versions, does not
of necessity mean anything more definite than subsequent days, future time. There is nothing _{The latter}
in the phrase itself to indicate whether the _{days}
later time to which it refers is proximate or remote or
eschatological.[1] It is used in writings of all dates, and
in connection with events of all dates. It is sometimes
used in the passages that speak of the victorious kingdom, and of the universal reign of Yahaweh's law and
of peace (Isa. ii. 2; Mic. iv. 1; Ezek. xxxviii. 8, 16).
There is nothing in the phrase itself to connect it with
"the day of Yahaweh," or with the idea of a judgment
scene, but this connection is sometimes made by the context.[2] And so the phrase comes to include the idea of
certain future times that shall be times of retribution to
Israel for his lack of fidelity to the promise-covenant,
but also times of the fulfilment of the promise, and of
overthrow to his enemies. We are not surprised to find
the term used in the New Testament to denote the times
then current and coming, with more or less distinct
eschatological implications (*e.g.* Acts ii. 17; Heb. i. 2;

[1] Jacob says that he will make known to his sons "what will befall you
in the latter days" (Gen. xlix. 1 J). Balaam proposes to advise Balak
"what this people shall do to thy people in the latter days" (Num. xxiv.
14 J). Moses is represented as saying : —
"For I know that after my death ye will act very corruptly, and will
remove from the way which I have commanded you, and the evil will
befall you in the latter days" (Deut. xxxi. 29).
"In the distress to thee, when all these words shall have found thee in
the latter days, and thou shalt turn unto Yahaweh thy God, . . . he will
not forget the covenant of thy fathers" (Deut. iv. 30–31).
See also Hos. iii. 5 ; Jer. xxiii. 20, xxx. 24 ; Dan. x. 14, etc.
[2] For example : "And my anger will burn with him in that day, . . .
and many and distressing evils will find him, and he will say in that day,
Is it not because my God is not in the midst of me that these evils have
found me ? And I for my part will surely conceal my face in that day"
(Deut. xxxi. 17–18, *cf.* 29).

I Pet. i. 20; 2 Pet. iii. 3); while a modification of it, "the last day" is specifically eschatological (*e.g.* Jn. vi. 39, 40).

Much more important in the prophetic writings is "the day of Yahaweh," variantly spoken of as "that day," and as a day in which Yahaweh "cometh." For some purposes it might be regarded as simply a specification under the more general term "the latter days," but it is a specification that has a character of its own.

We shall better understand this term if we look first at a different Old Testament form of expression. Yahaweh Yahaweh holding a judgment assembly in his character as chief magistrate of the nations is sometimes presented as holding a solemn assembly for adjudicating the cases that may arise. Look, for example, at this presentation : —

"Arise O Yahaweh in thine anger!
Uplift thyself at the aggressions of mine adversaries!
And be thou awake unto me, thou [who] hast commanded judgment,
A congregation of races surrounding thee!
And over it return thou on high " (Ps. vii. 6–7).

Here the adjudication is presented as a solemn pageant. Yahaweh is to arise and come from his lofty dwelling place to perform it. He is attended by the populations as a retinue, and when the court is over, they escort him in his return on high. With this compare the familiar picture in Daniel : —

" Thrones were placed, and one that was ancient of days did sit;
. . . thousand thousands ministered unto him, and ten thousand times ten thousand stood before him : the judgment was set, and the books were opened " (Dan. vii. 9–10 RV).

And with these compare the briefer description in Joel : —

"That the nations may come up unto the valley of Yahaweh-judgeth ; for there will I sit to judge all the nations from round about" (iii. 12 [iv. 12]).

Passages of this kind are not unfamiliar. The one just cited from Daniel is expressly connected with the promise-kingdom.[1] In most of the instances the connection is less direct. But in them all we have a way of speaking in which Yahaweh's judicial activities with men are pictured as special occasions, occurring at definite dates. This mode of figuring the matter prepares the way for another; any such occasion might naturally be called a day of Yahaweh; or, with reference to the particular matters to be adjudicated, the day of Yahaweh.

This phrase appears inchoately in the record of the exodus. After the sin of the golden calf, *History of the term "the day of Yahaweh"* Moses intercedes for the people, and at last obtains from Yahaweh this concession : —

"And now [I say to thee], Go, lead thou the people whither I spake to thee [saying], Behold my Angel will go before thee ; and in the day of my visiting I will visit upon them their sin " (Ex. xxxii. 34 JE).

The threat here uttered is terse, and likely to have made an impression. The impression would be deep in proportion as the Israelites were in the habit of looking forward to " the latter days " and expecting therein divine blessings or retributions.

It is a natural suggestion, though one hardly capable of decisive proof, that this clause is the original text of the sermons which the prophets preach concerning the day of Yahaweh. The sermons are many. Joel, Obadiah, Zephaniah, and several prophetic discourses in other books are monographs on this subject, and the day is frequently mentioned in still other prophecies. We cannot treat of them all, but we will follow the his-

---

[1] " Until the ancient of days came, and judgment was given to the saints of the Most High ; and the time came that the saints possessed the kingdom " (Dan. vii. 22 RV).

tory of the term a little way, on the theory that Joel is
the earliest of the books to which the names of prophets
are attached.[1]

The book of Joel has "The Day of Yahaweh" as its
subject; treating it, first, as a day of dread to Yahaweh's
people, demanding repentance from them
(i. 2–ii. 17), and, second, as a day of blessing
to them if they repent, and a day of judgment
to the nations (ii. 18 to close of book).

The day of
Yahaweh in
Joel

After picturing the locust calamity and the drouth
(i. 4–9, 10–13) the prophet challenges the calling of a
fasting assembly (14), and then pictures these calamities a second time, beginning thus : —

"Alas for the day !
Because the Day of Yahaweh is near,
    and like destruction from the Almighty it cometh !
Hath not food been cut off before our eyes ? " (15–16).

Then, after five verses descriptive of the drouth, the
prophet introduces his second sketch of the locusts : —

"Blow ye a trumpet in Zion,
    and raise a shout in my holy mountain.
Let all the inhabitants of the land tremble !
    for the Day of Yahaweh cometh, for it is near !
A day of darkness and gloom,
    a day of cloud and thick darkness " (ii. 1–2).

With this introduction the prophet describes the locusts
again, closing with the words : —

"For the Day of Yahaweh is great,
    and terrible exceedingly, and who may abide it ? " (11).

Thus far in Joel the day of Yahaweh is a day to be
dreaded by his people ; in the second half of the book
it takes on a different character.   We are told that

[1] The hypothesis that Joel is of later date would affect the history only
in details.

Yahaweh was jealous for his land (ii. 18–20), and gave a compassionate answer to his fasting people, promising relief, first from the crop failure, and second from the invading Northerner. In ii. 21–27 the promise concerning the crops is amplified, and that concerning the Northerner is amplified in ii. 28–iii. 17. This last section opens with the great passage cited by the apostle Peter at the pentecost, the passage concerning the outpouring of the Spirit upon all flesh.[1] In this passage the day of Yahaweh appears as great and terrible, but as a time of deliverance for those who call on the name of Yahaweh, and of retribution for others. A little further on we read of the nations summoned to the valley of Yahaweh-judgeth, where Yahaweh sits as judge, and again we find the day of Yahaweh, a dreadful day, attended by convulsions of earth and heaven, but a day of reassurance to his people.[2]

[1] " And it shall come to pass afterward
 I will pour out my Spirit upon all flesh,
  and your sons and your daughters shall prophesy,
 Your elders shall dream dreams,
  your choice young men shall behold visions.
 And even upon the bondmen and the bondwomen
  I will pour out in those days my Spirit.

" And I will give wonders in the heaven and in the earth,
 Blood and fire and columns of smoke.
 The sun shall be turned to darkness,
  and the moon to blood,
 Before the Day of Yahaweh come,
  the great and terrible [day].

" And it shall be that whoever shall call
  on the name of Yahaweh shall escape " (Joel ii. 28–32).

This is followed by details concerning the deliverance granted by Yahaweh to his people.

[2] " Multitudes, multitudes in the valley of Decision!
 For the Day of Yahaweh is near
  in the valley of Decision.

On the theory of the early date of the book of Joel, these are the earliest occurrences of the term "the day of Yahaweh." We have here also the fullest and most elaborate of the many presentations of this theme. And there is probably no other use of the phrase in the Old Testament that cannot plausibly be regarded as presupposing this treatment in Joel. But even in Joel the phrase is introduced as if it were not altogether unfamiliar. If we suppose that the prophet's generation had inherited prophetic utterances concerning "the latter days," and concerning Yahaweh's holding assizes for judgment, and that they believed that Yahaweh had said to their ancestors, —

"In the day when I visit I will visit their sin upon them,"

our supposition recognizes likely materials from which the prophet might construct just the treatment he has constructed.

The book of Obadiah is another monograph on the day of Yahaweh (8, 15), the day here being one of retribution on Edom, and of victory and reprisal on the part of Yahaweh's people. Amos addresses auditors who are familiar with just such a doctrine of the day of Yahaweh as Joel teaches, and who are gladly expecting the day; and he rebukes them, saying that for such as they the day is only dreadful.[1] Like Joel he insists upon it that men

The day of Yahaweh in the other prophets

> Sun and moon are darkened,
> while stars have withdrawn their shining,
> While Yahaweh from Zion roareth,
> and from Jerusalem giveth his voice,
> and heaven and earth are quaking.
> While Yahaweh is a refuge to his people,
> and a strong place to the sons of Israel " (iii. 14–16).

[1] " O ye that long for the day of Yahaweh! What is it to you, the day of Yahaweh? It is darkness and not light. As when a man fleeth from

will find the day of Yahaweh fortunate for themselves only in case they are repentant and faithful. Amos specifically appeals to the clause in Exodus : —

"For in the day of my visiting the transgressions of Israel upon him, I will visit upon the altars of Bethel," etc. (iii. 14, *cf.* Ex. xxxii. 34).

And with him "that day" is a frequent phrase.[1] Obadiah and Amos enable us to see that the doctrine of the day of Yahaweh had taken a deep hold upon the men of their generation, so that it could be appealed to in popular preaching. To them we might add prophet after prophet, in passage after passage.[2]

One notable phenomenon is that the day of Yahaweh is characteristically represented as "near," as impending (Joel i. 15, ii. 1, iii. 14; Isa. xiii. 6; Ezek. xxx. 3; Zeph. i. 7, 14, etc.). This representation is made by prophets who lived many generations apart, and therefore by prophets who knew that other prophets had made it generations before. Perhaps this indicates that the prophets thought of the day of Yahaweh as generic, not an occasion which would occur once for all, but one which might be repeated as circumstances called for it. However this

The day of Yahaweh always impending

before the lion, and the bear meeteth him. Or he entereth the house and leaneth his hand upon the wall, and the serpent biteth him. Is not the day of Yahaweh darkness and not light? and thick darkness, with no brightness to it?" (Am. v. 18-20).

[1] "And temple songs shall be howlings in that day" (viii. 3). "In that day . . . I will cause the sun to go in at noon" (viii. 9). "In that day the fair virgins shall faint, and the youths, for thirst" (viii. 13). "In that day I will raise up the fallen booth of David" (ix. 11). Compare the passages that speak of "the evil day," or that use the phrase, "Behold days are coming" (vi. 3, iv. 2, viii. 11, ix. 13).

[2] See articles in *Homiletic Review*, October and November, 1889, and February, 1890.

may be, the peculiarity in their representation exists. They picture the day as close at hand, not at one point of time only, but century after century.

We are all familiar with these modes of representation in the forms which they assumed in the New Testament times. The pictures of Yahaweh with his retinue coming to judgment are reproduced in what is said concerning the Son of Man coming " in his glory, and all the angels with him," or concerning the Lord descending from heaven " with a shout, with the voice of the archangel, and with the trump of God" (Matt. xxv. 31 ; 1 Thess. iv. 16), and in other like representations. No idea of the men of the New Testament is more marked than that of "the last days," as a period already reached in their time, but extending forward into eternity (Acts ii. 17; 2 Tim. iii. 1 ; Heb. i. 2, etc.). And "the day of the Lord," "the day of judgment," "that day," are expressions that occur scores of times (*e.g.* 2 Pet. iii. 10, 12; 1 Thess. v. 2, 4; Matt. vii. 22, xi. 22, 24). That these New Testament representations are those of the Old Testament in a widened form, and that they constitute an important part of the New Testament doctrine of the kingdom, are facts too obvious to require arguing.

The New Testament imagery

CHAPTER XIV

MESSIANIC TERMS. YAHAWEH'S *HHASIDH*. OTHER TERMS

In pursuing this subject, we will discuss somewhat in detail the term *hhasidh*, a term which in the prominence of its use in the Old Testament is surpassed only by the terms " Servant " and " Messiah " ; and will afterward deal more briefly with the terms that remain.

I. *Hhasidh* is in the English versions translated variously by "holy one," "merciful one," "godly one," "gracious one," and in the plural by "saints"; and in each of these translations the Hebrew word is liable to be confused with other words. Hence, it seems expedient here to use the transferred Hebrew word rather than any translation of it.

The word *hhasidh* is used only in poetry, never in prose. It occurs in the Psalms twenty-five times ; in the psalm-duplicates twice (2 Sam. xxii. 26; 2 Chron. vi. 41); and elsewhere five times (Deut. xxxiii. 8 ; 1 Sam. ii. 9; Prov. ii. 8 ; Jer. iii. 12 ; Mic. vii. 2).

Hhasidh is from the same stem with *hhesedh*, often translated " mercy," but properly "lovingkindness," the word that appears in the psalm-refrains, " for his mercy endureth forever," and in such phrases as " the assured mercies of David." The idea properly conveyed by the words of this stem is that of kindness or favor, or free grace — never that of mercy in the sense of compassion. We shall probably cling to the musical English phrase, "for his mercy endureth forever," but the exact rendering is, "his lovingkindness is to eternity."

When the words of this stem are translated by "holy" or "saint," that confuses them with the words of the very different stem, *qadhash*. The adjective of this latter stem denotes one who is holy in the sense of being separate by reason of his ceremonial or moral good character. Yahaweh himself is in this sense preëminently the Holy one, Israel is the one holy nation, angels or human persons may be holy (*e.g.* Lev. xx. 7,26; Dan. viii. 13, 13, 24; Job v. 1, xv. 15; Pss. xvi. 3, xxxiv. 9). As differing from this, the adjective from the stem *hhasadh* should denote a kindly loved one, a dearly loved one, a favored one, one who is in favor, a favorite one, who is the object of gracious love and is treated accordingly.

The lovingkindness denoted by the words of this stem may be that of any person to any other person,[1] but oftener than in all other uses combined it is Yahaweh's lovingkindness, under his promise, to Abraham, to Israel, to the line of David. This is, perhaps, exclusively the usage of *hhasidh*, as distinguished from the other words of the stem.

Hhasidh is properly the passive adjective of the stem, though it passes readily into a noun, and should, perhaps, in actual use, be always regarded as a noun. It denotes that wherein the quality denoted by the stem resides. That is, it denotes a person in whom lovingkindness is thought of as resident. When we find the word used of Yahaweh, he is presented as the person in whom his own lovingkindness dwells, whence it may be manifested for the benefit of his creatures. When we find it applied to men, it describes them as the de-

[1] For example, the lovingkindness of Abimelech or of Rebekah's family to Abraham (Gen. xxi. 23, xxiv. 49).

positaries of Yahaweh's lovingkindness. A *hhasidh* is a person to whom or in whom the divine graciousness and favor are especially manifested. If there is such a personality as "the *hhasidh*," then the *hhasidh* is he who is distinguished above all others in the matter of such manifestation. In nearly all the instances, the human persons who are called *hhasidhim* are expressly called Yahaweh's *hhasidhim*, and in the few remaining instances this is implied. It is safe to say that there are no exceptions. When the sacred writers thought of a man as *hhasidh*, they invariably thought of him as Yahaweh's *hhasidh*.

Further, it is clear in most of the instances that the lovingkindness implied in the word *hhasidh* is Yahaweh's lovingkindness, and there are no instances from which this idea is excluded. It goes without saying that persons in whom Yahaweh makes his lovingkindness known should themselves practise lovingkindness toward him and toward other beings; but they are *hhasidhim* not in virtue of this, but in virtue of his lovingkindness as shown in and through them.

These general statements prepare us to examine the instances. So far as the statements need proof, the proof will appear as we proceed.

The word *hhasidh* is used in the Old Testament seventeen times in the plural, eleven times in the singular, and four times where there are variant readings, the word being singular in some copies and plural in others.

Of the instances in which it is used without variant in the singular, there are probably three in which the meaning is subjective, the term being applied to Yahaweh himself. In each of the three he is presented as himself the repository of his lovingkind-

Yahaweh the *hhasidh*

ness to Israel.   In Jeremiah he urges his characteristic
kindly feeling as the reason why Israel should turn to
him.[1] In the great kingdom psalm, the character of
Yahaweh as *hhasidh* is made parallel with his character
as righteous.[2] A third instance, not so uniformly recognized, is found in Deuteronomy.[3] And this use of the
noun is paralleled by that of the verb in the Hithpael, in
the psalm in which David celebrates Yahaweh's having
rescued him from all his enemies.[4]

In the seventeen cases in which the word is used in
the plural, with no variant reading, the English versions
uniformly translate it " saints."   In these
passages the Septuagint translates by ὅσιος
except that in some copies, perhaps in the
best copies, υἱοί is used in 2 Chron. vi. 41.   The Vulgate, I believe, uniformly has " sanctus."   In fourteen
of these passages it is specified that the *hhasidhim* are
Yahaweh's *hhasidhim*, while in one place we have " her
hhasidhim," meaning Zion's (Ps. cxxxii. 16), and twice

*Hhasidhim
as used in the
plural*

---

[1] " Go thou and proclaim these words toward the north, and say :
> O turn back thou back-turning Israel, saith Yahaweh;
> I will not cause my face to fall with you,
> For I am *hhasidh*, saith Yahaweh,
> I will not maintain [my displeasure] forever " (Jer. iii. 12).
Here the Septuagint translates ἐλεῶν, the Vulgate " sanctus," and the
English RV " merciful."

[2] " Righteous is Yahaweh in all his ways,
> and *hhasidh* in all his deeds " (Ps. cxlv. 17).
Septuagint ὅσιος, Vulgate " sanctus," RV " gracious."

[3] " And in regard to Levi he said " — addressing Israel :
> " Thy Thummim and thy Urim are for the man of thy *hhasidh*,
> [Thy *hhasidh*] whom thou didst prove at Massah,
> and wert striving with by the waters of Meribah " (Deut. xxxiii. 8).
Here the Septuagint translates ἀνδρὶ τῷ ὁσίῳ, and RV has " thy godly
one," as if Levi were the *hhasidh*, instead of being " thy *hhasidh*'s man."

[4] " With a *hhasidh* thou wilt show thyself *hhasidh* " (2 Sam. xxii. 26;
Ps. xviii. 25).

we have simply *hhasidhim*, without the article or other limiting word (Ps. cxlix. 1, 5). If by saints we understand favorites of Deity, rather than holy persons, the translation conveys a correct idea. The idea itself is very intelligible, apart from all question of the road by which it is reached.

David is prominent in the *hhasidh* passages, though there is no uniformity in this. In the cases of undisputed plural use, the *hhasidhim* are primarily the Israelites, but the Israelites regarded as the depositaries of Yahaweh's lovingkindness, his own people, in covenant with him. At the same time, these passages have the same quality of universalness that we have found in the Servant passages in Isaiah. It is no perversion of most of them to apply them directly to the case of any persons who are in gracious relations with God. Note how these points are illustrated in the following three instances : —

" And he hath lifted up a horn for his people,
   A praise for all his *hhasidhim*,
   For the sons of Israel, the people that is near him" (Ps. cxlviii. 14).[1]

" He calleth unto the heaven from above,
     and unto the earth, for judging his people :
   Gather ye my *hhasidhim* to me,
     who made covenant with me by sacrifice " (Ps. l. 4–5).[2]

" I would hear
     what the God Yahaweh speaketh.
   For he speaketh peace
     unto his people and unto his *hhasidhim*.
   And let them not turn again to foolishness " (Ps. lxxxv. 8).[3]

---

[1] This psalm has no title, and David is not mentioned in the context.

[2] The title of this psalm is " A psalm. Asaph's." It does not mention David.

[3] The title is " To the leader. To the sons of Korah. A psalm." David is not mentioned.

In the use of this term it is quite common to emphasize faithfulness, and to put wickedness in contrast with
it. The *hhasidhim* are often those Israelites who avoid
transgression and are true to Yahaweh. This does not,
however, change the definition of the word as above
given. It is especially the faithful Israelites who constitute the Israel of the promise.

" Love ye Yahaweh, all ye his *hhasidhim.*
Yahaweh preserveth them that are trustworthy,
And, for the remaining part, requiteth a proud doer " (Ps. xxxi. 23).[1]

" For Yahaweh is he that loveth judgment,
and he will not forsake his *hhasidhim.*
Forever they are kept,
while a seed of wicked men is cut off " (Ps. xxxvii. 28).[2]

" Ye that love Yahaweh, hate ye evil.
He keepeth the souls of his *hhasidhim,*
From hand of wicked men he rescueth them " (Ps. xcvii. 10).[3]

It is sometimes alleged that the *hhasidhim* are a
particular sect or class or set of men, like the priests,
for example. The strongest instances that
can be adduced for this are the following, and
they are obviously inadequate. In particular, when the *hhasidhim* are mentioned in parallelism
with the priests, it is in the character of worshippers,
and not in that of an order like the priestly order.

Were the *hhasidhim* a sect?

" Arise, Yahaweh, to thy rest-place,
thou and the ark of thy strength.
Let thy priests be clothed with righteousness,
and let thy *hhasidhim* sing loudly.

[1] The title is " To the leader. A psalm. David's." It is apparently
written in the person of David, but does not otherwise mention him.

[2] The title is " David's," and the psalm seems to be written in the
person of David, but it does not directly mention him.

[3] This psalm has no title, and does not mention David.

For the sake of David thy Servant
turn thou not away the face of thine Anointed."

" And her priests I will clothe with salvation,
while her *hhasidhim* shall loudly, loudly sing "

(Ps. cxxxii. 8–9, 16).[1]

"Let thy priests, O Yahaweh God, be clothed with salvation,
while thy *hhasidhim* rejoice in the good " (2 Chron. vi. 41).[2]

" O God, nations have come into thine inheritance !
Have made unclean thy holy temple!
Have placed Jerusalem for heaps of ruins!

" Have given the corpses of thy servants
As food for the fowl of the heaven ;
The flesh of thy *hhasidhim* to beasts of earth!" (Ps. lxxix. 1–2).[3]

If in these last four instances we regard the *hhasidhim*
as a sect, we may perhaps admit the same usage in
some other passages ; but if the usage does not exist in
these four, it does not exist at all. And there is no
strong reason for admitting its existence here. If by
hhasidhim we here understand representative members
of Yahaweh's chosen nation, who are on that account
dearly loved by him, that meets all the conditions of
each of the contexts. There is no need of going further and regarding them as a sect or outwardly differentiated class.

The remaining instances of the undisputed plural use
are the following : —

[1] The title is " The song of the ascents." The psalm is full of the
mention of David. The name is in verses 1, 10, 11, 17, and there are
allusions to David in almost every verse.

[2] Here the Chronicler, in his account of the dedication of Solomon's
temple, makes a free citation from Ps. cxxxii, apparently implying that
the psalm was used on that occasion. Here the Swete text has "sons"
instead of "saints."

[3] The title is "A psalm. Asaph's." David is not mentioned.

" Sing psalms to Yahaweh, ye his *hhasidhim*,
  and give thanks to his holy memorial " (Ps. xxx. 4).[1]

" I will give thee thanks forever because thou hast done it,
  And I will wait for thy name, because it is good
    in the presence of thy *hhasidhim* " (Ps. lii. 9 [11]).[2]

" Precious in the eyes of Yahaweh
  is the death to his *hhasidhim* " (Ps. cxvi. 15).[3]

" May all that thou hast made give thee thanks, Yahaweh,
  while thy *hhasidhim* bless thee " (Ps. cxlv. 10).[4]

" Halleluia!
  Sing ye to Yahaweh a new song,
    his praise in an assembly of *hhasidhim*."

" Let *hhasidhim* be proud in glory,
    let them sing loudly upon their beds.
  The high praises of El in their throat,
    and a two-edged sword in their hand,
  To execute vengeance among the nations."

" To execute among them a written judgment,
    it is majesty for all his *hhasidhim*.
  Halleluia ! " (Ps. cxlix. 1, 5-7, 9).[5]

Of the instances in which the word is used without
variant in the singular, there is one in which the *hhasidh*
is a nation, that is, Israel.

" Judge me, O God, and plead
    my cause from a nation not *hhasidh* " (Ps. xliii. 1).[6]

---

[1] The title is " A psalm.   The song of the dedication of the house.
David's."   It is natural to understand it as written in the person of
David, though it does not mention him.

[2] The title is "To the leader.   *Maskil*.   David's.   When Doeg the
Edomite went in and told Saul and said to him, David went in unto the
house of Ahimelech."

[3] No title.   David not mentioned.

[4] Attributed to David in the title.

[5] No title.   David not mentioned.

[6] Septuagint ὁσίου, RV " an ungodly nation."

This non-*hhasidh* nation may be some other nation in contrast with Israel; or it may be Israel, the nation that ought to be *hhasidh* but is not. In either case we have by implication the conception of Israel as the *hhasidh*, the nation that is made up of *hhasidhim*.

In the remaining instances of use without variant in the singular, *hhasidh* denotes some human person. In these instances it is uniformly without the article, and without a limiting genitive. In most of the instances the English versions utterly fail to give the essential meaning.

A human *hhasidh*

We may begin with the following, attributed in its title to David : —

> " Bow down thine ear, O LORD, and answer me ;
>   For I am poor and needy.
>   Preserve my soul ; for I am godly :
>   O thou my God, save thy servant that trusteth in thee "
> (Ps. lxxxvi. 1–2 RV).

Changing this translation so that it may show the form of the original, it becomes : —

> "O keep thou my soul, for a *hhasidh* am I ;
>   Save thy servant, O thou my God,
>   who trusteth in thee."

That is, the speaker in the psalm declares himself to be a *hhasidh*. According to the earliest understanding of the psalm of which we are cognizant, we have here David claiming to be Yahaweh's *hhasidh*, and on that claim entreating the divine favor.

In the psalm in which David commemorates his deliverance from all his enemies, we have the couplet, as rendered in the revised version : —

> " With the merciful thou wilt shew thyself merciful ;
>   With the perfect man thou wilt shew thyself perfect "
> (Ps. xviii. 25 ; 2 Sam. xxii. 26).

The English makes the mistaken impression that "the merciful" is a plural term. Further, if one understands the word as meaning compassionate, he will be misled by it. He will see the true meaning if he puts the clause in the following form : —

> "With a *hhasidh* thou showest thyself *hhasidh*."

David is here represented as claiming, either directly or indirectly, that he is Yahaweh's *hhasidh*, and that Yahaweh treats him accordingly.

Look at a third instance : —

> "And know ye that Yahaweh hath distinguished to himself a *hhasidh* ;
> It is Yahaweh that heareth when I call unto him " (Ps. iv. 3).

Here again the title says that the speaker is David. The Septuagint translates " hath made his *hosion* wonderful." As in the preceding two instances, the speaker claims to be Yahaweh's *hhasidh*. He gives that as a reason why all attempts of men against him will be futile. As in the preceding instances it is possible to make this claim indirect : Yahaweh distinguishes as his own any person who bears the *hhasidh* character, and I am such a person. But it is simpler to understand the claim as direct : Yahaweh has distinguished one person as his *hhasidh*, and I am that person.

The following instance is somewhat different : —

> " Help, LORD, for the godly man ceaseth ;
> For the faithful fail from among the children of men "
> (Ps. xii. 1 RV).

The impression made on most English readers is that the failing and ceasing are in progress, that one godly man after another is ceasing to be, and that the faithful are failing, one after another. This impression is incorrect. The verbs are in the perfect, and the fact described is a fact thought of as complete. Further, the subjects are without the article. The following translation gives the form : —

" O save, Yahaweh, for a *hhasidh* hath ceased."

It is possible to regard the noun as collective, indicating that *hhasidhim* generally have gone out of existence. But the simplest interpretation is that the psalm laments the downfall (not necessarily the death) of some particular person who is here called a *hhasidh*. Possibly his restoration is spoken of in the fifth verse : —

" I will set him in safety at whom they puff."

A similar instance is found in the book of Micah.

" The godly man is perished out of the earth,
And there is none upright among men " (Mic. vii. 2 RV).

Give this its exact form, and its implications are different.

" A *hhasidh* hath perished from the earth,
while an upright one among mankind is not."

In this case the Septuagint has εὐσεβής instead of the usual ὅσιος. The natural understanding is that we have here a reference to the death of some distinguished individual, whom the prophet thinks of as Yahaweh's *hhasidh*, and whose departure opens the way for all license and wrong-doing.

There is one more instance : —

"For this let every one that is godly pray unto thee "
(Ps. xxxii. 6 RV).

Changing the form this becomes: " Concerning this every *hhasidh* prayeth," or " one who is wholly *hhasidh* prayeth." And again, either directly or indirectly, we have the speaker in the psalm, evidently David, counting himself as Yahaweh's *hhasidh*.

In most or all of these seven instances, the person
who is called a *hhasidh* is not indefinitely some one of
the *hhasidhim* taken at random, though that would be a
natural use of language, but is a person who is thought
of as having a preëminent right to be called *hhasidh*.
In most of the instances he is the speaker, and the
speaker is of the house of David. In other words, the
hhasidh is the person who would in other diction be
called the Anointed one.

This is still more marked in certain of the remaining
instances, those in which some copies have the word in

The cases
of variant
readings

the singular, and some in the plural. As we
have seen, there are four of these instances.
In each of them the word has a genitive pronoun. In two of them the evidence seems decisive in
favor of the reading in the singular. The first is from
the sixteenth psalm, attributed to David by its title and
by New Testament witnesses.

> " For thou wilt not abandon my soul to sheol,
> Thou wilt not give thy *hhasidh* to see destruction "
>
> (Ps. xvi. 10).

Here the documentary evidence preponderates in favor
of the singular. The two lines give in different words
the same meaning.   " My soul " — that is, " myself " —
in one line corresponds to " thy *hhasidh* " in the other.
Myself not being abandoned to sheol is the same thing
with thy *hhasidh* not seeing destruction. The *hhasidh*
therefore is here the speaker, represented to be David ;
and yet not David as a mere individual, but David as
the depositary of Yahaweh's lovingkindness. The
man David may die, but the *hhasidh* is eternal. Just
as David is the Anointed one, and yet the Anointed
one is eternal ; just as David is the Servant, and yet
the Servant is eternal ; so David is the *hhasidh*, and

yet the *hhasidh* is eternal. David as an individual went to the grave, and saw corruption there, but the representative of Yahaweh's eternal promise did not cease to exist. Peter's argument in the second chapter of Acts might be fallacious if his claim was that David in this psalm does not refer to himself; but this is not what Peter claims. He claims that David does not refer merely to himself in his ordinary character.

Peter and Paul are critically correct in arguing that the meaning is not exhausted when the words have been applied to the mortal man David, but extends on into the future, along the line of the eternal promise. And they are correct in claiming that the *hhasidh* is preeminently Jesus Christ (Acts ii. 25–31, xiii. 35).

As the word is used in the prayer of Hannah, the preponderance of proof is in favor of the singular.

> " The feet of his *hhasidh* he keepeth,
>
> *　　*　　*　　*　　*　　*
>
> Upon him in the heaven he thundereth,
>   it is Yahaweh that judgeth earth's uttermost parts;
> That he may give strength to his king,
>   and may exalt the horn of his Anointed one "
>
> (1 Sam. ii. 9–10).

If the word is here in the singular number, then the representation is that in the ideals of Hannah Yahaweh's *hhasidh* and his king and his Anointed one are all the same person.

In the eighty-ninth psalm is the familiar line : —

" Then thou spakest in vision to thy *hhasidhim* " (or *hhasidh*, ver. 19).

And in Proverbs : —

> " To preserve paths of judgment,
>   and the way of his *hhasidhim* (*hhasidh*) he keepeth " (ii. 8).

In these the word is probably plural. If so, the passages are like the other seventeen that use the word in the plural. If, on the other hand, you decide that the word is in the singular in these two places, then they are somewhat notable additional instances of the mention of Yahaweh's one preëminent *hhasidh*.

Summing up the results we have reached, *hhasidh*, though sometimes translated merciful, does not prop-
Summary of results erly denote a compassionate person, though the person in whom Yahaweh's lovingkindness dwells ought to be compassionate. It is translated pious, godly, godly one, holy one, but none of these translations are exact, though it is to be presumed that the person in whom Yahaweh's lovingkindness is displayed will be pious, godly, kind, holy. It is translated saint, gracious one, favorite, he whom Yahaweh favoreth, and, in a certain direction, these terms approach the true meaning; but the *hhasidh* is not properly the person in whom Yahaweh's lovingkindness in general dwells, but the one in whom dwells Yahaweh's particular lovingkindness as manifested in the eternal covenant with Abraham and Israel and David.

Like all the benefits of this eternal promise, Yahaweh's lovingkindness is for the nations, but for the nations through Israel. The principles on which he deals with one part of mankind are the principles on which he deals with all; the privileges of *hhasidhim* are not restricted to one race; but it is through Israel that they are offered to mankind. In all the representations that are made the *hhasidhim* are Israelite. The word in the plural is applied to Israelites, and in the singular it once denotes by implication the Israelitish nation. To this extent its use is parallel to that of the terms "servants" and "Servant" in the second half of Isaiah.

The word *hhasidh* in the singular, however, is like the word "Messiah" rather than like the word "Servant"; its use points to David rather than to Israel. Several of the passages where the word is used in the plural have a context that speaks of David, and about half of these passages are attributed to David, either in the psalm titles or otherwise. Six of the eight places where *hhasidh* in the singular denotes a man or a nation are in Davidic psalms, and the other two have possible Davidic affiliations. Usually the *hhasidh* denoted by the word in the singular is either David or the inheritor of the promise made to the eternal seed of David.

The representation is that this idea existed in the minds of some of the devout in Israel as early as the time of Hannah the mother of Samuel; that they believed in the promise that Yahaweh had made; that they expected that kings would descend from Jacob, and that the law of Moses concerning the kingdom would become operative; that they thought of this as the manifestation of Yahaweh's lovingkindness; that they looked forward to a future when Yahaweh's *hhasidh*, his king, his Anointed, should exist and reign. Afterward, in David's time and later, this idea became prominent. In their relations to the eternal promise Israelites came to think of themselves as *hhasidhim*, of the nation taken collectively as Yahaweh's *hhasidh*, of any particular obedient Israelite as a *hhasidh*, especially of David and David's promised eternal seed as a *hhasidh*, of the person who was at any time the inheritor of David's throne as preëminently the *hhasidh* of that generation. Those whose thinking was deepest thought thus of the Davidic *hhasidh*, not in virtue of his standing as an individual, but in virtue of his being the representative of the eternal promise to men through Abraham and Israel and David.

In the Maccabæan times there were Jews who called themselves *hhasidhim*, or, as the name has come to us through Greek sources, Asideans. They seem to have been a religious reform party, precursors of the Pharisees. They were commonly in sympathy with the political patriots, though apparently not always. They took their name of course from the scriptures. If it had been in the scriptures from the time of David and earlier, its ancientness fitted it all the better for their use. There is nothing in the history of the Asideans that necessarily calls for any modification of our exegesis of the passages.

The Asideans

There are critics, however, who regard the *hhasidh* passages as of late date, many of them having been written by the Asideans or their contemporaries. I do not accept this opinion. If I did, I should have to modify what I have said about the *hhasidh* only to the extent of saying that this was in Israel a comparatively late way of looking at the matter.

The men of the New Testament are not careful to keep the *hhasidh* line of expressions distinct. The word ὅσιος and its cognates they use but sparingly. Twice they quote from the sixteenth psalm the clause "Thou wilt not give thy *hosion* to see corruption" (Acts ii. 27, xiii. 35). Once they quote literally from the Greek of Isa. lv. 3: "The assured lovingkindness of David," τὰ ὅσια Δαυεὶδ τὰ πιστά (Acts xiii. 34). About eight times more they use ὅσιος or its derivatives in connections that make good sense equally whether we give the words the *hhasidh* meaning or not (1 Tim. ii. 8; Tit. i. 8; Heb. vii. 26; Rev. xv. 4, xvi. 5; Lc. i. 75; Eph. iv. 24; 1 Thess. ii. 10). But

Hhasidh expressions in the New Testament

it is possible that in the very numerous places where
they speak of being holy or of saints, using the word
ἅγιος and its cognates, they frequently had in mind
the ideas that the Hebrew expresses by words of the
hhasidh stem.   In particular, the New Testament
"saints" are often *hhasidhim* rather than *q'doshim*.

II. We must deal summarily with the remaining
messianic terms, though some of them are exceedingly
interesting.   The list here given makes no claim to
completeness.   It includes only such instances as I
have happened to note.

Christians are accustomed to speak of Christ as
Saviour and Redeemer.   These terms are not in this
especial sense applied in the Old Testament to the
messianic person.   Any person may supposably be a
saviour or a redeemer.   In the Old Testament "the
Saviour," "the Redeemer," is commonly Yahaweh.

In Isa. ix. 6 is a list of epithets which we apply
familiarly to the Messiah, — "Wonderful one, Counsellor, Mighty God, Everlasting Father, Prince of
Peace."   Whatever else we make of this diction, the
terms are descriptive epithets rather than technical
designations like Servant and Messiah and *hhasidh*.
The like may be said of Haggai's phrase "the Desire
of all nations" (ii. 7 OV), and of other similarly well-
known phrases.

Taking up the technical terms that are properly such,
we find that they arrange themselves in two classes, —
those which, like the term "Servant," primarily denote
Israel the promise-people, and those which, like " Messiah," primarily denote the king of the line of David.

1. Among the terms of the first of these two classes,
the one most to the front is probably "my Chosen one,"
"my Elect one."   The stem *bahhar* has a usage

extending to perhaps three hundred occurrences in the
Old Testament.   The verb is almost uniformly translated
Yahaweh's   by "choose," and is used with subjects and
Chosen one   objects of all kinds.   It is the verb that is
commonly used of Yahaweh's choosing Israel, or choosing Jerusalem to put his name there, or choosing David,
or choosing the Servant (*e.g.* Deut. vii. 6, xiv. 2; 1 Ki.
iii. 8, xi. 13, 32, 34; Isa. xli. 8, 9, xliii. 10).   The passive adjective *bahhir* denotes an object that is characterized by having been chosen.   It appears in the
plural seven times, always denoting Israelites (1 Chron.
xvi. 13; Pss. cv. 6, 43, cvi. 5; Isa. lxv. 9, 15, 22).   It is
used in the singular six times, once of Saul, once of
Moses, once of David, three times of the people Israel
(2 Sam. xxi. 6; Pss. cvi. 23, lxxxix. 3; Isa. xlii. 1, xliii.
20, xlv. 4).   When used of David and of Israel, it is
three times in parallelism with Servant.   The passive
participle is used as the equivalent of the noun in
Ps. lxxxix. 19.

This showing needs no comment.   Yahaweh's Chosen
one and his chosen ones are the same with his Servant
and his servants as presented in the last twenty-seven
chapters of Isaiah.   In the New Testament the term in
the singular is in a few places, some of them citations
from the Old Testament, applied to Christ (*e.g.* Matt.
xii. 18; Lc. xxiii. 35; 1 Pet. ii. 4, 6), and in both the
singular and the plural is often applied to Christians as
the inheritors of the promise.

Three additional terms of the same kind, though infrequently used in the records that have come down to
Jeshurun,   us, are Jeshurun (Isa. xliv. 2; Deut. xxxii. 15,
Meshullam,   xxxiii. 5, 26), Meshullam (Isa. xlii. 19), my
my Called
one   Called one (Isa. xlviii. 12).   Jeshurun is
commonly explained as a diminutive of endearment,

meaning upright one. Meshullam means "perfected one." Though it occurs only once in this use in our scriptures, it was not perhaps an infrequent term. It also occurs as the proper name of more than twenty different persons. My Called one appears as a singular use of a word of a very common stem.

In the places in which Israel or David or David's seed are designated as Yahaweh's son, that word is to be regarded as a messianic term. In Chap- Yahaweh's ter X we have already considered this term Son as marking slightly the records of the time of the exodus (Ex. iv. 22, 23; Deut. i. 31, xxxii. 6), and as marking more prominently the records of the time of David and later. In these later times the habit of representing the Israelitish people as Yahaweh's son still persists. Note a few examples : —

> "When Israel was a boy, then I loved him,
>   and from Egypt I called to my son" (Hos. xi. 1).[1]

> "Ephraim . . . is a son not wise" (Hos. xiii. 12-13).

"I said, How shall I put thee among sons ? . . . ye shall call me, My father" (Jer. iii. 19).

"I am a father to Israel, and Ephraim is my firstborn."
"Is Ephraim a precious son to me, or a child of caresses ? For altogether as I have spoken with him, I will surely still remember him" (Jer. xxxi. 9, 20).

In the matter of use in the singular and the plural, this term is like the terms "Servant" and *hhasidh ;* as in the singular it denotes Israel, so in the plural it

[1] When Matthew says (ii. 15) that this was "fulfilled" in the flight of Jesus to Egypt and his return thence, he means, of course, that it was fulfilled in the sense of there being an interesting coincidence between the experience of Israel and that of Jesus — not in the sense of an intended foretelling on the part of the prophet.

sometimes denotes Israelites who are true to their descent. See Isa. lxiii. 8, 16, lxiv. 8.[1]

The term is more conspicuous in the passages in which the seed of David is spoken of as the Son of Yahaweh, though here the conspicuity is due rather to the character of the passages than to their number. We have already looked at the expression as it occurs in the original account of the promise to David (2 Sam. vii. 14; 1 Chron. xvii. 13). It is equally prominent in the passages that cite that account, for example : —

"It is he that shall build a house to my name, while he himself shall be to me for a son, and I to him for a father " (1 Chron. xxii. 10),

or, —

> " He shall call me, My father thou,
> My God and the rock of my salvation,
> Yea, I myself will give him to be firstborn,
> A most high to kings of earth " (Ps. lxxxix. 26–27).[2]

So we are not surprised at finding in the second psalm a personage who is called Yahaweh's Anointed, but of whom Yahaweh says : —

> " Thou art my son, this day have I begotten thee " (7).[3]

The most jubilant passage in Isaiah is the exultation over the Son who is born to us, to sit on the throne of David, but who is to be called Mighty God and Ever-

---

[1] Other instances of this mode of representation may be found in Jer. iii. 4 ; Mal. i. 6, ii. 10, iii. 17.

[2] It is noticeable that the phrase " give thee to be a most high " seems to be taken from Deuteronomy (xxvi. 19, xxviii. 1), the author thus combining in one view the promise to David and that to the Israel of the exodus.

[3] In the English versions, this psalm also contains the exhortation to " kiss the son," that is, to do him homage (12). This is possibly correct, though the word is *bar*, and not *ben*, as in verse 7. Perhaps, however, the correct translation is, " Do ye homage sincerely."

lasting Father (ix. 6). Ezekiel represents Yahaweh as speaking of "the sceptre of my Son" (xxi. 10 [15]), and though the passage is obscure, Yahaweh's Son can here be no other than the occupant of the throne of the line of David.

The term "Son" is subject to certain modes of use that are peculiar to it. The "seed," whether of Abraham or of David, was to be perpetuated by Sons of fresh births in each generation. The promise promise is therefore in part a promise of perpetual parentage. Critical points in its history are marked by the gift of promised sons, such as Isaac, Ishmael, Samson, Samuel, Solomon. In these cases the mothers are made prominent, witness Sarah and Hagar and Manoah's wife and Hannah and Bathsheba. There is, so to speak, a sonship of human motherhood, as well as a sonship of divine fatherhood. And in connection with this a certain formula appears in the successive parts of the record. It is given most completely in connection with Hagar's bearing of Ishmael.

"And the Angel of Yahaweh said to her, Behold thou art pregnant and about to bear a son, and thou shalt call his name Ishmael" (Gen. xvi. 11).

Less complete versions of the formula appear in connection with the giving of Isaac and of Samson (Gen. xvii. 19; Jud. xiii. 5, 7).

These phenomena should not be neglected when we study the sign given through Isaiah to Ahaz, which Matthew cites as a prophecy concerning the The virgin virgin mother (Isa. vii. 14–16; Matt. i. 22–23). mother With only the substitution of Immanuel, "God with us," for Ishmael, "God heareth," Isaiah's words in the Hebrew are exactly the same with those uttered to Hagar: —

"Behold, thou the *almah* art pregnant and about to bear a son, and thou shalt call his name Immanuel."[1]

The sign given to Ahaz consists in the repeating to him of a familiar form of words promising the birth of a son, with the implication that certain events would come to pass before a child then soon to be born would be old enough to distinguish good from evil. The sign was proved true when, within a few years, the events foretold came to pass. Those who heard the prophet's words understood him to be preaching to Ahaz the familiar doctrine of the promise. There is no absurdity in supposing that the prophet himself knew by inspiration that he was foretelling a miraculous birth some centuries in the future. But if this seems to any of us improbable, we may find room enough for the disposal of all difficulties in the wide latitude of meaning with which Matthew frequently uses the phrase "that it

[1] The Hebrew verb "call" is here second person feminine (*cf.* Jer. iii. 4; Gen. xvi. 11; Isa. lx. 18, in contrast with the third person feminine in Gen. xxix. 35, xxx. 6; 1 Chron. iv. 9), and this controls the person of the preceding adjective and participle. The Greek translates the adjective and participle by verbs in the third person, but the verb "call" in the second person, the Greek not being able to distinguish the gender. Matthew follows the Greek, changing "thou shalt call" to the indefinite "they shall call."

Almah is not the distinctive word for virgin. So far as derivation goes, its proper meaning is young woman of marriageable age. But there is no trace of its use to denote any other than a virgin. It denotes Rebekah (Gen. xxiv. 43), the sister of Moses (Ex. ii. 8), timbrel players (Ps. lxviii. 25), young women as distinguished from queens and concubines (Cant. vi. 8), young women (Cant. i. 3). It occurs twice as a technical term in regard to the public songs (Ps. xlvi, title; 1 Chron. xv. 20). Finally, it appears in the clause "the way of a man with a maid" (Prov. xxx. 19). Here the allusion is to the mystery of "love's young dream," and the meaning is fine and worthy. It is absurd to make the meaning degraded and dirty, by regarding the *almah* as not a virgin. In fine, the Greek translators chose deliberately and correctly when they chose παρθένος as the translation here, and Matthew made no mistake when he so understood their translation.

might be fulfilled." Matthew was sure that the virgin birth of Jesus was a fact. He found that the words of Isaiah were in remarkable and interesting correspondence with this fact. This justifies his language, irrespective of the question whether the words are to be regarded as properly foretelling the fact.[1]

Returning from this digression concerning the sons of promise and the prophecy of the virgin mother, we note once more that when the word "Son" is used as a messianic term, the Son is either Israel or the existing representative of the house of David, thought of as the fulfilling of the eternal promise. The Son will always exist. Though he is explicitly said to be Israel, or is expressly identified with some member of the house of David, he is also in certain passages (*e.g.* Ps. ii or Isa. ix. 2–7) declared to be a superhumanly exalted person. We have here the same phenomena that we have in the case of the Servant, and they are to be accounted for in the same way. *Summary concerning the Son*

We must not delay to trace the later history of this term, or its relations to what the New Testament has to say concerning the Son of David, the Son of God, the Son of man, the fatherhood of God.

2. We have already crossed the line that separates the messianic terms which primarily denote Israel from those that primarily denote the Davidic king. The term "Son" is significant in both ways. We now take up other Davidic terms.

Words of two different Hebrew stems are in our English versions translated by our word "Branch," the word being in some bibles so printed as to indicate that it has a special use. One of these two is the noun *tsemahh* with its cognate verb. *The Branch, Tsemahh*

[1] See article in *Homiletic Review* for April, 1889.

The verb denotes the coming up of a shoot from a root or a seed, or the branching off of a shoot from a stem. For the noun we will use the traditional translation " branch." Examine first the passage in Isa. iv. 2–6 : —

"In that day the Branch of Yahaweh shall be for beauty and for honor, and the Fruit of the land for pride and for glory to them that are escaped of Israel ; and it shall come to pass that he that remaineth in Zion, and he that is left over in Jerusalem, shall be called holy, even every one that is written for life in Jerusalem ; when the Lord shall have washed away the filth of the daughters of Zion, and shall cleanse the bloodguiltiness of Jerusalem from the midst of her."

It is obvious that the terms " the Branch of Yahaweh " and "the Fruit of the land " may here be employed as designations for the dynasty of David, or for the reigning king in that dynasty. In other words, these phrases may be terms equivalent in signification to Anointed one or *hhasidh*. Some think, however, that these terms here have not this significance, but are mere expressions for the crops and for agricultural prosperity. It seems to me that the messianic interpretation is the correct one.

However it may be with this passage in Isaiah, the instances that follow are not open to doubt. To get the full meaning of the two passages now The Branch in Jeremiah to be cited from Jeremiah they should be read carefully in their contexts. The first is immediately introduced by two verses in which Yahaweh promises the return of " my flock out of all the countries whither I have driven them," and that he will place satisfactory shepherds over them. Then the promise proceeds : —

" Behold, days are coming, so saith Yahaweh, when I will raise up to David a righteous Branch ; and a king shall reign, and shall deal skilfully, and shall do judgment and righteousness in the earth. In his days Judah shall be saved, while Israel shall abide securely. And this is his name which one shall call him, Our-righteousness-is-Yahaweh.

"Therefore behold, days are coming, so saith Yahaweh, when they shall no longer say, As Yahaweh liveth who brought up the sons of Israel from the land of Egypt, but, As Yahaweh liveth who brought up and brought in the seed of the house of Israel from the land of the north, and from all the lands whither I had driven them, and they dwelt upon their own ground " (Jer. xxiii. 5–8).

In the second of the two passages in Jeremiah, the promise of the return is expanded to half a chapter (xxxiii. 6–13), and then follow the words : —

"Behold, days are coming, so saith Yahaweh, when I will establish the good word which I have spoken unto the house of Israel and concerning the house of Judah. In those days and in that time I will cause to branch forth to David a righteous Branch, and he shall do judgment and righteousness in the earth. In those days Judah shall be saved, while Jerusalem shall abide securely. And this is [the name] which one shall call her, Our-righteousness-is-Yahaweh.

"For thus saith Yahaweh, There shall not be cut off to David a man sitting upon the throne of the house of Israel " (Jer. xxxiii. 14–17).

This is followed by nine long verses magnifying the promise which Yahaweh has made to the Levite priests and to David and Abraham and Isaac and Jacob, and comparing the eternity and exactness of his covenant with them to the eternity and exactness of his covenant of the day and the night as exhibited in the movements of the heavenly bodies.

These passages need no comment. In both, the Branch is the representative of the line of David, reigning according to promise over Yahaweh's kingdom.[1]

[1] Some of the differences between the two passages are interesting. In both Israel is expressly included, as well as Judah. In one it is the Branch that is named Our-righteousness-is-Yahaweh, while in the other it is Jerusalem.

In the time after the exile when Zerubbabel and the highpriest Jeshua were building the temple, when the The Branch prophecies of Jeremiah concerning the return in Zechariah after seventy years were much in the thoughts of the Jewish leaders, we find Jeremiah's doctrine of the Branch applied to Zerubbabel, the representative for his generation of the house of David. In each case the prophet addresses the highpriest, but he speaks to him concerning Zerubbabel.

> " O Joshua the highpriest, listen, pray, thou and thy companions that sit before thee ; for they are men who are a sign ; for behold, I am causing to come to pass my Servant Branch " (Zech. iii. 8).[1]

In the fuller passage (Zech. vi. 9–15), the prophet is directed to make crowns for the highpriest and his companions (11, 14), and place one of them upon the head of the highpriest,[2] giving him this message : —

> " Thus saith Yahaweh of hosts, saying, Behold, [there is] a man, his name is Branch, and from beneath himself he shall branch forth and build the temple of Yahaweh ; it being he that shall build the temple of Yahaweh, and he that shall carry majesty, and he shall sit and shall rule upon his throne ; and there shall be a priest beside his throne, and peaceful counsel shall be between them two " (Zech. vi. 12–13).[3]

[1] " I will bring forth " (RV) is incorrect, and misses the meaning. "Bring in" would be correct. The Branch is spoken of as something that had been promised, and the promise is now to be made good.

[2] " And set [them] " (11). The object is not expressed. RV is incorrect in failing to italicize "them." Of course it was one crown only, and not all the crowns, that he was to set on the head of the highpriest. The crowns were apparently not kingly. The Persian government might have resented anything that looked like kingly state on the part of these men. The account specifies five men who are to have the crowns, and that seems to exclude Zerubbabel.

[3] In the last clause but one the translation might be "a priest upon his throne," which would give us a picture of a priestly throne in addition to the throne of the Branch. In any case there are two of them. The Branch is one and the priest is another, and the Branch is Zerubbabel and not Joshua.

Zechariah regards Jeremiah's prediction as fulfilled
in Zerubbabel, and he expects that through him will
come the building of the temple, and good government and prosperity, and a large immigration of returning Jews ; but that did not hinder his recognizing the
fact that Jeremiah had said that the Branch stands for
something that is as eternal as day and night.   Fulfilled in Zerubbabel, the promise concerning the Branch
still remained in existence, ready for whatever com-
pleter fulfilment Yahaweh might have in store.   There
is no clear recognition of the Branch in the New
Testament, but clearly the expression is parallel to
Anointed one and *hhasidh*. In the passage cited
from Zech. iii Servant is used as an equivalent
term, and the fact that David and Israel are from
the promise point of view identical is brought out in
the several passages.

The other word which our versions translate by
"Branch" is *netser*. "Flower" is a better rendering.

"Thy people being all of them righteous, . . . the
Flower of my plantings, the deed of my hands" (Isa.
lx. 21).

The Branch.
Netser

"And there shall come forth a bud-shoot out of the stem of Jesse,
while a Flower out of his roots shall be fruitful " (Isa. xi. 1).[1]

In one of these passages *netser* denotes the idealized
Israelitish people, and in the other the idealized Davidic
king. The last passage is so very marked as to make
the word conspicuous in spite of the paucity of the

---

[1] The word occurs elsewhere only twice : —
"Thou art cast out of thy grave like a discarded flower " (Isa. xiv. 19).
"And out of the flower of her roots shall one stand up" (Dan. xi. 7).
And it is the only word of the stem, though it may be akin to a stem that
denotes to preserve.

instances.   If one were to choose the one Old Testament messianic passage that would best serve as a type,
it is possible that his choice might fall upon Isa. xi.
1–10. This passage is cited in the New Testament often
indirectly and once (Rom. xv. 12) formally.   It presents
in a strong light "the root of Jesse that standeth for an
ensign of peoples" (10), and the "Flower from his
roots" that will surely become fruit; this Flower rested
upon by the Spirit of Yahaweh, wielding universal dominion, the result being good government and peaceful
prosperity and the knowing of Yahaweh throughout the
earth.   We must not delay upon the details.   In the
mind of the prophet's first hearers the *netser* may supposably have been Hezekiah, or have been an ideal king
of David's line, but he was so as a link in the promise
made for eternity by Yahaweh to Abraham and Israel
and David and mankind.

The word *hhoter*, translated "bud-shoot" in the passage just cited, is perhaps entitled to mention among
the messianic terms, but it need not delay us.

Not least important among these terms, though left
in the background in the English versions, is the word
nagidh, variously translated captain, ruler,
Nagidh, that is, Regent prince, chief ruler, leader, chief governor,
nobles, etc.   It is one of three words of a
stem that is much used.   One is a preposition signify-
ing in front of.   A second is the verb that signifies to
lay before one, that is, to announce, declare, make
known, tell.   The word *nagidh* is used in most parts
of the Old Testament, but its use is more frequent and
more varied in Chronicles than in the other books.   In
general it denotes a person or a tribe that is in front of
others, commanding attention and obedience; one that
is before others, not in the sense of being first in the

order of march, but in the sense of being looked to for orders ; one that is second only to the supreme authority ; one that has the primacy, a primate, viceroy, lieutenant, regent. The English word "regent" sometimes denotes a person who performs the duties of the sovereign because the sovereign is too young, or is otherwise incompetent. Excluding this use, the English word will translate *nagidh* wherever it occurs, and ordinarily with implications the same as those of the Hebrew word.[1] We have heretofore found that the human person who is over Yahaweh's kingdom on earth is called king, Yahaweh's Anointed. When the word *nagidh* is used, we have a different way of presenting the matter. In

[1] Five times the word is plural (2 Chron. xi. 11, xxxv. 8; Job xxix. 10; Ps. lxxvi. 12; Prov. viii. 6), the persons denoted being military or ecclesiastical officers or others of high rank. Three times the regent is an officer of the highest rank in a foreign nation (2 Chron. xxxii. 21; Ezek. xxviii. 2; Dan. ix. 26). About eleven times, besides instances in the plural, he is at the head of a department in Israel, the temple, the priesthood, the treasures, the house (1 Chron. ix. 11; 2 Chron. xxxi. 13; Jer. xx. 1; Neh. xi. 11; 1 Chron. ix. 20, xii. 27, xxvi. 24; 2 Chron. xxxi. 12, xxviii. 7; 1 Chron. xiii. 1). Four times the regent is of especially high rank, but is not otherwise designated (1 Chron. xxvii. 4, 16; Job xxxi. 37; Prov. xxviii. 16). Zebadiah, "the regent of the house of Judah" (not the tribe, but the royal house), was, next to the king himself, over the people "in all the king's matters" (2 Chron. xix. 11). Abijah was made regent at the head of his brothers the sons of Rehoboam (2 Chron. xi. 22).

This general use of the word may serve to define it when it is applied to the king of Yahaweh's kingdom. David is represented as saying that Yahaweh has chosen Judah for Regent (1 Chron. xxviii. 4). Though Reuben was the firstborn, Judah had the birthright, so that the Regent came from him (1 Chron. v. 2). Saul and David and Solomon and Jeroboam and Baasha and Hezekiah are in their kingly character each spoken of as Regent (1 Sam. ix. 16, x. 1, xiii. 14, xxv. 30; 2 Sam. v. 2, vi. 21; 1 Chron. xi. 2, xxix. 22; 1 Ki. i. 35, xiv. 7, xvi. 2; 2 Ki. xx. 5). And this way of speaking is employed in the passages that treat specifically of the promise (2 Sam. vii. 8; 1 Chron. xvii. 7; 2 Chron. vi. 5; Isa. lv. 4; Dan. ix. 25, xi. 22).

this mode of speech the king is Yahaweh, and the human monarch is Yahaweh's Regent, his grand vizier, his supreme representative, second in rank only to himself.

This list would be incomplete if we omitted the term " my Lord " as used in the opening of the one hundred My Lord, and tenth psalm. The one who uses the in Ps. cx phrase is speaking in the person of David, and the person of whom he speaks is Yahaweh's king or Regent. This would be clear even if we had not the word of Jesus and the writers of the New Testament for it (Matt. xxii. 43–45; Mc. xii. 36; Lc. xx. 42–44; Acts ii. 34–35; Heb. i. 13, x. 13; 1 Cor. xv. 25, etc.). Deferring to the next chapter our examination of the contents of the psalm, we now only note the name " my Lord " as here applied to this conquering king, who sits at Yahaweh's right hand, second in authority only to him.

In regard to each of the terms in the list we have been examining, we might repeat, with the requisite Common changes in details, certain things that have character of the messianic been already said concerning the Servant and terms the Messiah. Each one of them is so universal that it might be applied to any person or personified aggregate, thought of as representing Yahaweh's redemptive purposes for mankind. Each one was primarily understood to denote either Israel or the contemporary representative of the line of David, or both, thought of as standing for Yahaweh's promised blessing to mankind. But in each case this contemporary person or personified people is a link in an endless chain. The prophets never forget that the promise is for eternity. They taught that the Servant or the *hhasidh* or the Branch or the Son or the Regent belong to the present and the past, but also to future generations without limit. They looked forward to the future manifestation of the Servant or the *hhasidh* or the Branch or the Son or the Regent in such glory as should eclipse all earlier manifestations.

CHAPTER XV

Thus far we have been dealing with the direct statements made in the Old Testament concerning the promise. In the present chapter we are to look at certain less direct ways in which it gives testimony in the matter.

The central line of the Old Testament records is that of the history of Israel. We have traced the messianic promise in that history, up to the time when the psalmists and prophets whose works remain to us took up the doctrine. We have noticed how these poets and preachers of Israel found the promise in existence and made it the principal theme of their songs and sermons, regarding it as the central doctrine of their religion, and treating it accordingly. We have made a study of some of the terms which they created for the expressing of this doctrine: Servant, the Kingdom and the Anointed, *hhasidh*, Chosen one, Beloved one, Perfected one, my Called one, Son, Branch, Flower, Bud, Regent, my Lord. All this is what the records directly say concerning the promise as existing in the times of the patriarchs, of the exodus, of David, of David's successors. Now we come to the consideration of certain collateral ways in which this literature hands down this same doctrine of the promise.

As preliminary we need to look more closely at one or two aspects of the evidence as already presented.

344

Inevitably, as we consider these facts and terms one after the other, there arises in the mind a conception which we may describe as that of the Person of the promise. Each one of the messianic terms denotes either a person or an aggregate of people personified. We all have to agree in this, even if we differ in our opinions as to the identity of the person or the aggregate. For example, if one regards the Servant as Israel, and another regards him as the heir to David's kingdom, and another regards him as the prophet, and another as some typical Israelite, and another as a person who is to come, all alike have the conception of him as a person. They might use this conception in formulating their differences, one saying that the Person of the promise is Israel, another saying that the prophet himself is the Person of the promise, another saying that the Person of the promise is a coming Saviour, and so on.

The Person of the promise

We have already seen that certain extraordinary things are said concerning the Person of the promise, but we now need to attend to this more particularly. Under the title of the Servant the Person of the promise is in the same breath said to be Israel and to have the restoring of Israel as his mission (Isa. xlix. 1–6). Again, in a closely connected passage he is one moment presented as Israel, suffering for the wrongdoing of the nations, and in the next moment as stricken for the transgressions of " my people " ; at one moment as belonging to a particular generation, and cut off out of the land of the living, and in the next moment as prolonging his days and possessing to the full all that is included in Yahaweh's eternal covenant with Israel (Isa. liii).

Extraordinary statements concerning him

Perhaps the eternal and universal dominion ascribed

to the Person of the promise, under more than one of the titles by which he is designated, and the peace and happiness prevailing thereunder, should not be regarded as extraordinary, because the passages of this kind are so very frequent. But when we find applied to him, under the description of the Son that is born, such titles as Wonderful, Counsellor, God all Victorious, Eternal Father (Isa. ix. 6), these at least indicate something most unusual in his character as estimated by the prophet.

A very marked presentation of this idea of the wonderful exaltation of the Person of the promise appears in Jacob's blessing upon Judah : —

" Sceptre shall not be removed from Judah, nor lawgiver from his lineage, until that he come whose it is, and obedience of peoples be his " (Gen. xlix. 10).

Even if one does not venture to decide too dogmatically on a passage concerning which opinions differ so greatly, one may at least suppose that the poet has here in mind the conception of the Person of the promise. He says that the prerogatives of the promise shall descend through Judah, in a dominion that shall have no end. Compare Ezek. xxi. 27 [32].[1]

Jesus showed his insight into the scriptures when he selected the one hundred and tenth psalm as a typical instance for calling attention to the extraordinary char-

[1] The translation " until Shiloh come " (OV) is not bad. Shiloh is here not the familiar proper name, but the transliterated Hebrew phrase " whose it is." To a reader who understands this the meaning is clear. There is an old-fashioned interpretation that regards the verse as a prediction fulfilled in the fact that Judah under Herod retained some shadow of national prerogative till after the birth of Jesus. This is really quite plausible, but the meaning seems to me to be, rather, that the dominion vested in Judah will never cease, but will be merged into the " obedience of peoples " to the Person of the promise.

acter attributed to the Person of the promise.   Let us
look at this song more particularly.   Its title is " David's.
A Psalm."   There is no reason for disputing   The instance
that Jesus and the men of the New Testa-   selected by
ment are correct when they say explicitly that   Jesus
the words of the psalm are spoken in the person of David
(Matt. xxii. 44; Mc. xii. 36; Lc. xx. 42–43; Acts ii.
34–35).

> " The utterance of Yahaweh to my Lord :
>   Sit thou at my right hand
> Until I make thy foemen
>   a footstool for thy feet.

> " The sceptre of thy strength
>   Yahaweh stretcheth forth from Zion.
> Be thou conqueror in the midst of thy foemen.

> " Thy people are volunteers in thy muster-day.
> In holy splendors from the womb of morning
>   thy dew of youth are thine.

> " Yahaweh hath sworn, and will not repent,
> Thou art a priest for ever,
>   after the manner of Melchizedek.

> " It was the Lord upon thy right hand
>   that crushed kings in the day of his anger.
> He dictateth among the nations ; it is full of bodies ; [1]
>   he crushed one that was head over a wide land.

> " One drinketh from a brook by the way,
>   therefore one lifteth up his head."

The singer, apparently, has been reading the account
of the victory of Abraham over the four kings (Gen. xiv).
It is to him like drinking of a brook þy the way; he is
refreshed, and feels like holding his head high, when he
thinks how Yahaweh enabled the recipient of the promise, with his little band of retainers and allies, to defeat

[1] That is, the field of the battle is covered with bodies.

the armies of the "wide land" of the Babylonian-Ela-
mitic empire. He is reminded of what Yahaweh has done
for the Person of the promise from the time of Abraham
to his own time, and of what Yahaweh has promised for
future time without limit. No wonder he speaks of the
Person of the promise as "my Lord."[1] He sings of
the strong sceptre of "my Lord," reaching forth from
Zion, of his willing warriors, numerous and splendid as
the morning dewdrops, and of their victories. He remembers also that the promise-people is "a kingdom of
priests." The Person of the promise is a priest, as well
as a conqueror. In Abraham he paid tithes to Melchizedek, but he is himself a priest of the same rank with Melchizedek. It is not only in the phrase "my Lord" that
the psalm ascribes extraordinary exaltation to the Person
of the promise, but also in what it says concerning his
dominion, his subjects, his victories, his priesthood.

We must not make the mistake of understanding too
concretely this conception of the Person of the promise,
An idea   as if it steadily amounted to an expectation
rather than   of the coming of a concrete person. In itself
a concrete
person   considered it is an idea rather than a conception of fact, though like all such conceptions, it would
come to have, in many minds, more or less of the character of reality. We must remember that this stream of
teachings, on its way to us from its first fountains, flowed
through different belts of soil, and also received affluents ;
and from these derived not only greater fulness, but also
varieties of taste and coloring. There might supposably
come a time — actually there came a time — when the
conception of the Person of the promise assumed the
character of an actual expectation of a concrete person.
Of course Christians hold that the Person of the promise

[1] On this phrase see Chapter XIV, near the end.

became completely a reality in the person of Jesus Christ.

This conception of the Person of the promise, whether it existed at any given date as a mere form of thought or as the presentment of an expected actual person, became the heart of a more or less definitely formulated body of ethical and theo- *A nucleus of a doctrinal system* logical beliefs.   We have had occasion to notice the character of a suffering mediator attributed to the Person of the promise — to the Servant, for example, in Isa. liii. The idea in one form or another is not rare, and the redemption spoken of is not from disaster merely, but from sin and its punishment.   This presupposes familiarity with certain doctrines concerning obligation and right and wrongdoing, and the relations of Deity to men. The promise-doctrine, and especially the idea of the Person of the promise, became a nucleus around which crystallized an ethical theology.   Many of the points of Christian dogma concerning the extraordinary personality of Christ, his character, his atonement, his relations to the Holy Spirit, the privileges of those who are united to him, are more or less distinctly anticipated in what the Old Testament says concerning the Person of the promise.

As we have many times had occasion to notice, the Person of the promise is presented to us both as a typical Israelite and as a typical human person. *The Person both typical and antitypal* Or, using a mode of speech that is common among theologians, he is the antitype in antithesis to which much that appears in the dealings of God with man is typical.   The subject of type and antitype we have briefly considered in Chapter VI.   These terms will now afford us convenient phraseology for presenting what the present chapter has already described as the collateral lines of the promise-doctrine.

Some of these lines of information at least were in existence all through the period when the Psalms and the prophetic books were being produced, and served to illustrate the teachings of the prophets to their contemporaries.

I. The prophets were themselves typical men, men representative of the facts and the principles included in the promise, types with the Person of the promise for an antitype.

With the definition above given of the Person of the promise, this is not directly the same thing as to say that the prophets were types of the personal coming Messiah, though it may supposably amount to the same in the end.   So far as the coming Messiah is concerned, the proposition just stated is hypothetical.   Each prophet stood for the whole line.   He was a type of the chief prophet in case the line of the prophets should culminate in a chief prophet.   This is true alike of the whole succession and of each prophet in the succession.

In outlining the external history of the prophets, and again in outlining their functions, we have already (Chapters III, V) given some attention to the eighteenth chapter of Deuteronomy.   This passage has also a distinctly messianic character.   It promises that from time to time, as Yahaweh should see fit, he would raise up a prophet, so as to meet all the needs which his people might have for communication with the supernatural world.

Deut. xviii

"A prophet from the midst of thee, of thy brethren, like unto me, will Yahaweh thy God raise up for thee."

"A prophet will I raise up for them from the midst of their brethren, like unto thee, and I will put my words in his mouth, and he shall speak unto them all which I command him " (Deut. xviii. 15, 17–18).

COLLATERAL LINES OF PROMISE-DOCTRINE   351

Scholars are correct in saying that the word "prophet" is not here a collective, but denotes one prophet and no more. All the same, however, the word is here used distributively. The prophets will be a succession, and each one will have the typical character. As the word "Messiah" denotes the successive kings of the line of David, with the possibility that the line may culminate in a greater King, so there is the possibility that the line of prophets may culminate in a greater Prophet.

The Apostle Peter (Acts iii. 21, 24) connects this passage in Deuteronomy with the thought of the "holy prophets which have been since the world began," and with "Samuel and them that followed after." Evidently he understands that the passage refers to a succession of prophets. But in the same context (21–26) he claims that it is a messianic prediction, fulfilled in Jesus the Christ. Stephen (Acts vii. 37) puts the same interpretation upon it.[1] In other places, exceedingly numerous, the New Testament writers seem to have in mind the details of the Deuteronomic passage. Jesus is spoken of as he "of whom Moses . . . did write," as "the prophet that cometh into the world," as speaking only God's words (*e.g.* Jn. i. 45, vi. 14, iii. 34; Lc. x. 16), and thus as having made a record agreeing with the description in Deuteronomy. Great stress is laid on the

---

[1] The citations in the Acts are doubtless from the Septuagint, though they are somewhat free. They differ more from the Hebrew than does the Septuagint, though neither differs materially. That the citation is from a form of the text that was current among the disciples is to be inferred from the fact that the divergences which appear in Peter's speech are repeated in Stephen's.

In Acts iii. 26 (*cf.* iv. 2) there is apparently a play on words. Jesus Christ, here called Servant, is said to be raised up, not merely, like his predecessors, in the sense of being commissioned, but also in that of resurrection from death.

points of comparison and contrast between him and
Moses, as if the New Testament writers had in mind
the "like unto me" of Deuteronomy (*e.g.* Heb. iii. 2, 5,
ix. 19). The specification "of your brethren" is likewise made prominent (Heb. ii. 12, 17, etc.). In these
various ways they claim that the things that were typically true of each prophet were preëminently true of the
one great prophet, the culmination of the line.

In the fact that the prophet was regarded as especially the organ of Yahaweh's Spirit, we have an additional point that characterizes the antitype as it does the
type.

II. The line of passages in which the Old Testament
writers present the theophanic Angel of Yahaweh
— the Angel, as distinguished from angels — bears collaterally on the doctrine of the promise.

That there is such a line of passages no one would
question, nor that the Angel is especially to the front in
the theophanies that are described (see I, 2 (*d*) of Chapter VI). So much is easy to make out. It is less easy,
in some of the instances, to distinguish between the
Angel and any other angel;[1] and this we need not now

---

[1] The following are the passages in which the word "angel" appears
with the article or with a defining genitive. Whether the angel is in all
of them the same person, is another question. For the purposes now in
hand we need not take the trouble to distinguish between "angel of
Yahaweh" and "angel of Elohim."

The Angel (or angel) appears to Hagar, fleeing from her mistress, and
commands her to return ; and again appears for her rescue when Ishmael
is at the point of death (Gen. xvi. 7, 9, 10, 11, xxi. 17). He appears to
Abraham when Isaac is upon the altar, and, as we may probably infer, in
the great theophany just before the destruction of Sodom (xxii. 11, 15,
xviii). He is sent with Abraham's servant who seeks a wife for Isaac
(Gen. xxiv. 7, 40). He appears to Jacob in a dream, and is described
by him as "the Angel that redeemed me from all evil" (Gen. xxxi. 11,
xlviii. 16). Hosea represents Jacob as coming into contact with the

attempt.   Nor need we formulate a theological theory
as to the nature of the personage described as "the
Angel."[1]   It is sufficient to note that in several of the
instances the Angel is represented as appearing in human
form ; and in several of the instances he not merely speaks
in the name of Yahaweh, but is personally identified with
Yahaweh.   There are relations between the things that

Angel at Bethel, and also, evidently, at Peniel (Hos. xii. 3–5; *cf.* Gen.
xxviii. 10–19, xxxii. 24–30, xxxv).   He met Moses at the burning bush,
and protected Israel at the Red Sea (Ex. iii. 2, xiv. 19; Num. xx. 16, the
word being indefinite in Numbers).   It is promised that he shall go before
Israel into Canaan (Ex. xxiii. 20, 23, xxxii. 34, xxxiii. 2, the first and last
instances being indefinite).   He rebukes Israel at Bochim, and curses
Meroz (Jud. ii. 1, 4, v. 23).   He is prominent in the story of Gideon, and
in the account of the birth of Samson (Jud. vi. 11, 12, 20, 21, 22, xiii.
3, 6, 9, 13, 15, 16, 17, 18, 20, 21, all the instances being in the Hebrew
definite).   To him the Tekoite woman compares David (2 Sam. xiv.
17, 20), and Mephibosheth does the same (2 Sam. xix. 27).   He was
concerned with the pestilence and the threshing floor of Ornan the
Jebusite (2 Sam. xxiv. 16, 17; 1 Chron. xxi. 12, 15, 16, 18, 20, 27, 30),
and thus with the selection of the site of the temple.   He gave messages
to Elijah (2 Ki. i. 3, 15).   Apparently the destroyer of the one hundred
eighty-five thousand in the camp of Assyria (2 Ki. xix. 35; Isa. xxxvii. 36;
2 Chron. xxxii. 21) was "an angel," "the angel" that was commissioned
for this purpose, and not the Angel.   The Angel (or angel) protects those
who fear Yahaweh, and drives away their persecutors (Pss. xxxiv. 7, xxxv.
5, 6).   It is foolish to make excuses before the Angel (Ec. v. 6).   "The
Angel of his presence saved" Israel of old (Isa. lxiii. 9).   "The house
of David shall be as God, as the Angel of Yahaweh" (Zech. xii. 8).   The
word "angel" is used twenty times in Zech. i–vi, and it is merely a matter of painstaking here to distinguish the Angel from the other angels that
appear.   It was God's angel (or Angel) that delivered Daniel from the
lions, and his three friends from the furnace (Dan. vi. 22, iii. 28).   The
closing message in Malachi presents Yahaweh's Angel, "the Angel of
the covenant" (iii. 1).   "The angel" that appears ten times in the
story of Balaam (Num. xxii) is probably not the Angel.

[1] There is some plausibility in the idea that used to be advanced, to the
effect that the Angel is the Son — the second person of the Trinity, as
defined in Christian dogma — temporarily assuming human form, before
his incarnation in the person of Jesus.

are said concerning him and the New Testament doctrine of the incarnation.

The accounts of the theophanic Angel are a constitu-
ent part of the history of the promise. He is represented as in communication with Abraham in
some of the crises when the promise is mentioned (Gen. xxii, and by probable inference
xviii). He was with Jacob at Bethel, and when his
name was changed to Israel, and was remembered by
Jacob as "the Angel that redeemed me from all evil"
(Hos. xii. 3–5; *cf.* Gen. xxxii. 24–30, xxviii. 10–19, xxxv,
xxxi. 11, xlviii. 16). He is with Moses at the burning
bush, and with Israel in the pillar of cloud and fire (Ex.
iii. 2, xiv. 19). Evidently it is the theophanic Angel concerning whom Yahaweh says to Israel: "Behold I send
an Angel before thee," and again, "Mine Angel shall go
before thee" (Ex. xxiii. 20, 23). Yahaweh makes this
a great thing; the presence of the Angel with his people is his own presence with them.

> "If thou wilt indeed hearken at his voice, and do all that I speak,
> I will be enemy to thine enemies," etc. (22).

He adds threats that are correspondingly severe.

> "Take ye heed of him, . . . be not rebellious with him, for he
> will not pardon your transgression, for my name is within him" (21).

When Israel sinned with the golden calf, Yahaweh's
promise to go with him in the person of the Angel was
revoked. The intercession of Moses elicited only this
concession : —

> "And now, go thou, lead the people unto the place concerning
> which I spake to thee [saying], Behold my Angel shall go before
> thee. And in the day of my visiting I will visit their sin upon them"
> (Ex. xxxii. 34).

"Go thou up hence, thou and the people . . . unto the land which I sware . . ., saying, To thy seed will I give it, And I will send an Angel before thee . . .; for I will not go up in the midst of thee" (Ex. xxxiii. 1–3).

Observe that here is no renewal of the promise that the Angel should go, but, on the contrary, an implication that the promise is no longer in force. After further intercession, and after punishment inflicted on the people, and repentance expressed by them, Yahaweh relents and says : —

"My presence shall go, and I will give thee rest" (xxxiii. 14).

Apparently it is Yahaweh in the character of the theophanic Angel that rebukes Israel at Bochim, and that reveals himself to Gideon and to Manoah (Jud. ii. 1–4, vi. 11–22, xiii. 3–21). It is the Angel that deals with David in the matter of the pestilence, when Ornan's threshing floor was purchased to be the site of the temple (2 Sam. xxiv. 16–17; 1 Chron. xxi. 12–30). Various significant allusions are made to the Angel (Pss. xxxiv. 7, xxxv. 5, 6; Ec. v. 6; Isa. lxiii. 9; Zech. xii. 8). He appears very prominently, in company with other angels, in the first six chapters of Zechariah. And perhaps Malachi's mention of him is the most significant of all : —

"Behold, I send my Angel, and he shall prepare a way before me; and suddenly the lord whom ye are seeking shall come unto his temple, and the Angel of the covenant whom ye delight in, behold, he is coming, saith Yahaweh of hosts. And who may abide the day of his coming ? and who shall stand when he appeareth ?" (Mal. iii. 1–2).

The word here translated "the lord" is in the singular, and has the article. It differs from both "the Lord" and "the LORD," the two familiar forms in which this word is applied to Yahaweh; and yet the phrase

"his temple" indicates that the word here denotes
Yahaweh. There are a certain number of parallel instances (*e.g.* Isa. i. 24, iii. 1, x. 16, 33). What is said
here concerning the Angel is a repetition in modified
form of the promise made at the time of the exodus
(Ex. xxiii. 20, 23, xxxii. 34, xxxiii. 2). The question,
"Who may abide the day of his coming?" includes an
allusion to the warnings given in Exodus (xxiii. 21,
xxxii. 34c). As cited in the evangelists, it reverts in part
to its original form, as found in Exodus : —

> " Behold I send my Angel before thy face,
>   Who shall prepare thy way before thee "
>
> (Matt. xi. 10 ; cf. Mc. i. 2 ; Lc. vii. 27).

What Yahaweh says in Malachi is that his ancient
utterance to Israel holds good, and that he will signally
manifest himself in the person of the theophanic Angel.
Jesus says, as reported by Matthew and Luke, that the
movement in which he and John the Baptist are engaged
is this signal manifestation of Yahaweh. His words
have been commonly understood as also affirming that
John is the Angel (the messenger) sent before his face,
but this is not necessarily their effect.[1]

In fine, the theophanic Angel appears at all stages
of the history from Abraham to Malachi. He is represented as in relations with the kingdom, the last days,
the day of Yahaweh, the coming of Yahaweh. He is
especially prominent in giving to Yahaweh's people
their possession in the benefits of the promise.

---

[1] Of course it is a very natural way of understanding them. But it de-
mands the exercise of too much ingenuity for interpreting Malachi, and it
ignores the relation of the exodus passages with both the Malachi passage
and the New Testament citations. It is ingenious conjecture rather than
sound inference which makes " my angel " in Malachi to be a different
being from " the angel of the covenant," and one or both to be different
from the theophanic Angel.

III. As we have seen in Chapter VII, the scriptures represent that the whole of Yahaweh's law was given to Israel through the prophets. In addition to their direct utterances, they taught indirectly through the sanctuary and its furniture and the public worship and all religious observances. And the promise was so incorporated into the national institutions that these were a perpetual reminder of it to those who had the insight needed for understanding this lesson.

The heart of Israel's sanctuary, as described in the scriptures, was the ark standing in the holy of holies. The ark contained the two tables on which Deity himself had written the ten words. The lid of it, with the cherubim, constituted what we are accustomed to call the mercy seat. The ark is called the ark of the covenant, because the ten words, its contents, were the basis of Yahaweh's covenant with his people (Ex. xxiv. 3, 7–8). It was called the ark of the testimony because the two tables, Yahaweh's autograph, were the authenticated copy of the basis of the covenant. The covenant consisted in Yahaweh's acceptance of Israel as his own people on condition of obedience to the ten words in their religious and ethical and social obligations. But every Israelite who had insight knew that this was an impossible condition. He knew that neither Israel as a people, nor himself, nor other Israelites, were ever, in the eye of omniscience, perfectly obedient to the ten words. If that had been all, the covenant was a hopeless proposition. But that was not all. The mercy seat was significant, as well as the two tables. It signified that Yahaweh was gracious and compassionate as well as just, ready to forgive as well as strict, one who proffered atonement as well as one who required obedience.

The heart of the cult of Israel

The heart of the sacred year had the same significance with that of the sanctuary.   Once in the year the
highpriest entered the holy of holies, and placed on the
mercy seat the blood of the great annual sin-offering.
To this central solemnity were adjusted the three great
feasts and the new moons and the sabbaths and the
daily burnt-offerings, and all special and individual sea-
sons of worship.

Thus the mercy seat and its functions were the heart
of the whole sacrificial system.   This was carried out
in the ceremonial of all the various sacrifices.   The sin-
offering idea entered into the ritual in connection with
the disposal of the blood of all burnt-offerings and all
peace-offerings.   And the ideas that pervaded the sacrifices pervaded all the religious observances, the worship
by gifts that were not properly sacrificial, and by prayer
and song and fasting, and the reading of scripture and
the booths of the autumnal feast and the blowing of
trumpets and the resting on the sabbath.

This does not minimize any other significance which
may have belonged to the sacrifices or to the other worship.   It is impossible not to find in the burnt-offering
an emblem of self-surrender, accepted from the skies as
the smoke mounts heavenward.   In the sacrificial feasts
the worshipper found religious fellowship with his fel-
low-worshippers and with Deity.   But in the Levitical
scheme all other ideas are bound to those that centre in
the ark, with its tables of the covenant and its mercy seat.

Of course it is not claimed that all Israelites of every
period were fully aware of the spiritual meanings of the
rites they practised.   In our day the majority
of worshippers are deficient in spiritual insight, and very likely the ancient worshippers
may have been yet more deficient.   It is likely that there

Men who
were devout
and had
insight

were Israelites who thought of their sacrifices as a bribe to their God, or as a way of putting him into good humor by giving him a good feed. But however true this may be, it is certain that the cult itself was inspired by loftier meanings, and that some of the worshippers were, in a greater or less degree, conscious of these.

Further, it is, of course, true that the view which a modern person takes of these things will depend very much on the critical theories he holds. The One's ceremonial laws of Israel will have maximum critical point value in the mind of one who holds that they of view originated with Moses, and were actually, to some extent, in operation from his time. If one holds that they are mainly fiction, a presentation of ideas rather than facts, he, none the less, ought to recognize the principles that underlie the ideas. And even if one holds that the ceremonial laws are a chance aggregation of relatively late materials, coming into existence in different centuries and in connection with different movements, he is still under obligation to account for the fact that they may naturally be interpreted as the expression of these underlying principles. It is impossible so to interpret the laws as to eliminate these meanings utterly from them. My own opinion is that the meanings are in them through the design of the prophets who gave Israel the laws. But if they entered in some other way, at all events they are there.

The priestly laws of Israel may be regarded as an especial embodiment of the idea that Israel himself is "a kingdom of priests and a holy nation" Connected (Ex. xix. 6). The national priestly character with Israel's is exhibited in the functions exercised by the priesthood priests of the nation. When the psalmist says that the Person of the promise is "a priest for ever after the order of Melchizedek," he implies both comparison and contrast between that priest and the existing priests of Israel. The author of the book of Hebrews, in his long comments on this matter, has not failed to catch the spirit both of the psalm and of the ceremonial law.

As we have already seen, a different presentation of the sacrificial idea sometimes occurs. Israel, or the Servant, or the *hhasidh*, or the Person of the promise, appears as the victim rather than as the priest. Or, rather, inasmuch as his mediatorial sufferings are voluntary, he is both priest and victim.

The victim as well as the priest

On the whole, it is, perhaps, this phase of the promise-doctrine, this idea of vicarious suffering, the precursor of the New Testament doctrine of the atonement, that is principally emphasized in the Israelitish legislation. Every part of the national institutions, and in particular the worship, the sacrifices, the priesthood, the temple, has a typal value, is a presentation of the great truths of the doctrine of the promise. If the truths of sin and redemption are here most emphasized, emphasis is also placed on the separateness of Israel, and so on Yahaweh's eternal purpose for the nations through Israel. The institutions of Israel were themselves the perpetual fulfilment of the promise, and therefore a perpetual pointing forward to the coming stages of the fulfilment.

This was not a light thing. Imagine its influence over the worshippers who came from all parts of the earth to Jerusalem, in the generations just before the public ministry of Jesus. Was not the worship connected in their thoughts with the promise and with the future glories of Israel? Were they not ready to find in all its details illustrations of the hope that burned in their hearts? The author of the book of Hebrews knew what he was about. He knew how to select his arguments so that they would appeal to thoughts that were already in the minds of those for whom he wrote.

IV. To these lines of collateral testimony we may add a vast number of matters that are sometimes cited as instances of type or of prediction.

The quoting of Old Testament examples as types of the Messiah is a very common practice: Noah's ark, for example, or Noah himself, or Lot, or Melchizedek, or Joseph, or Jonah, and so forth. The representations of this kind that are currently made need careful sifting; but there can be no doubt that the prophets thought of many persons and objects as bearing some relation to the great national promise. *Persons or objects as types*

We should also class as collateral any predictive passages that may be found, which do not connect themselves directly with the main line of the promise. In these chapters we have examined a large number of the passages that are commonly quoted as messianic predictions, and we have found that they are not a miscellaneous collection of disconnected fragments, but parts of a continuous history. They are shoots from a common stem, the stem being the one never vanishing doctrine of the promise. Two additional questions arise. First: Have some of these passages, besides their value as statements of the promise-doctrine, an additional value as predictions of specific events in the career of the Person of the promise? Second: Are there other passages whose primary value is that of specific predictions? In the interest of brevity, I shall take the liberty of answering these questions hypothetically rather than categorically. *Disconnected predictions*

As an example under the first of these two questions
take the Canto of the suffering Servant (Isa. liii).   We
have seen that the Servant is the personified
idealized Israel, the people of the promise; and

Isa. liii

that he is equally any typical Israelite, and in particular
the one antitypal Israelite who beyond all others stands
for the promise idea.   In other words, the Servant is the
Person of the promise, and the Person of the promise
became a reality in Jesus the Christ.   But in addition
to this there are several matters of detail in the prophecy which correspond in a marked way to incidents in
the personal career of Jesus.   These have been often
pointed out, and we need not repeat them.   Are they
to be regarded as specific predictions of these particular
incidents?   An alternative reply is sufficient.   If one
so regards them, that need not change his opinion of
the main bearing of the passage; if one does not so regard them, the identification of the Servant with Jesus
as the Person of the promise remains unimpaired.

Or take the twenty-second psalm.   Except to one
who denies the existence of predictive inspiration, no
theory could be more plausible than that the
prophet was made to see in vision the events of

Ps. xxii

the humiliation and death of Jesus, and that he made the
song from what he saw.   On this theory, the parts of the
psalm that are cited in the New Testament, and other
parts along with them, are specific predictions.   The
prophet-singer in his vision heard the cry: "My God,
my God, why hast thou forsaken me?"   He saw the
enemies of Jesus shaking the head and laughing him to
scorn.   He heard them say: "Let him deliver him, seeing he delighteth in him."   He witnessed the thirst, and
the pierced hands and feet, and the projecting bones of
the body fastened to the cross.   He saw the garments

parted, with the casting of lots. And looking beyond, he saw the victory that the crucified one was winning through his humiliation, and he sang : —

"I will declare thy name unto my brethren :
In the midst of the congregation will I praise thee.

*   *   *   *   *   *   *   *

All the ends of the earth shall remember and turn unto the LORD :
And all the kindreds of the nations shall worship before thee.
For the kingdom is the LORD's :
And he is the ruler over the nations " (Ps. xxii. 22, 27–28 RV).

This is one theory of the song. Compare it with another. In these sufferings of his Jesus was, in his human nature, an antitypal man. There have been ten thousand other instances practically the same in type. Suppose that the prophet had primarily in mind some typical man or personified people of his own time, the representative of the promise for that generation ; and that the men of the New Testament simply applied to Jesus this presentation of the Person of the promise, as they applied other like presentations.

The question that we have to consider is this : Are these items concerning the outcry and the scoffing and the thirst and the pierced hands and feet and the parting of the garments to be regarded as specific predictions of these particular incidents in the crucifixion of Jesus ? If we say that they are, that is no more in conflict with the second of the two theories of the song than with the first. If we say that they are not, it will still be true, on the second of the two theories, that the song is a truthful presentation of Jesus as the Person of the promise, and that the use made of it in the gospels is exegetically sound.

As with details in the passages that formally teach the promise-doctrine, so with predictions that seem to

be isolated.   Is Balaam's utterance about the star that
shall arise out of Jacob (Num. xxiv. 17) of the nature of
Other   a prediction of a particular messianic event?
instances   Are the utterances, "Let their habitation
be desolate " and " Let another take his office " (Pss.
lxix. 25, cix. 8 ; cf. Acts i. 20), to be regarded as properly
predictions concerning Judas, or simply as scripture
phrases aptly applied to the circumstances ?   If you say
that they are predictions, you say nothing that contra-
dicts the view of the promise-doctrine that has here been
presented.   If you say that they are not, you put your-
self under obligation to explain the New Testament use
of them, but the doctrine of the promise is sufficiently
buttressed without them.

In fine, this body of literature which we call the Old
Testament is so thoroughly permeated with the idea of
the promise that this affects the whole of its contents.
Whatever in it is not of the nature of statement of fact
concerning the promise is likely to be connected with it
by way of illustration or suggestion.

CHAPTER XVI

MESSIANIC EXPECTATION AND FULFILMENT

We have been trying to interpret what the Old Testament records say concerning the giving of the promise. But if the promise is anything, it is a promise. It raised expectations in men's minds, and it was followed by fulfilments. We shall be able both to test and to illustrate the results we have reached if we can bring them into comparison with the expectations that existed in the time of Jesus, and with any fulfilments which the promise may have had.

I. We take up the question of the expectation of the Messiah as it existed in the New Testament times.

Sources of information on this subject are some of the later Old Testament Apocrypha, the Psalter of Solomon, the Sibylline books, the book of Enoch, Josephus, Philo, etc., with the traditions of the early $_{\text{Sources}}$ Christian fathers and the Talmudists. But it should not be forgotten that the New Testament is by far the most explicit and trustworthy source. The New Testament comes nearer than the other sources to being first-hand evidence on the subject. It is mistaken procedure to begin by gleaning stray information from other sources, and then, on the basis thus laid, to subject the New Testament evidence to modifying treatment before we accept it.

The statement commonly made is that the Jews, at the time of the Advent, were looking for a political

Messiah, who should free them from the Romans, and make them a dominant nation. In a rough way the

A temporal   statement is true. It has the same sort of truth
deliverer?   with other crude general statements — the
statement, for example, that the earth is round like an orange. But it needs to be much modified in order to render it accurate.

The nature of the expectation may be defined in the following propositions. First, the Jews of the genera-

The ex-   tion of Jesus were looking for a signal mani-
pectation   festation from Israel's God in fulfilment of
formulated   the promise. Second, this quite commonly
took the form of an expectation that the Person of the promise would appear among men as an actual person, Yahaweh's Servant, his *hhasidh*, his Chosen one, the Lord. Third, most prominently it was an expectation of the setting up of the kingdom, with the Anointed one, the son of David, as king. Fourth, beyond this, and in matters of detail, the expectation presented a great variety of aspects, according to the characters and the mental and spiritual habits of the men who held it. In the minds of political leaders and of others who made the most noise in the world, the idea of a political Messiah was doubtless to the front, but even these were uncertain on many points. In the minds of the more devout, of those who had greater insight into the scriptures, the spiritual mission of the hoped-for Coming one was clearly recognized. From the times of Jesus until now most Christian people have steadily held to the doctrine of the second coming of Christ; but that does not mean that they have uniformly held to some particular millenarian theory. There were many men of many minds in the generation of Jesus, as in the present generation. Let us look at a few

sections of the superabundant evidence by which these statements might be substantiated.

To begin with, the promise-doctrine, as we have already seen (Chapter VIII), is all-pervasive in the New Testament, and this fact shows the nature of The promise-doctrine in the expectation to which the first teachers of the New Christianity had to appeal. If we could take Testament the space for a fresh study of this matter, now that we have been prepared for it by our studies in the Old Testament, we should find that the New Testament is far more saturated with the promise idea than even the treatment in our eighth chapter would indicate. In that chapter we used mainly the passages where the word "promise" occurs; but the doctrine is taught in a vast number of other passages.[1]

The citations made in Chapter VIII for the New Testament doctrine of the promise were taken mostly from the book of Hebrews or the writings of Not a Pauline Paul. But the doctrine is not the opinion of view merely Paul and of the writer of Hebrews only, but of the other New Testament men as well. In affirming this matter, I use advisedly such phrases as "the New Testament," "the men of the New Testament." The nouns and verbs that specifically denote the promise appear in the utterances of James and John and Peter, and in the gospels. There is nowhere a more emphatic or explicit

---

[1] For example, the New Testament writers mention in a detailed way the accounts given in Genesis of Abraham and Isaac and Jacob, including their relations with Sarah, Rebekah, Hagar, Ishmael, Esau, Lot, and others. The several phrases in which the Old Testament affirms that Israel is Yahaweh's own people are repeated in the New Testament by citation from the Old. For instance, in Heb. xi. 16, the phrase, "And I will be to them for God," occurring first in Genesis (xvii. 8), and recurring throughout the Old Testament. Or the phrase "stars of heaven in multitude" (Heb. xi. 12). Or innumerable other descriptions or incidents or phrases.

statement of the doctrine than in the following from
Peter's sermon on the day of pentecost, though he does
not use the word " promise " : —

> " Ye are the sons of the prophets, and of the covenant which God
> made with your fathers, saying unto Abraham, And in thy seed shall
> all the families of the earth be blessed. Unto you first God, having
> raised up his Servant, sent him to bless you, in turning away every
> one of you from your iniquities " (Acts iii. 25–26).

It would be interesting to trace the variations of the
doctrine as seen from the different points of view of the
different men of the New Testament, and to trace its
growth in time in the mind of such a man as Paul
himself.   But these things would be mere matters
of detail.   The doctrine in its essential character is
taught by Jesus, and by all the original teachers of
Christianity.

The fact that they thus taught it indicates the nature
of the messianic expectation that existed among those
to whom they taught it. When they based their appeal
on the promise, they expected to be understood.   Their
ideas of the character of the promise were certainly
so far forth accepted, both in Palestine and in other
regions, as to furnish a basis for the arguments they
based upon it.

The generation to whom Jesus came were looking for
some great manifestation from God in fulfilment of the
ancient promise.   It does not follow that they all to a
man expected exactly the same thing, and that the thing
they expected was a military deliverer.   As we think
of it, it seems likely that we should find that different
persons expected different things.   Doubtless the idea
of a political Messiah loomed up large in the minds of
the politicians and their followers ; but these did not
constitute the whole Jewish population.

The beginnings of the gospel, as preached both by John the Baptist and by Jesus, included the announcement that the kingdom of heaven was at hand. This indicates the nature of the thing that their hearers were looking for, namely, a new manifestation of the kingdom that Yahaweh had anciently set up among men. This idea of the matter is traceable throughout the gospels. Late in the life of Jesus, his disciples were seeking positions of honor in the kingdom. The charge against him before Pilate is that he claims the sovereignty over a kingdom, thus placing himself in rivalry with Cæsar. The whole New Testament is an explanation of the nature of the kingdom. Doubtless this idea became modified during the interval between the birth of Jesus and the writing of the several parts of the New Testament; but it was in existence from the first. The first teachers of Christianity did not create it, they found it current among their compatriots. The common expectation of the fulfilment of Yahaweh's ancient promise took the form of this expectation of the kingdom.

An expectation of the kingdom

There was also, as we have already noticed, an expectation of the Person of the promise. At the very beginning of the public ministry of Jesus, we find Philip expressing to Nathanael his expectations in these words : —

And of a Person, its Anointed king

"We have found him of whom Moses in the law, and the prophets, did write, Jesus of Nazareth, the son of Joseph " (Jn. i. 45).

Philip is cautious, not venturing to say that they had found the Messiah, but only that they had found the Person of the promise as pictured in Moses and the prophets.[1] But Andrew the day before had been less

[1] See Chapter XIII, last paragraph of II.

cautious, saying to Simon: "We have found the Messiah" (ver. 41). And it is under this latter description as the Anointed king of the kingdom, that the expected Person is commonly presented. In proof of this, one might cite every one of the hundreds of New Testament passages that speak of Christ or of the kingdom.

It is made very prominent that in their expectations they thought of this Person of the promise, this Anointed king of the kingdom, as being of the royal line of David, and heir to the eternal throne which Yahaweh had promised to David and his seed. The Christ is in the New Testament about thirty times explicitly said to be son of David. The opponents of Jesus argued against him by appealing to this point in the current expectation : —

Descendant and heir of David

> "Doth the Christ come out of Galilee ? Hath not the scripture said that the Christ cometh of the seed of David, and from Bethlehem, the village where David was ? " (Jn. vii. 41–42).

When the wise men inquired for him that was "born king of the Jews," and Herod gathered "all the chief priests and scribes," and asked them " where the Christ should be born," the answer he received was based on the scripture concerning David's town of Bethlehem (Matt. ii. 2–6). In the annunciation to Joseph the angel addresses him as " Joseph, thou son of David " (Matt. i. 20). The book of Matthew begins with " the generations of Jesus Christ, the son of David, the son of Abraham " (Matt. i. 1). The genealogies of Jesus trace his line back to David, though also to Abraham, and in Luke to Adam (Matt. i ; Lc. iii). In the annunciation to Mary, Joseph is described as " of the house of David " (Lc. i. 27). We are told that Joseph and Mary went for enrolment " to the city of David which is called Bethlehem, because he was of the house and family of

David" (Lc. ii. 4). The angels are represented as saying to the shepherds : "There is born to you this day in the city of David a Saviour, which is Christ the Lord " (Lc. ii. 11). Surely, further citations are unnecessary.

But when we have looked at these facts, the case is still incomplete. The points thus far mentioned are very definite, but we also have glimpses of Uncertain points in which the expectation was marked elements in by indefiniteness and uncertainty. There were tion uncertainties as to whether the manifestation would be through one person or through several, and, indeed, a very general uncertainty as to the forms it might be expected to assume. Alike the first disciples and the priests in Jerusalem and the Pharisees and the people and Herod were conscious that they did not know whether to look for one person or more than one.[1] They were talking of the Christ, and Elijah, and "the prophet," and "one of the old prophets." So far as they knew, the kingdom might be manifested in one person sent from God, or in a group or succession of persons. They looked confidently for a certain great thing, but concerning the nature of that thing they were at many points in doubt.

[1] " And this is the witness of John, when the Jews sent unto him from Jerusalem priests and Levites to ask him, Who art thou? And he confessed, . . . I am not the Christ. And they asked him, What then? Art thou Elijah? And he saith, I am not. Art thou the prophet? And he answered, No. They said therefore unto him, Who art thou? that we may give an answer to them that sent us. . . . He said, I am the voice of one crying in the wilderness." "And they had been sent from the Pharisees " (Jn. i. 19–24).

"He asked his disciples, saying, Who do men say that the Son of man is? And they said, Some say John the Baptist; some Elijah; and others Jeremiah, or one of the prophets" (Matt. xvi. 13–14; cf. Mc. viii. 28, vi. 14–15). Luke has: "And others say that one of the old prophets is risen again " (ix. 7–9, 19).

John the Baptist shared in this consciousness of a lack of complete and specific knowledge. He knew that he was the voice in the wilderness. He knew that he was preparing the way for one that should follow him. He knew that Jesus was his mightier successor, and was the lamb of God. But he did not know that he was the Elijah of prophecy, and he did not know whether Jesus was "He that cometh," or was only, like himself, a precursor of the Coming one (Matt. iii; Mc. i; Lc. iii; Jn. i. 19–36, iii. 27–36; Matt. xi. 3; Lc. vii. 19, etc.).[1] And the disciples of Jesus were constantly asking questions concerning the kingdom, questions which showed that their minds were full of unsettled ideas on the subject. Their uncertainties were not cleared till after the resurrection (Lc. xxiv).

The New Testament accounts imply that the eternal and spiritual elements in the expected kingdom, its Spiritual elements in the expectation character as connected with redemption from sin, its mission for all mankind through Israel, were familiar to the minds of devout Israelites, to such persons as Zacharias and Elisabeth and Joseph and Mary and Simeon and Anna and John the Baptist and Andrew and Philip and Nathanael and Simon. It would be fruitless to inquire how large a proportion of the adult Jews living at the time of the birth of Jesus were of this type; but lofty ideas concerning the kingdom were prevalent enough so that one would be intelligible if he spoke of such things.

---

[1] The more common explanation is that John at first knew, but that afterward his faith grew dull, and then he did not know. This explanation is based in part on the mistaken theory that faith is a sort of pious guesswork which good people may substitute for evidence. Certainly John's course is more reasonably accounted for as resulting from the limitations of his knowledge.

The narratives of the earliest New Testament incidents assume the existence of a conception of the kingdom as part of a movement dating from Abraham or from the beginning of the world, and to last eternally. The angel says to Mary : —

"And the Lord God shall give unto him the throne of his father David ; and he shall reign over the house of Jacob for ever ; and of his kingdom there shall be no end " (Lc. i. 32–33).

Mary thinks of the revelation made to her as one in which God her Saviour remembers mercy : —

"As he spake unto our fathers,
Toward Abraham and his seed for ever " (Lc. i. 55).

Zacharias celebrates the " horn of salvation " which " the Lord, the God of Israel," has raised up —

"In the house of his servant David,
As he spake by the mouth of his holy prophets
Which have been since the world began ; "

"To remember his holy covenant,
The oath which he sware unto Abraham our father "
(Lc. i. 68–73).

The records imply that it was well understood that the kingdom and the salvation were for mankind as well as for Israel. They imply this in mentioning Abraham. They speak of the lamb that takes away the sin of the world. They represent Simeon as saying : —

"For mine eyes have seen thy salvation,
Which thou hast prepared before the face of all peoples ;
A light for revelation to the Gentiles,
And the glory of thy people Israel " (Lc. ii. 30–32).

The cosmopolitan character of this stanza becomes even more apparent when one looks it up in the context from which it is quoted (Isa. xlix).

We have found the Old Testament, in a few passages, attributing remarkable exaltation to the Person of the promise.   This feature is very prominent in the earliest New Testament incidents.   The representation is that in that generation it was a thing to be expected that the angel should say to Mary : —

"He shall be great, and shall be called the Son of the Most High" (Lc. i. 32).

It was not out of harmony with the expectations that prevailed to say that the wise men came to worship the child, and that Herod pretended to desire to worship him (Matt. ii. 2, 8, 11), or to represent his birth as miraculous, or as heralded by angels.

More prominently still these devout Jews are represented as expecting that the Anointed one will be a redeemer from sin.   When John said to his two disciples: "Behold the lamb of God that taketh away the sin of the world" (Jn. i. 29, 36), they understood him to imply that the lamb of God was the Messiah (41).   That the Messiah should be a remedy for sin was an idea intelligible to them. They understood that the Person who should follow John would baptize with the Holy Ghost and with fire. They believed that in preparing the way for him John was preparing the way for Yahaweh to rescue and comfort his people.   But the idea that John especially put in their minds was that of redemption from sin : not a warrior Messiah who should overthrow Rome, but "the lamb of God that taketh away the sin of the world."

In this representation of the matter the gospel by John is not alone.   Matthew tells us that the child was named Jesus because he should "save his people from their sins" (i. 21) — not from the Romans, but from

Redemption from sin as a part of the expectation

their sins. Luke represents Zacharias as saying that John was to —

"Go before the face of the Lord to make ready his ways;
To give knowledge of salvation unto his people
In the remission of their sins" (Lc. i. 76–77).

The forerunner was to be "filled with the Holy Ghost," and was to "turn the disobedient to" "the wisdom of the just" (i. 15–17). Personal holiness is insisted upon in the new movement. He that was to be born of Mary was to be "called holy" (i. 35). The purpose of it all is that men should serve God "in holiness and righteousness" (i. 75). Not to give further details, the great message was not merely that the kingdom was at hand. It was: "Repent, for the kingdom of heaven is at hand" (Matt. iv. 17).

There were false messiahs in that century, and these were political pretenders. This fact is sometimes cited in proof that the Messiah was expected to be False messiahs a political deliverer. But the false messiahs all belong to the later generations, after the career of Jesus had made the messianic idea a concrete one. This idea of a political Messiah existed. In time it became sharply defined as the idea of those who refused to accept Jesus as the Messiah. But among persons who were thoughtful, and had insight, and understood the scriptures, the messianic idea was not so simple or so crude as this. They expected a signal manifestation in fulfilment of the ancient promise, but one that included spiritual as well as temporal elements; and many of the details became definite in their minds only with the progress of events.

II. We turn to the question of the fulfilment of the promise — first, the nature of the thing we call fulfilment, and second, the fulfilment as a fact.

1. First, what do we mean by fulfilment when we think of it as sequent to a promise?

From some points of view there is no difference between performing something that has been promised or Fulfilment threatened and the coming to pass of some- of a promise thing that has been foretold; but from other *versus* a prediction points of view there is a great difference. For example, when we think of a promise and its fulfilment, we think of the means employed for that purpose. The promise and the means and the result are all in mind at once, and our conception of each is modified by our conception of the others. In the case of any fulfilled promise it would for certain purposes be proper to single out the foretelling clause in the promise, and to connect it in thought with the result foretold, describing the thing as a fulfilled prediction. If the promise involved a series of results, we might connect any one of the results with the foretelling clause as a fulfilled prediction. So far our thinking would be correct. But if we permanently confined our thought to these items in the fulfilled promise, we should be led to an inadequate and very likely a false idea of the promise and its fulfilment. To understand the predictive element aright we must see it in the light of the other elements. Every fulfilled promise is a fulfilled prediction; but it is exceedingly important to look at it as a promise, and not as mere prediction.

Throughout the Old Testament, as we have seen, the prophets give us the conception of a promise that is An eternal eternally operative. This necessarily implies fulfilment must be a cumulative fulfilment, and certain culmi- cumulative nating periods of fulfilment. At every date Deity has already begun to perform the great thing he has promised, and he will never cease performing it.

If one affirms that the promise is fulfilled in Jesus Christ, he ought not to separate that fulfilment from the rest of the eternal fulfilling movement. The idea of a long line of fulfilment is not a hypothesis offered for the solution of difficulties, but a part of the primary conception of a promise that is for eternity.

And if there is a long line of fulfilment, the nature of it may change as the ages go by. If the supreme Ruler of the universe begins the keeping of his promise by bestowing racial and political dominion, he may continue it by substituting a dominion of influence, a spiritual dominion. The transition from a racial to a spiritual seed of Abraham, or from a racial to a spiritual king of the line of David, may be a legitimate transition.

We have found that the promise is of a blessing at once cosmopolitan and national, and also that it is prevailingly expressed in personal terms. This threefold character must be taken into the account in considering the nature of the personal fulfilment. In other words, we have found the representation that it was given to Israel for the nations, and we have found it taking the form of the presentation of a Person, a person in some cases identifiable with Israel or with some Israelite, but of whom also are said things too wonderful to be applied to any ordinary man. In what they teach concerning the divine purpose through Israel, the prophets sometimes speak of his mission as a whole, and sometimes of parts of it. In speaking of the parts they sometimes treat them as typical, so that an assertion made concerning one part applies equally to other parts or to the whole ; and sometimes independently of their typical character, so that what is true of one part does not apply to the whole or to the other parts.

As the promise was for eternity and for mankind, the Person of the promise is a typical human person, thought of in his relations to Yahaweh. This is equally true whether you conceive of the Person as merely ideal, or as a personified people, or as a person existing when any particular utterance concerning the promise was made, or as a person then future ; whether you call him Servant or Messiah or *hhasidh* or Son or Regent or by some other technical name. The terms differ, but they are mostly capable of being thought of as alike.[1]

We must further have it in mind that a teaching that was uttered generation after generation, for centuries, by a succession of prophets, did not ordinarily come to its audience as something startling. It was perpetually the repetition in forms more or less changed of affirmations that were familiar and well known. And the repeating of it was not mainly the putting on record of predictions of events, so that these might be verified in the future ; it was the teaching of a practical theology for the enforcement of public and private duties.

A matter familiar and practical

If one claims that the promise is fulfilled in Jesus Christ, he should take these various matters into the

---

[1] Generally speaking each may, as we have seen, denote any person of any race or time, regarded as in close relations with Yahaweh. Each prevailingly denotes either the Israelitish race or the line of David, or either, but always with especial reference to their close relations with Yahaweh. In the use of each, stress is laid on God's purpose for mankind, on this as eternal, on this as already manifested, but to have its most glorious manifestation in the future. In the use of each the prophet ordinarily presents the Person of the promise from a subjective point of view as identical with Israel ; but each is capable of being presented objectively, so that the promise nation or the promise king, for example, will be thought of as differing from the nation or king actually existing, and as having a mission to these.

account, in defining his claim. The validity of his claim depends on its taking a form consistent with these facts. If the promise is fulfilled in Jesus, In what sense it is fulfilled as promise, and not barely as is Jesus the prediction; its fulfilment in Jesus is a part of fulfilment? its eternal and cumulative national and world-wide fulfilment. In the form of the unfolding of a divine promise, the prophets made a forecast of the future history of Israel in his relations to mankind. They made this forecast for the purpose of edifying their contemporaries. We need not attempt to answer the question how far they anticipated the actual details of external events. In many places in their forecast appears the figure of the Person of the promise, and in a few places he takes on an extraordinary character, very like that of the divine-human Redeemer whom Christians believe Jesus to be. From their point of view they must needs think of this Person as springing from Israel, and therefore as a part of Israel. If we suppose that some of the prophets had foreglimpses of the actual personal Jesus, they were compelled to think of him as a part of Israel. The apostles sometimes look from the same view-point, though they also have the conception of the Christ as greater than Israel, and of Israel as included in him.

In fine, if we are to regard Jesus as the fulfilling of the forecast of the prophets, we must follow the mode of thought of Paul and his associates, thinking of Jesus Christ as the greatest fact in the history of Israel, and as the culminating manifestation of God's purpose for mankind through Israel. If they were correct in this, then they were correct in applying directly to Jesus Christ whatever the prophets say concerning Israel the promise-people as distinguished from the merely ethnical Israel.   And I think that no intelligent student of history, of any creed, doubts that Jesus is the greatest fact in the history of Israel; and I see no room for doubt that Jesus is the culminating manifestation of God's purpose for the nations through Israel.[1]

[1] "In the sense in which it is true that the Servant is the Israelitish people personified, personification is not a mere figure of speech; it involves the recognition of the fact that a people is an organic unit. In law we speak of a business organization as a corporate person.   In its corporate personal character it has rights and obligations, and is subject to rewards and punishments.   We apply the same modes of speaking to other aggregates of individuals.   We speak of the German people or of the American church as organic wholes, having each a character and duties like a person."

"There is nothing to prevent such a personified aggregate from having relations with itself or its members, as well as with the world outside it. Even an individual has relations with himself, owes duties to himself, may be in conflict with himself, should respect himself.   In a more marked sense the same is true of a personified aggregate.   The German people has duties to itself, and to the persons that constitute it.   The American church has obligations to itself and to its members.   If the Servant is Israel personified, that does not exclude him from having a mission to Israel or to Israelites."

"When Deutero-Isaiah identifies the Servant with Israel, it is never with Israel as a mere political or ethnical aggregation of persons; invariably it is with Israel as the medium of Yahaweh's gracious purpose for the nations.   Giesebrecht is correct in saying that the personified Israel is not some part of the people, for example, not those who stand with the prophets, or the pious kernel within Israel, but the whole people.   Nevertheless it is the ideal Israel, the eternal Israel contemplated in Yahaweh's purpose and promise, and not merely the concrete Israel existing at any given point of time."

"Any Israelite, so far forth as he has Israelitish characteristics, may within limits be taken as a type of the whole people.   In particular, any Israelite who is imbued with the spirit of Israel's call for the sake of mankind, may so far forth be regarded as a type of the ideal Israel.   Within limits, that which is true of the people is true of any typical individual among the people."

"If the history of the world presents us with any one person who is peculiarly and uniquely a typical Israelite, who stands by himself as the representative of Yahaweh's promise to the nations through Israel, whose

2. Having attained to this conception of the nature of the fulfilment which we are to expect, we are ready to consider the fulfilment as a historical fact. The question may be divided. First, what are the historical facts, if any, that seem to correspond to the thing promised to Abraham and Israel? Second, is the correspondence a reality? We take up the first of these questions, leaving the second to be discussed in the following chapter.

What are the facts of history, if any, in which the supreme powers of the universe have kept the promise that was made to Abraham and Israel? An adequate reply would be a many-volumed history of Israel in his relations to mankind. A compact summary of the reply may be framed as follows, confining itself to a few general salient matters. If we leave Christianity out of the account, except as a medium through which Semitic ideas have disseminated themselves, it still remains true that the Israelitish race, both by what they have achieved and by what they have suffered, have been peculiarly a channel of benefit to substantially all races, and are likely to be increasingly so in the future. In this fact Yahaweh seems to be keeping the promise that he made of old, the promise that all the families of the ground should be blessed in Abraham and his seed. This fact is not erased, but on the contrary greatly magnified,

A summary as to the fulfilment

experiences and character and relations to the world are such that Israel's mission to the world culminates in him, then it is correct to apply directly to that person the statements made in Deutero-Isaiah concerning Israel the Servant. The writers of the New Testament regard Jesus Christ as such a person. Because they so regard him they apply to him the utterances concerning the Servant. Their doing so is not a matter of accommodating interpretation, but is as correct critically as it is magnificent in the conception of human history which it implies" (*Am. Jour. of Theol.*, July, 1903, p. 543).

when we recognize Christianity and Mohammedanism as movements growing out of Israel and constituting part of the mission of Israel. And these parts of the fulfilment of the promise to Israel, in their turn, sink into insignificance beside the fact that the person Jesus Christ came of the seed of Abraham and Israel — provided that Jesus is the God-man and the Saviour that Christians believe him to be. If there has been a fulfilment, it has been threefold : that in the race Israel, that in Israel's religion and its daughter religions, that in the person and work of Jesus ; and it is a mistake to neglect any one of these three factors.

A certain current interpretation claims that the seed of Abraham in whom the nations are blessed is Israel the race, set apart by Yahaweh as his especial organ for economic and ethical and religious revelation to mankind, and still kept separate by him for the further working out of these his beneficent purposes. No one need wonder at the great influence which this interpretation has, especially among the more reverent and appreciative of the rationalistic thinkers. But those who hold it sometimes draw the inference that since the national career of Israel is thus the fulfilment of the promise, therefore Jesus Christ is not its fulfilment. This inference is a gross *non sequitur*.

A Jewish interpretation

As opposed to the view just mentioned, a great body of Christian interpreters claim that the fulfilment is not, except incidentally, in Israel the race ; but in the Christian Messiah, perhaps with Israel the church, gathered from the nations, and abiding in the Christ. If the other conception was a large and worthy one, this is still larger and worthier. The mission accomplished by Israel through Jesus, his atonement, his church, his influence, his personality, is infi-

The exclusive Christian interpretation

nitely greater than that accomplished by Israel merely
as a race. But if the Christian interpreter persists in
excluding the ethnical Israel from his conception of the
fulfilment, or in regarding Israel's part in the matter
as merely preparatory and not eternal, then he comes
into conflict with the plain witness of both Testaments.
His interpretation is even less consistent with the text
than is the exclusive Jewish conception. Rightly interpreted, the biblical statements include in the fulfilment
both Israel the race, with whom the covenant is eternal,
and also the personal Christ and his mission, with the
whole spiritual Israel of the redeemed in all ages. The
New Testament teaches this as Christian doctrine, for
leading men to repentance and for edification ; and the
Old Testament teaches it as messianic doctrine, for leading men to repentance and for edification.

In the biblical idea of the Christ is included the idea
of his mission — his work among men in all the generations. From one point of view, seeing that the larger
includes the less, his mission includes that of Israel.
From a different point of view, one would say that
Christ and his mission came out of Israel, and were
germinally included in Israel. Genetically, the acorn
includes the oak, the less may include the greater.
Whether from the one point of view or the other, the
scriptures habitually identify both Israel and the Christ
as the fulfilling of the promise.

The exclusive Jewish interpretation and the exclusive
Christian interpretation are equally wrong. Each is
correct in what it affirms, and incorrect in An interpre-
what it denies. The Christian should never tation that is
say to the Jew : " Jesus Christ is the fulfill- and Christian
ing of the promise, and therefore you are shut out."
The truth requires us to say instead : " Your view is

correct as far as it goes, but it is incomplete. Large
and lofty as is your conception of the mission of Israel,
the true conception is still loftier and larger. You
Israelites have been kept in the world these thousands
of years, and your record as a whole has been a peculiarly splendid and beneficent one. Your vigor as a
race seems to be unabated. No one knows what magnificent possibilities the God of your fathers may have
in store for you. But you do your race injustice if you
claim that its career is circumscribed within even these
spacious boundaries."

Christianity came into the world, so far as its human
founders are concerned, as the joint product of Israel's
bible and of influences set in motion by men of Israelite
blood, who claimed inspiration from the God of Israel.
In a later century Mohammedanism sprang from the
two older forms of the religion of Yahaweh. As adherents of these two religions, several hundred millions of
the human race now profess to worship the God of Israel
as the only God; and these hundreds of millions include
the leading races and the leading civilizations of the
globe. These results are parts of the mission of Israel
in the world; and they are parts of it larger and more
important than those which have thus far been directly
accomplished by the perpetuation of Israel as a separate
race. Put the lowest possible estimate upon Mohammedanism and the corrupted forms of Christianity, and
even upon Christianity in its purer forms, and still the
blessing of Abraham, flowing and to flow to the nations
through these channels, is such as to be a worthy
fulfilment of even the promise of the infinite God.

That which Israel has achieved through the Israelite,
Jesus Christ, and through those other Israelites his
earliest disciples, and through their successors till now,

is not less the accomplishment of what Yahaweh promised to Israel than are the successes that Israel has achieved through Moses or David or Solomon or Isaiah or Nehemiah or Maimonides or the Rothschilds.

But even the view we have thus far been taking is comparatively a low and narrow view to take of the outcome of the promise made to Israel. It shows up dwarflike by the side of the outcome in the person of Jesus Christ. If the Christian doctrines be true, the doctrines of the incarnation, the trinity, the person of Christ, the atonement, salvation, immortality, then there is in the character of Jesus the Saviour, offspring of Jacob and of David, a fulfilment of the promise so vast that even the achievements of the religion that Jesus founded are by comparison insignificant.

Fulfilment in the person of Christ

Even from a theologically agnostic point of view the wonderful personality of Jesus, coupled with the unequalled acceptance he has had among men, render him a fact greater and more important than a whole cycle of other facts. Much more, if the doctrines of immortality and of the incarnation and the atonement are true, then the kingdom of the promise is eternal in the world of the blessed, and is as much beyond the largest temporal greatness as eternity is beyond time. If they are true, then the person of the divine-human Saviour, Deity incarnate in a man of Jewish blood, is as much greater than the great things we have been considering as God is greater than men. So far as duration is concerned there is no final fulfilment for an eternal promise ; but there was a climacteric fulfilment, one whose sublime height will never be exceeded, in the historical manifestation when the Word was made flesh and dwelt among us.

So much for the facts in which the promise made to Israel finds its accomplishment. When we are scanning the career of Israel in search of these facts, we should look at the whole historical process, and not at some relatively narrow and circumscribed portion of it.

Possibly we need to remind ourselves that the fulfilment is still in progress. It is not correct to say that it was accomplished on the cross and at the resurrection, with the implication that these were the last end of the process. If one holds that the culminating fulfilment is in the person of the divine-human Saviour, as manifested in Jesus Christ, he must none the less hold that there are remainders of the eternal fulfilment yet to be wrought out, alike in the Israelitish race, in the spread of the kingdom on the earth, and in the blessedness in heaven of the recipients of the promised blessing.

CHAPTER XVII

THE APOLOGETIC VALUE OF PROPHECY

VERY familiar among the theologians is the argument given in such works as Keith *On the Prophecies*, or Bishop Thomas Newton's *Dissertations on* the *Prophecies which have remarkably been* *Fulfilled*, or in its appropriate place in many of the full treatises on Dogmatics. It is to the effect that there are in the scriptures many hundred predictions which have come true. In particular, it is said that the Old Testament contains numerous predictions concerning a personage called the Messiah, who was to come at a certain time in the future; that these predictions sketch his character, give beforehand his biography, mention details in his career, his sufferings, his death, and that these details correspond remarkably to those of the career of Jesus Christ, as recorded in the New Testament. It is therefore inferred that, since it was beyond human power to foresee these details, the foresight of them must have been by divine inspiration; and thus that the facts prove at once the divine authority of the prophets who foresaw, and the divine mission of the Christ who was foreseen.

I do not attack or undervalue this argument. It has superficial defects, but it is in its essential nature impregnable. We cannot shut our eyes, how- Its ever, to the fact that it is now much less decadence influential than formerly. Some of the reasons for this

387

are not hard to find, and they show that the argument, however valuable, needs to be restated.

Its influence has been weakened by the indiscriminate claims which some of its advocates have made. When you claim instances and fail to make your claim good, your claim ought, logically, to go for nothing. Practically, however, it counts against you, bringing suspicion on any other claims you may make.

Again, many even of the valid instances used in this argument are instances whose validity is not at once apparent, but has to be argued in order to have it accepted. Instead of cogently using the instance, you have to exhaust your logical energy in vindicating your right to use it.

Again, the argument as commonly presented lacks unity. It deals with facts that seem to be disconnected and heterogeneous. Indeed, some of the presentations make the unconnected character of the facts an important part of the argument. They assume that marvellousness is a special proof of divineness. But our generation is not easily convinced by proofs of this sort. In its study of God and of miracles, as in its study of ordinary nature, it believes mainly the truths which it can classify and reduce to statements of law, and looks with suspicion on that which is incapable of being so treated.

Yet again, the argument as commonly presented is historically associated with the assumption that prediction is the main thing in prophecy. This our generation rejects. It is convinced that the prophet is a forthteller rather than a foreteller; that miraculous prediction, however real, is only one item in prophecy, and not the most important item. This doubtless diminishes for the time being — by suggestion, of course, and not by logical necessity — the influence which arguments from prediction have over us.

Further, the interpreters of the past have treated as predictions many passages that were not properly such, but expressions of fears or hopes or wishes or opinions, or statements as to existing tendencies. Confused habits of interpretation have been established. With similar confusion of thought, the opponents of the argument from prediction are now affirming that the prophets made many predictions that were proved false by the events; that the fulfilment of what the prophets foretold was a haphazard matter; that the thing sometimes came true, and sometimes not. There is at present enough of confusion of thought to dull the edge of the traditional argument.

When to considerations like these we add others based on the general sceptical and agnostic tendencies of our age, and on the effect of the current theories of criticism, whatever be the weight or the bearing any one may assign to these, we *The argument needs to be restated* reach at least one conclusion; namely, that it is not superfluous to inquire whether some better way can be found of stating the argument from prophecy. It seems to me that there is such a way, and that it is indicated by the treatment of the subject given in the preceding sixteen chapters.

In these chapters, let us remind ourselves, we have reached, strictly speaking, only provisional conclusions. We have been asking: What did the prophets claim? rather than: What were the actual *Our provisional conclusions. Are they true?* facts? We have taken the statements of fact as we found them, and have tried to get an orderly understanding of them. Now that we have been over the ground, we are ready for the inquiry whether the conclusions we have reached are genuine fact, or are falsehood or romance. And this question will closely connect itself with the question whether we can substantiate the claims of the religion that traces its existence back to the prophets.

In this region the one most important, indisputable fact which we possess is the scriptures themselves in the forms in which we have them. No one doubts that the scriptures are a fact, existing in some millions of details. Most of the statements made concerning their sources, their original form, their structure, the divine element in them, and other like matters, are more or less matters of inference, of conjecture, of opinion; but the scriptures themselves, including their contents, are a fact. Thus far we have been engaged in simply examining this fact. Apart from all questions of trustworthiness or inspiration, the scriptures are the original literary sources for information concerning the prophet, and we have been merely asking what they say concerning him. Now we are ready to ask whether what they say is sane and credible; and in asking that, to ask whether the religion taught by the prophets is a reasonable religion.

The effect of such an argument on the mind of any person will depend somewhat on the view which he already holds concerning God and the universe; but it will have weight with any one who is so far forth a theist that he regards the supreme energy of the universe as a Being that is intelligent and purposeful. We have found the prophets claiming to be in communication with such a Being. We have found them describing him as not merely the intelligent supreme energy of the universe, but as the Power that makes for righteousness, as exercising love

The lowest theistic presupposition

and preference and indignation, as having a plan in
human history, as the creator of nature, always everywhere present in that which he has created, but also as
transcending creation, and able at will to exercise powers different from those of nature as we understand it;
and in particular as interested in redeeming men from
sin. If we find reason to hold that what they say is
credible, that will be to us proof that their views of the
nature of the supreme energy of the universe are correct, and in particular that the offered redemption which
they proclaim is a reality.   These things will become
credible to us, both on the basis of their testimony and
through our own insight in the course of the processes
by which we are convinced that their testimony is
credible.

Upon this discussion we now enter, first recapitulat-
ing the results we have reached, and then inquiring how
these results bear on the question of apologetic restatement.

I. First, we make a brief recapitulation.

We have found that the scriptures present the prophet
as a citizen with a message from Deity; not a priest,
not a wizard of some sort, not an oracular *The prophet*
recluse, but eminently a man among men. *as we have*
We have found that the prophets were the *found him*
statesmen, the reformers, the writers and poets, the
preachers, of their times, as well as men who claimed
to be in supernatural communication with the unseen
world. We have found that the revelation which they
professed to bring from Deity was the product of their
human good judgment, as well as of special gifts
claimed by them to be superhuman.   Much of this so-
claimed revelation was written down, and is still extant
in the scriptures with which we are familiar; and thus

it is within our reach for purposes of testing and of judgment.

So far as the element of prediction enters into their utterances, we have found that it consists almost exclu-

Prophetic prediction as we have found it

sively of promises and threats uttered with a homiletical purpose. They appeal to fulfilled prediction as accrediting their divine authority, but their utterances contain very little prediction that purports to have been uttered merely or mainly for this purpose.

In particular, we have found that the foreshadowing of the Messiah, which constitutes by far the larger portion of

The messianic doctrine as we have found it

all the predictive element in prophecy, is the teaching of a doctrine, a doctrine in the form of a promise affirmed to have been given by Yahaweh. We have found the New Testament calling attention centrally to what it describes as " the promise," the one promise which it elsewhere designates as " the hope of Israel," — identifying this promise as the one originally made to Abraham, recognizing the specific promises into which it branched out, tracing its unfolding through the Old Testament narrative, preaching it as Christian doctrine, claiming that it finds culminating fulfilment in Jesus Christ, under it announcing salvation to the gentiles, and connecting it throughout with the redemptive and ethical and eschatological doctrines of the gospel. We have found their position fully justified by the testimony of the Old Testament. The Old Testament is the literature of Israel regarded as the people of the promise. We do not need to settle the critical questions that have arisen in order to justify this proposition. Many important details under it depend on questions of date and authorship ; but the proposition as a whole is true on any possible adjustment of dates and questions of authorship. At the beginning of the main line of the history recorded in the Old Testament, we found the record of the giving of this great promise which was so influential with the men of the New Testament — the promise that in Abraham and his seed all the nations shall be blessed. We found this promise emphasized in the story of the patriarchs. Again we found it in the records of the time when Israel came out of Egypt, made central in the form of the affirmation that Yahaweh, the God of all the peoples, has constituted Israel a separate and priestly nation. Later we found the same promise renewed to David and his seed — the promise that Israel shall be perpetuated as the eternal kingdom of God, reigned over eternally by the anointed king of the line of David. In this connection we found the promise described as "the *torah* of mankind," cosmopolitan as well as everlasting in its scope. And from David's time on we found the same promise presupposed in the songs and sermons of the prophets.

For we have found that the psalms and the prophetic discourses are simply the preaching of this gospel. They reiterate the promise. They unfold it in new lights, and present it in new aspects. They apply it each one to the circumstances of his own day. They call attention to past *The gospel in the Old Testament as we have found it* fulfilment, and affirm that what God has promised is sure for time to come. They make the truth vivid by new illustration. They do this in a main line of messianic prophecy, which can be traced, creating a vocabulary of terms in which to describe the great Agent of the promise — such terms as Servant, Messiah, Elect one, *hhasidh*, Branch; speaking at large of a kingdom, of universal peace, of the last days, of the always impending day of Yahaweh. They equally make the same truth vivid through the object lessons presented in their own persons, in the ceremonial law which they introduced, in all the institutions of Israel.

In their presentation of it the promise is not a mere forecast of a distant future, but is spiritual food for immediate use. It was fitted to be the central doctrine of the practical theology of Israel. If any descendant of Abraham believed that Deity had chosen his race for purposes of blessing to mankind, that was a reason why he should practise repentance and faith and obedience and deathless patriotism ; why he should never despair even when things were at their worst, but should be sure that God would carry out his irrevocable plans. In short, here was a preachable gospel — not merely a gospel like that which Christians have to preach, but the very same gospel, though in a less unfolded stage.

In current sermons and addresses in our day the messianic doctrine of the Old Testament is sometimes effectively illustrated by the minute scarlet strand said to exist in every rope of the cordage of the navy of Great Britain. In one respect the illustration fails. Rightly understood, the messianic element in the Old Testament is not a minute thread, difficult to discern ; it is everywhere the principal thing, that which underlies all the history, all the poetry, all the prophetic preaching, all the national worship, all the sayings of wisdom. It is at some points more discernible than at others, but the whole Old Testament is simply the record of the promise.

II. Does this view of the matter afford a practicable ground for restating the apologetic argument from prophecy ? Is there a basis here for proving the truth and the superhuman sanctions of the religion revealed in the scriptures ?

In answering this question, we must confine ourselves to four specific arguments, — those from the personality of the prophet, from the national ideal, from historical verisimilitude, from fulfilled prediction ; and in the case of each of these we shall be able to give no more than a brief illustrative sketch.

1. To me it seems that the personality of the prophet, as presented in the prophetic writings, is an argument of no small weight in proof of the genuineness of their mission and of the truth of their teachings.

The idea that God likes manliness in men, that manliness especially fits a man to interpret God, has in our day a good deal of currency. Our literature The biblical is full of this, and is busy in contrasting this ideal of a prophet is a idea with real or alleged ideas that have pre- true ideal vailed in the past. One pictures the ultra-professional minister of a few generations ago, or the minister of ultra-ecclesiastical type, or the grotesque and distorted types of holy men that are found somewhere, by way of illustrating the superiority of the type of Christian worker who depends solely on his own manliness and human sympathy and consciousness of divine mission. Many seem to suppose that this idea of the true character of a religious teacher is a twentieth-century idea — that it perhaps began to come in when the Young Men's Christian Association introduced athletics into their methods of work. Prophetic character of this type seems to be regarded by many as the crowning product of the current stage of evolution. And I suppose that none of us doubt the superior fineness of this type as compared with other types. It ought to stand for something, then, that this is the type of prophetic character set forth in the Old Testament, from the earliest parts of it to the latest.

That this is the Old Testament presentation of the prophet has been shown in the preceding chapters, particularly in the fourth chapter. The prophet is presented as the highest human religious authority, and yet he is simply a citizen with a message. We have traditional conceptions of the prophet in which he is robed or tonsured, or otherwise marked by external insignia, or by professional practices, and perhaps one cannot prove that these traditional ideas are at all points incorrect; but none of them are distinctly found in the Old Testament. So far as the primary record is concerned, they are importations, and many of them are importations that contradict the record. The Old Testament presentation of the highest type of religious teacher differs very little from the highest conception to which our century has attained.

This fact is the more marked because it is so in contrast with the ideas that have commonly prevailed among men. In all religions the teacher who has represented Deity has affected visible marks of distinction from other men. This is so among the American aborigines ; among the Africans and the Islanders of the sea; among the highly civilized Buddhists and Brahmans ; among Christian clergymen and scholars. It is so thoroughly the case that interpreters in all the past have assumed that the Old Testament prophet could not be an exception, and have supplied from inference or from imagination the details that the Old Testament omits. The uniqueness of the prophet of Israel in this respect is not to be lightly passed over. He is a class by himself.

These facts have a double bearing on questions of apologetics. First, this biblical idea of the typical religious man is a true idea. It appeals to our judgment

as to what ought to be.   We are sure that it is correct.
This judgment ought to carry with it our respect for
the records that present the conception. The Apologetic
writers of these records were persons who bearings
had attained to insight.   Their affirmations have a claim
on our confidence.   But this is not all.   We are compelled, in the second place, to raise the question how
they attained to such a conception.   The old-fashioned
opinion that it was revealed to them by divine inspiration
will account for the phenomena.   Can any one account
for them more reasonably?   Account for it as you may,
these men were, somehow or other, in remarkably close
relations with the supreme intelligent Energy that mani-
fests itself in the universe.

   The argument gains in cogency if we carry it over
into the region of the inspiration of the prophets, and of
divine revelation through them.   Tell a child God reveal-
that God gave the bible through the prophets, ing himself
the prophets writing it, and the child inevi- prophets
tably gets the notion of something like a dictating process.   That notion persistently clings to our minds, and
we find it difficult to prevent its vitiating any idea we
may form of the matter.   Our study of the prophets
offers a different form of conception.   We have before
us the conception of the supreme Energy of the universe
operating purposefully in human history.   In particular
we examine a block of history extending from Abraham
to the time when the New Testament was written.   God
causes the events of the history to be transacted, the
prophets themselves and their writings being portions
of the events; and he causes a record to be made of the
events transacted.   He is represented as raising up the
prophets, and as guiding them — guiding them in such
a way that each prophet distinctly continues to be him-

self, even while he is the agent of Deity. Here we have
a mode of conception not lax in its recognition of the
divine element and wide enough to include all the phenomena in the case.

2. If this argument from the Old Testament ideal of
the prophet is strong, yet stronger is the argument from
the national ideal which the promise-doctrine represents
as existing in the consciousness of Israel.

That ideal is that Israel is God's chosen channel of
blessing to mankind.

The details of the argument are partly dependent on
critical questions. If Moses wrote the pentateuch, then
Critical theo- the promise was already on record in his
ries and the time, whether one count the date as the thir-
national ideal teenth century before Christ, or the sixteenth,
and was in the consciousness of the family of Abraham
more than four centuries earlier. But how if one holds
that Moses did not write the pentateuch? Certain
scholars say that the earliest parts of the pentateuch
date from a time shortly before Amos, about 800 B.C.;
and that there is an element of fiction in the narrative,
so that we cannot be sure of the facts for the times
much earlier than that century. Now it is not a matter
of indifference which of these views we hold. One con-
tradicts the other, and one of the two is necessarily false.
In matters of apologetical detail the difference is important, and it is so in its bearing on many other questions.
Nevertheless, the main contention from the national
ideal stands firm on either view, or on any intermediate
view.

Whether it began in the twentieth century before
Christ, or the sixteenth or the thirteenth or the eighth,
it is on record that a certain national ideal existed in the
consciousness of Israel. Israelites held that the God

of all the earth had chosen Israel as his own especial
people, for purposes of blessing to mankind.   We need
not insist that every person was greatly under the influence of this ideal.   The majority were ignorant and
indifferent, as the majority in Christendom are to-day
ignorant and indifferent concerning the great truths of
religion.   But the doctrine of the promise was widely
enough understood so that the prophets could appeal
to it in their preaching; and devout souls in Israel
accepted it with the whole heart.

Think for a moment what a conception this was, to
stand as a nation's ideal.   Chosen of God for purposes of blessing to all mankind!   Had the   The signifi-
sages of China or India or Persia or Babylon   cance of such
any conception to compare with this?   Did   an ideal
Greek philosophy or that more wonderful thing, Greek
insight, ever attain to it?   Was it incorporated into the
Roman ethics of legislation?   In these modern times
we have borrowed the idea from the bible.   It is an
element of some importance in our religion, our philan-
thropy, our statesmanship.   In hours of supreme missionary enthusiasm we sometimes rise to a very distinct
consciousness that our nation, our race, our church, is
chosen of God for purposes of blessing to mankind.
But this consciousness, even on the theory of those who
date it latest, was on record in Israel when Rome was
founded; on record centuries before Plato or the pub-
lishing of the Greek drama with its wonderful theology
and ethics; existing and on record then, and then believed and preached as the ancient religious tradition of
the nation.   If the same consciousness existed in the
Abrahamic race twelve centuries earlier, that makes the
case so much the stronger; but it is strong enough if
we take the later date.

Such are the facts in this argument from the promise as the statement of a national ideal. They have two bearings. First, the ideal is a worthy one. It indicates mental largeness and moral fineness. The men who entertained and taught it deserve our respect, and deserve it both intellectually and spiritually. It is not reasonable to reject lightly the things which they affirm to be true. And secondly, we have to face the question how they attained to such an ideal. It is a remarkable phenomenon. In possessing it they are a class by themselves.

How shall we account for this wholly unique instance of national consciousness? this ideal of Israel as divinely chosen, not for his own sake, but for the sake of the nations? If one offers the hypothesis of miraculous divine inspiration, that will account for it. On this hypothesis, God gave Israel's ideal to him by superhuman revelation. And certainly the ideal is worthy of such an origin. If we thus account for it, it proves the divine mission of the prophets, the apostles, the scriptures. But suppose one refuses to entertain the hypothesis of an inspired revelation; suppose he tries to account for the phenomena from an agnostic point of view. The thing that he has to account for is the fact that this altruistic ideal existed, and that it constituted a part of the monotheism that has come to mankind through Israel. It existed, and it is so very marked a thing in human history that it amounts to a special and exceptional manifestation of the powers that control history. It shows something in regard to the nature of the powers that control history. Somehow or other, Israel and the prophets and apostles sustain this peculiar relation to the powers that control human history, whoever or whatever these powers may

How is this ideal to be accounted for?

be. It follows that Israel and the prophets and apostles and the scriptures have an especial claim to attention and credence, even from a theologically agnostic point of view. But the facts also constitute a strong argument against theological agnosticism, and in favor of the doctrine that the power in history is a personal and self-revealing God.

The strength of this argument from the national ideal will perhaps be the more apparent if we set it in contrast with a different ideal that has sometimes been A contrasting presented. Whoever has thoughtfully read ideal Mr. Kingsley's novel, *Hypatia*, doubtless has a certain picture deeply burned into his memory — the picture there so frequently sketched of all the millions of the human race who lived before Christ as now burning in hell. Whether or no Mr. Kingsley is correct in representing that this was current Christian doctrine in the time of Cyril, there can be no doubt that it is a doctrine that many Christians have taught. Probably there are those now living who regard it as a part of the scheme of Christian theology; who recognize no revelation of a redemptive divine purpose for any who lived before Jesus came save the obedient few in Israel. Such views of Christian doctrine as this have caused apologists to be at a great disadvantage when they addressed intelligent and humane minds. That disadvantage is turned to advantage when one notices what the ideal presented by the prophets actually is; for that ideal makes the divine redemption for men conterminous with human history.

An added consideration of some weight is to be found in the method in which the prophets present their ideal. It is easy to teach a great religious doctrine in such terms that it shall be intelligible only to persons of certain

attainments or habits of mind; in such terms that it
would be uninteresting to those who have not reached
Argument these attainments, or to those who have left
from their them behind. By putting their doctrine into
mode of
presentation the form of a promise, the prophets rendered
it intelligible to those to whom it was first given, and
yet expressed it in terms that could be retained age
after age as its truths unfolded themselves. They thus
made it a statement of doctrine that was fitted to be
central in religious teaching and practice for all time.
In this characteristic of the form of their teaching, we
have something that is of weight in apologetics.

In this matter of the national ideal, therefore, we
have an argument based on undoubted facts. It is not
open to the charge of being trivial. No one can belittle
it by placing "mother Shipton's prophecy" by the side
of it. Its facts are the grave and central things of history. Its force is obvious, I think, on the first presentation; and it grows weightier the more one reflects
upon it.

3. We turn to the argument from historical verisimilitude. The account of the prophets and of the promise,
as we have found it in the scriptures, commends itself
to the historical judgment as bearing the marks of truth.

Of course, the scholars of the so-called Modern View
would not wholly accept this affirmation. They regard
Marks of a large proportion of the statements of fact
historicity made in the bible as either fiction or falsehood. In the preceding sixteen chapters we have been
examining what purport to be facts. There are those
who would admit our conclusions to be biblically correct
and spiritually truthful, who would yet deny their truthfulness as matters of fact. And indeed it is supposable
that a statement may be true in its own proper sense,

and may have spiritual value, and may nevertheless be fiction. One who holds that many of the statements we have examined are unhistorical might also supposably hold that they are in their proper value truthful. We need not raise this question, however, unless we find reason for doubting their historical verity. If the view given by the testimony in the case is self-consistent and reasonable, and marked by such continuity as history ought to possess, we need not hesitate to accept it as true to fact.

(*a*) The question of self-consistency is largely a question of details. But if the view we have drawn from the bible has been correctly drawn, that very fact Self-shows that the records are mainly consistent; consistency for the view itself is certainly consistent. Records that are full of contradictions will not yield an agreeing view of a matter except by processes of elimination; and we have not found it necessary to resort to such processes.

The consistency of the record becomes impressive in proportion as one examines a large body of details; and the number of details which we have passed under review is very large. In them all we have found that the doctrine of the promise serves as a key. It has solved the difficulties before they arose, by the simple process of suggesting the true understanding of the text.

One difficulty with the argument from fulfilled prophecy, as sometimes presented, is that many of its citations from the Old Testament are not at Difficulties once obviously applicable. An apologist and the promise- cites a passage as applying to Jesus. One doctrine looks up the passage and finds that the words were spoken of Israel, or of some ancient historical personage, in a context that gives no hint of referring to a coming person who is to appear some centuries in the future. Just at this point there is often found a gulf between the apologist's premises and his conclusion, and he has to resort to some device for bridging the gulf. We are familiar, for instance, with the formula in which one says: Yes, it does indeed appear that the passage applies primarily to Israel or to David or to the author or to his hero, as the case may be; but this one of whom it was originally spoken is here to be regarded as a type of the personal Christ; and so the Antitype is signified through the type. Perhaps there is no greater fault to be found with this than that it opens the way for bringing in too large an element of personal opinion in interpreting passages of scripture. But this is only one of the many devices of apologetic exegesis, ranging all the way from the idea of generic prophecy, manifold fulfilment, progressive fulfilment, down to that of double meaning or of accommodated or allegorical interpretation. Some of these devices are legitimate processes for getting at the essential truth, and some are of a pretty desperate character.

In almost every one of these instances it simplifies the case, and renders it intelligible, to note that the prophet in the given instance is speaking of Israel as the people of the promise, or of some person as representatively related to the promise; and that the apostle who quotes him is speaking of Jesus as the fulfilment of the promise made to and through Israel. When we note that both are dealing with the promise, we see that they are on common ground.

With this in mind, read the New Testament through, comparing it with the Old at every suitable point. As you find that the difficulties vanish and the statements become luminous, in one case after another, your conviction of the thorough truth of the scriptures and their claims will grow deeper and more intense.

To put this in other words, the appeal of the New Testament to the Old in proof of the claims of Jesus is rather to a doctrine taught there than to utterances that were the mere foretelling of events; and when we understand this doctrine, the meaning of the appeal becomes clear. That which is not easily intelligible as long as we count it to be the foretelling of an event may become perfectly plain the moment we recognize it as a doctrinal statement. It was as competent for the apostles to appeal to the doctrines taught by the prophets as to any other prophetic utterances.

And so the fact that this is the nature of their appeal offers itself to us as a solution of problems that would otherwise be puzzling. It affords an improved way of stating whatever is true in the theories of generic prophecy. It presents itself as a reconciliation of the Jewish and the Christian interpretations of the prophecies, so far forth as both are tenable; as a reasonable substitute for all theories of a double sense; and, in fine, as a full refutation of most of the objections raised against the messianic claims of Jesus Christ, as set forth in the New Testament.

(*b*) But however consistent with itself the biblical presentation of the matter may be, is it rationally credible?

We are not to accept absurdities as fact, on the ground of their being self-consistent. If they are absurdities, their consistency may prove them to be fiction rather than falsehood, but it cannot prove them to be history. This question still remains: Is the account given by the prophets inherently unbelievable?

One's reply will depend in part on his mental attitude toward miracles. So we may begin by classifying the statements of the prophets into those which affirm the occurrence of miraculous events, and those which do not. For present purposes we have no need to define more closely than by saying that miraculous events are such as the human mind cannot account for as the product of natural law. Supposably what we call miracle may really come under natural law, and might be so accounted for by a superhuman mind, the divine mind for example ; but we do not now need to discuss this. We need not be troubled even if the definition thus given of miracle is a sliding definition, the human mind to-day being able to account for things that were unaccountable to men of earlier times.

The record as we have studied it has been almost exclusively concerned with events that are not, under this definition, miraculous. We have found it to be, not an account of a series of marvels, but of sober and believable facts, some of them remarkable and wonderful, but no one of them a miracle in the sense of being out of the ordinary and intelligible operations of nature. It is true that there are miraculous events described in the records, and that we have not disputed their reality ; but also we have not made use of them.

Most of the events un-miraculous

Of course, nothing could be more sane or open to credence than the affirmations of the prophetic writings in regard to ordinary unmiraculous events, provided these are taken by themselves. No one would allege against them any charge of inherent incredibility. And the history of the prophets, as we have traced it, is almost exclusively made up of events of this kind.

But how is it when these writings affirm events such as the human mind cannot account for as the product of natural law? They certainly make affirmations of this sort. Shall we accept these as fact? or shall we reject

them, and regard them as discrediting all other affirmations of the prophets ?   If one holds that every alleged
apprehension of the supernatural is irrational, Alleged
he must of course hold that the biblical miraculous
account of the prophets is irrational so far events
forth as they lay claim to the supernatural.   But even
such an one has no reason for holding that the prophets
are not in the main honest and truthful in the account
they give of themselves.   One might give them credit
for that, even if he regarded their claim to superhuman
revelations as a delusion.   But who knows that their
communion with the superhuman was a delusion? Most
men now living are not ready to take the sweeping position that all alleged communication with the superhuman is unreal.   What intellectual right has an agnostic
to affirm that the ordinary system of operations of the
ultimate powers of the universe cannot be interpene-
trated by a different system or by a different mode of
energy?   He who says that forsakes the ranks of agnosticism, and simply affirms something of which he has no
evidence.

In short, the question whether we are to believe those
parts of the prophetic records which, so far as we can
see, transcend natural law, is a question which depends
on the cogency of the evidence.   And here the uniqueness of the biblical accounts of miracle must not be
neglected.   Their simplicity and soberness and freedom
from grotesqueness, when they speak of miracle, differentiate them from most other accounts of miracle, and
are strong points in their favor.   Why should we disbelieve their testimony in this matter ?

But even from the point of view of one who is convinced that miracles do not occur, these records are not
incredible so far as they relate to unmiraculous events.

And so, really, in view of the facts in the case, miracle or no miracle, there is no reason for doubting that the

The history as a whole is true

recorded history of the prophets is true history, or that the record concerning the promise is a trustworthy record of a reality.

(*c*) When we turn to the question of historical continuity, this statement, " There is no reason for doubting," is changed to one more positive. There are overwhelming reasons for believing.

The historicity of a record, when attacked, may be defended by showing that the record is self-consistent and is free from incredible statements. These have more than a negative value, constituting a probability in favor of trustworthiness. If to this it can be added, in the case of any record, that it conforms to the tests of historical continuity, the probabilities in its favor become very strong indeed. They would be strong even in a record made by a single person, though in that case the continuity might be accounted for as the product of the constructive mind of the author. But where the record is made up of many independent writings, the proof from continuity is especially cogent.

Nowhere is this mark more distinct than in the writings of the prophets. They include many different

Historical continuity in the bible

documents of different authorship and dates. No writer of either the Old or the New Testament is properly a writer of history. Their historical narratives are uniformly selections from history made for the purpose of teaching religious lessons. These facts render it the more remarkable that we find among them in so high a degree a correct conception of the nature of historical movements. They treat history as a continuous process of dynamic ideas working themselves out in social movements. One ought to see that their method is correct, even if he disagrees with them as to the nature of the dynamic ideas. Further, they so present the events that they fit together in intelligible lines of antecedence and consequence.

Many are accustomed to say that the biblical writers are not scientific historians, and to ask indulgence for them on the ground that nothing of this kind ought to be expected from them. But they need no indulgence, provided the view we have taken of the promise and its place in the history is correct. A perfectly definite conception of historical unity and continuity underlies the New Testament interpretations of the Old Testament, and equally underlies the Old Testament itself. This conception makes the promise to be the centre, and arranges all the facts according to their relations to the promise. In this the best of the historians of our own time do not surpass the men of the bible, and most men who have treated of their themes are far behind them. Once more we come face to face with the fact of the uniqueness of these writings and these men. They are a class by themselves. And what a class it is!

For our purpose all this has more bearings than one. There is an argument from the nature of the facts. Their interfitting and continuity is proof that they are true to reality; for chance state- Bearings in the argument ments would not fit thus, and it is unimaginable that all these writers joined in fabricating a fiction. There are arguments from the character of the biblical men. The loftiness of their point of view is wonderful. If we account for it by their inspiration, we have in it direct proof of the divine authority of the men and of their writings. If we try to account for it otherwise, we have to attribute to them remarkable insight and rare trustworthiness, and we thus put ourselves under obligation to accept their testimony, both in regard to the history they narrate and when they claim divine authority for themselves.

It is remarkable that such a national ideal as that indicated in the promise should have been framed among such a people; but this ideal being given as one of the elements of this historical problem, we can see that the problem has wrought itself out congruously from the time of Abraham until now. With the view we have taken of the promise and its fulfilments, they constitute a historical movement, extending over some thousands of years of past time, and indefinitely into the future. This movement, whether considered in itself, in its relations with other history, or as the channel of a special revelation from God, is one that will stand the tests of all reasonable investigation.

4. We turn to a fourth argument from the facts we have traversed — the argument from fulfilled prediction. When we substitute the conception of one promise for that of many foretold events, this argument, far from becoming effete, gains immensely in strength.

The national ideal existed, let us remember, not merely as a conception of something which might be, but of Has the something which actually was. Israel's son-promise been ship with God, his priesthood between God kept? and the nations, his electness for the sake of the nations, his office as Yahaweh's Servant among the nations, his anointing for purposes of blessing to mankind—these are spoken of as matters of obligation; this is what Israel ought to be; but they are also spoken of as matters of fact. Israel is all these. He is so, no matter how unworthy he permits himself to be. The promise is essentially a statement of facts, largely a statement of future facts, a predictive statement. In this character has it turned out to be true?

Our present treatment of the question of fulfilled prediction must be restricted to the answering of this question. Of course, however, the prophets made many other predictions. Our argument does not destroy the instances that were cited in the older books on prophecy. Some of those instances it strengthens by binding them together. The others it leaves intact, provided they are in themselves tenable. It does not require the giving up of a single case of fulfilled prediction which is otherwise defensible. It simply places a distinguishing emphasis on the one body of fulfilled prediction which is central and all-embracing.

The promise is, remember, that the seed of Abraham shall be Yahaweh's channel of blessing to mankind. To this end, it was promised, Israel should be kept in existence and multiplied, even after he should become a people without a country. This was not a matter-of-course future career for Israel, such as any person could forecast. It was not the regular experience for all peoples to have. In the time of Abraham or Moses or Isaiah or Jeremiah, there were very many other peoples on the earth, each seemingly as distinctive and as likely to persist as Israel. Most of these peoples long ago became extinct, either by dying out or by mingling their blood with that of others. Where now are the Assyrians or Babylonians or Philistines? A few ancient peoples have persisted, for example the Copts in Egypt or the Greeks or Arabians, largely as subject races on the soil where their ancestors once were lords. As a rule, expatriated peoples have either perished or become incorporated into other races. A fractional percentage of such races

may have survived, the Gypsies being a supposable example, but not as a people having any significance in
history. There were scores of peoples whom the Assyrian and Babylonian conquerors deported to other countries, as they did Israel; but so far as we know not one
of them now remains as a distinct people. The destiny
foretold for Israel was not the ordinary destiny of all
peoples, such as a sagacious person might have predicted on general principles, but was one altogether un-
paralleled. Has the promise, nevertheless, proved to be
a true prediction ?

(a) This question must be answered in the affirmative,
even if we look no further than the secular history of
Israel.

The Israelitish race still exists, without a country, but
one of the greatest races on earth, the peer of any other
in wealth, in intelligence, in the power it wields. It is
the only expatriated ancient people that thus survives as
great and cosmopolitan. Its history, like that of other
peoples, includes things to glory in and things to be
ashamed of. Israelites have been and are of all shades
of character, from the meanest to the noblest. But
Israel is everywhere an international and a mediatorial
people. In matters of banking and commerce and
finance, the world owes Israel an immense
Finance,
science, art,   debt. In matters of statesmanship, particu-
monotheism   larly international statesmanship, the debt is
also large. From the time of Daniel until now Israelitish public men have been at the helm, sometimes in
one nation and sometimes in another. In science and
literature and music, the debt is likewise great. But
high above all these things, the literature of Israel's
prophets has been translated into all languages. Israel
has been made the channel for communicating to man-

kind the monotheism of the religion of Yahaweh, and the monotheism thus communicated now influences the thought and the welfare of hundreds of millions in every climate and of all races.

Suppose we stop at this point, and ask : Has the promise been kept ? Have all the families of the ground been blessed in Abraham and his seed ? Who can answer otherwise than in the affirmative ?

One might supposably object to this reasoning by raising the point that Israel is not the only people that has a mission. The fact is readily granted, but compare the missions. Egypt has a mission to the world. India has a mission to the world. So have Greece and Rome and Arabia. State this, if you please, in the diction of the Abrahamic promise. Yahaweh has blessed mankind through Arabia and Rome and Greece and India and Egypt. But the blessing through Israel is so utterly different from that through these others, different in kind, in quantity, in quality, in details, as to constitute it a thing unique in history. Further, the national mission to mankind was not preached in these other nations as it was in Israel; was not made central in the national religion for centuries; was not lifted up and exhibited as a national ideal; in short, is not, as in Israel, a matter of fulfilled prediction.

The promise to Israel was for eternity. We are not at the end of eternity yet, and are to this extent not qualified to say whether in this particular Eternal the promise corresponds with the fulfilment. fulfilment But inasmuch as ages of history have rolled by, and now, at the end of thirty or forty centuries, Israel seems more vigorous than ever, we have an impression of unlimited time that may well be taken into the account. And whatever stress any one may lay upon the physical possession of Palestine and kingly state there, as items in the promise, who dare say that these may not be resumed in time to come, and with such conditions of permanence that the current centuries of dispossession shall seem, in comparison, but a mere temporary interruption?

In the treatment of the promise-doctrine in the Old Testament much is made of the sufferings of the Agent Mediatorial of the promise—sufferings which are in some suffering sense mediatorial. This is especially the case in those consecutive chapters in Isaiah which treat of the Servant of Yahaweh — chapters that are more emphasized in the New Testament than anything else except the promise to Abraham. The Servant's visage is marred beyond measure, he is despised and rejected, led as a sheep to the slaughter, and this for iniquities not his own, and with the effect of bringing blessing to others. It is not wonderful that devout Jews see in this a characteristic mark of the history of their race. From Rameses II of Egypt to the reigning emperor of Russia, antisemitism has been one of the vices of the world. No other people has been so cruelly persecuted through so many centuries. Others have been persecuted, and have either conquered their persecutors or else become extinct or slavish; Israel alone has maintained his place in spite of persecution. The very cruelties practised have resulted in enlarging the benefits conferred on mankind through him. All mediation between God and sinful men is at the cost of suffering on the part of the mediator. Of this truth the history of God's priestly kingdom, Israel, has been emphatically typical.

Were this, then, all; were there no further fulfilment that could possibly be claimed, we might here safely

rest our case. Here is no trifling with marvellous trivi-
alities, no appeal to details that have a flavor of super-
stition in them ; but an appeal to great facts, The argu-
well verified and beyond dispute. It is an ment not
argument from prediction, indeed. It rests on trivial
the fact that certain things were foretold thousands of
years before they occurred. But it is prediction that
conforms to the law of historical continuity; and it is,
by reason of that fact, at once the more remarkable and
the more indubitable.

Concerning Frederick the Great of Prussia the story
is often told that he said one day to one of his chaplains :
" Give me in a word conclusive proof of the claims you
make for Christianity." The chaplain replied : " The
Jews, your majesty "; and the agnostic king was silent,
whether convinced or not. He was too well informed
in history not to feel the force of the reply. Even with
the crude, distorted, prejudiced notions that have prevailed in Christendom concerning Israel, the proof is
one that cannot be set aside; and it grows in strength
as one attains to correcter views of the glories of Israelitish history. As in biblical times, so now. Israel never
ceases to be God's witness in the world.

(b) The fulfilment in the civil history of Israel does
not stand alone ; note also the fulfilment in the religions
of Israel and Christianity and Islam.

Jesus of Nazareth was an Israelitish man. Those
who most strongly hold to the Christian doctrine that
he is God incarnate none the less regard him Their civili-
as a man of Israel, and to all others he is zational
simply a man of Israel. The first disciples results
and Paul and Paul's first coworkers were all Israelites.
The writers of the New Testament were of Israelitish
blood. Christianity, both in fact and in the claims of

its founders, is the extension of the influence of Israel in the world. So far as the words go, the Christ is simply the anointed king of the line of David. The Christian kingdom of God on earth claims to be the perpetuated eternal kingdom promised to David. Similar statements — similar though with a difference — might be made in regard to the religion of Mohammed. In strict truth, perhaps Christianity should be regarded as the religion of Israel itself; but Christianity and Mohammedanism are, in the common thought of men, daughter religions to the religion of Israel. We must not enlarge; but in one or another of the three forms several hundred millions of men and women acknowledge allegiance to the God of Israel, and profess to regard this allegiance as the greatest thing in their lives. Those who do this include the leading powers of the earth, and they are engaged in active and successful propaganda for persuading the rest of mankind. Whatever these three religions have done or are doing or shall do for civilization, for morality, for human well-being, is a part of the work that Yahaweh has wrought for mankind through Israel. Has he made good his promise that in Abraham and his seed all the families of the ground shall be blessed? The magnificent results achieved by Israel as a race sink into insignificance by the side of the greater results accomplished through the three religions, and all are alike parts of the blessing of the promise.

But in our estimate of these religions as a blessing we have not yet reached the end. There is something greater, namely, their spiritual values. The blessing bestowed through them on mankind has not been exclusively external or civilizational or temporal. Under the power of the religion of

Their personal and spiritual results

Yahaweh, especially in its purer forms, human hearts have been changed, human lives have been renewed, men have been sanctified, have been victorious over death, have had good hope of eternal blessedness. If spiritual character is of the nature of the highest good, how large an endowment of this good has come to men, directly or indirectly, through the people of the promise! All the nations have received spiritual blessing through Abraham and his seed.

(c) Once more, the fulfilment in the person of Jesus is so marked as to be classed by itself. He is the representative person of the promise and its accomplishment.

This argument doubtless seems more weighty to those who hold the Christian orthodox view of the person of Christ than to others, but it is not to Not proof for be despised by others. If the doctrines of the orthodox immortality and of the incarnation and the only atonement are true, then this range of the fulfilment of the promise is higher than those we have hitherto traversed, so much higher that they become low in the comparison. But does it not remain so, even if we waive the acceptance of these doctrines? Apart from the question of his divine-human character, who is there that fails to see that Jesus is, from the promise point of view, the typical Israelite? that the men of the New Testament were correct in claiming that the promise was culminatingly fulfilled in him? Thinking of Jesus, for the moment, as a reverent agnostic might think of him, does he not embody preëminently the idea that was in the promise to Abraham? In his character and work, in the cosmopolitan reach of his influence, in his experience as a suffering mediator, is he not the very antitype of Israel as the people of the promise?

We have spoken of the promise as fulfilled in the

three religions of Yahaweh, but we must not forget that the personality of Jesus is an element in those three religions. In Christianity he is supreme. In Islam he shares the throne with Mohammed. And as for Judaism, it is intensely conscious of his presence, even if it excludes him. Eliminate him utterly from the three religions, and how much that is of real value would remain?

In fine, is he not, more than all else combined, the channel through which the blessing of Abraham has flowed to the nations? Is not the blessing itself best described in brief by speaking of the earth-wide dominion of the anointed son of David?

Let me repeat this in the words published many years ago by the distinguished Jew, Benjamin Disraeli : —

"The pupil of Moses may ask himself whether all the princes of the house of David have done so much for the Jews as that prince who was crucified on Calvary. Had it not been for him the Jews would have been comparatively unknown, or known only as a high oriental caste which had lost its country. Has not he made their history the most famous history in the world? Has not he hung up their laws in every temple? Has not he avenged the victims of Titus, and conquered the Cæsars? What successes did they anticipate from their Messiah? The wildest dreams of their rabbis have been far exceeded. Has not Jesus Christ conquered Europe, and changed its name into Christendom? All countries that refuse the cross wither, while the whole of the new world is devoted to the Semitic principle and its most glorious offspring, the Jewish faith!" (*Interior*, Jan. 20, 1881).

Certainly there is no room for doubt. There is a correspondence between the word of promise spoken long ago by the prophets and the fulfilment which

Summary

we ourselves behold : that in Israel the people, that in the great religions in which men worship Yahaweh, that in the peerless personality of Jesus. This correspondence is sure proof both of the divine mission of the prophets and of the truths concerning him who is the supreme fulfilment of the promise.

If any one should raise the point that the preaching of the promise by the prophets, and afterward by the apostles and their successors, has had an in- A futile fluence in bringing about the result promised, objection the fact is admitted, but it has no weight as an objection. There is a difference between prediction in the form of a great promise and predictions in the form of disconnected bits of the marvellous. How did it happen that a like promise was not preached, with like results, in other nations than Israel? Even if you grant that the promise has wrought out its own fulfilment as naturally as in the case in which the acorn is a prediction of the oak, it is none the less true that the performing of the thing promised proves that the prophets were not mistaken in claiming that they had a revelation from the Promiser. It proves that both the revealing and the accomplishing of the promise are a part of the programme of the Intelligence that is supreme in human history. The proof is as convincing as it is wonderful.

The Apologetic of the twentieth century is disposed to deal with human experience and human ethical judgments rather than with histori- The Apologetic that surcal facts. Within limits this Apologetic has renders hisgreat advantages in point of direct applica- torical fact bility and convincingness. But if it surrenders the field of historical fact, it thus renders itself vulnerable. Win a man to Christianity by appealing to his spiritual perceptions and his sense of what is reasonable, and you will in turn lose him if he becomes convinced that Christianity originated in fraud. Open a person's eyes to behold the peerless personality of Jesus, and his vision will become blurred if he comes to think that Jesus habitually made assertions which he did not know to be true. If we surrender to the enemy the positions of historical Apologetics, that enables him seriously to disturb us in our possession of the other parts of the field.

We need make no such surrender. In arguing from the unique character of the prophet as presented in the scriptures, from the unique national ideal of the people of the promise, from the unique conformity of our record of them to the requirements of historical criticism, from the unique character of the promise as fulfilled prediction, we hold a position that is both impregnable and of strategic importance. It is impossible for one who has really studied the matter to disbelieve that the statements concerning the promise were on record, as then ancient, more than twenty-three centuries ago; or to disbelieve that the forecasts thus recorded have ever since been proving themselves to be realities. This establishes the fact of a central superhuman element in the history of the religion of Yahaweh. Account for it as you will in your philosophy concerning miracles, the fact is certain. And the reality of the transcendent divine element in this part of the field being demonstrated, the question of its existence in other parts of the field is simply a question of the sufficientness of the evidence. Holding this position, we command the field, so far as the defence of Christianity as a revelation from God is concerned. Having substantiated these claims, we are entitled to make other like claims covering the whole region.

Every advance in genuine knowledge of truth strengthens our reasons for holding that the truth is true. To this rule the truths concerning the prophets are no exception.

INDEX

When the references in this Index are to the chapters, many of the details are omitted from the Index. They may be found in the Table of Contents, and in the marginal cut-in notes.

Of the numerous scriptural quotations and references in the volume only a few appear in the Index.

Aaron, the prophet of Moses, 43.
Abraham, his prophetic character, 39; the promise to him, *see* Promise.
Acts ii. 16–18, 111; iii. 21–26, 38, 351, 368; iv. 25–26, 250; viii. 32–33, 283; xxvi. 6–7, 179.
Agrippa, 179, 190.
Ahab and the prophets, 97.
Ahab son of Kolaiah, 61.
Ahijah, 47, 49, 53, 100.
Amalekites and Canaanites, 225.
Amos, 57, 96, 161, 311.
Amos vii–viii, 118.
Amplifications of the promise, 246.
Angel, the, 24, 29, 45, 123, 145, 352–356.
Anointed, 298–303. *See* Messiah.
Antitype. *See* Type.
Apologetic value of prophecy. *See* Prophecy.
Apologetics, historical, 419.
Appearing of Yahaweh. *See* Theophany.
Argument from prophecy, 387.
Ark and mercy seat, 357.
Art, its presentment of the prophet, 67.
Asaph the seer, 22, 47, 49, 78, 100.
Asideans, 328.
Assembly of nations, 198.
Astrologers, 67.
Authority, prophetic, 169.
Azariah the prophet, 53.

Balaam, 43, 104.
Baruch, the law in, 139.
Baruch the scribe, 61.
Biography, prophetic, 36.
Book of the law, 145. *See* Torah.

Branch, messianic term, 335–340.
Burden. *See* Massa.

Caiaphas a prophet, 104.
Called one, 272, 330.
Canaanites and Amalekites, 225.
Casiphia, the place, 63.
Celebrations of events, 249.
Cessation of prophecy, 63.
Chosen one, 272, 329.
Christ. *See* Messiah.
Christocentric theology, 193.
1 Chronicles xvii, 229 and often; xxii, 229, 233, 246, 332; xxv, 49; xxix, 48.
2 Chronicles vi, 247, 253; xviii, 55.
Citizen with a message, 66–87.
Collateral presentations, 251, Chapter XV, 344–364. *See* Table of Contents.
College of Huldah, 80.
Coming person, 302. *See* Person of the promise.
Common false notions of prophet, 67.
Comparative religion, 12–14.
Conjurer contrasted with prophet, 93.
Consistency of bible record, 403.
Contemporary understanding, 211, 227, 239, 242, 251.
Continuity of the promise. *See under* Promise.
Cosmopolitan and local, the prophet both, 102.
Cosmopolitan, the promise. *See* Nations.
Costume of the prophets, 67, 69.
Covenant formula, 203, 217, 234.

421